Muslim Women, Domestic Violence, and Psychotherapy

Muslim Women, Domestic Violence, and Psychotherapy reconciles newly emerging Islamic practical theology with the findings and theories of contemporary social sciences. It is an inquiry about the lived experience of the Islamic tradition and its application in Islamic counselling and psychotherapy with Muslim women subject to domestic violence. By incorporating a holistic examination of the worldview, personhood, and understanding of social and religious obligations of Muslim women in psychotherapy, this book shows how practitioners can empower clients facing trauma and abuse to explore feasible solutions and decrease worry, anxiety, and other negative emotions.

Nazila Isgandarova, PhD, DMin, RSW, RP, is an instructor at Emmanuel College of Victoria University in the University of Toronto.

Muslim Women, Domestic Violence, and Psychotherapy

Theological and Clinical Issues

Nazila Isgandarova

Routledge
Taylor & Francis Group
NEW YORK AND LONDON

First published 2019
by Routledge
711 Third Avenue, New York, NY 10017

and by Routledge
2 Park Square, Milton Park, Abingdon, Oxon, OX14 4RN

Routledge is an imprint of the Taylor & Francis Group, an informa business

Library of Congress Cataloging-in-Publication Data
Names: Isgandarova, Nazila, author.
Title: Muslim women, domestic violence, and psychotherapy: theological and clinical issues/by Nazila Isgandarova.
Description: New York, NY : Routledge, 2019. | Includes bibliographical references and index.
Identifiers: LCCN 2018020033 (print) | LCCN 2018021096 (ebook) | ISBN 9780429469701 (eBook) | ISBN 9781138590595 (hardback)
Subjects: LCSH: Muslim women—Family relationships. | Muslim women—Counseling of. | Family violence—Religious aspects—Islam. | Psychotherapy—Religious aspects—Islam.
Classification: LCC BP173.4 (ebook) | LCC BP173.4 .I84 2019 (print) | DDC 305.48/697—dc23
LC record available at https://lccn.loc.gov/2018020033

ISBN: 978-1-138-59059-5 (hbk)
ISBN: 978-0-429-46970-1 (ebk)

Typeset in Bembo
by Apex CoVantage, LLC

I dedicate this book to all women who suffered/suffer domestic violence. I also celebrate, admire, and respect advocates who refuse to simply watch the suffering of these women but prefer to take action, fight against domestic violence, and empower these women physically, mentally, spiritually, and emotionally to have better lives for themselves and their innocent children.

Contents

	Abstract	viii
	Acknowledgements	ix
	Introduction	1
1	Defining Islamic Psychotherapy in the Context of the Islamic Tradition	18
2	Domestic Violence Literature Review: Definitions/ Discussions of Key Concepts	51
3	Divine Testing and Suffering	72
4	Satanic Interference and Evil Eye	95
5	Spiritual Diseases	122
6	Honour and Shame	145
7	Future Recommendations	177
	Conclusion	186
	Bibliography	195
	Index	217

Abstract

By using the case of domestic violence against Muslim women, this study attempts to reconcile the newly emerging Islamic practical theology with the findings and theories of contemporary social sciences and open a space for the discussion on *critical praxis*. From this perspective, this study should be treated as an Islamic practical theological inquiry about the lived experience of the Islamic tradition and its application in Islamic psychotherapy with Muslim women who are subject to domestic violence. It is especially concerned with the exploration of possible meanings and models of interventions in Islamic psychotherapy practice with women. I argue that in Islamic psychotherapy, the Muslim psychotherapist should support the client by engaging in a holistic examination of the worldview, personhood, and understanding of social and religious obligations of Muslim women in order to achieve optimal physical, mental, and spiritual health.

Acknowledgements

I want to acknowledge with gratitude the tremendous support I received from Prof. Pamela Couture, Prof. Nevin El-Tahry Reda, Prof. Pam McCarroll, and Prof. Ingrid Mattson. I also feel a deep gratitude to Ms. Anna Moore, the Project Manager Chris Mathews, and Dr. Kathy Edmisson for ongoing support. Not only did they supply me with right tools, research skills and knowledge to explore this timely and important theme, but they guided me through my feelings and frustrations and provided constructive challenges and positive reinforcement. The journey with them provided the spark that made the readings and case studies exciting. Their willingness to walk with me convinced me that it is worth it to contribute to the field of Islamic psychotherapy. Special recognition also goes to Emmanuel College and Forum for Theological Education who provided generous financial support that made this journey successful.

Introduction

Islamic psychotherapy (some may prefer to name it counselling) offers significant potential for empowering Muslim women who experience domestic violence to claim their voice and their power. By integrating theories and interventions from Islamic studies and counselling and psychotherapy, Islamic psychotherapy uses various psychological and theological/spiritual techniques to treat the person in distress and improve his/her emotional, mental, and spiritual well-being. Regardless how we call it, whether Islamic psychotherpay or Islamic counselling, this unique faith-based clinical approach to psychotherapy is a "contemporary response, in common with other therapeutic approaches," but "based on an Islamic understanding of the nature of human beings."[1] It has a potential to assist Muslim women by creating awareness of the consequences of their problems; exploring feasible solutions; and decreasing worry, anxiety, and other negative emotions associated with domestic violence.

This study begins by addressing several important questions. First, what is domestic violence? Second, what is distinctive about Islamic psychotherapy with women who are victims of domestic violence? And finally, what theories and methods does Islamic psychotherapy use and how do these approaches empower or disempower Muslim women? These questions are addressed by engaging in a careful analysis of heuristic stories of Muslim women who experience domestic violence. Key themes from these case studies are discussed in dialogue with relevant literature from the fields of Islamic studies and the social sciences and I recommend ways to respond to this crisis in the Muslim community.

Definitions

Domestic violence against Muslim women takes various forms including verbal, spiritual, physical, emotional, sexual, and/or economic abuse. It is also clear from both Islamic feminist scholarship and domestic violence literature that oppression is a contributing factor. We live in a world where women continue to be exploited, marginalized, and rendered powerless. Women provide unpaid labour in the form of housekeeping and childcare, they are persistently paid less than men for doing the same jobs, they occupy only a fraction of the decision-making positions in governments, and there continues to be a dearth of information in history books about women's achievements and contributions. If we take into consideration that Muslim women often belong to communities with histories of oppression, then they are even more vulnerable to violence due to an inequality of rights and power imbalance in the home, the community, and the society. The oppression of Muslim women afflicts the individual and the system in which she lives, contributing to deterioration within the social system and pathology within the individual. Oppression frequently leads to tragic outcomes such as domestic violence. Salma Elkadi Abugideiri, a well-known Muslim scholar and an active advocate and member of the Faith Trust Institute in the United States, explains how oppression operates to normalize domestic violence against Muslim women. A Somali war survivor told her: "My husband and I were both tortured in the camp. If he pushes me or hits me occasionally, it is nothing compared to what we have been through."[2]

Domestic violence experienced in the Muslim context parallels other forms of hostility in the society. Common contributing factors include the power dynamics within the family, the abuse of power and trust, the desire to control and dominate in intimate relationships, the use of intimidation, and the element of isolation. Furthermore, the complexities of Muslim cultures and religion create a unique environment in which violence against women is often tolerated and even encouraged. Misunderstandings of the key sources of Islam foster and sustain false beliefs about domestic violence in Muslim communities. These misinterpretations establish unhealthy patterns of power in Muslim families, dynamics that contradict foundational Islamic principles such as trust, loyalty, and mutual cooperation. Abugideiri cautions that these complex contributing factors be explored thoroughly before attempting to provide care for Muslim women who are victims of domestic violence and their families.[3]

The various definitions and descriptions of domestic violence usually incorporate wide-ranging holistic dimensions of abuse. For example, the definition of violence against women provided by the United Nations includes

> any act of gender-based violence that results in, or is likely to result in, physical, sexual or psychological harm or suffering to women, including threats of such acts, coercion or arbitrary deprivation of liberty, whether occurring in public or private life.[4]

From this broad statement, the definition becomes more detailed, outlining specific contexts where physical, sexual, and psychological violence occur and providing explicit examples:

1. *Within the Family*: including battering, sexual abuse of female children in the household, dowry-related violence, marital rape, female genital

mutilation and other traditional practices harmful to women, non-spousal violence, and violence related to exploitation.[5]

2. *Within the Community*: including rape; sexual abuse; sexual harassment and intimidation at work, in educational institutions, and elsewhere; trafficking of women and forced prostitution.
3. *Within the State*: including forced sterilization and forced abortion, coercive/forced use of contraceptives, female infanticide, and prenatal sex selection.[6]

The Department of Justice of the United States defines domestic violence "as a pattern of abusive behaviour in any relationship" including physical, sexual, emotional, economic, or psychological actions or threats of actions and is implemented for the purpose of gaining or maintaining power of control.[7] The Domestic Violence Protection Act of Ontario 2000,[8] defines domestic violence as:

1. An assault that consists of the intentional application of force that causes the applicant to fear for his or her safety, but does not include any act committed in self-defence.
2. An intentional or reckless act or omission that causes bodily harm or damage to property.
3. An act or omission or threatened act or omission that causes the applicant to fear for his or her safety.
4. Forced physical confinement, without lawful authority.
5. Sexual assault, sexual exploitation, or sexual molestation, or the threat of sexual assault, sexual exploitation, or sexual molestation.
6. A series of acts which collectively causes the applicant to fear for his or her safety, including following, contacting, communicating with, observing, or recording any person.

Simply put, the perpetrator uses "physical, sexual, emotional, and/or economic abuse" and "coercion, terrorism, degradation, exploitation, and violence" in order "to control and subordinate another in an intimate relationship."[9] By defining domestic violence in this way, I shift the focus from a single incident to a pattern of coercive behaviours and tactics. In this regard, Yasmin Jiwani employs a broad scope when examining the structural and systemic forms of violence in Muslim women's lives.[10]

In this study, domestic violence refers to a wide variety of aggressive and problematic behaviours on multiple levels. I purposefully do not use the term "battered women" that has been used extensively in the United States and Europe since the 1970s because it usually associates domestic violence with physical violence. I will also not use the term "spouse abuse" or "intimate partner violence" because these terms do not explicitly refer to female victims. I use the term "women who are victims of domestic violence" to refer specifically to the full range of abuses that male partners inflict against their female partners.

Rationale of the Study

As a relatively new profession, Islamic psychotherapy belongs to what might be called emerging Islamic practical theology within Islamic studies. Bonnie Miller-McLemore has described practical theology as "a general way of doing theology concerned with the embodiment of religious belief in the day-to-day lives of individuals and communities."[11] It is concerned with the practice of faith and tradition in daily life, how daily life practices gain an "epistemic weight" in the production of new knowledge, and where and how doctrine, tradition, philosophy, and the "living human document" become connected.

Nevertheless, a gap between theology and practice in Islamic studies is especially felt with the emergence of Islamic psychotherapy as a new field. For example, how do we capture a moment in Islamic psychotherapy with Muslim women to create a theological discourse and engage Islamic theology, psychology, spirituality, jurisprudence, and history? What approaches, practices, and rhetoric are used in Islamic psychotherapy that help us identify and understand a concern? How do we correlate Islamic studies and the social sciences to interpret human experiences and needs?

Recently, the practical theological wisdom within the Islamic tradition is gaining more importance[12] because theories and practices derived from the theological and social sciences produce positive contributions. In Islamic psychotherapy, we need straightforward and explicit approaches to help Muslim women who are subject to domestic violence express their understanding of the divine, express their fears and hopes, express their identity and self-understanding, and find solutions to their problems that leave them defenceless and unprotected. This requires not only responses from the social sciences but an active theological conversation. This thrust in Islamic psychotherapy can be informed by and inform a similar discussion in Christian practical theology in which religious-hermeneutics is widely used.

This must be the reason that at the start of 2000,[13] research and professional practice studies began to describe the role of Islamic psychotherapy in addressing domestic violence against Muslim women. A survey of this body of research reveals the necessity for best practices for addressing the complex issues of Muslim women who are victims of domestic violence. In contrast to Islamic psychotherapy literature, Christian textbooks often include a feminist critique, analyzing and challenging unequal power dynamics within families that are destructive to all and attempting to give a voice and power to women in the counselling process.[14] Through this study, I hope to expose systemic misogynist practices that prevent Muslim women from reaching out for support. As well, I will present a variety of effective counselling interventions in Islamic psychotherapy that will ultimately empower Muslim women who have been victimized by domestic violence.

I intend to facilitate a forthright dialogue between the basic beliefs, doctrines, psychotherapeutic theories, and practices and the difficult questions raised by Muslim women who are victims of domestic violence. These questions include:

1. What does the Qur'an teach about domestic violence? and
2. How did/do the classical and contemporary Islamic traditions (like Sufi counselling), and current psychotherapeutic theories and practices, deal with the controversial aspects of psychotherapy with women who were/are victims of domestic violence?

Although I believe that the Qur'an is the final Word of God to humans, God's words are not monolithic. Different interpretative approaches to the Qur'an[15] offer diverse views on how the Qur'an responds to these questions. There is no simple answer, particularly in the context of domestic violence.

Also, the behaviours and beliefs of women are influenced by culture and these issues must be addressed in spiritual counselling.[16] In this respect, domestic violence "is not inherent to any particular culture"[17] and reflects "systemic patriarchy and occurs across all cultural communities."[18] The phenomenon occurs more frequently when a system supports, tolerates, or justifies male violence against and/or dominance over women. Unfortunately, for a variety of cultural and theological reasons, Islamic psychotherapy literature does not adequately address the needs of Muslim women who are victims of domestic violence.[19] For example, many Muslim women who are asked why they refuse to seek support and accept domestic violence report their obedience to their husbands as a pious and religious duty or as a form of self-sacrifice. In many situations, Islamic religious leaders, laypersons, and spiritual counsellors justify male violence against women, citing historical and classical interpretations of Islamic traditions without critical reflection. Sadly, tragic stories about domestic violence against Muslim women appear regularly both within public media and scholarly circles.

This study:

- offers an important contribution to the body of Islamic psychotherapy literature to promote best clinical practices;
- advances a broader perspective on the meaning of domestic violence and mental health within the Islamic context;
- advocates for better access to effective support for Muslim women who are victims of domestic violence by encouraging social, community, and religious institutions to deliver culturally competent Islamic psychotherapy; and
- contributes to building a stronger and healthier community.

Islamic Psychotherapy vs. Islamic Counselling

The terms "psychotherapy" and "counselling" are sometimes used interchangeably in the literature. However, in this study I prefer to use the term

Islamic psychotherapy because distinctions can be made between the two. The International Organization for Migration describes counselling as:

> a process, organized in a series of steps, which aims to help people cope (deal with or adapt to) better with situations they are facing. This involves helping the individual to understand their emotions and feelings and to help them make positive choices and decisions. Counselling is an approach for assisting people to reduce initial distress resulting from a difficult situation, and to encourage short- and long-term adaptive functioning (positive coping).[20]

The College of Registered Psychotherapists of Ontario (CRPO) defines psychotherapy as "the assessment and treatment of cognitive, emotional, or behavioural disturbances by psychotherapeutic means, delivered through a therapeutic relationship based primarily on verbal or non-verbal communication."[21] Psychotherapy is an appropriate treatment modality for victims of domestic violence due to its effectiveness in treating common disorders that accompany this form of abuse such as post-traumatic stress disorder (PTSD), anxiety, and depression.

Nevertheless, since there is no consensus on the definition of Islamic psychotherapy and counselling, "Islamic psychotherapy" and "Islamic counselling" have been used interchangeably. Reflecting this dilemma, Sabnum Dharamsi and Abdullah Maynard even wonder "whether there is a model of counselling and psychotherapy that can be called 'Islamic.'"[22] They raise several challenging questions about the use of the term "Islamic." Does this term apply simply because Islamic concepts influence the therapeutic process? Does the fact that Muslim psychotherapists draw upon their faith in the counselling relationship and process justify using the term? Is the term relevant because Islamic knowledge and techniques are integrated into the mainstream model of psychotherapy?

Nevertheless, despite the ambiguity in the field, especially when it comes to the name of Islamic psychotherapy and articulating how the practice is associated with Islam, generally speaking, Islamic psychotherapy is not a new concept. Islamic psychotherapy uses a wide variety of contemporary psychotherapeutic and Islamic healing methods to help people confront their problems and establish meaningful and healthy lifestyles and relationships. A holistic practice, Islamic psychotherapy supports individuals as they explore the cognitive, behavioural, emotional, spiritual, and religious aspects of their lives. A South African Muslim scholar Somayya Abdullah, one of the founders of contemporary Islamic psychotherapy, speaks in terms of "a confluence of counselling and psychotherapy with the central tenets of Islam."[23] In a similar vein, Syed Azhar Ali Rizvi describes Islamic psychotherapy as "a long continuous evolutionary process of man's fight against spiritual/mental sickness, maladjustment, or any other similar disorder."[24] For Rizvi, Islamic psychotherapy involves a process that can help maladjusted individuals who may benefit from an Islamic understanding of psychotherapy. Islamic psychotherapy addresses not only emotional and mental health problems, but also provides a form of spiritual healing for self-purification and therapy of repentance, and educates the client in Islamic faith and *fiqh* (Islamic jurisprudence).[25]

Islamic psychotherapy draws upon a unique set of theories and interventions that are also based on the primary religious and spiritual sources of Islam; these include the Qur'an, *Sunnah* (the teachings and practices of the Prophet Muhammad), the *hadith* (the narrations by later generations about the sayings, approvals, and disapprovals of the Prophet Muhammad), and the works of classical and contemporary Muslim writers in nurturing the clients' personal growth and maturation. For example, practices such as *tarbiyya* (the process of developing individual potential through guiding and nurturing),[26] *ta'lim* (the process of gaining knowledge), and *ta'dib* (the process of learning good social and moral manners and improving personal conduct) are an integral part of Islamic psychotherapy. These three elements are part of the concept of *tazkiyyat al-nafs* (treating spiritual diseases by purifying the soul; the purification of the soul), which is the most used spiritual intervention offered within the Sufi tradition.[27] Islamic psychotherapy weaves together these sources with the various cultural customs that are practiced by Muslims as an integral part of their daily life.

Like many of the helping professions,[28] Muslim psychotherapists and counsellors embrace standards of practice, codes of ethical behaviour, and approaches and interventions based on various theories from the social sciences and through the membership in professional associations. It relies on the establishment of a therapeutic relationship between the psychotherapist and the client where the client's thoughts, feelings, behaviours, and relationships can be addressed.

Finally, a range of Muslim professionals including psychotherapists, counsellors, spiritual caregivers/practitioners, social workers, psychologists, psychiatrists, and religious leaders provide Islamic psychotherapy. They draw upon knowledge and skills that are based in social science disciplines such as psychology, psychotherapy, spirituality/religion, ethics, and family studies. These professionals also provide information, advice, and instruction to their Muslim clients by using various religious and/or spiritually based texts. Competent Islamic psychotherapists weave together these therapeutic skills and knowledge with the wisdom of the Islamic tradition and the social sciences. This process is complex and challenging, however, due to the diversity of interpretations and understandings of the Islamic traditions among Muslims and richness of social science theories and practices in psychotherapy in general.

Method and Methodology

Islamic psychotherapy sometimes gets "lost" between social sciences and theology when its interdisciplinary nature is not clarified. However, if we acknowledge the interdisciplinary nature of Islamic psychotherapy, and to claim the dominant role of emerging Islamic practical theology in Islamic psychotherapy, then we can solve the tension between the general theories and practices of Islamic psychotherapy. Also, the concerns of Muslim women are impossible to grasp without a lively conversation between Islamic theology, jurisprudence, Sufism, and history. Therefore, Muslim psychotherapists would benefit from theorizing Islamic psychotherapy not only as a psychological discipline but also as a discipline of practical theology.

This research brings clarity to the application of the Islamic tradition and social sciences in Islamic psychotherapy to address the dilemma of Muslim women who are subject to domestic violence. In order to do so, this study incorporates a variety of approaches, including heuristic case studies that characterize the lived experiences of Muslim women; the religious-hermeneutical method and the correlational method that are widely used in Christian pastoral and practical theology; theological reflection, classical and feminist Islamic theology; and the social sciences that provide the foundation for psychotherapy, clinical social work, and counselling.

Heuristic Case Studies

Heuristic case studies investigate the phenomenon of the subjects' experience, confirming what is known and/or seeking new meaning.[29] As an individual participates in the affairs of living, a situation may arise (phenomenon) that invites an expanding awareness of human experience. A psychotherapist (researcher) might encounter an individual in therapy, and subsequently engage in an investigation of that human experience through listening, observation, and discussion of the situation. Further clarification of the human experience might be gained through intuition or through exploration of similar stories in drama, biography and journals, and so forth.

Through these heuristic case studies, the reader enters imaginary Islamic psychotherapy sessions with the women in these stories. The subjects of these cases do not represent any specific individuals that I have seen in Islamic psychotherapy; rather, each case presents a composite of the many faces of Muslim women who experience domestic violence. Each story explores the primary and secondary sources of support and investigates the breadth and depth of interpretations in Islamic psychotherapy by examining the efficacy of various approaches in Islamic psychotherapy.

Religious-Hermeneutical Methods and Correlational Approach

Correlational approach, religious-hermeneutics and theological reflections allow interpreting case studies from practical theological/spiritual perspective.[30] David Tracy described practical theology as the mutually critical correlation of the interpreted theory and praxis of the contemporary situation in the Christian context.[31] Drawing heavily on Tracy's mutually critical correlational method, Don Browning[32] argued that practical theology, as a holistic discipline, should bind together theory and practice as a practical hermeneutic and take into consideration the experiences of daily living. Browning and Charles Gerkin,[33] who both specialized in pastoral counselling within the field of practical theology, integrated Anton Boisen's[34] notion of the "living human document." Browning and Gerkin also draw heavily on Hans-George Gadamer's[35] (d. 2002) philosophical hermeneutical method, especially his concept of "fusion of horizons."[36]

However, Gadamer is also criticized for overestimating tradition and authority, so philosopher Paul Ricoeur (d. 2005) introduced the concept of "hermeneutics of suspicion," emphasizing a critical approach to tradition. Ricoeur names prejudices as "naivete" or "hunch about meaning" that starts with an initial hunch that leads to the second one until the text becomes fully understandable.

Nevertheless, Hans-Goerge Gadamer, along with Paul Tillich[37] (d. 1965) and Paul Ricoeur[38] (d. 2005), have inspired practical theologians such as Browning and Gerkin and their readers to pay attention not only to "the earlier interest in what lay 'behind' the text to the text itself and what lies 'in front' of the text."[39] Therefore, practical theology "involves a process of the interpretive fusion of horizons of meaning embodied in the Christian narrative with other horizons that inform and shape perceptions in the various areas of activity in which Christians participate."[40] This process is an ongoing process of questioning, correcting, refining, and integrating.[41]

Theological Reflections

Theological reflections allow the elaboration of and reflection on the stories in this study to promote the liberative praxis in Islamic psychotherapy: that means grounding of knowledge about Islamic psychotherapy with Muslim women that offers a critical and action-oriented understanding of the use of Islamic tradition in Islamic psychotherapy. This kind of approach allows respect for the Islamic tradition, but also acknowledges a male-dominated version of the Islamic tradition with respect to Muslim women. In this regard, I engage in the practice of *tafakkur*, which literally means to think on a subject deeply, systematically, and *tadabbur* (contemplation, remembrance of God, thoughts of God).[42]

What would be the implication of this kind of theological reflection in the study of Islamic psychotherapy and domestic violence against Muslim women? The theological reflection on these arguments suggests that in Islamic psychotherapy the Muslim psychotherapists need to read, understand, and interpret the "living human document." In the Islamic tradition, such practice is a support of a client in the way of liberation from evil or destructive forces or trauma and the reestablishment of personal communication with the creator and self. It is the "seeing the same differently" which is "the moment of enlightenment in a living human document: a life story capturing its moment of truth when seen differently."[43] This kind of theological reflection enabled me to transcend the stories of domestic violence by offering a creative imagination or theological reflection to the stories in this study. Questions that stimulate creative theological reflection include:

- "Where is God in the stories of Muslim women who are subject to domestic violence?" and
- "Where in these stories does Islamic psychotherapy create hope?"

Islamic Feminist Discourse

The Islamic feminist discourse is yet not well presented in Islamic psychotherapy scholarship. However, a feminist discussion of patriarchy and its influence on interpretations of the Qur'an and the Prophet's traditions helps us understand the theological and social aspects of domestic violence and the submissive behaviour of certain Muslim women in abusive relations. As "an Islamic project of rereading the Qur'an,"[44] Islamic feminism claims that Islam does not differentiate between men and women. Also, Islamic feminism shows culture, tradition, religion, educational, and socio-economic factors affect Muslim women in the family and society and deconstruct and reconstruct patriarchal narratives in a client's story.

In this regard, Amina Wadud, one of the best-known American Muslim academic and activist women, advocates for a gender-inclusive reinterpretation of the Qur'an and dismisses the classical exegetical tradition, including its premises and methodology.[45] Wadud introduces the concepts of *tawhid* (divine unity) and gender justice. Also, Asma Barlas, a well-known American Muslim scholar of Pakistani origin, also offers a new methodology that reflects three aspects of God's Self-Disclosure, which are the principles of Divine Unity, Justness, and Incomparability.[46] Sa'diyya Shaikh's[47] notion of "hermeneutic of suspicion" as feminist hermeneutical methodology[48] allows examination of the religious framework of normative gender relations (*qawama*), the constructions of righteous women (*qanitat*) and the "disobedient" women (*nashiza*), and finally, the repentant women.[49] This approach is very intriguing since it grounds exegesis in the lived experiences of women, thereby inherently allowing for a multiplicity of exegetical expressions. Ayesha Chaudhry, a Canadian Muslim scholar, uses a perspective of "idealized cosmology" to locate the patriarchal and egalitarian positions on Q. 4:34.[50] Chaudhry demonstrates the clash between the hierarchical version of patriarchal cosmology and the "triangle" of the egalitarian idealized cosmology.

Thus, oppressive and restrictive readings of the Qur'an not only arise "from ignoring the contexts of the Qur'ans' teachings; rather, they arise also from specific epistemologies and methodologies employed to read the text."[51] A critical feminist theological framework of Islamic feminism helps us see the interconnectedness of gender, religion, and spirituality in Islamic psychotherapy with Muslim women and capture their historical and contemporary aspirations, challenges, desires, and wants. Islamic feminism empowers this study to deconstruct two discourses in Islam that influence submissive behaviours of Muslim women towards domestic violence: one is related to the famous, but at the same time one of the most controversial verses of the Qur'an (4:34), and the other is regarding the image of the modest Muslim women in relation to Q. 4:34. Furthermore, Islamic feminist discourse encompasses such topics as the male domination of family relations, cultural attitudes towards and expectations of women, unequal distribution of duties in the household, and gender discrimination in education, economics, and other areas of life.

Feminist Practical Theology

I also have to mention how feminist practical theologians such as Nancy J. Ramsay, Pamela Cooper-White, Pamela Couture, Maxine Glaz and Jeanne Stevenson Moessner, Sallie McFague, and Elaine Graham inspired me in this study.[52] Cooper-White expresses it as "to inform and be informed by both healing and liberation" in order to "be relevant to and ultimately grounded."[53] According to Graham, feminist practical theology is one

> of *protest* against the invisibility of women, followed by a task of *resistance* to the objectification and exclusion of women – as agents, as theological authorities, as authentic sources of experience – and of reconstructing tradition and practice in pursuit of a third goal, that of the *transformation* of church and society.[54]

Miller-McLemore offers a similar structure by naming these key terms as "critique, advocacy, and reconstruction."[55] Also, her reflection on the "living human web" provides a space for women's experience by letting their dramas be fully explored in a concrete way. Similarly, Riet Bons-Storm, a Dutch practical theologian, offers some prescriptive teachings and practices that allow self-actualization of women. For her, women are captive in the "narrow space," and they are lost in the "terrible silence" when they do not have a language or conceptual framework to name their oppression.[56]

The Organization of the Book

This book is organized as follows:

Chapter 1 addresses the general overview of Islamic psychotherapy and primacy Islamic sources for Islamic psychotherapy.

Chapter 2 presents a literature review and discusses key concepts related to domestic violence in the Islamic exegetical tradition in Muslim and Canadian cultures.

Having established the theoretical and methodological foundations that undergird my research, I present four heuristic case studies that address specific issues related to Islamic psychotherapy:

Chapter 3: Divine Testing and Suffering;
Chapter 4: Satanic Interference;
Chapter 5: Spiritual Disease and Spiritual Distress;
Chapter 6: Honour and Shame;
Chapter 7: Future Recommendations.

The characters in the case studies depict composites of real and fictional women. As a collective, they embody the universal countenance of Muslim women who have experienced domestic violence. Taking the approach of a Muslim psychotherapist, I employ a five-step process (DEEDS) to address the central problem/issue in each case:

1. **D**escribe the problem (assessing for spiritual distress);
2. **E**xamine the influences from the Islamic tradition;
3. **E**xplore the insights from the social sciences;
4. **D**evelop a spiritual care plan that addresses the presenting issue and empowers the Muslim woman to take appropriate action; and
5. **S**uggest specific Islamic psychotherapeutic interventions that focus on the "spiritual diagnosis," drawing upon sources from Shari'ah, Islamic theology, Sufism, and contemporary psychotherapy theories, as well as resources from within the community.

This process provides practical information about effective techniques and practices in Islamic psychotherapy that can empower Muslim women.

Notes

1. G. Hussein Rassool, *Islamic Counselling: An Introduction to Theory and Practice* (New York, NY: Routledge, 2016), 17.
2. Salma Elkadi Abugideiri, "Domestic Violence," in *Counseling Muslims: Handbook of Mental Health Issues and Interventions*, ed. by Sameera Ahmed and Mona M. Amer (New York, NY: Routledge, Taylor & Francis Group, 2012), 313.
3. Ibid., 309.
4. United Nations General Assembly, *Declaration on the Elimination of Violence Against Women*, in the 85th Plenary Meeting (Geneva, Switzerland, 1993). Also, see Abugideiri, "Domestic Violence," 309.
5. Domestic violence "occurs within the private sphere, generally between individuals who are related through intimacy, blood, or law. . . . [It is] nearly always a gender-specific crime, perpetrated by men against women." See Lisa Hajjar, "Domestic Violence and Sharia: A Comparative Study of Muslim Societies in the Middle East, Africa, and Asia," in *Women's Rights and Islamic Family Law: Perspectives on Reform*, ed. by Lynn Welchman (New York, NY: Zed Books, 2004), 233.
6. United Nations General Assembly, *Declaration on the Elimination of Violence Against Women*, 10.

7. United States Department of Justice, *Domestic Violence*. Accessed on January 26, 2018 from www.justice.gov/ovw/domestic-violence.
8. Domestic Violence Protection Act, *2000, S.O. 2000, c. 33 – Bill 117*. Accessed on February 21, 2017 from www.ontario.ca/laws/statute/S00033.
9. Oregon Domestic Violence Council, *A Collaborative Approach to Domestic Violence: Oregon Protocol Handbook* (Portland, OR: Oregon Domestic Violence Council, 1995), 3.
10. Jiwani states,

    > Dictionary definitions of violence embrace its physical, psychological, and discursive dimensions and underline the use of force and the abuse of power inherent in all forms of violence. What they fail to capture are the levels at which violence occurs and the differential treatment of various kinds of violence. Violence occurs within intimate relationships, between peers, at the societal level, within institutions, and within and between states.

    Yasmin Jiwani, *Discourses of Denial: Mediations of Race, Gender, and Violence* (Vancouver: UBC Press, 2006), 7.
11. Bonnie J. Miller-McLemore, *Christian Theology in Practice: Discovering a Discipline* (Grand Rapids, MI, Wm. B. Eerdmans Publishing, 2012), 103. Also see, Bonnie J. Miller-McLemore, "Toward Greater Understanding of Practical Theology," *International Journal of Practical Theology* 16 (1) (2012): 111. Accessed from http://dx.doi.org/10.1515/ijpt-2012-0009.
12. See Mohamed Ajouaou, *Imam Behind Bars: A Case Study of Islamic Spiritual Care in Dutch Prisons Towards the Development of a Professional Profile* (North Charleston, SC: CreateSpace Independent Publishing Platform, 2014); Amjad Hussain, "Muslim Theology and Religious Studies: Relational, Practical, and Inter-Faith Dimensions," *Religious Education* 104 (3) (2009): 239–242; Sophie Gilliat-Ray, "Body-Works and Fieldwork: Research With British Muslim Chaplains," *Culture and Religion* 11 (4) (2010): 413–432; Sophie Gillat-Ray, Mansur M. Ali, and Stephen Pattison, *Understanding Muslim Chaplaincy* (Surrey: Ashgate, 2013); Nazila Isgandarova, "The Role of Practice Based Education in Islamic Spiritual Care: The Clinical Pastoral Education (CPE) Training," *The Muslim World 108* (1) (2018); "Practical Theology and Its Importance for Islamic Theological Studies," *Ilahiyat Studies: A Journal on Islamic and Religious Studies* 5 (2) (2014). doi.org/10.12730/13091719.2014.52.109; "Music in Islamic Spiritual Care: A Review of Classical Sources," *Religious Studies and Theology* 34 (1) (2015). doi: 10.1558/rsth.v34i1.26326; "The Crescent of Compassionate Engagement: Theory and Practice of Islamic Spiritual Care," in *Multifaith Views in Spiritual Care*, ed. by Daniel S. Schipani, (Waterloo: Pandora Press, Society for Intercultural Pastoral Care and Counseling, 2013), 109-130; "Muslim Spiritual Care and Counselling," In *The Spiritual Care Givers Guide to Identity, Practice and Relationships: Transforming the Honeymoon*, ed. by T. O'Connor, E. Meakes and C. Lashmar (Waterloo, Belgium: WLU Press, 2008, 135-256); "Islamic Spiritual Care in a Health Care Setting, " in *Spirituality and Health: Multidisciplinary Explorations*, ed. by A. Meier, T. O'Connor and P. VanKatwyk (Waterloo, Belgium. WLU Press, 2005), 85 104.
13. See a sample of works: Ruksana Ayyub, "Domestic Violence in the South Asian Muslim Immigrant Population in the United States," *Journal of Social Distress and the Homeless* 9 (3) (2000): 237–248; Munira Merchant, "A Comparative Study of Agencies Assisting Domestic Violence Victims: Does the South Asian Community Have Special Needs?" *Journal of Social Distress and the Homeless* 9 (3) (2000): 249–259; Nawal H. Ammar, "Simplistic Stereotyping and Complex Reality of Arab-American Immigrant Identity: Consequences and Future Strategies in Policing Wife Battery," *Islam and Christian – Muslim Relations* 11 (1) (2000): 51–70; Muhammad Haj-Yahia, "Implications of Wife Abuse and Battering for Self-Esteem, Depression, and Anxiety as Revealed by the Second Palestinian National Survey on Violence Against Women," *Journal of Family Issues* 21 (4) (2000): 435–463.

14. A sample of Christian counselling literature that addresses women's issues in Christian counselling practice includes: Pamela Cooper-White, *The Cry of Tamar: Violence Against Women and the Church's Response* (Minneapolis, MN: Fortress Press, 2012); Jeanne Stevenson Moessner and Maxine Glaz, "Introduction: I Heard a Cry," in *Women in Travail and Transition*, ed. by Maxine Glaz and Jeanne Stevenson Moessner (Minneapolis, MN: Fortress Press, 1991); James N. Poling, *Understanding Male Violence: Pastoral Care Issues*, 1st ed. (St. Louis, MO: Chalice Press, 2003); Jeanne Hoeft, *Agency, Culture, and Human Personhood: Pastoral Theology and Intimate Partner Violence (Princeton Theological Monograph)* (Eugene, OR: Princeton Theological Monograph, Pickwick Publications, 2007); Pamela Cooper-White, *The Cry of Tamar: Violence Against Women and the Church's Response* (Minneapolis, MN: Fortress Press, 1995); Christie Cozad Neuger, ed., *The Arts of Ministry: Feminist-Womanist Approaches*, 1st ed. (Louisville, KY: Westminster John Knox Press, 1996); Christie Cozad Neuger, *Counseling Women: A Narrative, Pastoral Approach* (Minneapolis, MN: Fortress Press, 2001); Christine Cozad Neuger, "Women's Depression: Lives at Risk," in *Women in Travail and Transition: A New Pastoral Care*, ed. by Maxine Glaz and Jeanne Stevenson Moessner (Minneapolis, MN: Fortress Press, 1991), 146–161; Aruna Gnanadason and The World Council of Churches, *No Longer a Secret: The Church and Violence Against Women, Risk Book Series* (Geneva: WCC Publications, 1993); Patricia Sheerattan-Bisnauth and Philip Vinod Peacock, eds. *Created in God's Image: From Hegemony to Partnership: A Church Manual on Men as Partners: Promoting Positive Masculinities* (Geneva: World Communion of Reformed Churches, World Council of Churches, 2010); Riet Bons-Storm, *The Incredible Woman: Listening to Women's Silences in Pastoral Care and Counseling* (Nashville, TN: Abingdon Press, 1996); Pamela Cooper-White, *Many Voices: Pastoral Psychotherapy in Relational and Theological Perspecitve* (Minneapolis, MN: Fortress Press, 2007); Pamela Cooper-White, "Intimate Violence Against Women: Trajectories for Pastoral Care in a New Millennium," *Pastoral Psychology* 60 (6) (2011): 809–855. doi:10.1007/s11089-011-0354-7.
15. I.e., *ta'wil* (the esoteric interpretation addressing *batin* or the inner meaning of the Qur'an) and *tafsir* (the exoteric interpretation of the text).
16. Maxine Glaz and Jeanne Moessner Stevenson, *Women in Travail and Transition: A New Pastoral Care* (Minneapolis, MN: Fortress Press, 1991), 4.
17. Julie Macfarlane, *Understanding Trends in American Muslim Divorce and Marriage: A Discussion Guide for Families and Communities* (The Institute for Social Policy and Understanding, 2013), 25–26. Accessed on March 16, 2016 from www.ispu.org/getreports/35/2399/publications.aspx.
18. Ibid., 25–26.
19. The United Nations Population Fund (UNPF) identifies the key issues affecting women as reproductive health, stewardship of natural resources, economic empowerment, educational empowerment, political empowerment, and empowerment throughout the life cycle (*Gender Equality: Empowering Women*. Accessed from www.unfpa.org/gender/empowerment.htm).
20. International Organization for Migration (IOM), *Introduction to Basic Counselling and Communication Skills: IOM Training Manual for Migrant Community Leaders and Community Workers*, 2009. Accessed from www.iom.int/jahia/webdav/site/myjahiasite/shared/shared/mainsite/activities/health/pandemic_manual.pdf.
21. CRPO, *Psychotherapy Act* (Toronto: The College of Registered Psychotherapists of Ontario, 2007). Accessed from www.ontario.ca/laws/statute/07p10#ys4. According to European Association for Psychotherapy (EAP), psychotherapy commonly refers to a longer-term relationship that focuses on gaining insight into the problem. European Association for Psychotherapy (EAP), *Definition of the Profession of Psychotherapy* (Vienna: EAP, 2003).
22. Sabnum Dharamsi and Abdullah Maynard, "Islamic Based Interventions," in *Counseling Muslims*, 135–160.

23. See Somayya Abdullah, "Islam and Counseling: Models of Practice in Muslim Communal Life," *Journal of Pastoral Counseling* 42 (2007): 42.
24. Syed Azhar Ali Rizvi, *Muslim Tradition in Psychotherapy and Modern Trends* (Lahore: Institute of Islamic Culture, 1989), 1.
25. Rassool, *Islamic Counselling*, 19, 22.
26. Gilliat-Ray, Ali, and Pattison, *Understanding Muslim Chaplaincy*.
27. The term *tazkiyya* means to grow and flourish, or increase and augment, or enjoy the blessing and abundance of God, and to reform if used in conjunction with a person. Many great Muslim scholars such as al-Muhasibi and al-Ghazali explored this concept as a solution to spiritual diseases. Al-Muhasibi, who had skills in many disciplines, including the sciences associated with the Qur'an, *hadith* literature, '*ilm al-kalam* (scholastic theology), and moral (or ego) psychology, developed this concept as a crucial counselling intervention in traditional Sufi therapy. See Gavin Picken, *Spiritual Purification in Islam: The Life and Works of al-Muhasibi* (London: Routledge, 2011), 123.
28. Gerald Egan, *The Skilled Helper: A Problem-Management Approach to Helping*, 6th ed. (Pacific Grove, CA: Brooks/Cole, 1998).
29. Clark Moustakas established self-experience as the key element in the heuristic inquiry. The steps of his heuristic approach include: (1) Immersion (exploration of the question, problem, or the theme) through indwelling, internal frame of reference, self-search; (2) acquisition (collection of data) through tacit knowing, intuition, inference, self-dialogue, self-disclosure, signitive-symbolic representation; and (3) realization (synbook) through intentionality, verification, dissemination. Clark Moustakas, *Heuristic Research: Design, Methodology, and Applications* (Newbury Park, CA: Sage Publications, 1990). Also see Bruce G. Douglass and Clark Moustakas, "Heuristic Inquiry," *Journal of Humanistic Psychology* 25 (3) (1985): 45–46.
30. See Pamela D. Couture, "Introducing Practical Theology to English Canada," *Toronto Journal of Theology* 29 (1): 143–144 and *Child Poverty: Love, Justice, and Social Responsibility* (St. Louis, MO: Chalice Press, 2007), 151–152; and Miller-McLemore, *Christian Theology in Practice*, 3.
31. See David Tracy, *Blessed Rage for Order: The New Pluralism in Theology* (New York, NY: The Seabury Press, 1975); David Tracy, *The Analogical Imagination: Christian Theology and the Culture of Pluralism* (New York, NY: Crossroad Publishing Company, 1981); David Tracy, *On Naming the Present: Reflections on God, Hermeneutics, and Church* (Maryknoll, NY: Orbis Books, 1994), 37. Tracy suggested that the main task of Christian theology include: (1) To be ready for "the dramatic confrontation"; (2) to suggest "mutual illuminations and corrections", and (3) to offer "the possible basic reconciliation between the principal values, cognitive claims, and existential faiths of both a reinterpreted post-modern consciousness and a reinterpreted Christianity." David Tracy, "Foundational Theology as Contemporary Possibility," *Dunwoodie Review* 12 (1) (1972): 3. Also, see T. Howland Sanks, "David Tracy's Theological Project: An Overview and Some Implications," *Theological Studies* 54 (1993): 698–727.
32. Browning proposed that practical theology should be based on "a critical reflection on the church's dialogue with Christian sources and other communities of experience and interpretation with the aim of guiding its action toward social and individual transformation." Don Browning, *A Fundamental Practical Theology: Descriptive and Strategic Proposals* (Minneapolis, MN: Fortress, 1991), 36.
33. Charles Gerkin, *Widening the Horizons: Pastoral Response to a Fragmented Society* (Philadelphia: Fortress Press, 1986), 50; *The Living Human Document: Re-Visioning Pastoral counseling in a Hermeneutical Mode* (Nashville, TN: Abingdon Press, 1984).
34. Boisen suggested that pastoral caregivers must view and practice understanding of a "living human document" as a unique life story in conflict. He suggested that the "living human document" must be viewed from the point of view of a unique life story and conflict of the client. The books may help to understand the theories, but human stories must also be studied and interpreted as sacred texts. Anton Boisen, *Out*

of the Depths: An Autobiographical Study of Mental Disorder and Religious Experience, 1st ed. (New York, NY: Harper & Brothers, 1960).

35. Hans-Goerge. Gadamer, *Truth and Method*, 2nd rev., edited/translation revised by Joel Weinsheimer and Donald G. Marshall, Wahrheit und Methode (New York, NY: Continuum, 2004). (See Sally A. Brown, "Hermeneutical Theory," in *The Wiley-Blackwell Companion to Practical Theology*, ed. by Bonnie J. Miller-McLemore (London: Wiley-Blackwell, 2012), 114.
36. See Browning, *A Fundamental Practical Theology*; Charles Gerkin, *The Living Human Document: Re-Visioning Pastoral Counseling in a Hermeneutical Mode* (Nashville, TN: Abingdon Press, 1984). Gadamer's method became a way of interpreting the individual who comes for psychotherapy as a "living human document" who must be seen from various "horizons," including religious tradition, psychological theory, and counselling interventions. Gadamer inspired psychotherapists and pastoral counsellors to pay attention not only to "the earlier interest in what lay 'behind' the text to the text itself and what lies 'in front' of the text." Paul Ballard, "The Use of Scripture," in *The Wiley-Blackwell Companion*, 164. He also clarified Martin Heidegger's concept of *Dasein*, "there-being" or Being-already-engaged-in the world, which implies that the nature of human being requires active engagement in the world of experience. His concept of *Being* brings to our attention the average everydayness of life in the counselling practice. These concepts require reflection on "what it is to be" human, and how we live in the world through the medium of language. Gadamer considered interpretative experience more important than interpretative method: not only methods are important, but what we do and think during this process is also vital.
37. Paul Tillich, *Systematic Theology* (Chicago: Unviersity of Chicago Press, 2013).
38. Paul Ricoeur, *The Rule of Metaphor* (New York: Routledge, 2004).
39. Ballard, "The Use of Scripture," 163. For example, borrowing from Gadamer, Gerkin suggested developing a practice of pastoral counselling that allows a process of interpretation and reinterpretation of human experience where God's horizon fuses with human horizons in an analogical fusion within the framework of a primary orientation toward a Christian model of interpretation. Gerkin states that "practical theology is grounded in narrative . . . rooted in the faith that the Bible provides us with an overarching narrative in which all other narratives of the world are nested." However, human experience is also "the present experience of occasions for faithful adherence to the central metaphorical meanings of the grounding story of human identity." Gerkin, *Widening the Horizons*, 50.
40. Gerkin, *Widening the Horizons*, 61.
41. See Gerkin, *The Living Human Document.*
42. Both words are very often used in the Qur'an. In one of the narrations of the prophet Muhammad's (pbuh), it is said:

    > *Tafakkur* for an hour is better than a whole night's *salah*. So, reflect on the bounties of God and the works of His Power. But do not attempt to reflect on His Essence, for you will never be able to do that.

    However, the Prophet Muhammad was not in a silent reflection: God made him a man who stood up for social justice and prescribed solutions to major socio-economic and political crises during the age of ignorance (Q. 7: 29; 4: 58). By reflecting on these and similar narratives in the Islamic tradition, I conclude that as McCarroll states, "Paying attention to our performative participation in movements for justice and peacemaking is a means to recognize and experience the divine presence and agency."
43. Peter Van Katwyk, *Spiritual Care and Therapy* (Waterloo, ON: Wilfrid Laurier University, Press, 2003), 20.
44. Margot Badran, *Feminism in Islam: Secular and Religious Convergence* (Oxford: Oneworld Publications, 2009), 2.

45. Amina Wadud, *Qur'an and Woman: Rereading the Sacred Text From a Woman's Perspective* (Oxford: Oxford University Press, 1999), xiii.
46. The first principle symbolizes the idea of God's Indivisibility and God's Sovereignty; "thus, no theory of male (or popular) sovereignty that pretends to be an extension of God's Rule/Sovereignty, or comes into conflict with it, can be considered compatible with the doctrine of Tawhi d." The second principle of God's Self-Disclosure, Justness, means that as God's Speech, the Qur'an cannot be misogynist, or preach in favour of misogyny or injustice. The last principle refers to God as Incomparable and Unrepresentable. Therefore, "there also is no reason to hold that God has any special affinity with males (the positing of such an affinity allows men to claim God as their own and thus to project onto God sexual partisanship)." Asma Barlas, *Believing Women in Islam: Unreading Patriarchal Interpretations of the Qur'an* (Austin, TX: University of Texas Press, 2002), 13–15.
47. Sa'diyya Shaikh, "Exegetical Violence: *Nushuz* in Qur'anic Gender Ideology," *Journal for Islamic Studies* 17 (1997): 49–73; Sa'adiya Shaikh, "A Tafsir of Praxis," in *Violence Against Women in Contemporary World Religion*, ed. by D. C. Maguire and S. Shaikh (Cleveland, OH: The Pilgrim Press, 2007).
48. She borrows the concept from Elizabeth Schüssler Fiorenza and and Gerald West. See Elizabeth Schussler Fiorenza, *Bread Not Stone: The Challenge of Feminist Biblical Interpretation* (Boston, MA: Beacon Press, 1995), x; also see, Elizabeth Schussler Fiorenza, *But She Said: Feminist Practices of Biblical Interpretation* (Boston, MA: Beacon Press, 1992), 53; Gerald West, "Silenced Women Speak: Biblical Feminist Hermeneutics," in *Women Hold up Half the Sky*, ed. by Denise Ackermann et al. (Pietermarizburg: Cluster Publications, 1991), 76–77.
49. Shaikh, "Exegetical Violence," 49–73.
50. Chaudhry, *Domestic Violence and the Islamic Tradition*, 2013, 9.
51. Barlas, *Believing Women in Islam*, 168.
52. Nancy J. Ramsay, "Emancipatory Theory and Method," In *The Wiley-Blackwell Companion to Practical Theology*, ed. by Bonnie J. Miller-McLemore, (Maldan, MA: Wiley-Blackwell, 2012), 183–192; Cooper-White, Pamela. "Suffering," In *The Wiley-Blackwell Companion to Practical Theology*, ed. by Bonnie J. Miller-McLemore (Malden, MA: Blackwell Publishing Limited, 2012), 23–31; Pamela D. Couture, "Social Policy," in *Wiley-Blackwell Companion*, 153–162. Glaz and Moessner, *Women in Travail and Transition*; Sallie McFague, "The Theologian as Advocate," in *The Making and Remaking of Christian Doctrine: Essays in Honour of Maurice Wiles*, ed. by Sarah Coakley and David A. Pail (Oxford. Clarendon Press, 1993), 155.
53. Cooper-White, "Suffering," 24.
54. Elaine Graham, "Feminist Theology," in *The Wiley-Blackwell Companion*, 193.
55. Bonnie Miller-McLemore, "Feminist Theory and Pastoral Theology," in *Feminist and Womanist Pastoral Theology*, ed. by Miller-McLemore and Brita Gill-Austern (Nashville, TN: Abingdon, 1999), 79.
56. Riet Bons-Storm, cited by Graham, "Feminist Theology," in *The Wiley-Blackwell Companion to Practical Theology*, ed. by Bonnie J. Miller-McLemore (Malden, MA. Blackwell Publishing Limited, 2012), 197.

1 Defining Islamic Psychotherapy in the Context of the Islamic Tradition

Islamic psychotherapy, historically, was known as *nasiha* (sincerity, advise, counselling) and was based on the principles of Islamic belief and practices such as submission to God, integration of material and spiritual life, divine will, social obligation, mutual responsibility, repentance, and so forth.[1] In the prophetic period (610–632), when the Qur'an and the Prophet Muhammad first introduced many of the basic concepts and practices to Muslims, every Muslim considered it a duty to provide supportive counselling to other Muslims, although spiritual guidance remained the special responsibility of religious leaders such as imams and Sufi masters. *Nasiha* was *fard al-kifaya* (duty of the sufficiency or a collective obligation upon Muslims) as it was considered everyday duties of Muslims.[2] Later on, other healing practices based on Islam emerged including *al-tibb al-ruhani* (spiritual medicine), *al-tibb al-nabawi* (religious and traditional medicine that focuses on Muhammad's practices), and *ilaj al-nafs* (the treatment of mental health issues; in the Sufi tradition, it also refers to the treatment of the soul).

In an early account of Islamic psychotherapy and counselling, recorded in the *Kitab al-Uqala al-Majanin* (The Wise Fools) by al-Nishapuri, by using the wisdom of the Arabic language and poetry, a renowned Arabic philologist al-Mubarrad (d. 898) provided deep and meaningful counselling to a young patient who was chained to the wall of a hospital.[3] Later on, Sufi masters developed techniques that are still relevant in contemporary Islamic psychotherapy. For instance, in his *Kitab Sirr al-Asrar wa Mazhar al-Anwar* (The Book of the Secret of Secrets and The Manifestations of Light), Shaykh Abdul Qadir Jilani[4] (d. 1166) developed the concept of remembrance of God as a healing technique. For him, this remembrance could only be done outwardly by repeating the divine names and pronouncing them aloud so that the individual and others could hear and remember. Through this practice, the memory of God became deeply embedded, sinking into the heart and eventually becoming silent. The Qur'an also record that "Believers are those, when Allah is mentioned, feel a tremor in their hearts, and when they (see and) hear His manifestations their faith is strengthened" (Q. 8:2). In this context, tremor refers to a sense of awe, fear, and love of God; it is a sign of inner purity, which finds expression in the highest qualities of character, morals, and manners.[5]

Later, *madrasah* (Islamic colleges) and *khanqah* or *tekke* (Sufi centres) would appoint *shaykh al-ribat* or *shaykh al-khanqa* (the head or master of a Sufi lodge) and *arif* (student mentors) to counsel students on various matters and to give them advice. An example is found in Makdisi's report from Abd al-Latif al-Baghdadi (d. 1231), a scholar from Baghdad who worked at the al-Madrasa al-Aziziyya in Damascus and who was later involved in advising his students regarding their spiritual and emotional health in a traditional Sufi manner:

> when you have finished your study and reflection, occupy your tongue with the mention of God's name, and sing his praises, especially at bed-time, so that your very essence becomes soaked up and your imagination permeated with Him, and you talk of him in your sleep.[6]

A review of the early accounts of healing shows clearly that the Qur'an and the prophetic tradition constituted the original key foundations of the practice. Attempts to incorporate the intercession of the Prophet Muhammad in the healing of the person were also part of the Islamic practice of healing. In *Qasida al-Burda* (the Mantle Ode), Abu 'Abdallah Muhammad ibn Sa 'id al-Busiri al-Shadhili (d. 1297), the Sufi poet who belonged to the Shadhili Sufi order in Africa, describes how he called upon the Prophet as an intercessor on his behalf before God for strength and forgiveness. His vision of the Prophet giving him his mantle was interpreted as a sign of healing.[7]

Various schools of thought including Indian, Greek, and Christian influenced both distinct Islamic branches; consequently, Islamic psychotherapy developed as a highly complex field. For example, the treatises of Muslim scholars[8] demonstrate a blend of Western and Eastern thought. Not surprisingly, in the past, *nasiha* reflected the eclectic character of the theological, mystical, and philosophical trends that had infused Islamic thought in those times.[9]

During this time, Muslim scholars established a unique branch of science called Islamic psychology, which was known as *ilm-al nafsiyat* (the science of the soul/self or psychology). They studied concepts such as the self or the psyche in the modern context of psychology, psychiatry, and the neurosciences.[10] *Al-ilaj al-nafsi* (psychological therapy) aimed to cure or treat the soul and the mind. In mental hospitals in the medieval Muslim world, Muslim clinicians treated mental illness both as clinicians and researchers.[11] These professionals were called *al-tabib al-ruhani* or *tabib al-qalb* (spiritual physicians).[12] Their clinical practice included dream work by Muhammad ibn Sirin (d. 728), psychotherapy and music therapy by Abu Yusuf Ya 'qub ibn 'Ishaq al-Sabbah al-Kindi (Alkindus) (d. 873), clinical psychiatry by Ali ibn Sahl Rabban al-Tabari (d. 870), cognitive therapy and psychosomatic medicine by Abu Zayd Ahmed ibn Sahl al-Balkhi (d. 934), and physiological psychology by Ibn Sina (Avicenna) (d. 1037) whose research included investigations into self-consciousness.[13] Al-Balkhi, the Muslim psychologist, al-Razi, who was known for his medical encyclopaedia *Al-Hawi fi al-Tibb*, ibn Sina, and

Muhammad bin Muhammad Abu Hamid al-Ghazali (d. 1111), discussed common cognitive distortions and cultural beliefs to treat mental disorders.

Some of these scholars incorporated other sources besides the Qur'an and the Islamic tradition in their practice of healing and cure. For example, the Samanid[14] governor Amir Mansur b. Nuh b. Nasr (d. 976) suffered from chronic sadness and grief; in response, Rhazes dedicated to him, as a prescription, his famous medical treatise, *Kitab al-Mansuri* (The Book of Medicine), in which he offers detailed analyses and explanations of the scientific principles underlying psychological treatment.[15] Avicenna integrated his unique and original interpretation of human perception based on five external senses (hearing, sight, smell, taste, and touch) and five internal senses (precepts, the imaginative faculty, instinct, the sense of imagination, and intentions) with sense data (the *sensus communis* or the seat of all senses).[16] Al-Ghazali (d. 1111) further developed Avicenna's notion of five internal senses by adding a spiritual dimension. This new dimension considers the human's desire to attain spiritual perfection through *'aql* (intellect) and *irada* (will). What distinguishes him from Avicenna is his focus on the importance on *qalb* (the heart) as the seat of control of six powers (appetite, anger, impulse, apprehension, intellect, and will). He posited that, in contrast to humans, animals only have three of these (appetite, anger, and impulse) and this distinguishes him from Aristotle, Avicenna, Roger Bacon, and Thomas Aquinas who all believed that animals cannot become angry.[17] Al-Ghazali also differentiated between two types of disease: physical and spiritual. He believed that spiritual disease was more dangerous. He defines spiritual disease as "ignorance and deviation from God." For him, spiritual disease also included self-centredness, addiction to wealth, fame, and social status, ignorance, cowardice, cruelty, lust, doubt, envy, deception, and greed. He proposed a therapy of opposites whereby spiritual diseases could be treated by using the imagination to pursue the opposite. For example, ignorance could be countered by learning and hate could be countered by love.

The exemplary personal conduct of prominent Muslim scholars was also a source of inspiration for ordinary Muslims. Although we do not have detailed professional codes of conduct for early Muslim practitioners, the traditional code of practice for early Muslim doctors recorded by al-Majusi, a medieval Muslim doctor, sheds light on this subject. He writes that Muslim doctors:

> ought to be God-fearing, and faithful to their teachers. Their aim should be to help and heal the sick and not only to seek financial gains. . . . [They] should be chaste, intelligent, religious, kind and considerate.[18]

Several key Islamic psychotherapy concepts and their explanations were addressed in the writings of classical Muslim scholars, albeit some of the references were brief and incidental. Although Islamic psychotherapy theories and practices did not exist at that time as a distinct professional practice, writings from Islamic classical treatises influenced the direction of Islamic psychotherapy and counselling in the early and later stages of its development.[19]

While early discussions on Islamic thought were and continue to be essential as well, classical writings endure as a lasting influence on contemporary Islamic psychotherapy. A major contribution from this period is the distinction that humankind is not simply subject to heredity and left to the mercy of environmental forces; rather, a human is perceived as one being among others, primarily governed, sustained, guided, and controlled by God's infinite power and will.[20]

Currently, Islamic psychotherapy is transforming into a professional clinical discipline that is influenced by the spiritual and religious traditions of Muslims and the clinical work of Muslim professionals including psychotherapists, counsellors, spiritual care practitioners, clinical social workers, and psychologists. According to G. Hussein Rassool,[21] because of different ideologies and approaches there are several models of interventions in Islamic psychotherapy. He also argues that even traditional models of Islamic psychotherapy were also in various forms in the past and the most common form was sincere advice. This approach still is dominant in religious counselling and psychotherapy where traditional healing (based on cultural beliefs), and Muslim personal law based on the legal framework for regulating family life in Islam are applied. The latter focuses mainly on divorce, maintenance, child custody and inheritance, and Sufism.[22] In this regard, this model of Islamic psychotherapy is based on the Qur'an, the Sunnah, and the Tasawwuf.[23] From social work perspective, A. Barise explored the conceptual framework of helping, problem-solving and change with Islamic concepts such as consultation, contemplation, self-monitoring, awakening, seeking God's assistance, and so forth. Rassool also presents the 11-stage Islamic psychotherapy and counselling practice model using Ibn Qayyim al-Jawziyyah. These stages are: *qawmah* (awakening) and *niyyah* (intention); *istisharah* (consultation); *tafakkur*, *istikharah* (guidance-seeking), *'azm* (wilful decision); *basirah* (goal-and-route vision); *al-tawakkul 'ala – Allah* (absolute trust in God); *'amal* (action); *isti'anah* (help-seeking); *muraqabah* (self-monitoring); and *muhasabah* (self-evaluation).[24]

In sum, although the theological/religious/spiritual foundations of the discipline are rooted in the Islamic tradition, it also incorporates various theories from the social sciences. The diversity of interpretations of the Islamic tradition makes it challenging to pinpoint specific theories and practices pertaining to Islamic psychotherapy; and this rich variety is reflected in the literature.[25]

Islamic Tradition as the Primary Source for Islamic Psychotherapy

From this brief historical account, the Islamic tradition has had a tremendous impact on the historical and contemporary development of Islamic psychotherapy. This historical and contemporary development also suggests that Islam is "a human and historical phenomenon" that possesses "plenitude and complexity of meaning[s]."[26] More importantly, however, the Islamic tradition provides the very foundation for Islamic psychotherapy that is embedded in the human experience. For this reason, the Islamic tradition will now be explored with a careful attempt to present the notion of "Islam" in such a way that it "*comprehends* the integrity and identity of the complex historical and human phenomenon at play and at stake, rather than distorting or fracturing it."[27] Otherwise, it would give an impression that I also mispresent Islam as "religion," "culture," "civilization," "symbol system," or even "discursive tradition."[28] Furthermore, the challenge in defining the Islamic tradition is that "the existing conceptualizations and uses of 'Islam/Islamic' do not express a coherent object of meaning (or an object of coherent meaning)."[29] Therefore, everyone, including historians, anthropologists, sociologists, or scholars of art or religion, "are often frankly unsure of what they mean when they use the terms 'Islam/Islamic' – or whether, indeed, they should use the terms at all."[30]

A complexity of definitions for the meaning of Islam suggests that trying to define what the term "Islamic tradition" means, especially as it concerns Islamic psychotherapy, presents a considerable challenge. However, for the sake of clarity, we need to have a working term to define it and address diversity in Islam. In general, the term "tradition" refers to significant elements of the past or to beliefs or behaviours that hold symbolic meaning.[31] In many cases, traditions include customs, institutions, disciplines, and practices that are handed down to future generations. Alasdair MacIntyre suggests that a tradition can also be construed as:

> an argument extended through time in which certain fundamental agreements are defined and redefined in terms of two kinds of conflict: those with critics and enemies external to the tradition who reject all or at least key parts of those fundamental agreements, and those internal, interpretative debates through which the meaning and rationale of fundamental agreements come to be expressed and by whose progress a tradition is constituted.[32]

Following on Michel Foucault's (d. 1984) notion of "discourse" and Alasdair MacIntyre's notion of "tradition," a contemporary Muslim scholar and anthropologist Talal Asad describes the Islamic tradition as "discursive" and "diverse" that requires "an adequate concept."[33] More specifically, he asserts that Islamic tradition is "a tradition of Muslim discourse that addresses itself to conceptions of the Islamic past and future, with reference to a particular Islamic practice in the present."[34] For Asad, this "discursive tradition" provides guidance for its followers in terms of the correct form and purpose of a given practice based on the Qur'an and the *hadith*. Asad's concept of the Islamic tradition as "discursive tradition" is "prescriptive" that means that it is "oriented towards the prescription of correctness" that requires "authority as constituting Islam."[35] More specifically, the practice is Islamic only when "it is *authorized* by the discursive traditions of Islam, and is so taught to Muslims."[36] According to as late Shahab Ahmed (d. 2015), a Pakistani-American scholar of Islam at Harvard University, there is a subtle and crucial problem in Asad's definition of Islam as a discursive tradition because Asad presents it as "authoritative, prescriptive, and exclusivist discourse – including authoritative, prescriptive, and exclusivist reasoning" that "becomes, by definition, (more) Islam/ic than is non-authoritative, non-prescriptive, and non-exclusivist discourse/reasoning."[37]

The Islamic tradition should be perceived as a rich tradition as it is evident in the historical and contemporary expressions of Islam that suggest that "God does *not*, as the orthodoxizers would have Muslims have it, "speak with one tongue," but rather that He expresses and manifests Himself in a prodigious *variety* of mutually opposing statements and forms, the contemplation of which produces perplexity.[38] This is what we witness in our discussion of different aspects of the Islamic tradition(s) in our case studies because the logic of difference and contradiction is "coherent with and internal to Islam."[39]

In its earliest history, the divisions in Islam involved theological debates, religious issues,[40] and major political conflicts among the *sahaba* (Companions of Muhammad) and early Muslim scholars. At that time, there was no widely accepted Islamic council or ecclesiastical institution that could define and/or defend the principles of the true faith of Islam. No single authorized interpretation of the Qur'an or the *hadith* existed; however, Muslims could create an *ijma'* (consensus) which served to establish a wide area of agreement. Through processes of consensus, bridges were eventually built between the once hostile schools, i.e., Hanafite, Hanbalite, and the Shiite schools of thought (Zaydi and Ja 'fari/Ithna 'Ashari). In a spirit of understanding, almost all orthodox Muslim theologians stopped labelling other Muslims who also prayed towards Mecca, as infidels or *kafir* (disbelievers). Many scholars accepted the diversity of opinions within the Muslim community, conceding that "there will always be legitimate differences in interpretation."[41] This movement toward "orthodoxification," however, would keep in check any "wild growth of interpretations" which would most certainly not be seen as "a product of Islam."[42]

However, considering the diversity of the Islamic tradition(s), I engage the "Islamic tradition(s)" in this study in the context of the cultural and/or religious practices that relate to Islam's key sources: The Qur'an, the *hadith*, Shari 'ah, *kalam* (theology), and Sufism (Islamic mysticism). It may also refer to *'urf* or *'adat* (practices) that have become culturally embedded over time.[43] Most certainly, Islamic tradition situates itself in the present, living amid current practices, institutions, and social conditions.[44] As a historical institutionalized framework, the Islamic tradition weaves together the past, the present, and the future especially when established practices may have been lost, modified, or abandoned. Islamic psychotherapy practices draw upon the Islamic tradition to recover and apply traditional methods of religious and spiritual healing.

Due to the wide-ranging conflicts and contradictions that challenge the role and function of the Islamic tradition in the contemporary world, Islamic psychotherapy is undergoing a transformation. These contradictions invite the examination and reformulation of the role of the Islamic tradition in Islamic psychotherapy and the search for new methodologies that will respond to the challenges of Muslim women who experience domestic violence. Such an approach to Islamic psychotherapy requires innovation and resonates with early approaches in the Islamic tradition when lived experience helped to make sense of sacred sources and legal rulings. In the modern context, Islamic psychotherapy must innovate new ways to help Muslim women that consider the connections between their Islamic theology, the social sciences, and the lived experience of their faith.

Taking an innovative approach to the interpretation and application of a newly emerging field of Islamic practical theology parallels the process of revelation. In my understanding, God's conversation was not a linear monologue; rather, it was circular and systemic reflecting an active conversation between theory (revelation) and practice (the lived experience). This suggests that God was not indifferent to human needs; in many ways, the Qur'an represents a critical divine reflection on human needs. For example, many Qur'anic verses address everyday aspects of human experiences and activities in relation to the practice of the Islamic faith, as noted, for example, in the exegetical genre *asbab al-nuzul* (occasions of revelation).[45] They were intended to provide clarity to early Muslims regarding the nature of the divine and to offer guidance concerning their relationship with God and other human beings.

In addition to Qu'ranic exegesis, the early generations of Muslims developed *kalam* (discursive theology) and *fiqh* (jurisprudence). Although there was a strong support of *naql* (revelation) over '*aql* (reason), the early discussions on the use of human experience in the form of *'aql* suggested that the Islamic tradition accepted the production of knowledge based on the human perspective. Moreover, the integration of theory, practice, and spirituality as a human experience was embraced and embodied in classical Sufi tradition. This understanding and interpretation of the sacred using human experience has also laid a foundation for critical reflection on using a scientific or social sciences perspective within Islamic studies since the 1980s.[46]

At this point, different aspects of the Islamic tradition that continue to influence Islamic psychotherapy theories and practices will be discussed and it will be evident that the terms and concepts of the various aspects of Islamic tradition, including the exegetical, legal, theological, and mystical traditions, heavily dominate the field of contemporary Islamic psychotherapy. Also, this brief introduction to historical and contemporary approaches to the Islamic tradition lays a good foundation to understand the case studies where we analyze them in the context of the Islamic tradition and social sciences.

The Exegetical Tradition and Islamic Psychotherapy

The Qur'anic exegetical tradition provides a foundation for Islamic psychotherapy along with other branches of the Islamic tradition. Very often, Muslim psychotherapists consult with the Qur'an and its exegeses. However, Muslim psychotherapists need to be mindful in their selection of exegetical traditions as they are a "hybrid of more than one approach"[47] and their writers were motivated by the ideological tensions of their times.[48]

First of all, approaches to the Qur'anic interpretation can be classified as:

> analytical (*al-tafsir al-tahlili*), synoptic (*al-tafsir al-'ijmali*), legal exegesis, allegorical exegesis (*majazi*: esoteric or *batin, ta'wil, ishari*, etc.), comparative (*al-tafsir al-muqarin*), thematic or topic-based (*al-tafsir al-mawdu 'i*), literary and stylistic or a linguistic/rhetorical approach that is both textual and lexicographical and that is more interested in *gharib* works (foreign words, tribal dialect words, lexical oddities), *wujuh, naza'ir* and *ashbah* works (the multiple senses of Qur'anic expressions), *mutashabihat* (stylistically different but grammatically similar), quasi-syntactic (a brief grammatical analysis), and scientific.[49]

Al-Tafsir bil-ma'thur or *al-tafsir al-naqli* (traditional exegesis) provides critical explanations or interpretations of the Qur'an, the Sunna (prophetic tradition), and the insights of the companions of the Prophet.[50] *Al-Tafsir bil-ra'i* (the school of rational exegesis) draws on *al-'aql* (intellect) and *al-dirayah* (personal knowledge or judgement). The authors of these exegetical works use methodologies such as *al-insinbat* (deduction) to question the reliability of the *hadith* tradition. Although those in the mainstream exegetical approach to the Qur'an view rational exegesis as "fanciful," the Mu 'tazilite, the Sunni, many of the Shiite subsects, the Ibadi, the Sufi, and many contemporary Muslim scholars draw on these methodologies to provide insight into the Qur'anic verses, especially when more than two sources are needed (the Qur'an and the *hadith*). Rational exegesis "acquired a politico-religious overtone favouring esoteric shades of meaning of Qur'anic expressions and passages and adopting *hadiths* which are dubbed 'forged' or 'weak.'"[51] Nevertheless, many companions of the Prophet Muhammad, including Ibn 'Abbas and ibn Mas 'ud, used the rational approach. In addition, many Muslim jurists, linguistic exegetes, Mu 'tazilite scholars, Shiite scholars, and Sufi masters have adopted this approach in their interpretations.

The exegeses can also be classified as "Textualist," "Semi-textualist," and "Contextualist."[52] Such classification is based on whether the interpreters give preference to the linguistic criteria to examine the meaning of the text or to the socio-historical context of the revelation and needs and concerns of Muslims in different times. The Textualist[53] approach to the Qur'an ignores socio-historical contexts and rejects any attempts of those who impose a new meaning on the Qur'anic text. For them (i.e. traditionalists and Salafis), the Qur'an is "fixed and universal in its application." For the Textualists, the source of the interpretation – whether it is based on *manqul* (transmitted tradition) or *ma'qul* (rational exposition) – plays a significant role. In his *The Comprehensive Exposition of the Interpretation of the Verses of the Quran (Jami ʿal-bayan ʿan ta'wil al-Qur'an)*, Abu Ja'far Muhammad b. Jarir Yazid b. Kathir b. Ghalib al-Tabari (d. 923), uses etymology, grammar, and Arab linguistics to understand and offer a new meaning of each verse in the Qur'an. However, for the Hanbali scholar Taqi ad-Din Aḥmad ibn Taymiyya (d. 728/1328),[54] who did not extensively engage grammar and linguistics in his work, the desired intention behind speech to understand its meaning is important, "and not merely its individual word components; as such, the Qur'an as speech falls under this rule."[55] His approach did not make allowances for changing contexts and rejected openness to engage with the text, strongly critiquing the use of *ra'y* (reason, personal judgement or opinion) in exegesis.[56]

Semi-textualists, who also follow the Textualist approach, consider linguistic aspects of the Qur'an with emphasis on the ethico-legal context. Like the Textualists, they also argue that the Qur'anic message is immutable and eternal, and must be followed without questioning it regardless of the differences in the context. In addition, they give preference to the exegeses that are associated with the Qur'an and the Tradition over the exegeses based on reason. Such an approach also does not accommodate the socio-historical context as an important criterion in order to bridge the gap between the time of revelation and contemporary time.[57] In addition, the Semi-textualist approach that claimed but ignored the Universalist aspect of the Qur'an limited itself within the socio-historical context of the medieval centuries that very often engaged in "editing" the humanistic and universal messages and was strictly involved in the critical study of the legal content of the Qur'an at the expense of the socio-historical context.

On the other hand, Contextualists[58] consider the socio-historical context of the revelation and its interpretations and invite dialogue with various sources to better grasp the content of the Qur'an. The Contextualist approach was specifically developed and redeveloped by reformist thinkers.[59] They applied the principles such as contextual and situational analysis to reading and understanding the classical interpretations of the Qur'an for these works depended on the political, social, historical, cultural, and economic contexts in which their authors interpreted and applied the Qur'an.

These Muslim scholars argue that the Qur'an's ethico-legal content holds two aspects of the revelation: mutable (changeable) and immutable (unchangeable). Despite the differences in worldviews and perspectives, all these authors agreed that the Qur'anic text is open and relevant to various interpretations depending on the need and concerns of Muslims, and it addresses Muslims in different places and different times. Nevertheless, they also argued that to understand the intended meaning of the Qur'anic verses it is also important to consider the socio-historical context of seventh-century Arabia.[60] In contemporary Islamic scholarship, the Contextualists consider the socio-historical context of the ethico-legal content of the Qur'an important in our understanding of the Qur'an. For example, as Walid Saleh states, "One cannot study any given Qur'an commentary in isolation. It has to be seen in conjunction with the tradition that produced it and the influences it left behind."[61]

Also, Qur'anic exegeses are oriented either politically, scientifically, or linguistically. Literary exegesis appeared in the 20th and 21st centuries and was developed by scholars including Ayatollah Mahmud Taleqani (d. 1980), Sayyid Qutb (d. 1966), Muhammad al-Ghazali (d. 1996), Muhammad Mutwali al-Sha 'arawi (d. 1998), and Hasan al-Turabi (d. 2016).

Shari 'ah and Islamic Psychotherapy

Shari 'ah, the Islam's Legal Tradition, which literally means "the path" is also a strong foundation for Islamic psychotherapy. As we will see later on, many Muslim women who are subject to domestic violence also want Muslim psychotherapists to educate them in regard to their rights in Shari 'ah. This section will help Muslim psychotherapists again see how complex it is to use Shari 'ah as a source of Islamic psychotherapy.

A well-known Hanbali jurist Ibn Qayyim al-Jawziyyah (d. 1350–1), described Shari 'ah as God's will, mercy, and justice among the people.[62] It is generally accepted that the evolution of an Islamic judiciary as well as the formation of the legal schools constituted the first two of four major developments shaping Shari 'ah.[63] For example, Shari 'ah grew out of the analytical principles of the founders of four orthodox schools of law: Abu Hanifa an-Nu 'man ibn Thabit (d. 767), Malik ibn Anas ibn Malik ibn Abi 'Amir al-Asbahi (d. 795), Abu ʿAbdullah Muhammad ibn Idris al-Shafiʿi (d. 820), and Ahmad ibn Hanbal (d. 855). In addition, Shari 'ah was also influenced by the Shiite schools of law established by Imam Zayd ibn 'Ali (d. 740) and Imam Jaʿfar ibn Muḥammad al Sadiq (d. 765). Each of these schools of Islamic jurisprudence offers legal rulings about doctrines and practices. The main sources of the legal tradition of Islam include the Qur'an, the Sunnah (the normative practices of the Prophet Muhammad), the *'ijma* (consensus of Muslim authoritative scholars), and *qiyas* (analogy). Another source of the Islamic legal tradition is *ijtihad* (independent reasoning) by competent and qualified Muslim jurists because in certain situations the Qur'an and Sunnah do not provide sufficient information.

Muslim psychotherapists need to consider that in classical scholarship, the purpose of Shari 'ah was to maintain and protect the welfare of the people, which is expressed in the concept of *istislah/maslahah* (common good). The main values of the Shari 'ah or *al-daruriyyat al-khams* were and still are "(1) protection of al-din, (2) protection of life (al-nafs), (3) protection of dignity or lineage (al-'ird), (4) protection of intellect (al-'aql), and (5) protection of property (al-mal)."[64] In addition to these five values, the Maliki jurist, Shihab al-Din al-Qarafi (d. 1285) added the protection and preservation of *'irḍ* (honour, dignity) as a sixth objective to the theory of *maqasid*/objectives of Shari 'ah.[65] Some contemporary Muslim scholars such as Mohammad Hashim Kamali[66] and Tariq Ramadan[67] also contributed to Shari 'ah in the context of contemporary challenges: for them, Shari 'ah principles could be utilized in current legal and judicial processes.

These examples show how the early Islamic legal tradition provided the foundation for contemporary understanding of Shari 'ah and was heavily influenced by the socio-historical and political context. It was also open to manipulations to conform to state constrictions regarding freedom of thought; for those who resisted, their positions could easily be overridden by *'ijma* (a consensus) of Muslim scholars. Some scholars, such as Abu Bakr al-Sarakshi (d. 1090), argued that the ruling of an *'ijma* was equivalent to law, even going so far as to state that challenging such a decision constituted *kufr* (disbelief). According to Hamid al-Ghazali (d. 1111) and 'Abd al- 'Aziz b. Ahmad al-Bukhari (d. 1329), opposition against and rejection of *ijma* is *haram* (illicit). In his *Naqd al-Maratib al-'ijma*, Ibn Taymiyah also refuted Ibn Hazm (d. 1064), a famous Zahiri jurist of Andalusia, claiming that he contradicted *'ijma* on many occasions. Ibn Taymiyya believed that the consensus of the four imams of Sunni Islam constituted a definitive ruling because they possessed the truth of the Shari 'ah. He considered this *al-a'imma ijtima'uhum hujjatun qati'atun wa ikhtilafuhum rahmatun wasi'a* (divergence a divine mercy).[68] However, in his *Aqida Wasitiyyah*, he also argues that the *'ijma*, which is *jami' ma 'alayh al-nags* (everything which people follow) in matters of religion, should be limited only to the opinions of the *al-salaf al-salih* (the first pious generations). This approach to *'ijma*, however, restricts the divergences of opinions of Muslim scholars in the field of Shari 'ah and categorizes them as a deviation from the path of the "righteous generations." He took a similar approach towards the application of *qiyas* (analogical reasoning) in Shari 'ah, arguing that legal rulings based on it were *ishkal wa ifsad wa tadlis* (corrupt, ambiguous, and fraudulent). On the other hand, Fakhr al-Din al-Razi (d. 1209), Imam al-Haramayn al-Juwayni (d. 1085), and others, disagreed, however, arguing that the ontological authority of the *'ijma* was not clear.

Although most pre-modern jurists accepted the principle of consensus as a source of law, there is considerable disagreement regarding whose judgement should be held in highest esteem. Despite these discrepancies, however, one fact remains: the legal rulings of the Shari 'ah from the pre-modern era were never viewed through a gender-equal lens; consequently, much of what is reflected in the body of earliest Islamic legal traditions are misogynistic and androcentric.

Thus, Islam's legal tradition is neither static nor stagnant; instead, it is constantly influenced by Islam's intellectual tradition and subject to continuous interpretation and reinterpretation. Throughout history, it has played a central role in the implementation of legal rulings that responded to the socio-political, economic, and cultural needs of the time. Nevertheless, several points should be taken into consideration here. First, it is generally accepted that when the Qur'an or the Sunnah of the Prophet mandates a law, it cannot be changed or rejected. For example, the Shari 'ah ruling that *shirk* (idolatry) or consuming pork or alcohol are *haram* (forbidden), can never change in Islam's legal tradition because the source for this law is the Qur'an and the Sunnah. Specific types of practice are categorized as follows: *fard* (obligatory under law), *wajib* (obligatory through legal extrapolation but not accepted as sin if not performed), *mustahab* or *mandub* (not obligatory but recommended), *mubah* (neutral or permitted), and *haram* (forbidden). However, some aspects of the Islamic legal tradition are subject to change, such as legal rulings about domestic violence, which will be explained in detail later. Second, many Muslims generally see the legal tradition as the summative work of classical Islamic scholarship and they accept this as authoritative and authentic because it is approved by a consensus of Muslim scholars (*'ijma*). Consequently, Islam's legal tradition is considered binding on those who follow it. Third, the contemporary work of Muslim scholars is influencing the attitudes and behaviours of its followers and is gaining popularity as part of this legal tradition.[69]

Therefore, to draw upon the Shari 'ah as a source of empowerment in Islamic psychotherapy, it is necessary to accept that there is no definitive "Shari 'ah" or legal tradition in Islam. Just as pre-modern jurists and scholars could rule on the truth of an interpretation, individual Muslims and/or collective groups must be empowered to determine their own truth by choosing which interpretation of the tradition provides the best social and religious order. In order to make the Shari 'ah more empowering in Islamic psychotherapy, the focus should shift from the "morality of the process" to the "morality of the substantive results."[70] From this perspective, Shari 'ah is "the search for the beautiful because it is the search for God" and "the Divine Will through several avenues of evidence"; however, the ideal search is "through a moral and ethical inquiry."[71]

Viewing the Shari 'ah as a moral or ethical inquiry will free Islam's legal tradition to be interpreted in our contemporary context and will allow the Muslim psychotherapy to be developed into a framework for understanding various forms of domestic violence that are perpetrated against Muslim women. Such a close examination of the Islamic legal tradition in Islamic psychotherapy, alongside the reality of the damage wreaked by domestic violence – especially that which justifies itself by drawing upon discriminatory interpretations of Shari 'ah – will demonstrate how such violence includes psychological, emotional, and physical abuse, effectively robbing Muslim women of their sanity, safety, and a significant measure of the quality of life.

The *Kalam* Tradition and Islamic Psychotherapy

Kalam (scholastic/discursive theology) is another aspect of the Islamic tradition that Islamic psychotherapy might use, especially when Muslims want to make existential meaning of their suffering. In the past, *kalam* focused predominantly on revelation and its sources. It provided definitions for the primary tenets of the Islamic faith including doctrines such as the essence of God, free will, prophecy and prophets, eschatology, and *imama* (political authority). As well, it defended the Islamic faith against those who attempted to refute Islam as a true divine religion. *Kalam* tradition included the Mu 'tazilite, Jabrite, Jahmite, Ash'arite, and Maturudi schools among others. This tradition addressed theological controversies in Islam, particularly ontological and cosmological proofs of God's existence, the relationship between God and the world, the problem of evil with respect to free will, determinism, fate, good, evil, punishment, and reward, and the relationship between reason and revelation.[72] A classical Muslim philosopher, Abu Nasr Muhammad ibn Muhammad al-Farabi (872–950), did not believe that *kalam* could establish a truly theoretical and universal understanding of the nature of God and His attributes, and of man and his ultimate good.[73] Rather than a speculative science, Farabi depicted *kalam* as an art that aimed to "confirm adherence to the law on the part of those enquiring adherents of the religion who are not adept in philosophy."[74] Many prominent Muslim scholars such as Imam Abu ʿAbdullah Muhammad ibn Idris al-Shafiʿi (d. 820) and Imam Abu Ḥamid Muḥammad ibn Muḥammad al-Ghazali (d. 1111) defended *kalam* against such criticism, but ultimately, only a small circle of Muslim scholars studied this tradition.[75]

The Mu 'tazilites

Presenting themselves as *ahl al-tawhid wa'l- ʿadl* (the people of divine justice and unity), the Mu 'tazilites played an important role in the emergence and historical development of *kalam* tradition, developing theories of legal methodology,[76] and influenced the major branches of Islamic schools of thought from both the Sunni and the Shiite traditions.[77] Nevertheless, there are various and conflicting views about the role of the Mu 'tazilite on contemporary Islamic thought.[78]

According to Ignaz Goldziher, *mu'tazila* refers to "those who withdraw," basing his opinion on the fact that Wasil ibn 'Ata (d. 748) and many great Mu 'tazilites embraced *zuhd* (an ascetic way of life). Wasil ibn 'Ata's companion, 'Amr ibn 'Ubayd (d. 761), used to pray through entire nights; as well, he undertook the pilgrimage to Mecca on foot 40 times, and he addressed an ascetic sermon of admonition to the caliph al-Mansur (d. 775).[79] Later, the Mu 'tazilite joined the rationalist groups or "freethinkers of Islam," becoming a voice of opposition to other dominant expressions of belief.[80]

William Montgomery Watt agrees with the idea that the Mu 'tazilite engaged in withdrawal of an ascetic or monastic type; however, he points out that the term would most likely have been used in a pejorative sense.[81] He argues that asceticism is absent from the five principles that would have framed the Mu 'tazilite tradition and practice at that time:

1. *tawhid* (divine unity)
2. *'adl* (divine justice)

3. *al manzila bayn al-manzilatayn* (a position between two positions)
4. *al-wa'd wa'l-wa'id* (promise and threat)
5. *al-amr bi'l- ma'ruf wa'l-nahy 'an al-munkar* (commanding good and forbidding evil).[82]

Although the Mu 'tazilite began as an intellectual and religio-political movement, it became more prominent during the ninth century, a time when this school was influential in encouraging new developments in Islamic thought. For example, the Mu' tazilite made a significant contribution to the debates about the eternity of the Qur'an and the question of free will. They also wrestled earnestly with emerging issues that dealt with challenging topics such as the qualities of God and, later, with the Qur'anic promise of seeing God. Unfortunately, their spirit of theological revival was suffocated by rigid and inflexible dogmas that were incongruent with mainstream Islamic thought.

The Ash 'arites

Ash 'arite is one of the early and most popular and widespread rationalist schools of Sunni Islam that emerged in the tenth century. It was founded by Abu al-Hasan al-Ash 'ari (d. 936), who once followed Abu 'Ali al-Jubba'i (d. 915), the leader of the Basran Mu 'tazilities. The tradition portrays a famous debate between al-Ash 'ari and his Mu 'tazilite teacher Abu 'Ali al-Jubba'i that sheds light on the Ash 'arite theology of predestination in the context of the suffering of the innocent. Al-Ash 'ari asked his teacher whether God had performed "the optimum" in the case of three individuals: a believer, an unbeliever, and a child.

> Al-Jubba'i responded: "The believer is among the [honoured] classes; the unbeliever is among the doomed; and the child is among those who escape [perdition]." Al Ash 'ari: "If the child should desire to ascend to the ranks of the honoured, would this possible?"
>
> Al-Jubba'i: No. It would be said to him, "The believer simply earned this rank through his obedience, the likes of which you do not have to your credit."
>
> Al-Ash 'ari: If the child should respond, "This is not my fault. Had You allowed me to live longer, I would have put forth the same obedience as the [adult] believer?"
>
> Al-Jubba'i: God would respond, "I knew that had I given you [additional] life, you would have disobeyed Me, for which you would have been punished. So, I observed your best interest and caused you to die before reaching the age of majority [at which time you would have become responsible for obeying Me according to the religious law]."[83]
>
> Al-Ash 'ari: The unbeliever in the Hell would exclaim, "O Lord! Why did you not kill me as a child, too, so that I would not sin and then enter hell?"[84]

Al-Jubba'i could not respond to al-Ash 'ari's question how God's unlimited omnipotence, which is bound by values and principles as the Mu 'tazilite claim, works in the case of a believer, unbeliever, and a child. The tradition suggests that this incident resulted in the emergence of the mainstream Ash 'arite theodicy of determinism as the dominant "orthodox" perspective among Muslims who believe in God's absolute and autonomous power (*qudrah*), will (*iradah*) and knowledge.

As a Rationalist movement, Ash 'arism adopts the creed that God is acting in the best interest of humans but is not obliged to do so.[85] Ash 'arism, which later was adopted by the mainstream Sunni schools, also acknowledged that reason could recognize truth of revelation and achieve the highest perfection. Al-Ash'ari, the founder of Ash'arism, acknowledged the speculative inquires of *kalam* as a science with a purpose to study the fundamental principles of religion. Ash 'arism also considered *'amal* important which can be translated as action, practice or deed, and as a way of knowing faith. It is no wonder that multiple Qur'anic verses (i.e., Q. 103) also bring to attention the significance of *'amal* right after faith.[86]

Many Shaf 'i and Maliki scholars follow Ash 'arite school of thought.[87] Besides al-Shafi 'i, one of the most prominent member of this school of thought is Abu Hamid al-Ghazali who is also a well-known Sufi. Like some of the Mu 'tazilites, the Ash 'arites also used reason to understand the truth. As well, both schools openly questioned the source of truth and authority in Islam and two specific sources of knowledge in Islam – revelation and reasoning. This said, however, there are differences between the two. For al-Ash 'ari, reason can recognize the truth of a revelation and achieve the highest perfection. He valued the speculative inquiry of the *kalam* in studying the fundamental principles of religion. The Ash 'ariti School believed that although humans possess free will, God ultimately creates their actions. For them, the source of moral truth is revelation, something that is beyond what humans can achieve on their own. Ash 'arites, like Mu 'tazilites, recognized the importance of reasoning in non-religious issues. Al-Ash 'ari himself used cognitive judgement to explain religious principles.[88] For al-Ash 'ari, '*iman* (a belief) is *tasdiq* (confirmation) that God and His prophet have spoken the truth (revelation). He believed that revelation involved knowing/reasoning and he stressed that all humans have an obligation to know God.

The Maturidites

Abu Mansur Muhammad b. Muhammad b. Mahmud al-Maturidi (d. 944), a native of the northwest of the city of Samarqand in contemporary Uzbekistan, who followed the Hanafi legal tradition, was the contemporary of al-Ash'ari. He made major contributions to the *kalam* tradition, even though there were attempts to view the Maturidism as a failed or successful version of Ash'arism.[89] Nevertheless, the Maturidism differed from the Ash 'arite in a more substantive way or at least, constituted a bridge between Ash'arite and

Mu 'tazilite. For example, they agreed with the Mu 'tazilites that God cannot reward unbelievers nor God can do as God pleases; while they were in more agreement with the Ash'arites that humans cannot create their own actions nor God must observe human interest.[90] In his *Kitab al-Tawhid*, al-Maturidi asserted that *tawhid* (the oneness of God) is the heart of Islam. Together with the Ash 'arites, Maturidites tried to balance between free will and predestination through the doctrine of *kasb, iktisab* (voluntary acquisition) and by stating that in the Qur'an God declares, "God is the creator of everything."

Like the Ash 'arism, the Maturidism is one of the rationalist Sunni schools of thought. Also, they identified *al-'aql* (reason) and *al-sam'* (prophetic transmission) as the basic and main foundations of religious knowledge.[91] This school of thought is popular in Turkey, Central Asia, the Balkans, and also in some part of the Middle East and also, in the West, among the Muslim communities who immigrated from these Muslim countries.

The Traditionalist School or Ahl al-athar[92]

The traditionalists also played an important role in shaping the Islamic theology or leading the demise of the Islamic theological tradition.[93] The term "traditionalists" is open to various understandings and interpretations (i.e., can be understood as people who adhere to ancient customs and habits), but in the context of the Islamic theology, it refers to people who claim following the teachings of the Qur'an, the Sunnah, and the *ijma'* (consensus)[94] in opposition against Rationalism. In addition, the traditionalist school is based on "the religious content" that is "derived from the three devices mentioned here is homogeneous," and "the embracing of the scholars . . . are responsible for the application of these devices."[95] They claimed that those who did not adhere to these principles are blameworthy for *bid'a* (pl. *bida'*; innovations). However, the usage of the term "traditionalists" is also subject to criticisms because it should not be interpreted as if those Muslim scholars, who advocated using the reason, were against the tradition or the traditionalists or vice versa. For example, the Hanbali school of thought was against the application of reason simply because they refused to follow the Aristotelian reasoning.

Therefore, some prefer to call them "the Hadith folk"[96] or some also included in this school of thought Ash 'arites and Maturidities as well despite the fact that the Ash 'arite scholars used the Aristotelian reasoning in their practice of interpreting the scripture.[97] However, Binyamin Abrahamov suggests differentiating between "Traditionalism" and "Traditionalists" and uses the term "Traditionalists" to describe the scholars of *hadith*; whereas, Sherman Jackson[98] uses the term "Traditionalism" to refer to those who follow the Hanbali School of Thought. Therefore, I will use the term "Traditionalists" or "Traditionalism" as a technical term to describe those who literally interpret the Qur'an and follow the Sunnah.

Although the pure traditionalists rejected the use of rational arguments, the more moderate traditionalists used these tools to prove God's existence, unity, and attributes. The prominent members of this school, i.e., Ibn Hanbal, Yusnus b. 'Ubayd (d. 756–7), Ibn Qutayda (d. 889), Abu Zur'a 'Ubayy Allah b. 'Abd al-Karim al-Razi (d. 878) and Abu Hatim Muḥammad b. Idris al-Razi (d. 890) and so forth, were in explicit opposition against the Mu 'tazilites. They considered the Mu 'tazilite ideas, such as free will, the creation of the Qur'an, and the figurative interpretations of anthropomorphic expressions in the Qur'an and the Sunnah, deviance from the literal meaning of the Qur'an and Sunnah as these ideas corrupt Islam.[99] They also argued that '*iman* (faith) is composed of action and speech and can be increased or decreased. Further, they also viewed God as omnibenevolent, who created human beings with potential rather than as absolutes. Therefore, it

> is ultimately humans' failure or refusal to will or prefer good to evil and to petition God for the ability to carry this preference out that sets in motion the cycle of acts and impulses that generate and sustain evil.

Nevertheless, as we will see in this study, the theological arguments presented by the traditionalists, i.e., Hanbalites, the tradition that they claim to transmit was subject to mediation because the tradition itself is "the process of selectively endorsing and suppressing old and new ideas and practices."[100]

Sufism – Islam's Mystical Tradition and Islamic Psychotherapy

Sufism provides an essential foundation for Islamic psychotherapy as it is recognized as Islam's life-giving core since the emergence of Islam.[101] Many Muslim therapists draw upon Sufi concepts, especially Sufi psychology and its emphasis on the training of *nafs* (ego, self, soul)[102] and its approaches to emotional and spiritual diseases. For example, they encourage their Muslim clients to perform ritual activities such as *dhikr*[103] (the rhythmic repetition of God's names) prescribed by the Sufi masters. Some Muslims also visit the shrines of Sufi masters to seek healing.[104]

Although there is no consensus on what the name of Sufism refers to and it is beyond the scope of this study to present the diverse theories of Sufism's nature and origins, it is helpful to mention here that there are various explanations for the etymology of the term *tasawwuf* (Sufism). Some believe it is derived from *suf*, the word describing the rough woollen garments worn by many Sufis. Others draw a connection between the term and the *suffa*, an ascetic group of the Prophet's companions known as the People of the Bench. Due to the influence of Greek philosophy, the term is often associated with *sophos* (wisdom). It is also possible that the term is connected to the Syrian Sufi, Abu Hashim al-Sufi (d. 767). And finally, there may be a connection between the term and the *safwa* (chosen ones) who practiced *tasfiyat al-qulub* (the purification of the heart).

Sufism emerged during the political arguments after the death of the Prophet Muhammad, when Islam began to spread to the remote areas of the established Islamic caliphates. Some, especially the Hanbali School, argue that Sufism does not conform to Islam's legal tradition, theology, and/or mainstream schools of thought. However, abundant examples show that prominent Muslim scholars, such as Imam al-Shafi 'i, even Imam Hanbal, ibn Qayyim al-Jawziyyah, followed the Sufi path. As well, many *shaykhs* (Sufi leaders) were prominent Hanbali jurists; for example, 'Abd al-Qadir al-Jilani (d. 1166) founded the Qadiri Sufi order, one of the largest Sufi orders in the Muslim and Western world.[105]

Embracing a deeply spiritual aspect of Islam, Sufis seek to achieve direct experience of God through their devotional rituals and practices.[106] They desire *qurb* (to draw near to God) and *dhawq* (to taste God). In sum, Sufism infuses all Islamic doctrines with transcendental private experience. In this regard, Ibn 'Arabi described four levels of Sufi practice and understanding: *shari 'ah* (exoteric religious law), *tariqah* (the mystical path and a term that was used to refer to the Sufi orders), *haqiqah* (truth), and *ma 'rifah* (gnosis).[107] S*hari 'ah* provides the foundation for the practice because it offers genuine guidance for living ethically and morally in this world. Those who follow *Shari 'ah* and Sufism try to embrace "the earlier exemplary life of the Prophet Muhammad."[108] By integrating *Shari 'ah* and *tariqah*, the *salik* or *murid* (follower of a spiritual path) discovers esoteric knowledge, to experience God directly, and to follow the practice of *awliya Allah* (God's prophets and friends) in their private and public lives.

Currently, some of the most popular Sufi orders are the Qadiriyah, the Rifa'iyah, the Shadhiliyah, the Suhrawardiyah, the Jerrahi Sufi order, the Naqshibandiyah, the Tijaniyah, the Mawlawiyah in Anatolia, and the Ahmadayah in the Nile Delta.[109] What differs these Sufi orders is their distinctive identity in terms of some Sufi concepts, i.e., *fanaa'* (passing away) and *baqa'* (abiding or remaining in God) or *sukr* (drunkenness or intoxication) or *sahw* (sober). For example, the Yasawiyah and the Naqshibandiyah followed Abu Yazid al-Bistami (d. 874) who was famous for saying ecstatic utterances; whereas others (i.e., the Kubraqiyah and the Mawlawiyah) follow Abu al-Qasim al-Junayd (d. 910) who emphasized sober Sufism, external aspects of the Shari 'ah such as ritual purity and fasting.

Sufism enriched the conceptual vocabulary of Islamic tradition so that they became "an ingrained part of the idiom of the speech of Muslims, and especially of poetry."[110] Almost all the major languages of Muslims, i.e., Arabic, Persian, Turkish, and Urdu possess the Sufi concepts as a form of social communication and self-expression. The existence of the Sufi concepts among Muslims is also definitely related to the psychological aspects of Sufism. Although a detailed account of this aspect of Sufism will be provided in the chapter where we discuss spiritual diseases, it is important to mention here when we use the term "Sufi psychology" we refer to the psychology of *qalb* (heart),[111] *nafs* (self), and *ruh* (soul). This important aspect of Sufi psychology differentiates it from the traditional Western psychology that perceives human being as a physical body and a mind. Also, Sufi psychology does not treat the person as a material being only; instead, it recognizes the person as a spiritual being created by God. In Sufi psychology, as a divine temple, the heart is the seat of our deeper intelligence and wisdom, love, gnosis, and spiritual knowledge. On the other hand, the word *nafs* refers to the self, an aspect of the psyche where "begins our worst adversary but can develop into an invaluable tool."[112] It is also interpreted as the human potential to actualize the fullness of self-awareness, *aql* (the intellect) or as the "lower self," referring to spiritual impulses.[113] *Ruh* is also translated as the "soul," but unlike *nafs*, it is a "higher self" and primarily quoted in a positive sense. The soul has seven aspects of dimensions such as the mineral, vegetable, animal, personal, human, and secret soul, and the secret of secrets: every human being has these levels of consciousness. In sum, Sufi psychology recognizes both the spiritual and material components of human nature and recognizes their interactive relationship.

Culture and Islamic Psychotherapy

Islamic psychotherapy theories and practices must also consider the broad diversity of Muslim cultures. On one hand, these rich and vivid ethnic strands weave together a colourful tapestry of Muslim customs; on the other hand, many localized traditions sustain and support male dominance over women. For this reason, culture plays an important role in the phenomenon of domestic violence in Muslim families, and it is imperative to understand its role to address the problem effectively in Islamic psychotherapy.

The concept of culture varies considerably. Pointing to the complexity of meanings, Alfred Kroeber and Clyde Kluckhohn identify 164 definitions.[114] Edward Burnett Tylor defines culture as a universal human capacity, a "complex whole which includes knowledge, belief, art, morals, law, custom, and any other capabilities and habits acquired by man as a member of society."[115] Richard Velkley defines culture from the perspective of identity and looking back to the 18th-century German thinkers; he shows how two primary meanings of "culture" emerge: culture "as the folk-spirit having a unique identity" and culture as the "cultivation of inwardness or free individuality."[116] For Velkley, the former represents the mainstream interpretation of culture; whereas, the later is the ultimate goal of the individual or the human desire to achieve the full expression of the unique or "authentic self."[117] Other authors augment the definition of "culture" by adding characteristics such as the norms of behaviours, patterns of life, and social conventions that include mannerisms such as the way people dress, cook, and relate to each other. In general, all these definitions indicate that culture is an integral aspect of society.

With the passage of time, cultures evolve and change. Sometimes, local customs and practices become obsolete like outworn and useless "baggage."[118]

In other cases, the merging of the local customs with religious traditions is not congruent with Islam. For example, in Islamic traditions, *nikah* (the marriage ceremony) is followed by *walimah* (a gathering feast) where the Qur'an is usually recited. Islam discourages lavish and pretentious celebrations because they lead to pride and showing-off, and they place a financial burden on those who are not wealthy. However, in Azerbaijan, families opt for extravagant weddings due to the social stigma associated with unpretentious celebrations, despite the values of the Islamic tradition. Funeral and memorial services in Azerbaijan reflect a similar pattern. The family of the deceased provides rich and lavish food even though this contradicts the early teachings of Islam. As we know from the *hadith* literature, when the wife of Ja'far, a companion of the Prophet, died, the Prophet asked the neighbours to take food to his household, saying "what will keep them busy has befallen them."[119] As another example, among Yoruba Muslims in Nigeria, *iyale* (senior wives) hold more rights than *iyawo* (junior wives), which is contrary to the Islamic values of equality between wives.[120]

Generally, Islamic culture refers to a way of life that includes the religious and cultural practices of Muslims. In his three-volume work, *The Venture of Islam*, Marshall Hodgson proposes using the term "*Islamicate*" when referring to both religious and cultural practices of Muslims.[121] Ahmed, on the other hand, talks about the Islamic culture in terms of local *islams* that "conceive (even if *differently*) of universal Islam."[122] However, unlike Hamid Dabashi, who argues that "to call a culture Islamic" is "to deny its creative tension" and "to rob that culture of its most vital energy," Ahmed notes that assuming that some expressions are cultural rather than Islamic is not true as some cultural expressions cannot be understood without referring them to Islam. He gives example from the classical scholars such as al-Ash 'ari, who addressed these multiple expressions among Muslims. In his famous book *The Professions of the Islamic People, and the Disagreements among Those Who Perform the Prayer*, Al-Ash 'ari used the expression *al-islamiyyin* to refer to those who are "affiliated/associated with, or ascribed/attributed to Islam" despite the disagreements and differences.[123]

Although Islam "gathers them [Muslims] together" and "encompasses them all,"[124] this suggestion, however, does not clearly differentiate between religious and cultural aspects of Islamic traditions. To make a clearer distinction, I use the term "Islamic culture" when referring to the religious beliefs and practices of Islam and the term "Muslim culture" when describing the local customs and practices of Muslim communities, such as folk music, cultural holidays, visits to sacred places such as tombs of holy people, birthing and mourning customs, female genital mutilation (FGM), animism, and so forth.[125]

The Islamic tradition articulates the rich and unique cultural, philosophical, juridical, and religious traditions of Muslims who have experienced similar, yet distinctively different socio-historical, political, economic, and cultural transformations. Regardless of how Islamic tradition is defined, the various landscapes, languages, and social, historical, and religious constructions of Muslim communities contribute to a diversity of interpretations of the Islamic tradition. Throughout this study, I will move beyond the constriction of understanding the term "Islamic tradition" solely from the perspective of the legal tradition of Islam; rather, I will explore the parallels, similarities, and differences in the ways that the Islamic traditions have meaning (or not) for the Muslim women I encounter in Islamic psychotherapy.

Therefore, in this study, the Islamic tradition also embraces a set of cultural beliefs, lifestyles, assumptions, interpretations, rituals, and ceremonies that weave together to fashion the worlds of the Muslim women who seek Islamic psychotherapy. Islamic culture has the following common elements: first, it is God-centred or theocentric shaped under the strict concept of monotheism. Second, it is tolerant and fraternal because of the concept of brotherhood: it accepts people from various ethnic and racial backgrounds without forcing them to convert to Islam. Third, it is moralistic because of its emphasis on the dignity and morality of human beings, including truthfulness, honesty, modesty, etc. Fourth, it is dynamic, progressive, world-affirming and not world-denying or ascetic. Finally, it is non-exclusivist but *dawah* (missionary)-oriented and optimistic.[126] Unfortunately, in many cases, some cultural practices contribute to agonizing issues such as domestic violence. Within their specific social worlds, individuals and groups also overlay their own perspectives on relationships, social situations, and their unique identity, thereby creating their own traditions. This complicates the work of Islamic psychotherapy because our experience of reality is subjective, and, more importantly, our understanding of these "created" Islamic traditions are influenced by our own worldviews. Despite its complexity, culture must be embraced in Islamic psychotherapy because it embodies elements of the past, present, and evolving future. From that complex and pluralistic tradition, Islamic psychotherapy can draw great wisdom and guidance from the rich cultural practices of Muslims all around the world.

Notes

1. Rassool, *Islamic Counselling*, 18.
2. In Islamic jurisprudence, *fard* or its synonym *wajib* describes the duties of Muslims in everyday life. In general, there are two types of *fard*: *fard al-'ayn*, which is about individual duty of every Muslim such as five daily prayers, fasting during the month of Ramadhan, etc., and *fard al-kifaya*, which is about a communal obligation of a community of believers in Muslim legal doctrine. It implies that if one or enough members of the Muslim community take the responsibility of this obligation, the remaining Muslims are freed from the responsibility before God; otherwise, every individual Muslim carries responsibility for the problem. An example of *fard al-kifaya* is feeding the hungry, commanding good, and forbidding evil, or *janaza*, Islamic funeral ritual ("Fard al-Kifayah," in *The Oxford Dictionary of Islam*, ed. by John L. Esposito. *Oxford Islamic Studies Online*. Accessed on March 26, 2014 from www.oxfordislamicstudies.com/article/opr/t125/e625. Also see Abu Hamid al-Ghazali, *Revival of Religious Learning* (Ihya Ulum-id-Din), trans. by Fazl ul-Karim (Karachi: Darul-Ishaat, 1993).

3. See Michael Dol, *Majnun: The Madman in Medieval Islamic Societies* (Oxford: Clarendon Press, 1992).
4. In the Sufi tradition, he was entitled *al-ghawth al-a 'zam* (the supreme spiritual helper or the mightiest succor).
5. Shaykh Abdul Qadir Jilani, *Kitab Sirr al-Asrar wa Mazhar al-Anwar* (The Book of The Secret of Secrets and The Manifestations of Light), trans. by Muhtar Holland (Birmingham: Al-Baz Publishing, 2000).
6. Goerge Makdisi, *The Rise of Colleges: Institutions of Learning in Islam and the West* (Edinburgh: Edinburgh University Press, 1981), 88–89.
7. Abdal Hakim Murad, *The Mantle Adorned* (London: The Quilliam Press Ltd., 2009).
8. Mostafa al-Badawi, *Islamic Psychotherapy? Man & the Universe: An Islamic Perspective* (Amman: Wakeel Books, 2002), 137–141.
9. Those who were influenced by the rational school, for example, made references to the Qadari-Mu'talizes in the eighth and ninth centuries, especially Abu'l Hudhayl al-Allaf (d. 849), Bishr Ibn al-Mu'tamir (d. 825), Abu Ishaq Ibrahim ibn Sayyar ibn Hani' al-Nazzam (d. 845), Qadi 'Abd al-Jabbar ibn Ahmad ibn 'Abd al-Jabbar al-Hamadhani al-Asadabadi, (d. 1025) and others. Others, for example, were under the influence of the Asharities, such as Abu Bakr Muhammad ibn al-Tayyib al-Baqillani (d. 1013), Abd al-Latif al-Baghdadi (d. 1037), Imam al-Haramayn Dhia' al-Din Abd al-Malik al-Juwayni al-Shafi'i (d. 1064), Taj al-Din Abu al-Fath Muhammad ibn 'Abd al-Karīm al-Shahrastani (d. 1153), Abu Hamid Muhammad ibn Muhammad al-Ghazali (d. 1111), Fakhr al-Din al-Razi (d. 1209). The third group belonged to the anti-rationalist school, which were mainly represented by Abū Muhammad 'Ali ibn Ahmad ibn Sa'id ibn Hazm (also sometimes known as al-Andalusi al-Zahiri) from the Zahiri school (d. 1064), Taqi al-Din Ahmad ibn Taymiyyah (d. 1328), and others. The fourth group were inspired by the Sufis such as Hasan al-Basri (d. 728), Harith al-Muhasibi (d. 857), etc. The fifth group used the philosophical thought of Muslim scholars, especially Abu Yusuf Ya'qub ibn 'Ishaq al-Sabbah al-Kindi (801–873), Abu Bakr Muhammad ibn Zakariyya al-Razi or Rhazes (864–925), Abu Nasr Muhammad ibn Muhammad al-Farabi or Alpharabius (d. 950), Abu 'Ali al-Husayn ibn 'Abd Allah ibn al-Hasan ibn Ali ibn Sina or Avicenna (d. 1037), Yahya ibn 'Adi (d. 974), the Brethren of Purity (*Ikhwan al-Safa*) of the tenth century, Abu 'Ali Ahmad ibn Muhammad ibn Ya'qub ibn Miskawayh (d. 1030), the Shiite Nasir al-Din al-Tusi (d. 1274). Many of these philosophers were under the great influence of Greek thought. Al-Farabi and al-Razi, for example, represented the Neo-Platonist school; ibn Rushd and Ibn Sina, on the other hand, represented the Aristotelian thought. A rich tradition of Eastern thought also enriched Islamic counselling approaches. The translation of Ibn Miskawayh's Persian philosopher Buzurgmihr, Anushirwan, Hushay, and others, and the translation of *Kalila and Dimna* (the Fables of the Lion, the Fox, and the Donkey) by Abu Muhammad 'Abd Allah Ruzbih ibn Dādūya (also known as Ibn al-Muqaffa') (d. 759), the translation of the Patanzali by Abu al-Rayhan Muhammad ibn Ahmad al-Biruni (also known as Alberonius) (d. 1048), for example, allowed them to incorporate the religious and ethical concepts of Indian and Persian thought into Islamic counselling.
10. Majed A. Ashy, "Health and Illness From an Islamic Perspective," *Journal of Religion and Health* 38 (3) (1999): 241–258; N. Deuraseh and M. Abu Talib, "Mental Health in Islamic Medical Tradition," *The International Medical Journal* 4 (2005): 76–79.
11. Angelisa V. Paladin, "Ethics and Neurology in the Islamic World: Continuity and Change," *Italian Journal of Neurological Science* 19 (1998): 257.
12. See Deuraseh and Abu Talib, "Mental Health in Islamic Medical Tradition."
13. See Amber Haque, "Psychology From Islamic Perspective: Contributions of Early Muslim Scholars and Challenges to Contemporary Muslim Psychologist," *Journal of Religion and Health* 43 (4) (2004): 357–377.
14. The Samanids were the Sunni state in the territory of current Iran that ruled between 819–999.

15. Abubakr Muhammad ibn Zakariyya al-Razi, *The Spiritual Physick of Rhazes*, trans. from the Arabic by Arthur J. Arberry (London: John Murray, 1950), 4.
16. Haque, "Psychology From Islamic Perspective," 365.
17. Simon Kemp and K. T. Strongman, "Anger Theory and Management: A Historical Analysis," *The American Journal of Psychology* 108 (3) (1995): 397–417.
18. Munawar A. Anees, "Al-Majusi's Observations and Instruction on Medical and Public Health," in *Health Sciences in Early Islam*, ed. by S. Hamaerneh and M. Anees (n.p.: Zahra Publications, 1984), 317.
19. See Abu-1-Hasan Muhammad al-'Amiri, *Al-sa'ada wa-l-is'ad* (The Book of Happiness and Making Happy), ed. by M. Minovi (Tehran: Wiesbaden, 1957); Roxanne D. Marcotte, "Ibn Miskawayh's Tartib al-Saadat (The Order of Happiness)," in *Monotheism and Ethics: Historical and Contemporary Intersections Between Judaism, Christianity, and Islam*, ed. by Y. Tzvi Langermann (Leiden: Brill, 2012), 141–162; al-Razi, *The Spiritual Physick of Rhazes*; Abu 'Ali al-Husayn ibn Sina, *The Canon of Medicine* (al-Qanun fi al-Tibb). Accessed on August 25, 2016 from http://sekretariat.beacukai.go.id/data/aplikasi/Buku/Ibn%20Sina/Canon%20of%20Medicine%20Book%201.pdf; Abu al-Hasan al-Mawardi, *Kitab Aadab al-Dunya wa'l-Din* (Right Conduct in Matters Worldly and Religious) (Beirut, 1978); Abu Hamid al-Ghazali, *Mizan al-'amal* (The Balance of Action), ed. by S. Dunya (Cairo: Dar al-Ma'arif, 1964); *Ihya' 'Ulum al-Din* (The Revival of the Religious Sciences) (Cairo: Matba'ah Lajnah Nashr al-Thaqafah al-Islamiyya, 1937–8), 5 vol.; Abu Hamid al-Ghazali, *al-Munqidh min al-dalal* (The Rescuer from Error), ed. by J. Saliba and K. Ayyad (Damascus: Maktab al-Nashr al-'Arabi, 1934); Abu Hamid al-Ghazali, *Mishkat al-Anwar*, (Niche of Lights), ed. by A. Afifi (Cairo, 1964); *Al-Ghazali on The Ninety-Nine Beautiful Names of God* (Al-Maqsad Al-Asna Fi Sharh Asma' Allah Al Husna), trans. by David Burrel and Nazih Daher (London: Islamic Texts Society, 1999); Fakhr al-Din al-Razi, *Kitab al-nafs wa'l-ruh wa-sharh quwahuma* (Book on the Soul and the Spirit and their Faculties), ed. by M. S. H. al-Ma'sumi (Islamabad: Islamic Research Institute, 1968); Ahmad ibn Taymiyya, *Diseases of the Hart and Their Cures* (Birmingham: Daar us-Sunnah Publishers, n.d.); *The Relief From Distress* (Birmingham: Daar us-Sunna Publishers, 2006); Muhammad ibn Abi Bakr Ibn Qayyim al-Jawziyah, *Shifa' al-'alil* (Misr: al-Matba'at al-Husayniyya, 1905); *Hadi al-Arwah ila Bilad al-Afrah* (Spurring Souls on to the Realms of Joy), ed. by Yusuf Ali Badawi and Muhyiddin Mustu (n.d.: Dar Ibn Kathir & Dar Taybat al-Khudra) (also published in Beirut: Dar Al-Kutub Al-'Ilmiyya); *Mukhtasar al-sawa 'iq al-mursala 'ala al-Jahmiyya wa'l-Mu'attila* (Bayrut: Dar al-Nadwa al-Jadida, 1984); Yahya ibn Sharaf an-Nawawi, *Kitab al-Adhkar* (The Book of Remembrances) (London: Turath Publishing, 2014); Constance E. Padwick, *Muslim Devotions: A Study of Prayer-Manuals in Common Use* (London: S.P.C.K., 1969). Also cited by Gilliat-Ray, M. Mansur Ali, and Stephen Pattison, *Understanding Muslim Chaplaincy* (Surrey: Ashgate, 2013); Nurdeen Deuraseh and Mansor Abu Talib, "Mental Health in Islamic Medical Tradition," *The International Medical Journal* 4 (2) (2005): 76–79.
20. For a detailed account of the historical development of Islamic counselling, see Salisu Shehu, "Towards an Islamic Perspective of Developmental Psychology," *Islamic Online* (2002). Accessed from www.islamonline.net/english/Contemporary/2002/05/article7-a.shtml.
21. Rassool, *Islamic Counselling*, 18.
22. Abdullah, "Islam and Counseling," 42–55.
23. Shabnum Dharamsi and Abdullah Maynard, "The Interaction of Self and Soul in the Islamic Counselling Relationship," paper presented *at Spirituality, Theology and Mental Health: Myth, Authority and Healing Power*, Durham University, 13–16 September 2010; Malik B. Badri, *Contemplation: An Islamic Psychospiritual Study* (London: International Institute of Islamic Thought, 2000).
24. Rassool, *Islamic Counselling*, 208.
25. See note 13.

26. Shahab Ahmed, *What Is Islam? The Importance of Being Islamic* (Princeton, NJ: Princeton University Press, 2016), 5.
27. Ibid., 302.
28. Ibid.
29. Ibid., 9.
30. Ibid.
31. Thomas A. Green, *Folklore: An Encyclopedia of Beliefs, Customs, Tales, Music, and Art* (Santa Barbara: ABC-CLIO, 1997), 800.
32. Alasdair MacIntyre, *After Virtue*, 3rd ed. (Notre Dame, IN: University of Notre Dame Press, 2007), 257.
33. Talal Asad, *The Idea of Anthropology of Islam* (Washington, DC: The Center for Contemporary Arab Studies at Georgetown University, 1986), 5.
34. Ibid., 20.
35. Ahmed, *What Is Islam*, 272.
36. Ibid., 272.
37. Ibid., 274.
38. Ahmed, *What Is Islam*, 278. Ahmed states that

    > Perplexity, which is, of course, precisely a condition on non-resolution of truth, is thus valorized as an appropriate and positive response for the Muslim to have to Divine Truth – that is, as a normative Islamic value (albeit a little-studied one).

39. Ibid., 542.
40. Bernard Lewis, "Some Observations on the Significance of Heresy in the History of Islam," *Studia Islamica* 1 (1953): 44.
41. Rahman, "Approaches to Islam in Religious Studies," in *Approaches to Islam in Religious Studies*, ed. by Richard C. Martin (Tucson: University of Arizona, 1985), 195.
42. Ibid.
43. *Adat* also refers to the moral code in oral form in a particular society that sets the limits of a proper conduct or "a maximal limit to what could be tolerated by a particular, local community." Wael Hallaq, *Sharīʻa: Theory, Practice, Transformations* (Cambridge: Cambridge University Press, 2009), 90.
44. Ibid., 20.
45. Andrew Rippin, "The Exegetical Genre '*asbab al-nuzul*': A Bibliographical and Terminological Survey," *Bulletin of the School of Oriental and African Studies* 48 (1) (1985): 1–15.
46. Fazlur Rahman, *Islam and Modernity: Transformation of an Intellectual Tradition* (Chicago, IL and London: The University of Chicago Press, 1982); Isma'il Raji al-Faruqi, "Islamizing the Social Sciences," in *Social and Natural Sciences: The Islamic Perspectives*, ed. by Isma'il Rājī al-Faruūqi and Abdullah Omar Nasseef (Jiddah: Islamic Education Series, 1981); Sayyid Waqqar Ahmed Husaini, "Humanistic–Social Sciences Studies in Higher Education: Islamic and International Perspectives," in *Social and Natural Sciences: The Islamic Perspectives*, ed. by Ismā'īl Rājī al-Fārūqī and Abdullah Omar Nasseef (Jiddah: Islamic Education Series, 1981); Seyyed Hossein Nasr, "The Teaching of Philosophy," in *Philosophy, Literature, and Fine Arts*, ed. by Seyyed Hossein Nasr (Jiddah: Islamic Education Series, 1981).
47. Abdul-Raof Hussein, *A Practical Comparative-Contrastive Analysis* (London: Routledge, 2012), 2.
48. Walid Saleh, *The Formation of the Classical Tafsır Tradition: The Qur'an Commentary of al-Thalabi* (Leiden: Brill, 2004), 16.
49. Huseein Abdul-Raof, *Theological Approaches to Qur'anic Exegesis: A Practical Comparative-Contrastive Analysis* (New York: Routledge, 2012), 3–4.
50. Those who had a significant influence on traditional exegesis include the companions: 'A'isha (d. 678), Ibn 'Abbas (d. 687), the founder of the Makkah school, Ubai

b. Ka 'b (d. 649), the founder of the Madinah school, and Ibn Mas'ud (d. 653), the founder of the Kufah school; and early Islamic scholars such as Mujahid b. Jabr (d. 722), Sa 'id b. Jubair (d. 713), 'Ikramah al-Barbari (d. 723), 'Ata' b. Abi Rabah (d. 732), and Hasan al-Basri (d. 728).

51. Ibid., 29.
52. Abdullah Saeed, *Interpreting the Qur'an: Towards a Contemporary Approach* (New York, NY: Routledge, 2006), 3.
53. Walid Saleh calls this approach "radical hermeneutics," which he defines as the claim of those "to take *tafsir* back to its roots in the *salaf*." See Walid Saleh, "Ibn Taymiyya and the Rise of Radical Hermeneutics: An Analysis of an Introduction to the Foundations of Qur'anic Exegesis," in *Ibn Taymiyya and His Times*, ed. by Yossef Rapoport and Shahab Ahmed (Oxford: Oxford University Press, 2010), 148. In addition,

> At the heart of this radical hermeneutics is a restriction on the ability of exegetes to say anything by way of interpreting the Qur'an that has not been believed to have been said by authorities in the first three generations of Islam. (ibid., 148–149)

For Saleh, it started with Ibn Taymiyya and culminated to its peak with the publication of *al-Durr al-manthur fī al-tafsir bi-al-ma'thur* by al-Suyuṭi. Although it sounds "radical," at the heart of the "radical hermeneutics" lies attempts to reform Sunni hermeneutics. Saleh explains this "necessity" with three factors: (1) the paradoxical nature of the Sunni hermeneutics; (2) the rise of Shi'ism; and (3) the increase of tradition-based resources (Saleh, 151–152).

54. Taqi al-Din Ahmad b. 'Abd al-Halim b. Taymiyah, *Majm'at al rasa'il wal-masa'il* (Bayrut: Dår al-Kutub al- ̧Ilmiyyah, 1983); *Muqaddimah fi usul al-tafsir*, ed. Adnan Zarzour, 2nd ed. (Bayrut: n.p. 1972); *An Explanation of Shayhkh al-Islam Ibn Taymiyyah's Introduction to the Principles of Tafseer Explanation by Shaykh Muhammad Ibn Salih al-Uthaymin* (Birmingham, UK: Al-Hidaayah Publishing Ltd., n.d.). Accessed from http://alsiraat.co.uk/wp-content/uploads/2014/12/Ibn-Taymiyahs-Principles-of-Tafseer.pdf. Such an emphasis on the role of the words resonates with Gadamer's emphasis on *logos* and meanings. The literal meaning of *logos* is "an opinion," "word," "speech," "account," "to reason"; however, it is used in various disciplines as a "discourse" or "the argument." See, Christof Rapp, "Aristotle's Rhetoric," in *The Stanford Encyclopedia of Philosophy*, ed. by Edward N. Zalta (Spring 2010 Edition).
55. Saleh, "Ibn Taymiyya and the Rise of Radical Hermeneutics," 129. Ibn Taymiyya developed *qawa'id kulliyyah* or the methodological principles of the textualist approach in classical Islamic scholarship. According to his classifications, Qur'anic exegeses belong to these groups: the *tafsir bil-ra'y* (exegesis based on personal judgement), or *tafsir bil-ma'thur* (exegesis by transmission of the tradition). Ibn Taymiyya gave preference to the second form of exegesis over the first one and emphasized that the Qur'an must be a primary source in understanding the Qur'an. If it does not assist, then the Sunnah or the Prophetic tradition and the words of the *sahaba* (companions) must be used. In his *Muqaddima fi usul al-tafsir*, Ibn Taymiyya argued that the Qur'anic interpretations are four kinds: (1) the exegesis of the Qur'an by the Qur'an; (2) the exegesis of the Qur'an by hadith; (3) the exegesis of the Qur'an by companions such as Abdullah ibn Abbas (d. 68/687); and finally, (4) the exegesis of the Qur'an by the *tabi 'un* (immediate successors of the companions) such as Mujahid ibn Jabr al-Makki (d. 104/722), who studied the exegesis of the Qur'an from the companions of the Prophet.
56. As the tradition developed, exegetes refined the notion of *tafsir bi'l-ra'y* (exegesis based on personal judgement), accepting some forms and rejecting others, as can be noted in the work of al-Dhahabi, who gave several examples of acceptable and unacceptable forms of *tafsir bi'l-ra'y* among other things. Ibn Taymiyya's

hermeneutical framework also became extensively discussed in the monumental works on Qur'anic exegetical sciences by Badr al-Din Muhammad ibn 'Abdallah al-Zarkashi (d. 794/1392), and Jalal-al-Din al-Suyuti (d. 911/1505) although both Zarkashi and Suyuti followed the Shafi 'ite school of jurisprudence. Moreover, Ibn Taymiyya's hermeneutical framework opened the door for modern exegesis, which located itself within his first category, *tafsir al-Qur'an bi'l-Qur'an*, thereby highlighting their continuity with the tradition, but also the epistemological superiority of their interpretations to traditionalist interpretations. It also occurs in the widely disseminated modern work by Muhammad Husayn al- Dhahabi, which further indicates the significance of Ibn Taymiyyah's hermeneutics. See Muḥammad al-Dhahabi, *al-Tafsir wa'l-mufassirun*, 3 vol. (Cairo: Maktabat Wahbah, 2003), vol. 1, 72.

57. Some modern neo-revivalist movements, such as the Muslim Brotherhood (Egypt) and Jama'at Islam (Indian subcontinent), rely on this methodology when they interpret the Qur'an. I would suggest that certain elements of the both textualist and semi-textualist methods of interpretation are very distant from our current, lived realities and are not compatible with the needs and concerns of Muslims of our time, especially their emphasis on the tradition-based interpretation. In addition, adhering to the textualist or semi-textualist approach would eliminate my capacity to look at the "meanings" produced during the analysis of the stories. This is explained by the fact that the textualist approach to the Qur'an was interested in "narrowing the range of meanings available for the text." Saeed, *Interpreting the Qur'an*, 153.
58. A vivid example for this stream of interpreters of the Qur'an is Fazlur Rahman whose work extensively influenced "new-modernists, as well as Ijtihadis, the so-called 'progressive' Muslims and more generally 'liberal Muslim thinkers today.'" See Saeed, *Interpreting the Qur'an*, 4. We will talk more about the application of this approach by Muslim scholars later.
59. Muhammad Rashid Rida and Muhammad ˛Abduh, *Tafsir al-Qur'an al-hakim al-shahr bi-tafsir al-Manår*, 12 vols. (Bayrut: Dår al-Ma ˛rifah, n.d.); Muhammad Iqbal, *The Reconstruction of Religious Thought in Islam* (Lahore: K. Bazar, 1958); Sayyid Abul A'la Mawdudi, *Towards Understanding the Qur'an*, trans. by Zafar Ishâq Ansari (Leicester: Islamic Foundation, 1995); Ismail R. al-Faruqi, "Towards a New Methodology for Qur'anic Exegesis," *Islamic Studies* 1 (1) (1962): 36–52; Fazlur Rahman, *Islam* (Chicago, IL: University of Chicago Press, 1966); "Towards Reformulating the Methodology of Islamic Law: Sheikh; Yamani on 'Public Interest' in Islamic Law," *New York University Journal of International Law and Politics* 12 (2) (1979: 219–224; *Islam and Modernity*; *Major Themes of the Qur'an* (Minneapolis, MN: Bibliotheca Islamica, 1994); *Revival and Reform in Islam*, ed. by Ebrahim Moosa (Oxford: Oneworld, 2000); Abdolkairm Soroush, *Qabz o bast-e teutik-e shariat – nazariye-ye takamol-e marefat-e dini (Theory of Extension and Concentration/Evolution and Devolution of Religion – the Theory of Religious Knowledge's Development)*, 3rd ed. (Tehran: Sarat, 1994); Khaled Abou El-Fadl, *Speaking in God's Name: Islamic Law, Authority and Women* (Oxford: Oneworld, 2001); Abu Zayd, Nasr Hamid, *Falsafat al-ta'wıl* (Dåı al-Bayda': al-Markaz al-Thaqâf al- ˛Arab, 1996); *al-Na, wa al-,ulfah wa al-aaqiqah* (Dår al-Bayda': al-Markaz al-Thaqâf al- ˛Arab, 2000); Farid Esack, *Qur'an, Liberation and Pluralism: An Islamic Perspective on Inter-Religious Solidarity Against Oppression* (Oxford: Oneworld, 1997); *The Qur'an: An Introduction* (Oxford: Oneworld, 2002); Saeed, *Interpreting the Qur'an*.
60. For example, Rahman argues that to "try to see things from another person's point of view . . . is impossible," because an observer must share at least some part of the experience. However, this is not a "legitimate demand." On the other hand, he argues that an observer does not need to share the experience to make judgements and come to a conclusion. For him, what is important in this process is to obtain some "understanding" and "being meaningful to someone." Second,

Rahman argues that truth is very subjective; therefore, Muslims' approach to Islam is different from the Orientalist approach to Islam. Moreover, literary criticism is not enough to understand the religion of Islam. The hermeneutical exercise and historical criticism to analyze the historical texts such the Qur'an and Hadith is required. If such a method inspires Rahman's Muslim readers to practice Islam's five pillars, then, it also inspires Western scholars to grasp the understanding or appreciation of Muslims, who are committed to have faith and practice scriptural values from the level of the individual to society at large. Rahman, "Approaches to Islam in Religious Studies – Review Essay," 192. Also, Abdolkarim Soroush's concept of the changeability of religious knowledge suggests that our religious knowledge is subject to constant transformations because of the change that takes place in our cognitions. He explains the nature of the change of our religious knowledge with the human need to fit the context in which the interpreter lives. In addition, Soroush also argues about the role of our "biases" which he calls as the interpreter's preconceptions that have a tremendous impact on the way we interpret the text. See Abdolkarim Soroush, *Reason, Freedom, and Democracy in Islam: Essential Writings of Abdolkarim Soroush*, trans. and ed. by Mahmoud Sadri and Ahmed Sadri (Oxford: Oxford Univeristy Press, 2000).

61. Saleh, *The Formation of the Classical Tafsır Tradition*, 15.
62. Ibn Qayyim al-Jawziyyah, cited in El-Fadl, *Speaking in God's Name*, 14.
63. Hallaq, *Sharī'a*, 18.
64. Muhammad Adil Khan Afridi, "Maqasid al-Shari'ah and Preservation of Basic Rights Under the Theme 'Islam and Its Perspectives on Global & Local Contemporary Challenges,'" *Journal of Education and Social Sciences* 4 (2016): 275–285.
65. *Maqasid* or the main purpose of the Shari 'ah is *maslahah* (the fulfilment of some good) and/or *mafsadah* (the avoidance of some mischief). In Islamic law, the term *maqasid* (plural: of *maqsad*) refers to a purpose, objective, principle, intent, goal, end. See Afridi, "Maqasid al-Shari'ah and Preservation of Basic Right"; Mohammad al-Tahir Ibn Ashur, *Ibn Ashur-Treatise on Maqasid Al-Shariah*, trans. by Mohamed El-Tahir El-Mesawi, vol. 1 (London and Washington, DC: International Institute of Islamic Thought (HIT), 2006), ii. See also: Jasser Auda, *Maqasid Al-Shariah: An Introductory Guide* (Herndon, VA: IIIT, 2008). It is also often used interchangeably with the word *masalih* or interests. The main contributors to the development of the *maqasid* are Al-Tirmidhi al-Hakeem (d. 908); Abu Zaid al-Balkhi (d. 933), Abdul Malik al-Juwaini (d. 1185); Abu Hamid Ghazali (d. 1111), Fakhruddin al-Razi (d. 1209), al-Amidi (d. 1234); Shihab al-Din al-Qarafi; Maliki Abu Ishaq al-Shatibi, Shafie al-Izz Ibn Abd al-Salam and Hanbali Ibn Qayyim al-Jawzi, and so forth. Some of the contemporary Muslim scholars who extensively wrote on this subject are Rashid Rida (d. 1935), Muhammad al-Tahir ibn Ashur (d. 1907), Mohammad al-Ghazali (d. 1996), Taha al-Alwani, Yusuf al-Qaradawi, Hayrettin Karaman, and so forth. In his famous book *Al-Muwafaqat fi Usul al-Shari'ah*, al-Shatibi characterized *maslahah*

    > as being the only principal objective of the Shari'ah which is broad enough to comprise all measures that are beneficial to the people. He placed a great emphasis on the objectives of the Shari'ah (Maqasid al-Shari'ah), so much so that his unique contribution to the understanding of the objectives and philosophy of the Shari'ah is widely acknowledged.

    See Afridi, "Maqasid al-Shari'ah and Preservation of Basic Right," 275.
66. Mohammad Hashim Kamali, *Shari'ah Law: An Introduction* (Oxford: Oneworld, 2008). Also see Mohammad Hashim Kamali, *Principles of Islamic Jurisprudence* (Cambridge: Islamic Texts, 1991).
67. Tariq Ramadan, *Radical Reform: Islamic Ethics and Liberation* (Oxford: Oxford University Press, 2009).
68. Taqi al-Din Ahmad b. ibn Taymiyyah, *Mukhtasar al-fatawa al-misriyya* (Cairo, 1980), 35.

69. Examples include the works of Shah Wali Allah (d. 1762), Rashid Rida (d. 1935), Mahmud Shaltut (d. 1963), Muhammad Zakariyya al-Kandahlawi (d. 1968), 'Abd al-Halim Mahmud (d. 1978), Muhammad al-Ghazali (d. 1996), Yusuf al-Qaradawi, and Hayraddin Karaman.
70. El-Fadl, *Speaking in God's Name*, 63.
71. Ibid., 70–71.
72. See John L. Esposito, *The Oxford Dictionary of Islam* (New York, NY: Oxford University Press, 2003).
73. See Richard M. Frank, "Reason and the Revealed Law: A Sample of Parallels and Divergence in Kalam and Falsafa," *Recherches d'Islamologie; Recueil d'aricles offert a Georges C. Anawati et Louis Gardet par leurs collegues et amis, Bibiliotheque Philosophique de Louvain no. 26* (Louvai: Peetes, 1977), 127–128; *Philosophy, Theology and Mysticism in Medieval Islam: Texts and Studies on the Development and History of Kalam*, vol. 1, ed. by Dimitri Gutas (Aldershot: Ashgate, Variorum, 2005); *Early Islamic Theology: The Mu'tazilites and al-Ash'arī. Texts and Studies on the Development and History of Kalam*, vol. 2 ed. by Dimitri Gutas (Aldershot: Ashgate, Variorum, 2007).
74. Frank, "Reason and the Revealed Law," 134.
75. Mashhad Al-Allaf, "Islamic Theology," in *The Bloomsbury Companion to Islamic Studies*, ed. by Clinton Bennett (London: Bloomsbury, 2013), 119–134.
76. See Sherman Jackson, *Islam and the Problem of Black Suffering* (New York, NY: Oxford University Press, 2009); Josef van Ess, *The Flowering of Muslim Theology* (Cambridge, MA: Harvard University Press, 2006).
77. Massimo Campanini, "The Mu 'tazila in Islamic History and Thought," *Religion Compass* 6 (1) (2012): 41–50. Known as the rational and liberal school of Islamic theology, the Mu 'tazilite views may be identical "to those of contemporary liberalism." See William Montgomery Watt, *The Formative Period of Islamic Thought* (Oxford: Oneworld Publications, 1998), 232.
78. For example, some argue that some schools of thought, i.e., the Zaydi and Twelver Shiite of the Shiite sect were adopted within the Mu 'tazilite thought. Oliver Leaman and Sajjad Rizvi, "The Developed Kalam Tradition (Part II: Later Shi'i Theology)," in *The Cambridge Companion to Classical Islamic Theology* ed. by Tim Winter (Cambridge: Cambridge University Press, 2008), 77–96. For example, Sajjad Rizvi explains why the Mu 'tazila doctrine could not influence other schools of thought. One of the reasons was the popularity of Ash 'arism, Maturidism and moderate Hanbalism. Therefore, the Mu'tazilite doctrines became more prominent in among many Shiite theologians such as Sadid al-Din al Himmasi al Razi (d. after 1204), Naslr al-Din al-Tusi (d. 1274), Maytham al-Bahram (d. 1300), Ibn al-Mutahhar al-Hilll (d. 1325), and later al-Miqdad al-Suyuri (d. 1423) were at the forefront of his school. Nevertheless, Rizvi also suggests that the adoption of Mu 'tazilite doctrines by Shiite schools was never wholesale or uncritical. For example, the Shiite's mystical principles such as the principle of the *imamah* (imamate), the belief in prophecy, miracles, intercession, etc., the status of sinners, intercession, and the afterlife, "remained distinctive; different." Ibid., 92. The word imamate is derived from "imam" and refers religious-political leadership of the Muslim community after the Prophet Muhammad passed to any member of the *ahl al-bayt* (the Prophet's family). In the Shi'ite tradition, it is generally believed that the imams are infallible leaders and authoritative teachers of the Muslim community. However, there are various positions within the different Shiite schools. For example, for the Twelver Shiites, the imamate belongs only to Fatima's and 'Ali's descendants through his son al-Ḥusayn ibn 'Ali, and the last Imam was Imam Muhammad bin Hassan- al-Mahdi who assumed the imamate when he was 5 years old and disappeared in 874. However, the Isma 'il Muslims still believe in continuation of the linage of imams. See Abdulaziz Sachedina, "Imamah," in *The Oxford Dictionary of Islam.* Accessed on February 9, 2017 from

www.oxfordislamicstudies.com.myaccess.library.utoronto.ca/article/opr/t236/e0357?_hi=0&_pos=1.

Leaman and Rizvi, "The Developed Kalam Tradition," 92. However, Rizvi's and other's attempt to emphasize on the Mu 'tazilite fading within the Shi'ite is not supported by other scholars. For example, according to Sherman A. Jackson, the Mu 'tazilite actually became lost in Sunnism. Jackson, *Islam and the Problem of Black*, 23. Also, the Mu 'tazilite's rational approach to religious doctrines still attracts many Muslim intellectuals. See Esposito, *The Oxford Dictionary of Islam*. Therefore, it is my conclusion that both many classical and contemporary Sunni and Shiite Muslim scholars use the rationalism of the Mu 'tazilite and its principles hoping "to give new life to Islamic thought, seeking to equip it to face the challenges of history." Campanini, "The Mu 'tazila in Islamic History and Thought," 41. For example, there were also many Sunni Mu 'tazilite theologians, particularly associated with the Hanafite School of law. They also influenced non-Muslim thinkers, such as Saadia Gaon, a Jewish Egyptian, (d. 942) and the ninth century Yusuf al-Basir). Ibid., 47. Further, it is important to consider that many of the early Mu 'tazilites were clearly anti-Shiite, or at least did not agree with the fundamental Shiite doctrine of the imamate. Ibid., 47. In sum, it is our conclusion that the acceptance of some of the Mu 'tazilite ideas by the Shi 'ite school does not mean that the contemporary Shiite are the Mu 'tazilite. Therefore, any scientific study of the Mu 'tazilite and its influence on contemporary Islam must involve a comparative analysis of the sources as the question of the relationship of Mu 'tazilite to Shiite "is delicate one." Ibid., 42. Any attempt to link Shiite with Mu 'tazilite is a vivid example of the desire of contemporary Muslim scholars (both Shiite and Sunni) to rediscover and revive elements of rationalism to better answer to the challenges of modernity. Ibid., 41.

79. Ignaz Goldziher, *Introduction to Islamic Theology*, transl. by Andras and Ruth Hamori (Princeton, NJ: Princeton University Press, 1981), 87.
80. Ibid., 86.
81. Watt concludes that the name – Mu 'tazilite – was a later invention after Hasan al-Basri (d. 728), Wasil ibn Ata's teacher. He emphasizes that the Mu 'tazilite adopted a neutral ground, "not participating in either of the two contrary fractions" (orthodox and Kharijite), especially when it came to consideration of the politico-religious question of determining the *fasiq'* (those who transgressed Islamic law). Watt argues that the name was first used by the proto-Shiite to describe those who were neutral to 'Ali and who claimed it is not lawful either to fight against 'Ali or to fight with him. Watt, *The Formative Period of Islamic Thought*, 216.
82. Jackson, *Islam and the Problem of Black Suffering*, 50–51, Watt, *The Formative Period of Islamic Thought*, 212; also See Watt, *Free Will and Predestination in Early Islam* (Luzac: Univrsity of Minnesota, 1948), 64; Khalid Bankinship, "The Early Creed," in *The Cambridge Companion to Classical Islamic Theology*, 33–54; Campanini, "The Mu 'tazila in Islamic History and Thought," 45. In sum, born in the seventh century, the Mu 'tazilite developed as an outstanding intellectual movement and during the ninth century, the dogmatic system of the Mu 'tazilite emerged under the auspices of the 'Abbasid caliph Harun al-Rashid (786–809). Campanini, "The Mu 'tazila in Islamic History and Thought," 41. In the early 800s, some of the Abbasid rulers, such as 'Abd Allah al-Ma'mun (d. 833), were personally close to a number of distinguished and leading Mu 'tazilite scholars, and was moved by the doctrine of the createdness of the Qur'an. John A. Nawas, "A Re-examination of Three Current Explanations for al-Mamun's Introduction of the Mihna," *International Journal of Middle East Studies* 26 (4) (1994): 616. Known as the Golden Age of the Mu 'tazilite, this period ended in 848 (or possibly in 851). The Silver Age followed, lasting until the death of Abu Hashim in 933. See Watt, *Formative Period of Islamic Thought*, 215. During this time, the Mu 'tazilite had two important schools: one was in Basra and was under the leadership of Abu al-Hudhayl al-'Allaf (d. 841); the other was

in Baghdad under the leadership of Bishr ibn-al-Mu'tamir (d. 825). There were over a thousand contentious issues about which these two main schools disagreed; frequently, they would accuse each other of *kufr* (disbelief). Esposito, *The Oxford Dictionary of Islam*, 21. The Basra school was more prestigious, tracing its historical roots back to Hasan al-Basri; as well, important adherents including Dirar ibn Amr (d. 815), Abu-l-Hudhayl, Ibrahim an-Nazzam (d. 846), and al-Jahiz (d. 867) distinguished themselves by integrating Greek ideas with Islamic thought. Watt, *Formative Period of Islamic Thought*, 219–220. The Baghdad school was in the capital of the empire and from this vantage point considerable influence could be exercised upon imperial policies and doctrines. Two important examples of their influence include the doctrine that was proclaimed during the time of Abbasid al-Ma'mun declaring that the Qur'an was created (as opposed to co-eternal with God) and *Mihna* (the Inquisition). Ibid., 221. The Baghdad school also looked more favourably upon the Rafidites than the Basra Mu 'tazilite. The Basra leader, Abu-l-Hudhayl, considered that Abu Bakr (d. 834), Umar (d. 644), and Uthman (d. 656) were *afdal* (most superior) when they became caliph. By contrast, the Baghdad school, especially Bish ibn-al-Mu'tamir (d. 825), claimed that Abu Bakr was *mafdul* (having lesser merit) and as such, was not a rightful imam. The Baghdad school differed from the Rafidites, for whom Abu Bakr was never considered to be an imam. Ibid., 227. The Baghdad school also introduced the principle of *'illa* (some ground) to appoint *mafdul* caliphs.

83. Jackson, *Islam and the Problem of Black Suffering*, 75–76.
84. Erik L. Ormsby, *Theodicy in Islamic Thought: The Dispute Over al-Ghazali's 'Best of All Possible Worlds'* (Princeton, NJ: Princeton University Press, 1984), 23.
85. Ibid., 77.
86. See Frank, "Reason and the Revealed Law," 127–128.
87. Jackson, *Islam and the Problem of Black Suffering*, 80.
88. Frank, "Reason and the Revealed Law," 127–128.
89. Jackson, *Islam and the Problem of Black Suffering*, 103; Also see Khaled El-Rouayheb, "Al-Māturīdī and the Development of Sunni Theology in Samarqand," *Journal of Near Eastern Studies* 75 (2) (2016): 413–416.
90. Jackson, *Islam and the Problem of Black Suffering*, 104.
91. The famous Muslim scholars who contributed to the Maturidism are Abu al-Yusr al-Bazdawi (d. 1099), Abu al-Mu'in al-Nasafi (d. 115), Abu al-Thana' Mahmud b. Zayd al-Lamishi (d. beginning of the 12th century), Majm al-Din 'Umar al-Nasafi (d. 1142), Kamal al-Din Muhammad b. Muhammad b. Abi Sharif al-Maqdisi (1499), and many others.
92. The word *athar* means "the remnant," or "narrative."
93. See Jeffry R. Halverson, *Theology and Creed in Sunni Islam: The Muslim Brotherhood, Ash'arism, and Political Sunnism* (Basingstoke, UK: Palgrave Macmillan, 2010), 36.
94. Binyamin Abrahamov, "Scripturalist and Traditionalist Theology," in *The Oxford Handbook of Islamic Theology*, ed. by Sabine Schmidtke (Oxford: Oxford University Press, 2016), 264–265.
95. Ibid., 270.
96. See Marshall G. S. Hodgson, *The Venture of Islam, Volume 1: The Classical Age of Islam* (Chicago, IL: University of Chicago Press, 2009), 8374.
97. See Racha El Omari, "Theology," in *The Princeton Encyclopedia of Islamic Political Thought*, ed. by Gerhard Böwering and Patricia Crone (Princeton, NJ: Princeton University Press, 2013).
98. Jackson also notes that before the ninth century, no school of thought could purely be identified as the Traditionalist. However, the *Mihna* (Inquisition) during the Abbasids became the turning point: with the strong opposition of Ahmad b. Hanbal (d. 855) against the Mu 'tazilite doctrine of the createdness of the Qur'an, the Traditionalism started to be associated with the Hanbali School of Thought. Today

the traditionalists are also known as the Salafis (Primitivist) who claim to be the *salaf* (the pious ancestors) of the earliest generations of Islam, including the companions of the Prophet Muhammad. Besides, Ahmad b. Hanbal, Ibn Taymiyah (d. 1328) is the most prominent representative of this school of thought. Jackson, *Islam and the Problem of Black Suffering*, 127.

99. Abrahamov, "Scripturalist and Traditionalist Theology," 275.
100. Jackson, *Islam and the Problem of Black Suffering*, 27.
101. See William C. Chittick, ed., *The Inner Journey: Views From the Islamic Tradition* (Sandpoint, ID: Morning Light Press, 2007); William C. Chittick, *Sufism: A Short Introduction* (Oxford: Oneworld Publications, 2001); Sachiko Murata and William C. Chittick, *The Vision of Islam* (New York, NY: Paragon House, 1994); Seyyed Hossein Nasr, *The Garden of Truth: The Vision and Practice of Sufism* (San Francisco, CA: Harper, 2007); Carl W. Ernst, *Sufism: An Introduction to the Mystical Tradition of Islam* (Boston, MA: Shambhala, 2011); Fazlur Rahman, *Islam*, 2nd ed. (Chicago, 1979); Annemarie Schimmel, *Mystical Dimensions of Islam* (Chapel Hill, NC: The University of North Carolina Press, 2011); Michael A. Sells, *Early Islamic Mysticism: Sufi, Qur'an, Mi'raj, Poetic and Theological Writings* (New York, NY: Paulist Press, 1996).
102. The word *nafs* refers to the "soul" or "the self." It is described as a spiritual reality of all living beings. In the Islamic tradition, it is also interpreted as the human potential to actualize the fullness of self-awareness, *aql* (the intellect) or as the "lower self," referring to spiritual impulses. See John L. Esposito, *The Oxford Encyclopedia of the Islamic World* (Oxford: Oxford Unviersity Press, 2009).
103. As a ritual activity, *dhikr* is mentioned in the Qur'an (i.e., Q. 33: 41–42). It is either performed in the group or individually.
104. For example, some Muslims visit the shrine of al Shadhili (d. 1465), who was a prominent Sufi master and founder of the Shadhiliyah Sufi order in southern Egypt. More about the importance of these rituals will be discussed in the chapters where we analyze traditional healing practices and spiritual diseases.
105. See Mansoor Ahmad Bhat, *The Sufi Thought of Shaikh Sayyid Abdul Qadir Jilani and Its Impact on the Indian Subcontinent* (New Delhi: D.K. Printworld, 2010); 'Abd al-Qadir Al-Jilani, *The Secret of Secrets*, trans. by Shaykh Tonsun Bayrak al-Jerrahi al-Halveti (Cambridge: The Islamic Texts Society, 1994); *Utterances (Malfuzat)*, trans. by Muhtar Holland (Kuala Lampur: S. Abdul Majeed & Co., 1992); Jacqueline Chabbi, "ʿAbd al-Qadir al-Jilani," in *Encyclopaedia of Islam: Three*, ed. by Kate Fleet, Gudrun Krämer, Denis Matringe, John Nawas, and Everett Rowson (Brill Online, 2015). Accessed on March 10, 2016 from http://referenceworks.brillonline.com.myaccess.library.utoronto.ca/entries/encyclopaedia-of-islam-3/abd-al-qa-dir-al-ji-la-ni-COM_22592.
106. Abu Bakr Siraj (Martin Lings), "The Origins of Sufism," *Islamic Sciences* 13 (2) (2015): 59–76; Robert Frager, *Heart, Self & Soul: The Sufi Psychology of Growth, Balance, and Harmony* (Wheaton, IL: Quest Books, 1999), ix.
107. Frager, *Heart, Self & Soul*, x.
108. Nile Green, *Sufism: A Global History* (Malden, MA: Willey Blackwell, 2012), 4. The leading and the most prominent Sufi masters are Al-Hasan al-Basri (d. 728), Muqatil ibn Sulayman al-Balkhi (d. 767), Abu-Said-al-Kharraz (d. 899), Abu Abdullah Harith bin Asad al-Basri al-Muhasibi (d. 857), Husain ibn Mansur al-Hallaj (d. 922), Abu Bakar Abi Ishaq bin Ibrahim bin Yakub al-Bukhari al-Kalabazi (d. 990), Aby 'Abd al-Rahman al-Sulami (d. 1021), Abu Talib al-Makki (d. 996), 'Abd al-Karim ibn Huzan Abu al-Qasim al-Qushayri al-Naysaburi (d. 1074), Khawaja Muhammad ibn Muhammad ibn Hasan Tusi, also known as Nasir al-Din Tusi (d. 1274), Abul Hassan Ali Ibn Usman al-Jullabi al-Hajveri (d. 1077), Abu Ḥamid Muḥammad ibn Muḥammad al-Ghazali (1058–1111), Hakim Abul-Majd Majdud ibn Adam Sana'i Ghaznavi (d. 1131 or 1141), ʿAbd al-Qadir al-Jilani (d. 1166), Abu al-Najib al-Suhrawardi (d. 1168); Fakhraddin Razi (1149–1209), Rizbahab (or al-Baqli) (d. 1209),

Mu'in al-Din Chishti (d. 1142), Abu Ḥamid bin Abu Bakr Ibrahim (d. 1221), Shihab al-Din al-Suhrawardi (d. 1234), Muhyiddin Ibn 'Arabi (1165–1240), Jalal ad-Din Muhammad Rumi (d. 1273), Muhammad Bahauddin al-Baytar, Sadraddin al-Konevi (d. 1274), Aḥmad al-Rifa'i (d. 1182), Abu al-Ḥasan al-Shadhili, d. 1258), Abdurrezzak Kemaleddin b. Ebi'l-Ganaim el-Kashani (d. 1329), Ali ibn Muḥammad ibn 'Ali al-Ḥusayni al-Jurjani (al-Sayyid al – Sharif) (d. 1413), Abd al-Karim al-Jili (d. after 1408), Aḥmad al-Bakka'i al-Kunti (d. 1504), Muḥammad Ghawth (d. 1517), Ismail Haqqi of Bursa (d. 1724), 'Abd al-Ghani ibn Isma'il al-Nablusi (an-Nabalusi) (d. 1731), al-Alusi (d. 1853), and many others.

109. The Qadiriyah order is established around the teachings of 'Abd al-Qadir al-Jilani (d. 1166) in Baghdad; the Suhrawardiyah is based on the teachings of Abu al-Najib al-Suhrawardi (d. 1168) and his nephew Shihab al-Din al-Suhrawardi (d. 1234); the Rifa'iyah is founded by Aḥmad al-Rifa'i (d. 1182); the Shadhiliyah is founded by Abu al-Ḥasan al-Shadhili (d. 1258) in Egypt and North Africa, and the Chishtiyah by Mu'in al-Din Chishti (d. 11420 in Central and South Asia. For more information, see Rahman, *Islam*; Schimmel, *Mystical Dimensions of Islam*; Ernst, *Sufism*; Sells, *Early Islamic Mysticism: Sufi, Qur'an, Mi'raj, Poetic and Theological Writings.*
110. Ahmed, *What Is Islam*, 21.
111. In the Qur'an, the heart is expressed in various terms depending on the context. For example, *sadr* (breast) is used in the context of conversion or openness to Islamic message (Q. 39:23); *qalb* (heart) is the seat of *iman* (faith) (Q. 49:7; 16:106); *fuad* (heart) relates to *marifa* (gnosis) (Q. 53:11); and *lubb* (innermost heart) is the seat of *tawhid* (unity) (Q. 3:190).
112. Robert Frager, *Heart, Self, and Soul: The Sufi Psychology of Growth, Balance and Harmony* (Wheaton, IL: Quest Books, 1999), 1, 2.
113. See Esposito, *The Oxford Encyclopedia of the Islamic World.*
114. Alfred L. Kroeber and Clyde Kluckhohn, *Culture: A Critical Review of Concepts and Definitions* (Cambridge: Peabody Museum Papers, 1952), 149. Accessed on September 2, 2016 from www.pseudology.org/Psyhology/CultureCriticalReview1952a.pdf.
115. Edward Burnett Tylor, *Primitive Culture*, vol. 1 (New York, NY: J. P. Putnam's Sons, 1920 [1871]), 1.
116. Richard Velkley, *Being After Rousseau: Philosophy and Culture in Question* (Chicago, IL: The University of Chicago Press, 2002), 11–30.
117. Ibid., 11.
118. Tylor, *Primitive Culture*, 16. In other cases, customs live on or transform into a fusion of religious and secular practices. In some cases, the resulting synbook is compatible with Islam, as in the celebration of *Nowruz*, the spring holiday of many Sunni and Shiite Muslims in Iran, Azerbaijan, and Central Asia. As a cultural holiday, *Nowruz* has pre-Islamic origins. It is often linked to the Zoroastrian religion in Iran and to the ancient Turkic legend of survival in Central Asia, Azerbaijan, and Turkey. As it has blended with Islamic culture, however, it has acquired religious motifs. For example, placing the Qur'an on a *Nowruz* table has become a widespread custom. Some Shiite groups even associate this ancient holiday with the survival and succession of the *Ahl al-Bayt* (the Prophet's family). For many Muslims in Iran, Central Asia, and Azerbaijan, *Nowruz* is as significant as Islam's two foremost celebrations: *Eid al-Adha* and *Eid al-Fitr.*
119. Abu Bakr Jabir Al-Jazairi, *Minhajul Muslim*, 3rd ed. (Morocco: Dârul baidâ', n.d.), 283.
120. A. O. Omotosho, "Islam, Custom, Culture and Tradition: The Dilemma of the Nigerian Muslim," *Jurnal Syariah* 15 (1) (2007): 6–7. Accessed on March 16, 2016 from http://e-journal.um.edu.my/filebank/published_article/6648/ISLAM%20CUSTOM%20CULTUR%20AND%20TRADITION%20THE%20DILEMMA%20OF%20THE%20NIGERIAN%20MUSLIM.pdf.

121. Hodgson, *The Venture of Islam*.
122. Ahmed, *What Is Islam*, 148.
123. Ibid., 105.
124. Ibid.
125. Many cultural practices, especially FGM and certain matrimonial customs (early, forced, or arranged marriages, for example) are based on abuse of Muslim women and exploitation of their rights. Female genital mutilation (FGM) is practiced in approximately 27 countries in Sub-Saharan and Northeast Africa, in the Middle East, and in some parts of Asia. In some situations, efforts are made to link this practice to Islam. For example, in Sudan, FGM is practiced as the *sunna circumcision*; however, the Qur'an does not mention the circumcision of females and the prophetic practice is not so clear. See United Nations Children's Fund [UNICEF], *Female Genital Mutilation/Cutting: A Statistical Overview and Exploration of the Dynamics of Change* (New York, NY: UNICEF, 2013). Accessed from www.unicef.org/media/files/FGCM_Lo_res.pdf.
126. Muzammil H. Siddique, *Five Features of Islamic Culture*. Accessed on February 15, 2017 from www.thekhalids.org/index.php/newsletter-archive/1160-5-features-of-islamic-culture.

2 Domestic Violence Literature Review

Definitions/Discussions of Key Concepts

Domestic violence is not simply a family matter: it is a complex web of social, cultural, and religious challenges. This section focuses on a review of literature within the Islamic tradition, particularly on the problematic text Q 4:34, of theories of culture that intertwine with tradition to normalize domestic violence, and of social scientific approaches to domestic violence. This chapter does not provide a full literature review as I will engage more literature from the Islamic studies, counselling and the social sciences in the case studies. However, this chapter focuses on some key aspects of domestic violence that will provide a background for our analysis of the case studies later.

Domestic Violence: What Is It in the Islamic Context?

Domestic violence includes not only physical abuse but other forms:

> verbal abuse (name-calling, insults); psychological abuse (threats, intimidation, humiliation, isolation, stalking, and so forth); sexual abuse (forced sexual acts, forced pornography viewing, withholding sex); financial abuse (deprivation from access to money); and spiritual abuse (misusing religious teachings to manipulate behavior, interfering with worship practices).[1]

However, a large percentage of Muslim men do not consider economic and emotional control as abusive behaviours;[2] and, many Muslim men and women do not recognize other domestic abuses. To understand what makes domestic violence against Muslim women distinctive, the phenomenon must be examined from an Islamic perspective. For example, some Muslims assume that in Islam, a husband is obliged to provide financial support, including food, clothing, lodging, etc.; in return, he literally gets *milk* (authority, ownership, and dominion) over his wife's reproductive capacity.[3] She is obliged to be sexually available to the husband at any time or place he chooses. Some Muslim women assume that their husbands have the right to beat them for discipline, often believing that their punishment carries a potential for spiritual reward. Some Muslim men believe that their overprotective attitudes serve to guard the family against "outside" influences and keep it pure from an Islamic point of view. In many cases, they do not recognize progressive laws that offer protection to women from assault by any man, including family members nor the egalitarian version of Islamic teachings.

Domestic Violence and Islam's Exegetical Tradition

In many Muslim cultures, patriarchal and androcentric readings of the Qur'an are used to justify domestic violence against women. Islam's exegetical and legal traditions play a role in perpetrating domestic violence against Muslim women, and new exegesis seeks to correct this problem.

The Problematic Translation in Some Exegetical Traditions

Some pre-modern Muslim scholars, including exegetes and jurists, gave men rights, or even religious duties, to discipline their wives when they were rebellious.[4] In classical exegetical tradition, *daraba* in Q. 4:34[5] was usually translated using verbs such as "to strike," "to hit," "to beat," "to scourge," or "to spank." Abu Jafar al-Tabari (d. 922) suggests that *daraba/wadribuhunna* ("beat them [women]") be used "as a last resort toward a disobedient wife and stated that it involved striking her without hurting her."[6] In contrast, Abu Qasim al-Zamakhshari (d. 1144), recommends that a husband put the whip where the family can see it which contradicts what Ingrid Mattson argues that al-Zamakhshari applied the primary principle – justice and unity – of his theological school (Mu'tazilite) to interpret the Qur'an.[7] Others, like Sa'adiya Shaikh, suggest that al-Zamakhshari based his interpretation on the socio-political and economic demands of his time.[8]

Some pre-modern exegetes, like Fakhr al-Din al-Razi (d. 1210), avoided endorsing *daraba* as a physical discipline by quoting a *hadith* which views men who beat their wives as inferior. Furthermore, he stated, "Know that those who strike are not better than those who refrain."[9] Al-Razi was clear that the hitting should not be extreme; its effect must be like the strike by a folded handkerchief or *miswak* (a small twig used as a toothbrush) or "a folded scarf."[10]

The classical exegetical tradition has a tremendous impact on contemporary exegetical works among Muslims. An influential modern exegete in Turkey, Elmalili Hamdi Yazır (d. 1942),[11] interprets *nushuz* as a wife's disobedience to her husband. He points out that classical exegetes interpreted *nushuz* as a wife's rebellion against her husband (Ibn Abbas), rejecting a husband's desire to have a sexual relationship with her or changing her high manners to undesirable manners ('Ata' ibn Rabah), and feeling aversion against her husband or a wife's preference to situate herself in a different location against her husband's will (Abu Mansur al-Maturudi). For Yazir, in the ideal family, the husband is the authority, and the wife is subordinate. However, he cautions husbands not to use excessive physical force against their wives, reminding them that God's power is stronger over them than their power over women. Moreover, a husband's sin against God is greater than a woman's transgression against her husband. God is ever forgiving and merciful towards men; therefore, it follows that husbands should be merciful and gentle towards their wives.[12] Nonetheless, when the wife does not meet the rights of her husband, she was blamed for *nushuz*, considered not consistent with the character of a God-fearing woman.

An influential 20th-century translator of the Qur'an, Abdulla Yusuf Ali (d. 1953), interpreted the word *daraba* in the light of classical exegetical tradition and also in respect to *qawwamun* ("one who stands firm in another's business, protects his interests and looks after his affairs or it may be, standing firm in his own business, managing affairs, with a steady purpose").[13] His commentary on Q. 4:135 argues that

> Justice is Allah's attribute, and to stand firm for justice is to be a witness to Allah, even if it is detrimental to our own interests (as we conceive them) or the interests of those who are near and dear to us. According to the Latin saying, "Let Justice be done though heaven should fall."[14]

Muhammad Asad (d. 1992) interprets *qawwam* as the intensive form of *qaim* ("one who is responsible for" or "takes care of a thing or a person"). In this sense, *qawwam* refers to physical maintenance, protection, and moral responsibility. Considering this meaning, Asad interprets Q. 4:34 as: "men shall take full care of women."[15] He translates *daraba* as "to beat" but in his commentary, he notes:

> It is evident from many authentic Traditions that the Prophet himself intensely detested the idea of beating one's wife, and said on more than one occasion, "Could any of you beat his wife as he would beat a slave, and then lie with her in the evening?"[16]

When the verse 4:34 was revealed, the Prophet is reported to have said: "I wanted one thing, but God has willed another thing – and what God has willed must be best."[17] However, shortly before his death, he stipulated in his Farewell Pilgrimage sermon husbands should "beat" wives only if the wife "has become guilty, in an obvious manner, of immoral conduct," and that it should be done "in such a way as not to cause *ghayr mubarrih* (pain)." By these Traditions, this "beating," if resorted to at all, should be more or less symbolic – "with a toothbrush" (Tabari, quoting the views of scholars of the earliest times), or even "with a folded handkerchief."[18] Some of the greatest Muslim scholars, such as Ash-Shafiʿi, are of the opinion that it is just barely permissible and should be avoided. They justify this opinion by the Prophet's personal feelings about this problem.[19]

Some contemporary Muslim writers continue the pre-classical and conservative interpretations of Q. 4:34. Farid Esack, a Muslim scholar from

South Africa, uses Q. 4:34 to argue that Islam is a patriarchal religion because it grants men control over women. Also, he asserts that "The Qur'an's essential audience is males . . . [women] are essentially subjects being dealt with – however kindly – rather than being directly addressed."[20] Accepting the argument that the main audience of the Qur'an is men raises thought-provoking questions. Does the Qur'an assume that men were more corrupt than women and needed more reform? Does the Qur'an favour men in some areas (like inheritance, for example) or all areas of life?

Islamic Feminist Response

Muslim feminist scholars deconstruct the patriarchal understandings of Q. 4:34. Some consider the linguistic, historical, and social contexts of classical exegesis to understand why Muslim scholars endorsed wife-hitting.[21] Others draw on traditional precepts to develop new principles to guide the Islamic feminist inquiry.

First, Muslim feminists reinterpreted the word *nushuz* as "an act of rebelliousness." They argued that the husband can also be blamed to commit the act of rebelliousness. Unfortunately, the term *nashiz*, that is, the one who committed *nushuz* (disobedience) was always used in reference to women because some Muslim scholars took women's obedience to their husbands for granted. These scholars were concerned with specific actions related to the wife's fulfilment of the marital obligations to which maintenance was linked: accepting restrictions and making herself physically available. Even actions that did not constitute *nushuz*, such as travel with the husband's permission, could nonetheless lead to loss of maintenance. Lama Abu-Odeh observes that the wife in the medieval marriage was the "provider of sexual pleasure (obedience) in return for her right to maintenance."[22] Therefore, pre-modern Muslim jurists usually discussed the concept of *nafaqa* (maintenance) in the context of a wife's obedience to her husband.[23] They also articulated women's legal rights and obligations in marriage in the context of two concepts: *tamkin* (obedience; also *ta 'a*) and *nafaqa* (maintenance). The concept of *tamkin* was always defined in regard to sexual submission as a man's right and thus a woman's duty; whereas *nafaqa*, defined as shelter, food, and clothing, became a woman's right and a man's duty.[24]

Against the pre-modern interpretation of the term *nushuz*, Wadud argues that the Qur'an uses *nushuz* for both the male and the female: therefore, it cannot be used only in reference to a wife's "disobedience to the husband."[25] Based on Sayyid Qutb's[26] interpretation of the word *nushuz* as "a state of disorder between the married couple," she considers it more correct as "recalcitrance," or "disruption of marital harmony."[27] Based on her interpretation of *nushuz*, Wadud also re-interprets the word *daraba*. She argues that according to the *Lisan al-'Arab* and *Lanes's Lexicon*, *daraba* does not necessarily mean "force" or "violence." Elsewhere in the Qur'an the word is used for "set an example," "when someone leaves," or "strikes out on a journey."[28] She also suggests that Q. 4:34 actually prohibits violence against females and put a severe restriction on existing practices against women who were blamed for being disobedient. Wadud argues that the Qur'an never endorses violence against women for being disobedient, nor does it require obedience to their husbands: it does not imply that obedience is "characteristic of the 'better women' (66:5), nor is it a prerequisite for women to enter the community of Islam (in the Bay'ah of the women: 60:12)."[29] Rather, the Qur'an suggests resolving marital difficulties peacefully. If all peaceful efforts fail, the Qu'ran permits equitable divorce.

Chaudhry cannot reconcile interpretations of classical Muslim scholars who found wife-hitting ethically and morally wrong but sanctioned "non-extreme" hitting. Chaudhry also draws on a *hadith* to derive multiple meanings of *daraba*, including: to walk, to run, to rape, to whip/flog, to slap, to present an example, to behead, to play the *daff* (drum), to knock on a door, to wear a *hijab* (a dress that covers a woman's body, except her face and hands), to pitch a tent, and to apply a poll tax. Challenging the patriarchal readings that suggest hitting wives lightly, she argues that hitting, regardless if it is done with "a toothbrush or a rose," still risks harming a woman physically, psychologically, and emotionally.

The position of Barlas on Q. 4:34 is closer to Wadud's interpretation. Barlas argues that misogynistic interpretations of Q. 4:34 are misleading as they lead to sexual inequality and male privilege by interpreting *qawwamun* as "managers," *qanitat* as "wifely obedience," and *nushuz* as "the wife's disobedience." She concludes that "the Qur'an does not use this concept or term [*qawwamun*] to speak about either husbands or fathers [superiority over women]."[30] Also, she agrees with Wadud that *nushuz* is not disloyalty and ill-conduct on the wife's part but "a general state of marital disorder."[31] Therefore, regarding the word *daraba*, Barlas also states that "it is questionable whether *daraba* even refers to striking a wife, even if symbolically."[32]

Barlas provides an extensive analysis of the image of a "believing woman," a term from the Qur'an itself, and helps us question the legitimacy of patriarchal readings "on the basis of a distinction in Muslim theology between what God says and what we understand God to be saying."[33] Her intention is not to question an "ontological status as Divine Speech or the claim that God Speaks, both of which Muslims hold to be true."[34] Barlas advocates for the Qur'an "as a dual-gendered text, that is, a text that has both male and female voices in it" by taking the Qur'an as God's Speech only, and not as the voice of either men and women, because "God is beyond sex/gender."[35] She challenges the Qur'an's patriarchal exegesis of conservative males by emphasizing the idea that only God knows the true meaning of the Qur'an. Such an approach to the Qur'an sheds doubt on the authenticity of the male-dominated Islamic classical tradition that very often "underwrites sexual oppression in Muslim societies and therefore needs to be contested."[36] Barlas argues that despite differences between text (the Qur'an), tradition (the narrations of the Prophet Muhammad), and reason, the classical religious authority has distorted the original meanings for its own advantage and to the disadvantage of female believers. She applies "a creative engagement with texts, traditions, and reason" that may yield a hermeneutic of the Qur'an that is founded on liberation.

Barlas also provides an extensive discussion about the obstacles that patriarchal Muslim societies pose to a new and creating rereading of the Qur'an by women because only male scholarly elite can claim "to speak authoritatively in God's name."[37] These societies effectively suppress women's ideas from being developed and their voices from being heard to protect the male dominance in the interpretation process. Barlas's work "will be among those egalitarian and antipatriarchal readings of Islam that will, in time, come to replace misogynist and patriarchal understandings of it."[38] However, she is also aware that she belongs "to no sanctioned interpretive community," nor she is a male or even a recognized scholar of Islam who is a master of the Arabic language. Nonetheless, as a "believing" Muslim woman, she embarks on a mission to combat repressive readings of the Qur'an and offers a new image of Islam that "is not based on the idea of male epistemic privilege, or in a formally ordained interpretive community."

Fatima Mernissi, a Moroccan feminist writer, and sociologist, uses the historical example of the Prophet as authoritative to examine certain Qur'anic injunctions and see the problematic areas in the Qur'an and the tradition. Regarding Q. 4:34, Mernissi claims that Islam is an egalitarian religion with a strong intent to liberate women; however, its project of liberation faced strong opposition from Meccan men, including the Prophet's companions. Mernissi particularly names 'Umar b. al-Khattab (d. 644) for his being more at ease with pre-Islamic traditions.[39] She also gives examples from the outspoken "feminist" women of that time, especially Umm Salama (d. 680), one of the Prophet's wives, who expressed her frustration by questioning why Allah addresses only men in the Qur'an and who received the revelation of Q. 33:35, which promises forgiveness and great reward for believing men and women. For her, Q. 33:35 is a manifesto of gender equality in the Qur'an. Although the Qur'anic promise of equality was not realized, the Prophet's conduct as described by Ibn Sa'd is a prescription against gender violence. Ibn Sa'd reported that "The Prophet never raised his hand against one of his wives, nor against a slave, nor against any person at all."[40] Mernissi quotes the *hadith* that prohibits the beating of women: "The Prophet abhorred violence toward women and stubbornly adhered to that attitude."[41] Mernissi also applies feminist hermeneutics to interpret *nushuz*. For her, *nushuz* is a positive act of defiance and self-fulfilment of the wife in the family and public space. To prove her statement, she gives an example from Sakina bt. al-Husain, the great-granddaughter of the Prophet Muhammad, and 'Aisha bt. Talha, the granddaughter of Abu Bakr, whose behaviours challenged the Qurayshi nobility, therefore, they were *nashiz* (disobedient). *Nushuz* affirms women's individuality, uniqueness, and capacity to disagree. She interprets the word *nushuz* as a gender-specific term that signifies only women's rebellion and dismisses male's *nushuz* in the Qur'an and tradition.

Laleh Bakhtiar, the first American Muslim woman who translated the Qur'an into English, points out that the patriarchal approach to the Qur'an contradicts the understanding of the Qur'an's equal treatment towards women, represents a violation of human rights, and leads to one of the major sources of criticism of Islam.[42] Looking carefully at the linguistic features of the Arabic language, she generates new meanings for *daraba*. For her, the root letters of *daraba* – *d r b* – have different meanings when accompanied by a preposition. For example, with the preposition *fi*, it means to travel; with the preposition *'ala*, it means to stomp; with the preposition *'an*, it means to turn something away; with the preposition *bayn*, it means to set up between, to separate.

In Q. 4:34, *daraba* is used without any modifying preposition. Therefore, several other meanings should be considered:

> it might imply to encompass; to cast, throw or fling upon the ground; to engender; to make a sign or to point with the hand; to prohibit, prevent or hinder from doing a thing one has begun; to seek glory; to avoid or shun; to be with shame; to be in a state of commotion; to be in a state between hope and fear; and to go away.[43]

Bakhtiar translates *wa-d·ribuhunna* as "to go away" as opposed "to hit." To substantiate her translation, she describes a situation where the Prophet Muhammad chose to leave his wives for one month instead of hitting them when he was displeased with them. Bakhtiar's suggestion for dealing with *nushuz* includes three steps: admonishing, abandoning, and going away.

Approaching the challenge from a different perspective, Laury Silvers uses Ibn al- 'Arabi's (d. 1240) ontology, ethics, and hermeneutics to deconstruct Q. 4:34.[44] In her argument, Silvers draws attention to the empowering aspects of the Sufi tradition, which encourages individual ethical and moral responsibility about the application of faith in real-life situations. Her approach to Islam and its key sources emphasizes the individual believer's critical position of responsibility regarding the available interpretations of the Qur'an and other sources of Islam. Like Silvers, other Muslim women scholars concur that Ibn 'Arabi established a hermeneutical approach to the Qur'an that placed "a great ethical burden on the believer who must take responsibility for choosing which interpretation is the right one."[45]

Thus, Q. 4:34 is sufficiently ambiguous. Reading Q. 4:34 as a permit to beat wives or to compel them to obey their husbands is not the best meanings of the Qur'an. Most importantly, such a reading is against the Qur'an's principle of sexual equality and its teachings that "marriages should be based in love, forgiveness, harmony, and *sukun*."[46]

In the light of these new insights, it is reasonable to conclude that the word *nushuz* means "violating and breaching the marital relationship with wife through unfaithfulness in her relationship with her husband, i.e., adultery, love triangle, and so forth."[47] In addition to Mernissi, Wadud, Barlas, and others that I used above, we can also add the names of Nimat Hafez Barazangi,[48] and the recent contribution by Ziba Mir-Hossieni, Mulki Al-Sharmani and Jana Rumminger that I used extensively in my discussion of the case studies in following chapters.[49] The new methodologies and scholarship of Muslim feminists unlock innovative interpretations of *nushuz*, *daraba*, and Q. 4:34 in general. They do not restrict themselves to classical methodologies, such as *asbabal-nuzul* (where it is argued that many verses of the Qur'an were revealed to address specific historical situations). Muslim feminists take an even more radical approach than secular feminists by questioning and investigating classical and secular sources. By doing so, they provide a strong scholarly foundation that challenges the traditional beliefs that disciplining women – even at the risk of abusing them – is a religious duty of Muslim men, and that tolerating abusive relationships is a valid spiritual practice for Muslim women.

Domestic Violence and Culture

Any discussion of domestic violence towards Muslim women must consider the traditional customs and cultural aspects of the problem because these influences play a major role in an already complex and controversial issue. Cultural interpretations of gender roles shape not only the understanding but also the responses to domestic violence among Muslims.[50] Broadly speaking, Muslim culture comprises a diversity of social, economic, and political contexts from around the world. The multiplicity of expressions of Muslim culture ranges from conservative and traditional to liberal. Although these various cultural expressions often reflect geographic or regional patterns – for example, Middle Eastern and Asian cultures tend to be more conservative and traditional, while those in Europe may be more liberal – one cannot generalize.

Marwan Dwairy, a psychologist and cross-cultural researcher, has made an extensive study of the similarities and differences among Arab/Muslim cultures. For the most part, he did not find a significant deviation within the cultural and religious worlds of Arab Muslims or Turkic-speaking Muslims.[51] Most of the differences among Muslims can be attributed to psychological, historical, and social factors. Within the broad spectrum of Muslim culture, however, several important polarities create helpful categories for understanding vital differences. First, from the ideological perspective, Muslim culture can be divided into two contrasting groups: totally traditional-religious or predominantly secular. Second, from the social system perspective, Muslim culture is either collectivistic or individualistic. In general, Muslims can be categorized as traditional (strongly practicing), bicultural (moderately practicing), acculturated (marginally practicing), assimilated (non-practicing), and recommitted (strongly practicing).[52]

When researchers describe Muslim culture as collectivistic,[53] the term implies that an individual places the needs of the community above any individual desires. Collectivistic societies promote values such as humility and interdependence and any deviation from these attributes carries the risk of bringing shame or guilt to the family, the clan (*hamala*), and/or the tribe. Even worse, not conforming to the established imperatives within a collectivistic system may imperil the survival of the larger group. A strong gender and generational hierarchy characterize collectivistic communities; as well, everyone in the collective has a well-defined sense of their role and the limits of their status and knowledge. In these societies, women and younger members usually have a lower status than males and elders. Women are expected to marry within the extended family, to take care of domestic affairs, and in many cases, to give birth to many children. Abuse towards women is often accepted as "family business," meaning that violence against women should not be disclosed to outsiders. In some Muslim cultures, confinement and isolation of women is a standard practice. Although the rapid cultural transformation that is occurring in the Muslim world means that many women now enter the workplace, they still must carry "their traditionally mandated household and childcare duties."[54]

While acknowledging that specific local influences contribute to differences in all cultures, Dwairy argues that collectivism and authoritarianism play a crucial role in understanding the fundamental differences between Arab/Muslim and Western cultures.[55] In his research, he found that Muslim communities in the Middle East, Asia, and Africa exhibit higher levels of collectivism and authoritarianism when compared to those in Europe and North America where individualism is stronger. Dwairy suggests that there is a correlation between collectivism and the need for social interaction between individuals in the society. More specifically, collectivistic norms and practices in the Muslim world reflect the continuation of *'asabiya* (the ancestral tribal heritage) and the individual's extreme reliance on the family, *hamula* (clan), and tribal system for basic needs such as food, shelter, and safety. According to Dwairy, individuals in collectivist social systems must choose between two poles: "(a) to be submissive to gain vital collective support, or (b) to relinquish the collective support in favor of self-fulfilment."[56]

Cultures are dynamic and susceptible to external and internal influences. Muslim cultures have been influenced by the influx of Western ideologies since the colonialism of the 19th century and the more recent exposure to urban lifestyles. In response to these formidable influences, many Muslim cultures have experienced a rapid shift from collectivism to individualism. As well, a process of acculturation has occurred because of the encounters between these different cultures. Anthropologist Conrad Kottak explains that when two diverse groups meet, they remain distinct but their original cultural patterns may be altered because of the exchange.[57] A continuous process of change, acculturation involves the adoption of the cultural traits or social patterns of another group. By contrast, assimilation entails a more radical form of change that necessitates abandoning old traditions and replacing them with the cultural practices and traits of the more powerful group.

Many Muslim communities have been attracted to the novelties of Western culture – the technology, the dress, the art and music, the languages, and the individualistic and liberal attitudes. Exposure to Western culture has resulted in rapid changes within Muslim cultures. As Dwairy points out, in the face of such powerful influences, many Muslims found themselves in a position of submission and helplessness. Essentially, this process of acculturation "gave rise to inferiority feelings and brought about a process of identification with that oppressor."[58]

Even though many Muslims share a similar collective experience and heritage, their unique socio-historical situations and *adat* or *'urf* (local customs and practices of particular communities) contribute to the complexities and variations within Muslim cultures. A Tunisian Muslim scholar al-Tahir Ibn Ashur (d. 1907) stated that

> Islamic law does not concern itself with determining what kind of dress, house, or mount people should use. . . . Accordingly, we can establish that the customs and mores of a particular people have no right, as such, to be imposed on other people as legislation, not even the people who originated them. . . . This method of interpretation has removed much confusion that faced scholars in understanding the reasons why the law prohibited certain practices . . . such as the prohibition for women to add hair extensions, to cleave their teeth, or to tattoo themselves. . . . The correct meaning of this, in my view . . . is that these practices mentioned in hadith were, according to Arabs, signs of a woman's lack of chastity. Therefore, prohibiting these practices was aimed at certain evil motives. . . . Similarly, we read:. . . "believing women should draw over themselves some of their outer garments" (Surat al-Ahzab). . . . This is a legislation that took into consideration an Arab tradition, and therefore does not necessarily apply to women who do not wear this style of dress.[59]

In his ground-breaking work *What Is Islam*, Ahmed (d. 2015) also points out that

> the logic of applying the same principal – namely, the ontological and spiritual equality of all humans – to the question of the legal and social rights of women has not persuaded the vast majority of modern practitioners of Islamic law.[60]

Some customs and practices may not be purely Islamic, although they still fit within the rich fabric that constitutes Islam, critiquing conceptualizations of Islam as "religion" or "culture" or even those that emphasize its legal dimension. These remnants of pre-Islamic culture reflect the capacity and flexibility of Muslims to acculturate and to adopt local customs and practices within their expression of Islam, which he conceptualizes very broadly as "meaning-making for the self in terms of hermeneutical engagement with Revelation to Muhammad as Pre-text, Text and Con-text."[61]

However, not all Muslim communities respond with such tolerance and flexibility when confronted with the prospect of cultural innovation. Some Muslim communities respond to such transformations with vehement rejection and unbridled revolt, referring to these influences as *bid 'ati sayyi'a* (bad innovations) for Islam. Regrettably, in the name of Islam, these Muslims brandish a similar attitude of rejection towards *bid 'ati hasana* (good innovations, like those that address social and cultural repression and the oppression of women). In these areas of the Muslim world, marriage customs and family structures are based on patriarchies where men are in control. Sadly, the women in these communities have the highest risk for domestic violence; by contrast, women in marriages based on equal rights comprise the lowest risk.

For the most part, Muslim cultural customs and practices continue to coexist with Islamic religious traditions in a parallel world. In Islamic psychotherapy, however, it is important to differentiate between culture and religion and how these two factors impact the phenomenon of domestic violence against Muslim women. For Islamic counsellors, it is also vital to understand the power dynamics that operate within individual Muslim marriages and families to assess effectively the risks and evidence of domestic violence and more importantly, to create care plans that respond with cultural sensitivity.

Domestic Violence and the North American Society

The phenomenon of domestic violence occurs in all sectors of the society. However, certain factors make the problem even more complex for Muslim women in North America. Many Muslim women in the United States and Canada are immigrants of colour who find themselves marginalized for a variety of reasons including racism, poverty, language difficulties, and cultural stereotyping. These factors complicate the phenomenon of domestic violence and make it difficult for these women to access resources.

In her contribution to the Fatih Trust Institute project, Abugideiri[62] reports that the professionals need to pay attention to multiple barriers when they work with Muslim immigrant women because of "additional layers that add complexity to their case." For example, these women might find themselves "caught between the cultural norms of their native culture, American societal expectations, and their religious beliefs." In addition, they also have language barriers, and do not know how to access existing services. Most of these women relied on family support in the back home but it may or may not be available now.

Although her research is based on American statistics, McCue has identified a variety of complicating societal factors in the United States that also apply in the Canadian and other Western contexts as well:

- racism in the legal, healthcare, education, shelter, and welfare systems;
- lack of people of colour in the medical, law enforcement, social service, and justice systems;
- attitudes and stereotypes about the prevalence of domestic violence in marginalized communities;
- assumptions about gender roles and acceptability of domestic violence in other cultures;
- fear by battered women of colour that their experience will reflect poorly on or will confirm the stereotypes placed on their ethnicity;
- added pressure to keep the family together because of societal stereotypes and one-parent households.[63]

Research suggests that women of colour tend to stay longer in abusive relationships for many of the reasons that have been cited above. Furthermore, classism and lack of financial opportunities for people of colour increase the "sense of shame and self-blame for the abuse."[64] Jiwani points out that "the healthcare system as a hierarchical structure not only mirrors the dominant structures of violence inherent in the wider society but also perpetuates them in particular ways,"[65] favouring some patients and making it difficult for immigrants to access and/or navigate the system. Jasmine Zine shows how some Muslim students prefer Islamic schools because they have been made to feel like outsiders in public schools.[66] If Muslim youth feel like strangers in the school system, it is quite likely that their mothers feel even more alienated when trying to navigate larger social networks like government agencies.

Some healthcare practices contravene the principle of cultural safety,[67] a concept that is based upon the belief that "each person's knowledge and reality is valid and valuable."[68] Care is unsafe "if the patient is humiliated, alienated, or directly or indirectly dissuaded from accessing necessary care."[69] More than simply honouring the individual, cultural safety "insists that mainstream service providers recognize themselves as the bearer of their own culture and attitudes that either consciously or unconsciously exercises power over patients."[70] In addition to encouraging self-awareness among healthcare practitioners, this standard reinforces the importance of the safe and effective use of self (SEUS), a primary foundation for psychotherapy practice.

From a social systems perspective, the experience of most Muslim women in North America is fraught with complexities. Immigrants can easily be triggered into an uneasy "outsider-insider" relationship that mirrors the dynamics of conquest and domination over visible minorities. This dynamic can be further exacerbated by the intentional and unintentional ways in which the political entities within the society establish the terms and conditions that define success or failure to blend into the social fabric.

In order to provide counselling support to Muslim women, psychotherapists must work within a web of diversities that can include complexities related to class, race, gender, age, disability, sexual orientation, religion, culture, health, geography, expectations, and outlook on life within the Muslim community. In the face of such intricacies, a well-meaning counsellor could easily be tripped up by the religious and cultural variations within the Islamic tradition. Unfortunately, a considerable number of mental health professionals who work with Muslim women who have experienced domestic violence are at risk of practicing from a framework that is culturally unsafe. A psychotherapist who has an unconscious internalized fear of Islam may begin feeling anxious in the counselling session. This kind of anxiety can easily become an undercurrent that undermines the effectiveness of the therapeutic relationship between the woman and her counsellor. Furthermore, the media often portray Muslim women who wear traditional attire as evidence of a backward and inferior Islamic culture.[71] Unaware of such a "blind spot," a counsellor could unconsciously attempt to emancipate a Muslim woman from her supposedly backward traditions and practices and suggest she simply wear Western-style clothing.

As well, psychotherapists need to be sensitive to the ways in which hate crimes, discrimination, and stereotyping stigmatize the lives of Muslim women, especially those who are victims of domestic abuse. Erving Goffman identifies three forms of the stigma that Muslim women commonly experience: the stigma of character traits, the stigma of physical deformity, and the stigma of group identity. The first stigma refers primarily to the experience of mental illness (or the imposition of such a diagnosis); the second type is related to deformity or an undesired physical difference; and the third type is related to an association with a race, religion, or belief.[72] In a therapeutic relationship, stigma and discrimination occur when the counsellor is blind to a cultural norm that defines "who is and who is not a member of the group."[73]

At its best, psychotherapy supports and respects ethnic and religious minority cultures and their traditions. In a therapeutic relationship, it is common for the psychotherapists and the client to view the situation from different perspectives; however, the psychotherapist bears the weight of responsibility for the creation and maintenance of the relationship. The actions of the psychotherapist always reflect his/her therapeutic approach/framework, values, biases, and stereotypes, and these all play a role in the ultimate effectiveness of the relationship. Ultimately, the therapeutic plan of the psychotherapist has the potential to influence the next stage in the client's life. First impressions or initial perceptions in the counselling process have been found to be tenacious and affect the process and the outcome of the psychotherapy session.[74] For these reasons, the psychotherapist must be intentional and conscious of the implicit and explicit power dynamics and underlying interpersonal subtleties.

Theories for Understanding Domestic Violence From the Social Science Tradition

Six general theories shed light on the nature of domestic violence and why some men become abusive in relationships: psychopathology theory, social learning theory, biological theory, family systems theory, deficit theory, and feminist theory.[75] To date, Islamic psychotherapy has not offered a unified theory on domestic violence. However, Muslim advocates against domestic violence, including Muslim psychotherapists, have tried to raise awareness with respect to the toxic impact of domestic violence on Muslim women. They also provided education on Islam's position against violence.[76] Nevertheless, theories of domestic violence in the social sciences are also helpful to understand this problem in the Muslim community.

Psychopathology theories suggest that men tend to be more abusive if they have anxiety disorders, post-traumatic stress disorder (PTSD), and/or personality disorders, especially borderline personality and anti-social personality disorders. Also, men with a tendency towards abuse display more shame-based rage and project this blame on their wives.[77] These men are usually psychologically dependent on their wives. When triggered, they engage in furious outbursts, especially when they have a fear of abandonment.[78]

Some sociologists argue that violence is a learned social behaviour. This theory is based on behaviourism – a prominent idea in the social sciences since the first half of the 20th century – and on Bandura's social learning theory. According to social learning theory, men who come from families where violence was tolerated tend to be more abusive; by contrast, women who come from families where the mother capitulated in the face of violence tend to be more submissive in abusive relationships.[79] Essentially, the environmental conditions nurture future development. In many Muslim families, men are accorded preferential treatment and have access to more economic and social opportunities than women; they learn to be the breadwinners of the family and, in exchange, expect women to be subordinate. By contrast, women learn how to be responsible for the family honour; ironically, a dynamic that patriarchal societies often use to control them. Social behaviour theory argues that cultural norms and practices lead to compliance or conformity; consequently, many women learn to acquiesce to the power of the physically stronger member of the family. This learning is not solely cognitive; more often, the process is heavily laden with complex emotions, especially when women feel responsible for holding the family unit together and protecting the cultural and religious norms in the family and society.

Biological theories suggest that organic causes of behaviour contribute to violence. These theories focus on the role of etiology, genetic defects, brain injury, neuropathology, brain infections, and medical illnesses. These illnesses and injuries may cause functional changes in the brain secondary to trauma. Some studies argue that individuals who have sustained a brain injury or childhood trauma tend to be more violent due to the physiological changes in the brain.[80] These physiological changes may be one of the contributing factors of domestic violence against women by men.[81] However, some biological studies examining the relationship between these neurotransmitters and domestic violence have also produced inconsistent findings.[82] Some studies report a strong positive association,[83] some a moderate or weak association,[84] while some could not identify any relationship at all.[85]

Family systems theories emphasize the impact of the family dynamics and processes (communication, relationship, problem-solving skills, and so forth) on abusive relationships. They also suggest that since both the wife and the husband "play some role" in domestic violence, interventions should target both individuals.[86] Such perspective may also blame the women in part for domestic violence. Nevertheless, this theory may help us understand the pattern of violence within a family system as the family theorists also suggest that system processes alone are not only factors that contribute to domestic violence against women.[87]

Deficit theories focus on a lack of the character, functions, and skills of the perpetrator. In the context of domestic violence, a deficiency within the perpetrator differentiates him from those who do not tend to be violent. K. Corvo found that a deficit in the frontal lobes affects the process of cognition and impulse control, leading to a lack of capacity to control one's impulses and triggering violent and abusive behaviours.[88] The assessment of executive function is necessary to understand possible deficits. Such perpetrators may develop skills to identify affective arousal to violence and use adaptive strategies to manage it.[89]

Although these theories offer important insights for understanding domestic violence, they often reflect the male gender bias that exists in many psychological and developmental theories. However, the feminist theory offers a crucial counterbalance for understanding how patriarchal ideologies (inequality, male power, and female subordination) contribute to domestic violence.[90] Furthermore, feminist theories focus on the inequality within social structures that creates an environment where men can exercise absolute power and control women.[91] Offering a new paradigm for counselling women, Christie Cozard Neuger addresses the dynamics of gender that exist at cultural, institutional, familial, and personal levels and shows how a feminist analysis provides important correctives for patriarchal constructions.[92]

Contrary to several of the theories that were discussed above and like social learning theory, feminist theories argue that violence is a learned behaviour. Unfortunately, many religious institutions reinforce this behaviour by accepting male dominance and the patriarchal structures that increase risk factors for domestic violence within the broader culture.[93]

Feminist theories provide an opportunity for learning from women's experiences that lead to awareness of gender dynamics and sensitivity in everyday life.[94] They suggest that the society is structured along the lives of gender where men have more power over women. They call this arrangement patriarchal which allows "men have access to material and symbolic resources, while women are devalued as secondary and inferior."[95] They also pay attention to the early socialization conditions which make girls more submissive while boys are perpetrators of violence.[96]

Also, the domestic violence literature also discusses the role of the male privilege and male control that breeds violence against women.[97] The Duluth Model, also called the Power and Control Wheel, was created in 1984 by Domestic Abuse Intervention Project in Duluth (DAIP).[98] Based on feminist and socio-cultural concepts of domination and control, the tool describes how men use male privilege, emotional, and economic abuse, violence, intimidation, and isolation to control women via a pattern of tactics that involves threats, intimidation, and coercion to make his partner fear and obey. Also, as an educational tool, the Duluth model incorporates cognitive-behavioral techniques and provides information about the importance of the coordination of community responses.[99] However, it is also important to state here that the tool was created by a small group of activists against domestic violence not by qualified healthcare professionals, and therefore lacks scientific evidence.[100] One of the important aspects of the tool is that it mainly focuses on power and control and does not provide sufficient insight into the role of anger and other psychological and social factors in domestic violence. Also, one also needs to take into consideration that its application with a diverse population is questionable as it is considered appropriate if utilized with Caucasian, African American, Native American, and Latino populations.[101] Pastoral theologian Pamela Cooper-White differentiates forms of power by introducing the concepts such as "power-within," "power-over," and "power-with." For her, unlike power-within and power-with, power-over is death-dealing that does not recognize or respect mutuality, justice, responsibility, and care. Power-within (such as powers of reason) is the strength of the women to resist the attack. Power-with is the power to respect and a manner "that negates neither self nor other." It adds dignity of power-within into relationship through negotiation and consensus. However, she also talks about the pitfalls of power-with and power-within such as indecisiveness, manipulation, solipsism, covert-exercises of power-over.[102]

Viewing domestic violence solely as a product of patriarchy or any other physical, mental, emotional, or social problem, including religion and culture, ignores the additional risk factors that can be identified through other theoretical sources (biological, psychological, previous trauma, a family of origin violence, and so forth). In order to get an accurate picture of domestic violence, it is vital to consider the complex web of contributing factors.

Conclusion

This literature review has exposed the complex socio-economic, political, religious, and cultural factors that together contribute to the phenomenon of domestic violence towards Muslim women. Difficult to grasp, the phenomenon is like a chameleon that blends into a specific historical, social, or cultural background. For instance, against a patriarchal background, it takes on overtones of male domination and female submission. Ubiquitous and insidious, it spreads like a bruise, discolouring the essence of our social systems. Like a thief, it robs Muslim women of their dignity, their mental, physical, and spiritual health, and their capacity to draw life from their religious beliefs and practices. It denies families an environment where they can experience *mawaddah* (love and compassion), *rahmah* (mercy), and *sakinah* (mutual tranquillity).[103] Put simply, domestic violence can best be described as *zulm* (oppression) against women – a violation that breaches the essential and Universalist principle of equality in the Qur'an.

Notes

1. Abugideiri, "Domestic Violence," 311.
2. Mohammed Baobaid and Gahad Hamed, *Addressing Domestic Violence in Canadian Muslim Communities: A Training Manual for Muslim Communities and Ontario Service Providers* (London, ON: Muslim Resource Centre for Social Support and Integration, 2010).
3. Kecia Ali, *Marriage and Slavery in Early Islam* (Cambridge, MA: Harvard University Press, 2010), 6.
4. Chaudhry, "The Ethics of Marital Discipline," 126.
5. According to Ibn 'Abbad, the verse was revealed on the occasion when Sa'd ibn Rabi', one of the chiefs of al-Ansar (the Prophet's companions from Medina), smacked his wife, who was the daughter of Muhammad ibn Salama. She "turned away from him in their bed and with the mark of the blow on her face, went to the Prophet to request *qisas* (retribution according to the Shari 'ah)." When the Prophet initiated the terms of *qisas*, the verse "men are in charge of women" was revealed. The Prophet then stated, "I wanted something and God wanted something other than that and whatever God wills is benignant." See Chaudhry, *Domestic Violence and the Islamic Tradition*, 116.
6. Shaikh, "A Tafsir of Praxis," in *Violence against Women in Contemporary World Religion*, ed. by D.C. Maguire & S. Shaikh (Cleveland, OH: The Pilgrim Press, 2007), 72.
7. See Ingrid Mattson, *The Story of the Qur'an: Its history and Place in Muslim Life* (Oxford: John Wiley & Sons, 2012), 195.
8. Ibid. Others, like Sa'adiya Shaikh, suggest that al-Zamakhshari based his interpretation on the socio-political and economic demands of his time.
9. Mohammad Mazher Idriss and Tahir Abbas, *Honour, Violence, Women and Islam* (New York, NY: Routledge, 2011) quoted by Gabriella Alziari, 4:34: *Is Domestic Violence Acceptable?* Accessed from https://authoristo.wordpress.com/2011/12/17/verse-434-is-domestic-violence-acceptable/.
10. Muhammad Asad, *The Message of the Qur'an*, translation and commentary of the Qur'an (Gibraltar: Andalus Press, 1980), footnote 45, p. 167. Accessed from http://muhammad-asad.com/Message-of-Quran.pdf.
11. Elmalili Muhammed Hamdi Yazri, *Hak Dini Kur'an Dili*, vol. 2 (the Qur'anic exegesis and translation of Qur'an in Turkish) (Istanbul: Eser Nesriyat, 1971), 1352.
12. Ibid., 1352.
13. Abdulla Yusuf Ali, *The Holy Quran-Text*, trans. and commentary (Beltsville, MD: Amana Corporation, 1989), foot No, 545, 195. His commentary states:

    > As to those women On whose part ye fear Disloyalty and ill-conduct [*nushuz*] Admonish them (first), (Next), refuse to share their beds, (And last) beat them [*daraba*] (lightly); But if they return to obedience, Seek not against them Means (of annoyance).
    >
    > (ibid., 195)

14. Ibid., 229.

15. Asad, *The Message of the Qur'an*, 109.
16. Asad, *The Message of the Qur'an*, footnote 45, p. 167. Accessed from http://muhammad-asad.com/Message-of-Quran.pdf.
17. Ayesha Chaudhry, "'I Wanted One Thing and God Wanted Another . . .': The Dilemma of Prophetic Example and Wife-Beating," *Journal of Religious Ethics* 39 (3) (2011): 416–439.
18. Sa'adiya Shaikh, "Transforming Feminism: Islam, Women and Gender Justice," in *Progressive Muslims: On Justice, Pluralism*, ed. by O. Safi (Oxford: Oneworld Publications, 2003), 154.
19. Ibid., 109–110.
20. Farid Esack, "Islam & Gender Justice: Beyond Simplistic Apologia," in *What Do Men Owe to Women? Men's Voices from World Religions*, ed. by John C. Raines and Daniel C. Maguire (Albany: SUNY Press, 2001): 187–210.
21. See Leila Ahmed, *Women and Gender in Islam: Historical Roots of a Modern Debate* (New Haven, CT: Yale University Press, 1992); Amina Wadud, *Qur'an and Woman* (New York, NY: Oxford University Press, 1999); Barlas, *Believing Women*; Fatima Mernissi, *The Veil and the Male Elite: A Feminist Interpretation of Women's Rights in Islam*, trans. by Mary Jo Lakeland (Reading, MA: Addison-Wesley Publishing Co., 1993); Hadia Mubarak, "Breaking the Interpretive Monopoly: Re-Examination of Verse 4:34," *Hawwa* 2 (3) (2005): 261–298; Sa'diyya Shaikh, "Exegetical Violence: *Nushuz* in Qur'anic Gender Ideology," *Journal for Islamic Studies* 17 (1997): 49–73; Shaikh, "A Tafsir of Praxis."
22. Lama Abu-Odeh, "Modern Family Law, 1800-Present. Arab States," in *Encyclopaedia of Women in Islamic Cultures*, vol. 2, ed. by Joseph Su'ad (The Hague: Brill 2.005), 459.
23. Judith Tucker, *Women, Family, and Gender in Islamic Law* (Cambridge: Cambridge University Press, 2008), 50.
24. Ziba Mir-Hosseini, "Towards Gender Equality: Muslim Family Laws and the Shari'ah," in *Wanted: Equality and Justice in the Muslim Family*, ed. by Zainah Anwar (Petrailing Jaya: Musawah, 2009), 31.
25. See Wadud, *Qur'an and Woman*, 74.
26. Sayyid Qutb, *Milestones* (Cedar Rapids, IA: The Mother Mosque Foundation, 1981).
27. Ibid., xxvi, 74.
28. Wadud, *Qur'an and Woman*, 76.
29. Ibid., 77.
30. Ibid., 187.
31. Ibid., 188.
32. Ibid.
33. Barlas, *Believing Women in Islam*, 19.
34. Ibid., 58.
35. Ibid., 21.
36. Ibid., 19.
37. Ibid., 41.
38. Ibid., 209.
39. Fatima Mernissi, *The Veil and the Male Elite: A Feminist Interpretation of Women's Rights in Islam*, trans. by Mary Jo Lakeland (Reading, MA: Addison-Wesley Publishing Co., 1993), 142.
40. Ibid., 156.
41. Ibid., 155.
42. Bakhtiar, "The Sublime Quran," 431–439.
43. Ibid., 432.
44. In her words: "Ibn al- 'Arabi claims that whatever meaning one can take from the Qur'an within the semantic boundaries of the accepted recitations must be intended by God." From this perspective, no amount of interpretive finesse would

be able cover over a reading of God's prescription in v. 4:34 as obliging husbands to hit their wives if necessary to control them. Following Ibn al- 'Arabi's hermeneutic, I suggest that the verse comprehends all possible meanings including "beat them." Laura Silvers, "In the Book We Have Left out Nothing: The Ethical Problem of the Existence of Verse 4:34 in the Qur'an," *Comparative Islamic Studies* 2 (2) (2006): 171–180; Laura Silvers, "Religion, State Power, and Domestic Violence in Muslim Societies: A Framework for Comparative Analysis," *Law & Social Inquiry* 29 (1) (2004): 1–38.

45. See Mattson, *The Story of the Qur'an*, 208.
46. *Sukun* means love but also "a deeper intimacy ensuing from sexual gratification and mental peace," Mir, 1987, cited by Barlas, *Believing Women in Islam*, 153.
47. Rabha Isa Al-Zeera, "Violence Against Women in Qur'an 4:34: A Sacred Ordinance?" in *Muslima Theology: The Voices of Muslim Women Theologians*, ed. by Ednan Asla, Marcia J. Hermansen, and Elif Medeni (New York, NY: Peter Lang Edition, 2013), 226.
48. Nimat Hafez Barazangi, *Woman's Identity and the Qur'an: A New Reading* (Gainesville, FL: The University Press of Florida, 2006).
49. Ziba Mir-Hossieni, Mulki Al-Sharmani and Jana Rumminger, *Men in Charge? Rethinking Authority in Muslim Legal Tradition*, ed. by Ziba Mir-Hosseini, Mulki Al-Sharmani, and Jana Rumminger (London: Oneworld Publications, 2015).
50. Maha B. Alkhateeb and Salma Elkadi Abugideiri, "Introduction," in *Change from Within: Diverse Perspectives on Domestic Violence in Muslim Communities*, ed. by Maha B. Alkhateeb and Salma Elkadi Abugideiri (Alexandria, VA: The Peaceful Families Project, 2007), 6.
51. Marwan Dwairy, *Counselling and Psychotherapy With Arabs and Muslims: A Culturally Sensitive Approach* (New York, NY: Teachers College Press, 2006), 10.
52. Alkhateeb and Abugideiri, "Introduction," 5.
53. Dwairy, *Counselling and Psychotherapy With Arabs and Muslims*; Hooman Keshavarzi and Amber Haque, "Outlining a Psychotherapy Model for Enhancing Muslim Mental Health Within an Islamic Context," *The International Journal for the Psychology of Religion* 23 (2013): 230–249; Abugideiri, "Domestic Violence," 2012; Baobaid and Hamed, *Addressing Domestic Violence in Canadian Muslim Communities*, 2002.
54. Laeth Sari Nasir, "Globalization, Health and Culture," in *Caring for Arab Patients: A Biopsychosocial Approach*, ed. by L. S. Nasir and A. H. Abdul-Haq (Oxford: Radcliffe Publishing, 2008), 21.
55. Dwairy, *Counselling and Psychotherapy With Arabs and Muslims*, 11.
56. Ibid., 23.
57. Conrad Phillip Kottak, *Window on Humanity* (New York, NY: McGraw Hill, 2007).
58. Dwairy, *Counselling and Psychotherapy With Arabs and Muslims*, 21.
59. In his *Kitab Ta'rifat*, 'Ali b. Muhammad al-Jurjani defines *'urf i* as "[Action or belief] in which persons persist with the concurrence of the reasoning powers and which their natural dispositions agree to accept [as right]." It refers to unwritten customs as opposed to established law, shar' though attempts have not been lacking to regard it as one of the *usul* (principles) cited by Auda, *Maqasid Al-Shariah*, 49. Auda, *Maqasid Al-Shariah*, 50.
60. Shahab Ahmed, *What Is Islam? The Importance of Being Islamic*, 513.
61. Ahmed, *What Is Islam*, 405.
62. Salma Abugideiri, "Immigrant Muslim Women," Faith Trust Institute. Accessed on January 26, 2018 from www.faithtrustinstitute.org/resources/articles/Immigrant-Muslim-Women.pdf/?searchterm=None.
63. Margi Laird McCue, *Domestic Violence: A Reference Handbook* (Santa Barbara, CA: ABC-CLIO, 2008), 42.
64. Ibid., 42.
65. Jiwani, *Discourses of Denial*, 146.

66. Jasmine Zine, *Canadian Islamic Schools: Unravelling the Politics of Faith, Gender, Knowledge, and Identity* (Toronto: University of Toronto Press, 2008).
67. Baobaid and Hamed, *Addressing Domestic Violence in Canadian Muslim Communities*, 35.
68. Ibid., 35.
69. Ibid.
70. Ibid.
71. Sangeetha Dhami and Aziz Sheikh, "The Family: Predicament and Promise," in *Caring for Muslim Patients*, ed. by Sheikh A. Gatrad (Abingdon: Radcliffe Publishing, 2000).
72. Erving Goffman, *Stigma: Notes on the Management of Spoiled Identity* (New York, NY: Simon and Schuster Inc., 1963), 7.
73. Derek Truscott and Kenneth H. Crook, *Ethics for the Practice of Psychology in Canada* (Calgary: University of Alberta, 2004), 114.
74. Ahmed Nezar Kobeisy, *Counseling American Muslims: Understanding the Faith and Helping the People* (Westport, CT: Praeger Publishers, 2004), 86.
75. Ibid., 12.
76. Alkhateeb and Abugideiri, "Introduction," 2.
77. Donald. G. Dutton and Mark Bodnarchuk, "Through a Psychological Lens: Personality Disorder and Spouse Assault," in *Current Controversies on Family Violence*, ed. by D. R. Loseke, R. J. Gelles and M. M. Cavanaugh, 2nd ed. (Thousand Oaks, CA: Sage Publications, 2005); Neil S. Jacobson and John M. Gottman, *When Men Batter Women: New Insights Into Ending Abusive Relationships* (New York, NY: Simon and Schuster, 1998).
78. Jacobson and Gottman, *When Men Batter Women*, 127.
79. McCue, *Domestic Violence*, 13.
80. Ibid., 13.
81. Ibid., 14.
82. Parveen Azam Ali and Paul B. Naylor, "Intimate Partner Violence: A Narrative Review of the Biological and Psychological Explanations for Its Causation," *Aggression and Violent Behaviour* 18 (3) (2013): 373–382.
83. Hosanna Soler, Preeti. Vinayak and David Quadagno, "Biosocial Aspects of Domestic Violence," *Psychoneuroendocrinology* 25 (7) (2000): 721–739.
84. John Archer, "Testosterone and Human Aggression: An Evaluation of the Challenge Hypobook," *Neuroscience and Biobehavioral Reviews* 30 (3) (2006): 319–345; Angela S. Book, Katherine B., Starzyk, and Vermon L Quinsey, "The Relationship Between Testosterone and Aggression: A Meta-Analysis," *Aggression and Violent Behavior* 6 (2001): 579–599.
85. Justin M. Carré and Cheryl M. McCormick, "Aggressive Behavior and Change in Salivary Testosterone Concentrations Predict Willingness to Engage in a Competitive Task," *Hormones and Behavior* 54 (3) (2008): 403–409.
86. McCue, *Domestic Violence*, 14.
87. Ibid., 14.
88. Allen Jenkins, *Invitations to Responsibility: The Therapeutic Engagement of Men Who Are Violent and Abusive* (Adelaide, AU: Dulwich Centre Publications, 1990).
89. Ibid., 350.
90. R. Emerson Dobash and Russell P. Dobash, *Violence Against Wives: A Case Against the Patriarchy* (New York, NY: The Free Press, 1979).
91. K. A. Yllo, "Through a Feminist Lens: Gender, Diversity and Violence: Extending the Feminist Framework," in *Current Controversies on Family Violence*, ed. by D. R. Loseke, R. J. Gelles, and M. M. Cavanaugh, 2nd ed. (Newbury Park, CA: Sage Publications, 2005).
92. Neuger, *Counseling Women*, 2001.
93. See Dobash and Dobash, *Violence Against Wives*; Cooper-White, *The Cry of Tamar*.
94. McCue, *Domestic Violence*, 15.

95. Ibid., 15.
96. Ibid.
97. Shelly M. Wagers, "Deconstructing the Power and Control Motive: Moving Beyond a Unidimensional View of Power in Domestic Violence Theory," *Partner Abuse* 6 (2) (2015): 230–230; Kristin L. Anderson and Debra Umberson, "Gendering Violence: Masculinity and Power in Men's Accounts of Domestic Violence," *Gender and Society* 15 (3) (2001): 358–380; Kristy Candela, "Protecting the Invisible Victim: Incorporating Coercive Control in Domestic Violence Statutes," *Family Court Review* 54 (1) (2016): 112–125.
98. See McCue, *Domestic Violence*, 65; Cooper-White, *The Cry of Tamar*, 128.
99. Greg Bohall, Mary-Jo Bautista, and Sabrina Musson, "Intimate Partner Violence and the Duluth Model: An Examination of the Model and Recommendations for Future Research and Practice," *Journal of Family Violence* 13 (8) (2016): 1029–1033.
100. Ibid.
101. Ibid.
102. Ibid., 55–59.
103. Abugideiri, "Domestic Violence," 310.

3 Divine Testing and Suffering

Asma is a 25-year-old born in Azerbaijan, with Azeri being her first language. She resided in Turkey for five years where she followed the Hanafi school of jurisprudence. She always dreamed of getting a university education in Canada. She is the fifth of five siblings, having one brother and three sisters. She reported that being a younger child in her family had always been a roadblock, and she had to give up her dreams for the sake of her older sisters because her parents demanded that she do the cleaning and household chores since her sisters were not available to help. Asma married her husband when she was 17 years old in order to escape her family duties. She had two children in this marriage.

Asma's marriage was one of the violent ones. Each time her husband showed her his anger, she would pray to God to save her life. She resisted getting help, hoping that one day he would improve. She felt immense pressure of social expectations; when she wanted to divorce her husband, some family members told her to be a better wife, not to do anything wrong, and that they did not want gossip to reach the extended family. So instead of considering divorce, she tried to pray harder than she used to. She hoped that it would "save" her marriage. She thought that a good wife never divorces her husband. She had a secular marriage and *kabin* (religious marriage) at the same time.

For the most part, Asma's only confidante was her sister in Turkey who advised her to be patient, to trust in God, and to accept her fate for the sake of her children. Gradually, she learned to show *rida* (willingness to accept; acceptance) of God's divine writ (*qadar*) and discover *hikmah* (divine wisdom) behind her *musibah* (evil, afflictions, and disasters that cause pain, suffering, agony, anguish). She also learned that sometimes these tests might be rare chances to change *qaza* (destiny). She thought that reflecting on her miseries might help her to be aware of her weaker qualities that might cause a test by God, and improve them to change her *qaza*.

The intensive cycle of verbal, emotional, spiritual, and physical abuse caused Asma to develop emotional problems that manifested themselves as anxiety, panic attacks, and insomnia. As a coping strategy, she tried to read the Qur'an at night, especially when her husband mistreated her, but the abuse interfered with her ability to concentrate. In desperation, Asma prayed for God's guidance. She believed that God was preparing her for something and hoped that there would eventually be some wisdom in this misery. She reminded herself that patience is a virtue, but, deep in her heart, she was afraid of losing faith and hope.

Asma reported that she escaped to the books of prominent religious leaders. She hoped that her patience in response to her husband's violence would elevate her status and she would be part of the group of steadfast people who show patience for the sake of God and are convinced that everything comes from God.

Psychotherapy sessions with Muslim caregivers helped her strengthen her faith and improve her character as a Muslim; she learned how a strong faith made her resilient, with a deep belief that God might test humans in different stages of their lives. However, she still struggled to find an answer to the question of whether her experience of domestic violence was part of testing her faith. She wanted to know whether her test was due to God's anger towards her – or due to His love.

Divine Test and Suffering in Islamic Studies and Islamic Psychotherapy Literature

Asma's question of suffering in her life may be one of the well-known subjects in Islamic theology, especially in relation to God's power, human freedom of will, divine omnipotence, divine justice/divine omnibenevolence (*'adl*), and divine destiny such as *ajal* (the appointed time of death) and *rizq* (sustenance). In theology, these concerns are addressed by theodicy,[1] which is a branch of theology concerned with the formal and ontological problem of evil and answers to the question of "God's concern and solicitude for creation."[2]

This section discusses how the major theological schools of Islam – the Mu 'tazilite, the Ash 'arite, the Maturudite, and the Hanbalite (also known as the "Traditionalists" because they are known as the strict traditionalist school of jurisprudence in Sunni Islam) – might clarify Asma's problem in Islamic psychotherapy. Such an ultimate wisdom from the teachings of these schools may also produce horizons (like Gadamer's) through which Muslim women "can pursue greater self-truth and greater self-understanding."[3] Although Asma follows the Maturudite school of thought, I first introduce the Mu 'tazilite approach to suffering, then outline the Ash 'arite, Maturudite, and Hanbalite responses in dialogue with each other.

The Mu 'tazilite School

In the context of suffering like Asma's, many Muslim women try to understand domestic violence in relation to divine justice. They ask: how does the suffering due to domestic violence promote concrete, *gharad* (palpable interests; pl. *aghrad*) for women? If God inflicts suffering in order to benefit or constitute an earned reward, how does the suffering due to domestic violence avert other sufferings? The Mu 'tazilites have a unique answer to these questions.

Early forms of the theology of suffering in Islam are associated with the Mu 'tazilite, which was one of the Qadariyyah (proponents of free will) sects and the dominant "orthodox" school of Islamic theology from the 10th to the 12th centuries. However, even before the attempt of the Mu 'tazilite to defend God's attributes against the objections resulting from the existence of evil, Muslim intellectuals as well as ordinary Muslims tried to understand divine justice in the context of suffering. The Ummayyads' persecution of the Prophet's family, particularly Imam Hussain, who was the grandson of the Prophet and the son of the fourth caliph Imam Ali, intensified the discussions of the most pious members of the Muslim community on the meaning and purpose of suffering.

During these debates, in reaction to the exaggerated emphasis on predestination of the Jabriyya sect, the Mu 'tazilites interpreted sheer destiny as "knowledge of what men by their own activity would in fact do."[4] They tried to reconcile the two opposites: God's attributes of omnibenevolence/justice and omnipotence to the existence of suffering. In order to do so, they began by divorcing evil from God, and declared humans the masters of their own actions (*yakhluq*), including their own suffering. In this capacity, they argued that humans not only possess the "*ability to choose*" but also have "the autonomous *power to translate* their choices into reality."[5] Even if God is the creator of all acts, all these acts serve in the interest of humanity.[6] In the context of suffering, such a position suggested that even amid our suffering God must have intended the best interest of the creatures.[7]

Nevertheless, they also suggested judging all acts (whether God's or humans' or good and evil) on the basis of their source: i.e., their inherent properties or their effect. This position was known as the doctrine of *al-husn wa al-qubh al- 'aqliyan* (objective good and evil).[8] They claimed that humans are responsible for their acts because on the basis of revelation or by sound reason and rational argument, they have the capacity to know if their acts are beneficent or maleficent and if they are violating the moral dictates. Further, the Mu 'tazilites explained the concepts of *lutf* (divine grace) and *'iwad* (indemnification, compensation, or restitution for harm) to reconcile between divine omnipotence and human suffering.[9] For them, their concept of *lutf* promotes human choices via God's ability to guide, direct, and offset; whereas, the concept of *'iwad* proposes that for every pain and suffering humans must be indemnified by God in this life or the Hereafter "in the form of intensified pleasures or diminished punishments."[10]

Although the Mu 'tazilite largely "faded as a formal movement within Sunnism,"[11] by the 14th century in favour of the Ash 'arite and Maturudite schools of thought, their approach to the problem of suffering still has meaning for many Muslims in our contemporary time and also is reflected in works of many Muslim scholars. For example, Abdulaziz Sachedina, who is a prominent contemporary Shiite scholar but also examines the Mu 'tazilite and Ash 'arite sources, presents the Mu 'tazilite perspective and points out that human behaviours, specifically human disobedience, and transgression, produce evil. His argument is that "God owes no obedience to anyone and is bound by no commandment," therefore "no evil can be imputed to God."[12] On one hand, he refers to the Qur'an to support his argument and states that the Qur'an holds human beings responsible for being the authors of their evils. However, on the other hand, he states that the Qur'an, i.e., Q. 57:22, also reminds us that suffering is "fixed" in the "Book," and God has "foreknowledge of suffering."[13] He concludes:

> the Qur'an is dealing with very different claims about evil and suffering: that (a) some suffering is not evil and is from God, being a station on the path of spiritual and moral maturity; (b) some suffering is evil and is from God, perhaps as punishment for sin; (c) some suffering is evil and not from God (deriving from human arrogance); (d) some suffering is not evil and not from God (e.g., a doctor-administered inoculation).[14]

Sachedina also addresses the contradictions in the Qur'an with respect to free will and destiny. He concludes that despite the ambiguity in the Qur'an, it is still the ultimate source to guide Muslims on how to prevent or eliminate "evil," including natural disasters and human evil, by learning and understanding God's "tradition" (*sunnatallah*) of natural laws and human nature (*fitra*).[15]

Although Asma is not Mu 'tazilite, this understanding may help Asma see her suffering as not coming from God. This belief can make a big difference in her experience of domestic violence. In sum, the Mu 'tazilite formulation of the free-will theodicy and the link between free will and divine justice may suggest to Asma that God "neither commits nor chooses evil" because of God's omnibenevolence. God is knowledgeable of the evil nature of evil acts, free of any need to commit evil acts, and aware of being free of any need to commit evil acts.[16] Such an approach to God's omnibenevolence helps Asma realize that the Mu 'tazilite thought invites her to apply free will in order to reflect on her experience. Also, from the perspective of the Mu 'tazilite principle of *al-husn wa al-qubh al- 'aqliyan*, Asma may conclude that domestic violence against her is evil and the evil nature of domestic violence can be known by its harmful consequences. Since domestic violence is evil, God then cannot cause the suffering to Asma through domestic violence. Nevertheless, as per the Mu 'tazilites, even though Asma's suffering is the direct effect of domestic violence and does not promote any good, the indirect effect may benefit her through practicing humility, gratitude, and obedience to God.

The Mu 'tazilite position of free will presents a very clear reason why we are responsible for our acts. However, I realize that because many ordinary Muslim women, including Asma, believe in predestination, Asma may find more solace in the belief that humans do have a capacity to understand and explain how God's wisdom is manifested in the suffering of the innocent. The mainstream understanding of evil and suffering among the Muslim women is very well explained in a famous Sunni saying by Abu Hasan al-Ash 'ari (d. 935), who initially followed the Mu 'tazilite ideas: "Whatever God wills happens, and whatever He does not will does not" ("*ma sha'Allahu kana wa ma lam yasha' lam yakun*"). In addition, it shows the earliest extreme response of Sunnis against the Mu 'tazilite understanding of evil and suffering. The common assumptions of the Ash 'arites in this regard are described below and may be used in Islamic psychotherapy to understand Asma's dilemma, even though she is Maturudite by creed.

The Ash 'arites

Although Asma follows Maturudite theology, like many Ash 'arites, she also believes in God's absolute power and knowledge.[17] The Ash 'arites, in general, argued that whatever happens, "happens for the best," but they also defended the idea of God's omnipotence and absolute will and power against the idea of human freedom to make a choice.[18] Their doctrine of *kasb* (pl. *iktisab*) (voluntary acquisition) which became a distinct feature of the Ash 'arites may help Asma to change her suffering.

The doctrine of *kasb* implies that God creates human actions while humans appropriate them. In another word, although humans still have a limited autonomy (especially in these aspects of human life: sustenance, span of life, pleasure, and pain, as a created power belongs only to God), they can acquire the power to act with God's will via *kasb* and they are responsible for their actions. Through the doctrine of *kasb*, the Ash 'arites taught that when humans make a choice and intend to do the act, they acquire (*iktisab*) either the reward by making the right choice or punishment by making the wrong choice. Adhering to this thought, they reinforced "the distinction between God's wishes and those of humans," and recognized "human choice as an entity separate and distinct from God's."[19]

Ash 'arite theology also does not belittle the importance of human choice. For example, via the doctrine of *kasb*, the Ash 'arites encourage Asma to practice her free choice even though she depends upon God for her power to eliminate her suffering due to domestic violence. The Ash 'arite theology assures Asma that God does not endorse and is not pleased with her suffering. In general, there is nothing in Ash 'arite theology that would imply that God is or must be pleased with any socio-political oppression against women or obliges women to be pleased with such. Al-Ash 'ari said:

> There are afflictions, such as natural catastrophes, illness, disease, and loss of money, children and the like, that we must bear with patience. And there are afflictions, such as unbelief and all the various forms of disobedience that we are not to bear with patience.[20]

Thus, from al-Ash 'ari's perspective, Asma does not have any obligation to be patient in her suffering due to domestic violence. Also, she must exercise her *ikhtiyar* (choice) to remove her suffering and God will translate her choice into reality.

Often what first comes to mind regarding the Asha 'arite thought is the works of Abu Hamid al-Ghazali (d. 1111), a prominent representative of this school of thought and a famous theologian and mystic. Due to the contributions of al-Ghazali, the mainstream Ash 'arite theodicy of determinism became the dominant orthodox perspective of divine testing, suffering, and the problem of evil among Muslims. Al-Ghazali extensively talked about occasionalism, the doctrine ascribing the connection between events to the continuing intervention of God, by explaining the first cause and secondary causation, and stating that the interaction between causes are so complex that it is beyond human capacity to understand and explain everything occurring in life.[21]

However, one also may refer to Bediuzzaman Said Nursi (d. 1960) to understand the Ash 'arite approach to the problem of suffering as relevant to contemporary Muslims. He, first of all, tried to present the aforementioned questions in conversation with contemporary issues. Second, Nursi examined suffering in relation to God as the Creator of causes and God's ability to perform miracles by breaking the cycle of patterns or forces of nature. Third, he suggested looking for an "epistemological wholeness" and organic relations between suffering and its causes based on other categories of knowledge, revealed and scientific, and art, ethics, and belief.[22] Fourth, Nursi reconciled the causes of any suffering with the concept of an omnipotent God, for it is God who creates causes to happen and with the concept of divine justice.

In Asma's case, Nursi would probably invite her to see common patterns of causes in nature, human life, etc., via the divine law (i.e., it is God who makes the earth spin, causes worlds to revolve, and the solar system to travel through space). He then would likely invite Asma to see "goodness" in evil and suffering in order to be safe from pride with the gift of choice or admit responsibility. However, although for Nursi, it is God who is the source of both good and evil, but it is Asma who acquires (*kasb*) good or evil acts by her own free will. Unlike Muslim scholars such as al-Tabari (d. 923), the Mu 'tazilite al-Zamakhshari (1075–1144), and the Asha 'raite scholar al-Razi (d. 1209), who endorsed misogynistic *hadith* traditions,[23] Nursi's perspective would encourage Asma not to rely on some *hadith* traditions that promote misogynistic ideas and endorse her suffering. He also would not diminish her creational rank over that of her husband nor would he support the belief that holds her responsible for humankind's primaeval act of disobedience against God.[24] Such an approach to the tradition is important in Asma's case, as we know that blaming women for man's disobedience against God causes more suffering to women. Further, again, within the limits of the Ash 'arite position, he would encourage Asma to understand her suffering in the context of the Day of Judgement when the innocent will be rewarded, and the guilty will be punished. The reason why Nursi insists so strongly on the Day of Judgement is because he wants to assure the believers that there is divine wisdom and justice, and one may have eschatological hope via the belief in an afterlife.[25]

In general, the Ash 'arite thought acknowledges the evil aspect of Asma's suffering, including pain, incapacity, illness, or poverty. They also do not deny the painful realities of existence. However, for them, the pain and suffering Asma experiences on earth is not the result of social inequality or an accident or human wickedness. Instead, they are part of God's plan: as God intends wealth, well-being, and belief of others, he also intends poverty and pain for others.[26] From this perspective, if we adhere to the Ash 'arite principle that God is the sole creator of all actions, do we suggest that Asma's suffering due to domestic violence is God's plan for her? If so, would then God be unjust in punishing the violent husband for the damage he causes to Asma? Further, if we apply al-Ghazali's theistic determinism, would it mean that if God determines Asma to be happy for eternity, God will also create its causes to make her happy? And if God determines suffering and pain to her, then would she believe that her action against violence will not change her condition? Such an approach to causality does not appreciate Asma's free choice to decide to eliminate her suffering due to domestic violence.

These questions suggest that the Ash 'arites' insistence on divine omnipotence raises more questions than answers especially regarding identifying a clear demarcation between absolute divine omnipotence and human responsibility. However, this does not also imply that Islamic psychotherapy cannot find anything helpful in the Ash 'arite thought that may empower Asma in her suffering. For example, Islamic psychotherapy can re-interpret the Ash 'arite approach to causality in such a way that Asma may see her suffering in the context of causes and conditions in the society. For example, a Muslim counsellor can argue that removing suffering due to domestic violence is bound to divine rules. In this regard, Asma has to make some effort to change her destiny because the change occurs from a causal relationship which is brought either by God or by God's agent. In this case, change might occur by reporting violence to police or getting counselling to deal with the effects of violence, including suffering. Also, although the Ash 'arites, including al-Ghazali and Nursi, did not encourage discussing certain themes, including the divine decree, their discussion of causes and effects of events may also inspire Asma to reflect on the causes and effects of her suffering due to domestic violence. Such a reflection may lead to gaining more insight that may also inspire her to take firm action to remove her suffering.

The Maturudites

Since Asma follows the Maturudite thought, we also need to examine this school in order to find out how they circumvented the problem of evil. We also need to determine how the Muslim counsellor can use their perspective to bring clarity to Asma's question of suffering and reconcile God's omnibenevolence with God's refusal/failure to intervene. Therefore, alongside presenting the articulation of the problem of suffering and evil in the Mu 'tazilite and Ash 'arite schools, we also need to mention the role of al-Maturudi in further elaboration of divine testing and suffering in Asma's dilemma.

Abu Mansur Muhammad b. Muhammad b. Mahmud al-Maturidi (853–944), one of the leaders of orthodox Islam in the Sunni school of thought, followed strict guidelines to resolve the tension between the "affirmation of God's existence and the reality of existent evil in what He created."[27] For him, "this opposition impregnates the whole of reality – the cosmos (*al-'alam*) and man, the microcosm (*al-'alam al-saghir*)."[28] Al-Maturidi rejected the idea of physical evil as merely metaphor and declared that

> God is the creator of the substance of evil and of good, the creator of the act of the creature as evil or as good, for it is impossible that anything exists in the realm of His power which He did not create.[29]

Against the Ash 'arite attempt to rank God's omnipotence above and beyond all other divine attributes such as justice (*'adl*), wisdom (*hikmah*), mercy (*rahmah*), al-Maturidi generated fresh insight on the reality of evil by isolating God's wisdom (*hikmah*) as an effective denominator of God's omnipotence. He defined this wisdom as "*wad'u kulli shay'in mawdi'ah*" ("placing everything in its proper place"). His follower Abu al-Mu'in al-Nasafi, on the other hand, defined it as "that which promotes a praiseworthy result" ("*kullu ma lahu 'aqibah hamidan*").[30] Regardless of how the Maturudites define wisdom, it is important to mention that their understanding of wisdom does not limit God's power like the Mu 'tazilite doctrine of justice nor does it claim that wisdom can be known by reason. Instead, they suggest that the wisdom behind God's actions may be beyond human comprehension. Therefore, the believers must embrace the belief that "God's actions serve a wise purpose."[31]

In his *Kitab al-Tawhid*, Maturidi discussed the theological problems of his time, including the existence of evil and the human responsibility and religious obligations in this world. In the context of wisdom, al-Maturidi examined the problem of evil, *al-qada'* (the divine decree) and *al-qadar* (divine fore-ordination).[32]

For al-Maturidi, the divine decree is a two-fold decision ("one, that the thing be, and two, that it should be in a way appropriate to it") and creational and creative ("bring into being what was not").[33] Furthermore, for al-Maturidi, there are multiple meanings of *al-qadar*: being either

> (a) good or evil; (b) beautiful or ugly; (c) wise or foolish. In the second sense, it means (a) time and place; (b) truth and falsehood; (c) reward and punishment. In this second sense, *qadar* is called not *al-hadd* but *al-bayan*.[34]

For al-Maturidi, the former meaning of *qadar* refers to the intrinsic qualities of the creation; whereas the latter implies the externals of the action in relation to time and place, truth and falsehood, rewards and punishments. Thus, for al-Maturidi, evil was a thing that God created, and should not be accepted as a negation of being. He pointed out that humans cannot fully comprehend the wisdom of creation because "one does not necessarily come to know (*ta'arruf*) His modality (*kaifiya*) or quiddity (*ma'iya*)."[35] Therefore, humans should accept the creation of goodness and evil as the aspects of *al-mihna* (the trial).

Al-Maturidi also strongly argued that it is against reason to think that the world is not grounded in anything other than wisdom, nor is without *qasd* (purpose).[36] For him, "reality is rational and therefore subject to reasonable analysis."[37] He equated *'adl* (justice) with wisdom and supported the idea that God's creation does not deviate from fairness.

Al-Maturidi also introduced a new interpretation of the doctrine of *al-kasb*, which implies that "regardless of any obscurities in it, is nevertheless the affirmation of the reality of human action as the human agent's, not God's."[38] In other words, although God creates evil, based on their degree of intellect and *ikhtiyar* (free choice), it is human beings who perform evil. Such a position may resemble the Ash 'arite understanding of voluntary acquisition; however, there is also an important difference: in the Maturidism, the concept of *kasb* suggests that humans are more implicated than God regarding retaining a power to withdraw or suspend their initial decision to act. Also, for the Maturudites, the created power that humans acquire via *kasb* is "an *enabling* power, not a *compelling* one."[39] This idea suggests that the freedom of action comes from *min nafsihi* (from one's own consciousness). Such an approach, however, does not free God from the "responsibility" for the evil which Asma experiences because still, it is God who gives the capacity to human to perform evil.

In the Sufi tradition, suffering can be explained within a larger metaphysical context. Classical Sufi concepts, such as *qabd* (contraction) and *bast* (openness), to explain distress and suffering may help Asma to a certain degree. *Qabd* is severance of the link between an individual and the source of his or her spiritual gifts and radiance for a certain period. A believer, who experiences *qabd* depending on his/her spiritual and emotional capacity, suffers from spiritual obstruction and blockage. For example, when a believer experiences fear and hope, the first station for her is to seek God's knowledge. Therefore, Asma needs *bast* – expansion, development, relief, and being freed from spiritual blockage through knowledge. Asma might have certain wisdom and benefits of *qabd*, including waking up from her heedlessness and loss of spiritual energy, sins, or neglect of spiritual and religious duties.

However, this perspective still does not answer to Asma's question, which is "What is the wisdom behind the violence against her?" The most likely answer to this question according to the Maturudites would be that domestic violence is decreed for Asma, i.e., God has created it and passed judgement on her to accept or reject it. Also, God assigned truth and falsehood, and the reward or punishment to domestic violence. Asma may not have the power of knowledge to determine her acts in terms of time and place in her experience of domestic violence. Her act depends on God as the Qur'an declares: "We have determined in their regard the journey" (Q. 34:18). However, Asma can act within the limits of *kasb*, i.e., tolerating her suffering or eliminating it through her actions. Finally, although God did not intervene to stop Asma's suffering, her suffering might have a wise/good end, i.e., she might stop the violence, reinforce her humanity, create awareness about the damage of domestic violence, or at least, God will reward her in the hereafter. Therefore, the Maturudites may help Asma gain insight into what God promised and threatened in the hereafter, and into her capacity (such as the intellect, reason, and understanding the revelation) to eliminate her suffering. Her choice of action based on this capacity is then her free choice. The Maturudite theology also encourages Asma to be responsible for her decisions, i.e., either she must decide to end her suffering or to remain in a violent relationship and suffer more. In addition, according to the Maturudites, since all acts are judged by their ultimate effect, domestic violence is ultimately evil for it is devoid of good, just, and wise effects.

Also, one of the suggestions for Asma from the Maturudites' perspective would be to use *qiyas* (analogical reasoning). For example, al-Maturudi's analysis of God's names in the context of God's uniqueness can be an example for Asma. Al-Maturudi points out that there is nothing like God. Therefore, God cannot be evil because evil is a created thing.[40] Therefore, Asma's suffering should be understood not in respect to God's direct relationship or responsibility to domestic violence that may imply that we put God on trial for domestic violence against Asma but in respect to God's alleged use of domestic violence (i.e., domestic violence as a function of wisdom).

The Hanbalites

Like the Ash'arites and Maturudites, the Hanbalites affirmed God's omnipotence and omnibenevolence. First, the prominent members of the Hanbali School that represented itself as the traditionalist theological movement,[41] such as Ahmad ibn Hanbal, the founder of the school, and Taqi al-Din Ahmad ibn Taymiyya (d. 1328), rejected any attempt to reconcile the meaning of the Qur'an with speculative meanings. Ibn Taymiyya, for example, is famous for stating that "Whatever God wills happen, and whatever He does not will not."[42] He also differentiated between *iradah kawniyah* (God's ontological will) and *iradah shari 'iyah* (God's deontological will) which was similar to the concepts of ontological command (*amr al-takwin*) and deontological command (*amr al-taklif*) of the Ash'ari scholar imam al-Haramayn Dhia' ul-Din Abd al-Malik ibn Yusuf al-Juwayni al-Shafi'i (1028–1085). The concept of *iradah kawniyah* implies that everything that God desires to happen, including evil, will happen (Q. 36:82). On the other hand, according to the concept of *iradah shari 'iyah*, the rightness of any action depends upon what God has ordered humans to do and an action is an intrinsic object (i.e., regardless of the consequences or the actor who performs it, the evil is inherent to the act). These concepts also defended the idea that God may permit the circumstances that permit people to harm others; however, not everything that God approves reflects God's pleasure or God's preference in the creation of that thing. Although Ibn Taymiyya argues that the Ash 'arite did not possess the similar approach, Jackson argues that both the traditionalists and Ash 'arites distinguished God's will from God's preference. However, Ibn Taymiyya interpreted the concept of *al-kasb* differently than the Ash 'arites: for him, *al-kasb* does not mean humans have power but simply means "an *indication* or *guarantee* of where God would place God's own efficient power."[43] In addition, he introduced the concept of "theory of complementarity" that referred to God's bestowing inherent capacity to everything God created that becomes effective when "comes into a relationship with its complement."[44]

In the context of human will, he calls it a "qualifying capacity" (*qudrah musahhihah*), which includes human's

> primordial knowledge of God, an instinctual love of pleasure, praise, power; the inclination to indulge the "lower" desires; self-absorption; and heedlessness . . . a general will (*iradah*), the basic instincts (fear, hope) and a modicum of quasi-efficient agency (*qudrah*).[45]

Such a presentation of the qualifying capacity may resemble the Mu 'tazilites' concept of free will; however, unlike them, Ibn Taymiyya did not agree that God grants *lutf* in the form of the equal amount of capacity to everyone to stimulate internal decisions or capacity. Therefore, there must be "special something" or the causative complement, i.e., psychological impulses in the human self, that promote good or bad deeds by God's will. Ibn Taymiyya also states that everything has an inherent capacity instilled by God and gets activated in the presence of a complement, i.e., fire burns in the presence of paper or wood.[46] Therefore, from Ibn Taymiyya's perspective, Asma has also an inherent capacity and in the presence of a necessary complement, i.e., at least her desire to eliminate her suffering, hope, and so forth, it will enable her to remove domestic violence.

In addition, Ibn Taymiyya's treatment of evil and suffering of women is in the context of his concern for the stability of the family and the right of a wife to social justice.[47] His questioning of theological and legal stances of his time with respect to divorce, forced marriage, and treatment of women explicitly demonstrated that he was interested in issues that affected women.[48] By providing the *hadith* narrations against forced marriages and the importance of seeking the women's (both virgin and non-virgin) consent for marriage, Ibn Taymiyya concluded that even the father of the woman cannot force her to agree with what she disagrees. Although he did not explicitly disapprove forced marriages, he clearly rejected the force used in these marriages by stating that "she is still very much the hostage."[49] Such a courageous and critical position against forced marriages demonstrates how Ibn Taymiyya challenged his own intellectual predecessors. Nevertheless, we should also not forget that like other Muslim scholars of his time, Ibn Taymiyya also supported the idea that even in forced marriages, the husband's rights come after those of God and the Prophet.[50]

If we apply this understanding to Asma's dilemma of suffering and divine testing, it would imply that her suffering is due to the first evil or *dhanb* (sin) which is the failure to obey God and become heedless. However, unlike the Mu 'tazilite, Ibn Taymiyya suggests that performing good and avoiding evil is for the interest of the person and others. Also, probably, in Asma's case, the existence of domestic violence as an evil and suffering has *hikmah* (a purpose or wisdom). From Ibn Taymiyya's perspective, it might be "functional" and steers "humans away from routinized lives of heedlessness that result in perdition, in this world, the next, or both."[51] In sum, for the Hanbalites, Asma's desire and practice of obedience to God increases her chance of removing evil and suffering.

Thus, the Qur'an is not that explicit in terms of divine decree. The early discussions among Mu 'tazilite, Ash 'arite, Maturudite, and Hanbalite theologians also do not bring a clear explanation. They might not provide direct response to the inquiry about how Asma may find herself in a difficult position in terms of determining where the will of God ends in her situation and where God wants her to be active in changing the fate. It sounds as if, in both classical and contemporary Islamic thought there is a general tendency to find a spiritual lesson in every suffering, for a believer needs to be tested to discover his/her true essence. Also, there is an attempt to find fault in human experience instead of in the Almighty.

Islamic Feminist Responses

The analysis of the responses of Islamic schools of thought once more demonstrates the complexity of the system in which Muslim women live.[52] There is no doubt that Islamic theological schools play an important role in understating how Asma perceives her suffering. They offer some understanding of the root of suffering and the path to end suffering. Therefore, like many other Muslim feminist scholars,[53] I do not state that the entire Islamic theological schools are invalid and wrong. For example, taking into consideration the historical contexts of the Qur'anic exegetes, Wadud proposes her feminist theory of justice based on her understanding of the Qur'an. From this perspective, her "gender jihad" may encourage Asma to challenge the societal *status quo* and attempt to change her status.[54] By presenting this idea to Asma's Muslim counsellor, as Wadud explicitly points out, will try "to change the immutable words we grapple with and challenge the inherent sexist biases of the historicity of words."[55] Also, Barlas's idea of a "believing woman," a term that she borrows from the Qur'an, may be very empowering for Asma who presents herself a Muslim woman who has a strong faith in her religion. As Barlas points out, a "believing woman" is not sceptical of the ontological status of the Qur'an and accepts it as a Divine Speech. However, like many feminists, she questions the legitimacy of the Qur'an's patriarchal readings with a purpose to differentiate between "what God says and what we understand God to be saying."[56]

Such affirmative approach to the Islamic tradition does not mean that the Muslim counsellor is not against the Qur'an's patriarchal readings and the traditional understanding of the Islamic authority (*ulama*), which are only conservative males. The introduction of Islamic feminism in previous chapters has also suggested that Islamic feminist scholars have made a shift from the apologetic approach to Islamic teachings; they hold even the Qur'an responsible for the contradictory verses within the Qur'an.[57] Asma's question of suffering makes it important not only to analyze the social contexts of Islamic teachings, including the influence of patriarchal interpretations that "result from the exclusively male constitution of much institutional Islam,"[58] but also question the tension between patriarchal and egalitarian values in the Islamic tradition, including within the Qur'an itself, and the divine wisdom and plan for suffering and inequalities in human society. Based on feminist discourse and core principles of gender justice, equality, and freedom from oppression, Islamic feminist perspective in Islamic psychotherapy suggests consciously utilizing an Islamic discourse to problematize gender justice in the context of Qur'anic values, such as "divine justice, compassion, egalitarianism and liberation from slavery or submission to any being other than God."[59] For this purpose, the Muslim psychotherapist can use Islamic feminist theories to engage in a call for reclaiming religious discourses and practices concerning Asma and deconstructing Islamic history and tradition by producing alternatives and new solutions inspired by feminist and Islamic values. As "believing" Muslim women, Muslim psychotherapists can teach Asma how to provide a critical lens to suffering in the Qur'an and the aforementioned four schools. Such an approach may inspire Asma to create a new understanding of her suffering. Further, the Qur'an-centred Islamic feminist discourse encourages understanding a pure and essential message of Islam and its spirit in the context of Asma's suffering, especially how it was presented by the Prophet Muhammad himself. Meanwhile, the Prophet Muhammad's treatment of his wives, daughters, and women companions cannot be undermined or overlooked, for during his lifetime Muslim women were extremely outspoken and active members of the Muslim community.

However, as we mentioned before, Islamic feminist perspective suggests that we also need to practice a more affirmative position in understanding and examining these schools. The discussions of God's omnipotence, omnibenevolence, and wisdom in the aforementioned schools of Islamic thought, which still need to be elaborated by Islamic feminist theology, suggest that God in Islamic theology is not a mere static concept. From Islamic feminist perspective, Asma must engage these concepts in her relationship with God both on the individual and collective level. However, the muteness or indirect responses to women's suffering due to domestic violence in Islamic theology should not be perceived that Islamic theology promotes silence before injustice and evil. Intense and active discussions of human free will and choice should encourage Asma to act against her suffering. For example, according to the Mu 'tazilite, Asma has an obligation to fulfil her duty to command right and forbid wrong. They also teach Asma should seek help which also includes receiving counselling.

Therefore, through the focus of Islamic feminism on gender equality and social justice, i.e., "an Islamic project of rereading the Qur'an,"[60] "women-centred readings of religious texts," and "Muslim women's gender activism,"[61] the important theological teachings of these schools may help Asma to understand her question of suffering in the context of both one on one and collective responsibility towards God to prevent evil and maintain justice. They also suggest that in order to awaken the hidden human qualities inside our personalities we need to endure before *qabd* that is an essential and most important dimension of servanthood to God, and carries the potential to elevate a person to the highest spiritual rank in the sight of God. Further, the Qur'anic notion of human morality holds us ethically responsible for our thoughts and actions even if one may excuse that these actions are utterly dependent upon God for the ability and power to act comes from God. It creates and sustains "communal contemplation"[62] and awareness to be embraced by Muslims.

However, if we neglect to treat these discussions in the context of their socio-cultural and historical context, their arguments might not be enough to resist domestic violence as many women may draw a conclusion that the pre-modern Muslim scholars reconciled with domestic violence rather took a radical stance against it. In order to answer to this dilemma, we need an Islamic feminist perspective used by Barlas, Wadud, Hassan, and others that motivates to take into consideration the lived experience of Muslim women when we interpret the Islamic sources. Although Muslim feminist scholars also come from various religious and cultural traditions, they use primarily the legal, exegetical, and mystical sources of Islam to challenge gender issues. Their consideration of the socio-cultural and historical context of classical sources is helpful to examine the stance of theological sources. In sum, Islamic feminism offers another possible response to Asma's suffering due to domestic violence by not attributing its cost to the theological schools of Islam, but to deviation or degradation in the social or cultural context that normalizes women's suffering due to domestic violence. The Muslim feminist scholars suggest that the end of women's suffering is possible only when we address the root causes of the problem, i.e., domestic violence, patriarchal culture, social oppression, and the underlying assumptions and structures of oppression. Such a position helps to obtain a new theological understanding of suffering that may help structural changes take place in order to improve women's lives. In general, the Qur'an also encourages individual interpretations based on lived human experience[63] to find out answers to these important questions above because we experience God's goodness, power, and wisdom "not through theology but through our relationship with God."[64]

Suffering in Social Science Literature

In this subsection, we discuss the correlation between Islamic theology, the domestic violence literature, and psychotherapy theories with regard to the meaning and treatment of suffering. Therefore, I use the domestic violence and counselling literature to understand how Muslim women find a meaning in their suffering and resist domestic violence from a social sciences perspective.

The domestic violence literature clearly documents how women suffer because of the negative impact of violence.[65] The movements against violence against women emphasize women's suffering due to sexism, cultural and religious factors, and patriarchy.[66] Also, loss of hope and suffering result from relational difficulties and social adversity. For example, Pamela Cooper-White, who talks about spiritual abuse against women in the Christian context, draws our attention to a collective denial of women's suffering and the collective notion of blaming women for their suffering.[67] She argues that women "do *not* invite, nor do they consent to, the violence that is perpetrated upon them."[68] She also states that God does not cause women to suffer; instead, God stands with women in their suffering. She states that empowerment, relationship, justice, and change are important to relieve the suffering of women.

Cooper-White's approach to suffering due to domestic violence resonates with the position of Salma Elkadi Abugideiri, a Muslim counsellor who co-leads the Peaceful Families Project in the USA. Abugideiri cites different forms of violence due to sexism, patriarchy, and social injustice, and states that all the forms of violence are prohibited because the Qur'an and *hadith* identify them as *zulm* (oppression).[69,70] Also, there is a strong correlation between suffering and various emotional and mental health issues such as nightmares, self-blame, PTSD, and so forth.[71] Women who are victims of violence express their suffering by asking questions such as: "Why did God let this to happen to me?" and "Where was God when I called out to Him?" These questions explicitly describe a wavering relationship between the women who are victims of violence and God. For example, these women may feel that God has betrayed and abandoned them.

However, along with these mixed feelings, these questions also express women's strong longing for God and a desire to feel protected by their religious community.[72] Further, beyond questioning their faith, they also express the extent of their trauma. Questioning the faith demonstrates women's suffering amid the violence and the beginning of the healing process. This is a normal feeling: after the stages of denial, shock, and resistance, acknowledging one's own suffering leads to more complicated issues such as "self-blame and recognition of the complexities of one's own actions and reactions."[73] However, the struggle with finding meaning in the suffering by questioning the role of God may be powerful, too. For example, the victims may feel that their faith has been strengthened through their doubts.[74]

The Declaration on the Elimination of Violence against Women also states domestic violence causes suffering due to physical, sexual, and psychological harm.[75] The legal actions to eliminate the suffering of women, such as protective orders, criminal prosecution, or tort litigation, may help women obtain a remedy for the suffering.[76] Although the domestic violence literature highlights the question how women who are victims of domestic violence can resist domestic violence, it does not adequately respond to the question of suffering. Therefore, existential therapy may be more relevant because it focuses on finding meaning in human experience.

In existential therapy, the interpretation of suffering is closer to the Islamic understanding of suffering. Based on the philosophies of existentialism and psychoanalysis,[77] existential therapy, which is a unique approach to counselling and psychotherapy,[78] suggests that existential crisis causes mental suffering and tries to answer the question whether life has a meaning in suffering. Despite the differences between the diverse strands of the existential tradition in counselling (i.e., the American schools such as existential-humanistic and existential/contemporary psychoanalysis and the British School, including the well-known Daseinsanalysis and Logotherapy), the existential therapy applies a phenomenological approach to explore the client's whole existence as being-in-the-world.[79] The most appealing aspect of the existential therapy is that it is interested in the historical and contextual embeddedness of concrete lived experience: it is "more inclined to perception than abstraction, to sensation than conjecture, to description than theory, existential psychotherapists gravitate to ontology rather than metaphysics."[80]

Viktor Frankl, the survivor of the Jewish Holocaust and one of the influential figures of existential therapy, for example, concluded that suffering itself is anything but meaningful, but meaning can be found even amid suffering. He suggests that there are times that suffering is unavoidable; however, the causes of suffering can be removed or eliminated. Also, Frankl suggests that despair is suffering without meaning.[81] In order to deal with suffering one needs to live according to one's real nature and be free from conforming to the demands of others. However, what is more important is to find meaning in suffering; otherwise, it would be suffering with no meaning.

In the context of domestic violence, the answers to the questions of suffering can be found in the everyday vicissitudes of human experience. For the existential therapist, it means allowing women who are subject to domestic violence to speak for themselves "without seeing them through some theoretical lens."[82] For example, the existential therapist does not assume that the suffering is the beginning of a spiritual awakening that usually starts during the middle stage of life. Instead, they apply a phenomenological approach which means "to be open to the details of thought, feeling, imagination, and behaviour precisely as they occur and to understand them on the grounds of their 'self-showing.'"[83]

Furthermore, existential therapy thinks about human nature and suffering in an understanding of the human *qua* human, rather than humanity as an object like all other natural objects fit for calculative and natural scientific investigation. Therefore, it is helpful to understand the women's perception of suffering due to domestic violence simply as part of their world, or simply *being-in-the-world* and in the whole human existence.

Also, existential therapy may help women who experience domestic violence explore the potency of being conscious rather than the power and impact of what is unconscious. We suffer from our very awareness of our all-too-contingent human existence. What is also important in this therapy is that it believes that women who are subject to domestic violence have the capacity to perceive, understand, and reply to their experience of violence. This capacity can fundamentally alter old deterministic, cause and effect models of human behaviour as it offers to find out *situated freedom* which we experience in every moment of our lives. Therefore, it aims not only to bring awareness to the past experience but also aims to explore "future possibility that shapes our present purpose and direction."[84] Such a notion in the existential therapy differentiates it from psychodynamic therapy which suggests that one needs to be aware of the elements of the past that cause suffering and transform those elements from a weakness into a strength.

Interventions to Relieve Suffering

In the light of multiple approaches to and explanations of the Qur'an and other sources of Islam, these women seek counselling to find out how to make sense of the divine testing and suffering. Existential therapy can help to deal with the complexity of the question of meaning in suffering in the context of Asma's physical, emotional, cognitive, and behavioural states. This therapy is especially more appropriate for the clients who feel marginalized in the society.[85] For example, by using Logotherapy,[86] interventions aim to help Asma to address a *restricted existence* (i.e., limited awareness of herself and often being vague about the nature of the violence).[87] The psychotherapist assists Asma in moving toward authenticity, learning to recognize when she is deceiving herself, facing her anxiety, and engaging in action to create a worthy existence. Without being authentic to herself or as Islamic theology suggests, following *fitra* (primordial nature), it is impossible to create the meaning in the suffering. As Frankl states, "What matters, therefore, is not the meaning of life in general but rather the specific meaning of a person's life at a given moment."[88] In order to discover hope and meaning, he suggests to be self-aware of our responsibility to self and society by three primary ways: (1) by creating a work or doing a deed, (2) by experiencing something such as positive values, i.e., love, and (3) by practicing the attitude toward unavoidable suffering. Therefore, the main interventions with Asma may focus on spiritual need and also seeking and finding meaning, transcending hardship and suffering by (1) helping her become more present to her needs, (2) assisting her to identify ways that block her capacity from being more fully present, (3) challenging her to assume more responsibility how she is currently choosing to deal with their suffering, and (4) encouraging her to choose more expanded ways of being in her daily life. Also, by applying a compassionate approach, Muslim psychotherapist who applies the existential therapy can help Asma alleviate suffering and benefit physical and psychological health, and turn her suffering into spiritual growth and achieve personal and interpersonal goals.

Furthermore, without being too lofty and elusive or placing emphasis on a subjective understanding of Asma's suffering, the existential approach would be the most useful approach to helping Asma who uses Islamic concepts to describe her suffering. Therefore, the Muslim psychotherapist can also use Islamic thought to increase Asma's self-awareness that is talking about suffering or complaining should not be perceived as against divine will or questioning God's omnipotence, omnibenevolence, and wisdom. When the Muslim psychotherapist notices that Asma tends not to see how her own thoughts and behaviours produce unviable results, the counsellor can place responsibility back on Asma's shoulders, like the Islamic schools of thoughts attempted to do. For example, they can ask her "What have you done to try to solve the problem related to divine testing and your suffering?" "And then what did you do?" "What have you done about it in the past?" and "What are you going to do about it?" These questions may challenge Asma to examine her own thought process and behaviour. The purpose is to assess the client's placement of responsibility and whether she views herself as playing as an active role in the process.[89]

For the purpose of assisting Asma in finding the meaning in her suffering and empowering her to take more responsibility, the Muslim psychotherapist can incorporate a few of techniques of existential therapy into the Islamic psychotherapy practice. For example, the Muslim psychotherapist can use inspirational resources such as stories/parables and autobiographical narratives of the prophets and saints from the Islamic tradition. The Muslim theologians, i.e., al-Ghazali, Nursi, Ibn Taymiyya, and so forth, extensively used these stories to help Muslims see how these saints experienced God's goodness, power, and wisdom in their suffering. These stories of suffering are the most popular types of the Islamic tradition, written for the believers to develop or heighten feelings of devotion toward God, the prophets, and Muslim mystics. Although the main purpose of these stories in Islamic theology is to depict the exemplary Muslim life, emphasizing the relationship between the individual and the community and the individual and the divine, in Islamic psychotherapy, these resources can be used to give strength and comfort to Muslim women and provide spiritual uplifting for them.

One of the stories of suffering in the Qur'an is the story of Job (Ayyub) who was one the prophets. In the works of Muslim theologians, e.g., Nursi,[90] this story holds a special place in order to theologically prove that God is good and wise and powerful. The Qur'an describes how Job cries unto God and expresses his dissatisfaction and emotional and spiritual pain. His words such as "affliction has befallen me," or "Behold, Satan has afflicted me with weariness and suffering!" (Q. 38:41–44; 21:83) clearly demonstrate the fact that complaining does not mean accusing God of causing afflictions or evil; instead, it is the sign of pure commitment to one's faith through sharing and sincere supplication and a strong desire for support for a radical change. Muslim women who are subject to domestic violence can act like Job when they find that their suffering is unbearable: this act includes seeking refuge in God who Job describes "the most merciful of the merciful" (Q. 21:83). In addition, God's response to Job's prayer also advises to seek out earthly means for salvation with patience: "Strike (the ground) with your foot: here is cool water to wash and to drink!" (Q. 38:42).

Similarly, the stories of Maryam and Asiya, the Pharaoh's wife can also be used to inspire Muslim women to deal with their quest for the meaning of suffering and resisting domestic violence. The Muslim psychotherapist, for example, can use the narrative of the Prophet Muhammad's daughter Fatima, whom the Muslim women always find as a source of inspiration and strength in their suffering. For them, Fatima is a woman with great compassion, generosity, and nurturing nature as a daughter, mother, and wife.

However, Fatima's presentation as a "queen of sorrow" may not be helpful in Islamic psychotherapy with Asma. We need her presentation as a woman of courage and spiritual power to speak the truth. Therefore, Muslim psychotherapists may use the argument of some Muslim scholars, i.e., Ali Shari 'ati, who refused to depict Fatima only as a symbol of sorrow and unhappiness and did not lament on Fatima's miseries. For Shari 'ati, Fatima was and is a true revolutionary model along with other members of the household, whose life is an example for a virtuous life of poetical awareness.[91] Fatima was depicted as a mother and daughter who stood against injustice from childhood, which continued after the death of her father. Thus, Fatima should not only be remembered as a wife with unconditional loyalty and fidelity to her husband Ali who also stood up against injustice in society, but also "the very epitome of love, devotion, courage, and steadfastness."[92]

One of the models for Asma who seeks answers to divine testing and suffering is Zaynab, the granddaughter of the Prophet, Imam Hasan and Husayn's sister, who emerges as an important female figure of the tragedy of Karbala. She is described as the most important *shahadat* (evidence, testimony) and the voice of the tragedy and a wise and learned woman who stood up against unjust rulers after the death of her father, Ali. As Muhammad Husayn al-Tabataba'i, an Azerbaijani Turk from Tabriz, remarks:

> the event of Karbala, the capture of the women and children of the Household of the Prophet, their being taken as prisoners from town to

town and the speeches made by the daughter to Ali, Zaynab, . . . disgraced Umayyads.[93]

Where is the therapeutic role of these stories for Asma? First, these resources from the Islamic tradition play an important role in the lives of Muslim women. Specifically, the gender themes carry a potential to empower Muslim women by embedding a significant space for feminine sanctity. Second, these male and female sacred figures in the Islamic tradition were not passive and submissive before their suffering. Therefore, not only men's but also women's images in these stories carry a deep transformative power. Finally, Muslim women give these stories great value and significance because their life gets changed and shaped by these images even though some of these images are symbols of pain, conflict, and deep wound. Through these stories, the Muslim psychotherapist may help Asma, as Van Deruzen states, to get better at reflecting on her own situation, to deal with the dilemma she faces, to challenge her predicament, and to "think for" herself.[94]

Notes

1. Ormsby, *Theodicy in Islamic Thought*, 3; Gottfried Wilhelm Leibniz, *Theodicy: Essays on the Goodness of God, the Freedom of Man and the Origin of Evil* (La Vergne, TN: Lightning Source Incorporated, 2006).
2. Ormsby, *Theodicy in Islamic Thought*, 3.
3. Jackson, *Islam and the Problem of Black Suffering*, 124.
4. See Watt, *The Formative Period of Islamic Thought*, 233.
5. Jackson, *Islam and the Problem of Black Suffering*, 53.
6. Ibid., 56.
7. Abdul Aziz Sachedina, *Islamic Biomedical Ethics: Principles and Application* (Oxford: Oxford University Press, 2009), 96.
8. Ibid., 56, 96.
9. Jackson, *Islam and the Problem of Black Suffering*, 62–63.
10. Ibid., 64.
11. Ibid., 124.
12. Sachedina, *Islamic Biomedical Ethics*, 87.
13. Ibid., 89.
14. Ibid., 90–91.
15. Ibid., 90.
16. Jackson, *Islam and The Problem of Black Suffering*, 59.
17. Ibid., 77.
18. Sachedina, *Islamic Biomedical Ethics*, 83, 97.
19. Jackson, *Islam and the Problem of Black Suffering*, 94.
20. Cited by Jackson, *Islam and the Problem of Black Suffering*, 93.
21. Al-Ghazali, *Ihya'*, vol. IV, p. 318, 1.5; Binyamin Abrahamov, "Al-Ghaz l 's Theory of Causality," *Studia Islamica* 67 (1988): 75–98.
22. Mehmet S. Aydin, "The Problem of Theodicy in the *Risale-i Nur*," in *Islam at the Crossroads: On the Life and Thought of Bediuzzaman Said Nursi*, ed. by Ibrahim M. Abu Rabi (New York, NY: State University of New York Press, 2003), 219–222; Bediuzzaman Said Nursi, *The Words: The Reconstruction of Islamic Belief and Thought*, trans. by Hesyin Akarsu (Clifton, NJ: The Light, Inc., 2005), 711.
23. See Shaikh, "A Tafsir of Praxis," 72.

24. Barbara Freyer Stowasser, "Theodicy and the Many Meanings of Adam and Eve," in *Theodicy and Justice in Modern Islamic Thought: The Case of Said Nursi*, ed. by Ibrahim M. Abu-Rabic (Surrey: Ashgate, 2010), 16.
25. Thomas S. J. Michel, "The Resurrection of the Dead and Final Judgment in the Thought of Said Nursi," in *Theodicy and Justice in Modern Islamic Thought*, 40.
26. Sachedina, *Islamic Biomedical Ethics*, 97.
27. Jerome Meric Pessagno, "The Uses of Evil in Maturidian Thought," *Studia Islamica* 60 (1980): 65.
28. Ibid., 63.
29. Ormsby, *Theodicy in Islamic Thought*, 67.
30. Jackson, *Islam and the Problem of Black Suffering*, 109.
31. Ibid., 110.
32. Pessagno, "The Uses of Evil in Maturidian Thought," 69.
33. Ibid., 71.
34. Ibid.
35. Ibid., 79.
36. Ormsby, *Theodicy in Islamic Thought*, 63.
37. Ibid.
38. Pessagno, "The Uses of Evil in Maturidian Thought," 77.
39. Jackson, *Islam and the Problem of Black Suffering*, 117.
40. Pessagno, "The Uses of Evil in Maturidian Thought," 79.
41. Ibid., 128.
42. Cited by Jackson, *Islam and the Problem of Black Suffering*, 137.
43. Ibid., 139.
44. Ibid.
45. Ibid., 140.
46. Ibid., 137.
47. Carolyn Baugh, "Ibn Taymiyya's Feminism? Imprisonment and the Divorce Tafwas," in *Muslima Theology: The Voices of Muslim Women Theologians*, ed. by Ednan Aslan, Marcia K. Hermansen and Elif medeni (New York : Peter Lang Edition, 2013), 181.
48. Ibid., 189.
49. Baugh, "Ibn Taymiyya's Feminism," 193.
50. Ibid., 193.
51. Jackson, *Islam and the Problem of Black Suffering*, 155.
52. See Julie Macfarlane, *Islamic Divorce in North America: A Shari'a Path in a Secular Society* (Oxford: Oxford University Press, 2012); Ali, *Marriage and Slavery in Early Islam*; Ali *Sexual Ethics and Islam: Feminist Reflections on Qur'ān, Hadith and Jurisprudence* (Oxford: Oneworld Publications, 2006); Judith Tucker, *Women, Family, and Gender in Islamic Law* (Cambridge: Cambridge University Press, 2008).
53. Riffat Hassan, "Feminism in Islam," in *Feminism and World Religion*, ed. by Arvind Sharma and Katherine K. Young (Albany, NY: State University of New York Press, 1999); Wadud, *Qur'an and Woman*; Barlas, *Believing Women*; Barlas, *Believing Women: Unreading Patriarchal Interpretations of the Qur'an.*
54. Wadud, *Qur'an and Woman*, 66.
55. Ibid., 206.
56. Barlas, *Believing Women*, 19.
57. See Ali, *Sexual Ethics and Islam.*
58. Sa'diyya Shaikh, *Sufi Narratives of Intimacy: Ibn'Arabi, Gender and Sexuality* (Chapel Hill, NC: University of North Carolina Press, 2012), 23.
59. Abu Bakr, Omaima, "Islamic Feminism: What's in a Name? Preliminary Reflections," *AMEWS Review* xv, xvi (Winter/Spring 2001): 1.
60. Margot Badran, "Towards Islamic Feminisms: A Look at the Middle East," in *Hermeneutics and Honor: Negotiating Female "Public" Space in Islamic/ate Societies*, ed. by Asma Afsaruddin (Cambridge, MA: Harvard Middle Eastern Monographs, 1999), 2.

61. Shaikh, "Transforming Feminism."
62. Jackson, *Islam and the Problem of Black Suffering*, 162.
63. See also Mulki Al-Sharmani and Jana Rumminger, "Understanding Qiwamah and Wilayah Through Life Stories," in *Men in Charge: Rethinking Authority in Muslim Legal Tradition*, ed. by Ziba Mir-Hosseini, Mulki al-Sharmani and Jana Rumminger (London: Oneworld Publications, 2016), 219–255.
64. Jackson, *Islam and the Problem of Black Suffering*, 163.
65. McCue, *Domestic Violence*, 6, 18, 42, 82.
66. Ibid., 42.
67. Cooper-White, *The Cry of Tamar*, 19.
68. Ibid., 136.
69. Abugideiri, "Domestic Violence," 310, 314.
70. Abugideiri, "Domestic Violence," 317; Inga Rudolfsson and Lisa Tidefors, "I Have Cried to Him a Thousand Times," *Mental Health, Religion & Culture* 17, 9, 910–922.
71. Annette Mahoney, Layal Abadi, and Kenneth I. Pargament, "Exploring Women's Spiritual Struggles and Resources to Cope With Intimate Partner Aggression," in *Religion and Men's Violence Against Women*, ed. by Andy J. Johnson (New York, NY: Springer, 2015), 52.
72. Rudolfsson and Tidefors, "I Have Cried to Him a Thousand Times," 910.
73. Cooper-White, *The Cry of Tamar: Violence Against Women*, 12.
74. Rudolfsson and Tidefors, "I Have Cried to Him a Thousand Times," 921.
75. UN General Assembly, The Declaration on the Elimination 1991, Articles 1, 2a.
76. McCue, *Domestic Violence*, 197.
77. Existential therapy is influenced by these philosophers and therapists: Søren Kierkegaard (1813–1855), Friedrich Wilhelm Nietzsche (1844–1900), Martin Heidegger (1889–1976), Jean-Paul Charles Aymard Sartre (1905–1980), Edmund Husserl (1859–1938), Maurice Merleau-Ponty (1908–1961), Victor Frankl (1905–1997), Rollo May (1909–1994), Irvin Yalom (1931–), Jacques Derrida (1930–2004), and James Bugental (1915–2008). For example, Ludwig Binswanger (1881–1966) and Medard Boss (1903–1990), two influential existential therapists, borrowed terms such as *amor fati* from Nietzsche, Sartre's view of a person's relationship to the dead in their "necropolis," and Derrida's "*heritage*." (See Laura Barnett and Greg Madison, "Introduction," in *Existential Therapy: Legacy, Vibrancy and Dialogue*, ed. by Laura Barnett and Greg Madison (New York, NY: Routledge, 2012), 3; and Erik Craig, "Existential Psychotherapy, Discipline and Demarche: Remembering Essential Horizons," in *Existential Therapy*, 11.
78. See Laura Barnett and Greg Madison (eds.), *Existential Therapy*; Viktor Frankl, *Man in Search of Meaning* (Phoenix, AZ: Zeig Tucker and Theisen, 2003).
79. Barnett and Madison, "Introduction," 2.
80. Craig, "Existential Psychotherapy, Discipline and Demarche," 7.
81. See Viktor Frankl, *The Will to Meaning* (Phoenix, AZ: Zeig, Tucker and Theisen, 2003).
82. Craig, "Existential Psychotherapy, Discipline and Demarche," 9.
83. Ibid., 9.
84. Ibid., 17.
85. Gerald Corey, *Theory and Practice of Counseling and Psychotherapy*, 9th ed. (Belmont, CA: Brooks/Cole Cengage Learning, 2008), 159.
86. Ibid., 143.
87. Ibid., 154.
88. Victor Frankl, *Man's Search for Meaning: An Introduction to Logotherapy*, ed. by Harold S. Kusher and William J. Winslade, trans. by I. Lasch (New York, NY: Beacon Press, 2006), 131.
89. Thor Johansen, *Religion and Spirituality in Psychotherapy: An Individual Psychology Perspective* (New York, NY: Springer Publishing Company, 2010), 131.

90. Zeki Saritorpak, "The Creation of Evil Is Not Evil: Theological Approach to the Existence of Evil," *The Fountain* 50 (2005). Accessed on September 25, 2016 from www.fountainmagazine.com/Issue/detail/The-Creation-of-Evil-is-not-Evil-Nursis-Theological-Approach-to-the-Existence-of-Evil.
91. See Hamid Dabashi, *Theology of Discontent: The Ideological Foundation of the Islamic Revolution in Iran* (New York: New York University Press, 1998), 123; Karen Ruffle, "May Fatimah Gather Our Tears: The Mystical and Intercessory Powers of Fatimah al-Zahra in Indo-Persian, Shi'i Devotional Literature and Performance," *Comparative Studies of South Asia, Africa and the Middle East* 30 (3) (2010): 395.
92. Ibid., 125.
93. Muhammad Husayn Tabatabi, *Shi'ite Islam* (Herndon, VA: SUNY Press, 1975), 200. See also Diane D'Sousa, *Shia Women: Muslim Faith and Practice* (New Delhi: Zubaan, 2012), 43.
94. Van Deurzen, quoted by Corey, *Theory and Practice of Counseling and Psychotherapy*, 158.

4 Satanic Interference and Evil Eye

Hagar is a 41-year-old Muslim woman who was born in Pakistan. She immigrated to Canada a few years ago to join her extended family, including her mother who lives with her brother. Soon after immigrating, she married one of her cousins. She was happy to marry him, as she was on good terms with his side of the family. Her cousin was in a relationship with someone else before her, but his family wanted him to marry Hagar. Soon after the engagement, they began to spend more time together. Initially, he expressed his love and support and encouraged her to improve her English. He also was attentive and liked to listen to her when she had something to share.

However, after the wedding, Hagar had difficulties with normal everyday functioning due to physical pain and mood swings because her husband started to force her to do what he wanted her to do. He ignored her suggestions and desires and forced her to spend less time with her parents and siblings. He blamed her spending too much time trying to look nice, and spending too much time with her mother. In the beginning, Hagar did not want to accept that her own cognitive, emotional, and functional problems were related to her husband's emotional violence. She was afraid of making him angry by not following his demands as he had big mood swings – he would get angry and yell at her one minute but was sweet and apologetic the next.

Hagar was strongly convinced that both she and her husband were in the trap of *jinn* (unseen creatures), who tempted her husband to be violent and aggressive. She thought that the *jinn* who might have possessed her husband and forced him to behave violently towards her also touched her and caused mental health issues such as anxiety and depression. Her husband's odd and strange behaviours also reinforced her belief that the *jinn* touched him: her husband claimed to see and talk to unseen creatures and hear voices. He became more restless and sleep-deprived and even once told her that he was afraid to sleep as he felt something was "strangling" him. He also stated that he believed both she and their two sons (ages 2 and 5) were evil. Hagar felt even more hopeless, sad, and lethargic. She had a lack of concentration and extreme worries about the future, as well as being indecisive as to how to deal with her husband's behaviour.

However, the difficulties increased. Hagar told her mother that every night after her husband yelled at her or threatened her she felt as if dark and evil forces possessed her body and soul. Her family agreed that she has been inflicted with *nazar* or *isabat al-'ayn* (evil eye), *hasad* (envy), *sihr* (black magic), and mischief of *jinns.* They also told her that *jinn* might have also touched her husband; therefore, he displayed symptoms of madness. Her mother instructed her to go to an Imam who practiced *ruqyah* (a special chanting) and seek a cure for any illness by reciting the Qur'an and making *du'a* (prayer) to God.

Therefore, Hagar decided to try traditional healing methods for her husband's violent behaviour and mental health issues. During her childhood, she had witnessed some women in their village whose husbands were cheating or violent, and they found these healing practices effective and powerful over *jinn.* The traditional healers claimed to be more experienced than psychiatrists and psychologists in dealing with the effects of domestic violence. These women would usually say that the healers knew what happened to the women without requiring them to tell everything. They healed these women and their husbands' spiritual disturbances from the satanic interference which occurred through (1) demonic possession by *jinn*; (2) *jinn* whispering into the victim's mind, as a kind of negative muse; (3) evil eye; or (4) magic. These healers provided special amulets consisted of Arabic letters and numbers and written with ink and made from the mixture of *misk* (musk), *anbar* (amber), *safran* (saffron), *ıtır* (attar), and rose water as one of the most effective "prescriptions" for the touch of *jinn.* In addition, they taught those who used their services that since the spirits never completely abandon a person and may later on to wish to possess them, they had to continue the "prescription" from the Qur'an (Q. 1:1–5; 2:163–164, 255–256, 185–186; 3:18–19; 7:54–56; 55:33–36; 59:21–24, 72:1–9; 112; 113; and 114). One of the prescribed *du'a* was "*Ya Mubdiʾ al- baraya wa-muʿiduha baʿda fanaʾiha bi-qudratihi bi-hurmati Muhammadin wa-ahli bayti Muhammad*" (O the One who raises humans when they are alive and after the death, give the healing for the sake of Muhammad and His family!).

However, after she disclosed to her husband that she thinks that *jinn* possessed both of them and she is looking for a traditional healer, her husband threatened to kill her and her sons. So, she decided to seek help from her family doctor without telling that her husband was threatening to kill them because they were "evil." After she had disclosed to her doctor that she was tired all the time and had lost interest in activities she previously enjoyed, and that she believed her husband was possessed by *jinns*, she referred her to a psychiatrist. Her psychiatrist diagnosed her with depression with psychotic features. However, she was not happy with her diagnosis, as it did not immediately help "treat" her husband's possession problem. So, she decided to consult with a Muslim psychotherapist in the local mosque. In the counselling session with a Muslim psychotherapist, Hagar told her that she did not believe she was suffering from depression with psychotic features, and that all her symptoms were not organic as her doctors claimed. She asked her Muslim psychotherapist whether she could guide her to someone who has experience dealing with the unseen creatures.

Satanic Interference and Evil Eye in Islamic Studies and Islamic Psychotherapy Literature

Hagar's case presents the story of a Muslim woman who interprets domestic violence as satanic interference, magic, and an evil eye. In this section, I mainly talk about her reference to her husband's possession problem, her belief that her husband has been involuntarily taken over and controlled by alien spirits or para human forces that cause various diseases/ailments, including physical and mental health diseases, which we present here as satanic interference. I highlight the role of traditional healing practices, such as *al-ṭibb al-nabawi* (prophetic medicine that refers to traditional religious medicine based on Prophet Muhammad's practices) and folk medicine, which Hagar attempts to use to deal with the problem of possession and indirectly with domestic violence. Satanic interference is usually defined as affliction by evil spirits who inflict people with maladies and cause harm to their well-being.[1] The afflicted person may be possessed either through sorcery or from *jinn*'s desire for a person and for a long period of time, the afflicted person may not know that he/she has been possessed.

The guiding questions for this section are: How do the Islamic traditional healing practices, such prophetic medicine, and folk medicine, explain the phenomenon of satanic interference causing harm to women like Hagar? How does this theoretical knowledge of Islamic studies in this area contribute to the improvement of the practice of counselling with Hagar who is subject to domestic violence?

Prophetic Medicine and Its Legal-Ethical Context

Within the traditional healing practices, prophetic medicine would hold a special place for Hagar. Although prophetic medicine emerged a few centuries after the Prophet's death, it was especially well-known since the 13th to the 15th century, when the first manuscripts on the subject appeared in the Muslim world.[2] The vast body of prophetic medicine suggests that this practice was one of the most recommended therapies for physical, mental, emotional, and spiritual distress and illness such as fevers, leprosy, plague, poisonous bites, protection from night-flying insects, protection against the evil eye, rules of coitus, theories of embryology and anatomy, the proper conduct of physicians, and the treatment of minor illnesses such as headaches, nosebleeds, cough, colic, and sciatica. Their arguments were mainly based on the *hadith* literature, which contains some narrations that directly approve the application of various remedies and interventions for any illness, including mental and emotional problems.

As Hagar's case presents, prophetic medicine also contains materials relevant to the issue of satanic interference as it is vastly used for relationship problems between the husband and wife. In Q. 2:102 and the prophetic tradition the marital problems are usually presented as the work of Satan. One of the well-disseminated prophetic narrations reports that:

> The Satan places his throne upon water; he then sends detachments (for creating dissension); the nearer to him in rank are those who are most notorious in creating dissension. One of them comes and says: "I did so and so." And he says: "You have done nothing." Then one amongst them comes and says: "I did not spare so and so until I sowed the seed of discord between a husband and a wife." The Satan goes near him and says: "You have done well." A'mash said: He then embraces him.[3]

Although the aforementioned *hadith* does not elaborate how the satanic interference directly or indirectly causes domestic violence, it highlights the direct result of domestic violence as the seeds of discord between the husband and wife.

The Prophet taught his companions to practice *taʿwidh* (means for protection from illness, evil eye, *jinn*, etc.) against the satanic interference. For example, he used the *ruqyah sharʿiyya* (lawful incantation), which generally involved reciting Qur'anic verses and prayers for seeking a cure for effects of satanic interference, physical, and mental illnesses. The Prophet and his companions also read the Qur'an and asked for a cure from God for an afflicted person. The companions strongly believed that the Prophet's touch was the act of wishing the sick person to heal faster or carried a message of a personal blessing.

The Muslim scholars, who explored prophetic medicine, including Suyuti (1445–1505) and Zarkashi (d. 1392), suggested that surah *Fatihah* (the opening chapter of the Qur'an) is the cure for every disease. Other specific chapters from the Qur'an (i.e., Q. 36), were used to treatment madness and fear. A medieval Muslim scholar Ibn al-Tin even suggested that *muʿawwadhatayn* (the last two chapters of the Qur'an) and other prayers are the strongest spiritual medicine that are even efficient in physical illnesses.[4] Later, the list of prayers and incantations were extended names of God, angels, prophets, and even the poems written by Muslim poets (i.e., *Qasidat al-Burda* [Poem of the Mantle]). Some even prescribed *tamima* (an amulet and talisman) and *nushra* (a charm).

Nevertheless, there were strict guidelines of practicing prophetic medicine. Most of the Muslim scholars generally stated that the practice of prophetic medicine must be preceded with a proper physical and spiritual preparation by the healer and the sick, which is also very important in the context of domestic violence which Hagar struggles. Some of these guidelines included suggestions such as having a strong faith by the healer and the ones who seeks help that the practice will be responded to either in this world or in another form in the Hereafter. Also, before applying prophetic medicine (i.e., lawful incantation, saying a prayer, and so forth), both the healer and the sick needs to take *wudu'* (ablution) and ensure that the area and clothes were clean. In addition, the healer must have the ability to encourage their patients to be optimistic about the results of the healing process. In order to promote optimism, the healers usually perform prophetic medicine during auspicious times of the day, week, month or year, such as during times of distress, when travelling, on Fridays, during Ramadan, on holy nights, i.e. *Laylat al-Qadr* (the Night of Power, which is believed to be the night before the 27th day of Ramadan), and after obligatory prayers or in certain places such as in the Ka'bah in Makkah, the Prophet's Mosque in Madinah, or Masjid al-Aqsa in Jerusalem was also recommended. Finally, acquiring a *halal* (lawful) livelihood and consuming *halal* food is a key in getting the positive result of prophetic medicine.

As Hagar's case displays, prophetic medicine is still popular among Muslims to treat the satanic interference, mental and physical illnesses, and marital problems via the evil eye and sorcery. According to Khadher Ahmad, Ishak Suliaman, and Sedek Ariffin Khadher, there are at least 20 methods to heal the effects of the satanic interference.[5] These practices are an integral part of services in many Islamic treatment centres in some Muslim countries. However, not all of these 20 treatment approaches and methods are mentioned in the traditional sources. Ibn Qayyim suggested the following methods to treat the sorcery: (1) search, discharge, and omit the sorcery; (2) purify the body suffered from the sorcery; and (3) use *ruqyah al-shar'iyyah* to treat the patient. Regardless of the lack of research whether *ruqyah* practice helps or not, it is becoming more popular not only among Muslims.

Currently, there is no agreement among contemporary Muslim scholars on the direct or indirect impact of satanic interference. Some interpretations, which sometimes contradict each other, have been under the heavy influence of Jewish and Christian legends, scriptures and thought, which is briefly labelled as *isra'iliyyat.*[6] In addition, the Jewish, Christian, Zoroastrian, and Hindu legends also influenced Muslim understanding of Satan and its harm to humans. Therefore, each version of the Satan narratives must be read and interpreted within its own context of its full Qur'anic chapter.[7] So, Hagar may benefit from finding out the contemporary interpretations of satanic interference.

In general, with respect to using prophetic medicine against satanic interference, Muslim scholars' position can be categorized under three categories: (1) those who advocate for unrestricted use of prophetic medicine, (2) the opponents of prophetic medicine, and (3) those who hold a middle position and allow only the restricted use of prophetic medicine. The first group of Muslim scholars, i.e., 'Umar Sulayman al-Ashqar, those who are represented in the Permanent Committee for Scientific Research and Issuing Fatwas in Saudi Arabia (such as Ibn Baz), 'Abdullah Ibn al-Siddiq al-Ghumari (1910–1993), and many others are ardent advocates of using the Qur'an and the prophetic tradition as a spiritual medicine for all diseases. Ibn al-Siddiq, especially, criticizes the "reformists" who, according to him, deny the healing aspect of the Qur'an and the prayers.[8] The opponents of using prophetic medicine usually consider the Qur'anic references to Satan and its mischievous nature. However, these references have been interpreted in different ways, too.[9] From this perspective, many Muslim scholars tend to criticize the inappropriate application of prophetic medicine with respect to the satanic interference.

For example, in his *Masalih al-Abdan wa al-Anfus* (*Sustenance for Body and Soul*), Abu Zayd al-Balkhi (d. 934), the Muslim psychologist, discusses cultural beliefs such as satanic interference that are usually simple common mental disorders. He includes mental health issues such as fears and anxiety under four main categories: anger (*al-ghadab*), sadness and depression (*al-jaza'*), fears and phobias (*al-faza'*), and, obsessional disorders (*wasawes al-sadr*).[10] His entire chapter on obsessional disorders (including obsessive beliefs about *jinn*) includes his thoughts on fear and worries that prevent individuals from enjoying life, performing daily activities, and concentrating on other aspects of life. Under the influence of intrusive, recurrent, and persistent thoughts, the person expects that the worst will happen in the near future. Taking into consideration the common myth among Muslims in his time indicates three major barriers to a proper treatment: cultural beliefs, attitudes towards seeking help and loss of hope in finding a treatment before effective prevention and treatment of mental health problems. He argued that many people believe that *jinns* afflict fears and concerns, but the afflicted person still needs to resist these thoughts and replace them with positive thoughts.

A more contemporary Muslim scholar Muhammad Abduh (d. 1905), on the other hand, tried to interpret *jinn* (unseen creatures) as the microbes in the context of modern science.[11] Such an interpretation allows seeing the satanic interference emerging as a physical illness. Abduh's student Rashıd Rida (d. 1935), on the other hand, held a strict opposition against the practice of *ruqyah* (incantation) because for him, it was originally a pre-Islamic tradition and was forbidden by the Prophet, except in the case of evil eye, bites and sting of a snake and blood that will not be staunched. Rida also pointed to the violation of an important ethical principle *tawakkul* (the principle of trust) in the practice of *ruqyah.* Nevertheless, Rida concluded that allowing the practice of *ruqyah* is only *rukhsa* (a legal concession) rather than the Prophet's belief in its effectiveness.[12]

Fazlur Rahman encouraged seeing the dilemma of satanic interference in the context of the principle of evil. For example, Rahman stated that Satan

> rebels against God's command but as rival and enemy of man rather than God, since God is beyond where the devil can touch him; it is the man who is his aim, and it is the man who can either conquer him or be vanquished by him.[13]

He mentioned that "Satan does not exist in man except metaphorically . . . there can be no Satan independent of human nature."[14] The Qur'an's main image of Satan highlights weakness in human character (i.e., fallible, gullible, disobedient) and the one who is being used to test human righteousness.[15]

In the spirit of the aforementioned positions, Mahmud Shaltut (d. 1963), the late grand imam of al-Azhar, invited Muslims to be mindful of (*bid'ah*) (false innovations and heresies in Islam). He included the practice of reciting incantations in false innovations and stated that it is inappropriate to use the Qur'an in these practices because who those do so are ignorant of the true reason of the Qur'anic revelation.[16]

Despite the contradictory approach to prophetic medicine and using the Qur'an and other prayers to ward off satanic interference, Muslims have a strong belief in the effectiveness of prophetic medicine in dealing with almost all kinds of problems. For example, Hagar seeks indirect help for treating impacts of domestic violence such as her anxiety, fear, and so forth, which she interprets as the satanic interference, and invokes the authority of the Prophet in respect to the healing of her and her husband's mental health issues due to the impact of the satanic interference. For Hagar, his sayings, deeds, or attitudes are a fundamental source of reference for making decisions and judgements on the process of healing. It is no wonder that his authority is still relevant for Muslims, including the Muslim doctors who refer to the Qur'an and the *hadith* for advice. However, the healing process takes some time. The Prophet also presented the healing process as a gradual process rather than a result of "magic." Therefore, the third group of Muslim scholars usually allows the restricted use of lawful incantation. Yusuf al-Qaradawi and Muhammad 'Uthman Shubair, for example, consider these practices valid; however, they also suggest that the Qur'an should be used for purely spiritual purposes rather than treating physical diseases. Some others suggested that *ruqyah* (incantation) should include only the last three chapters in the Qur'an alone. In addition, Qaradawi condemned the so-called practitioners known as *mu'alijun bi al-Qur'an* (Qur'an healers) who operated special Qur'an clinics.[17]

In sum, it is my conclusion that the *hadith* literature is not explicitly clear whether the Prophet's companions believed that the Prophet had a special healing power or whether he was acting as a medium in transferring divine healing to the sick person. Nevertheless, I assume that many of the companions did not ascribe a healing power to the Prophet himself because they were aware that for the Prophet such a belief was strictly against the *tawhid* (the unity of God) principle of Islam. However, later generations of Muslims did not view prophetic medicine as a symbolic and formal way of invoking a blessing from God; instead, they put the Prophet Muhammad as an intercessor between God and humans; some of them even ascribed a divine power to the Prophet.

Despite the complications above with respect to practicing prophetic medicine, Islamic psychotherapy with Hagar can apply some of its elements within the limits of the ethical/legal framework of the Islamic tradition because it promises an alternative option for Hagar to express herself and find help for domestic violence.

Although the Qur'an does not directly link domestic violence to the satanic interference, Hagar's case suggests that the majority of Muslims tend to link Satan with different kinds of harm by unseen creatures. Hagar knows that there is a strong emphasis in the Qur'an on Satan's enmity with humankind, and Satan uses every situation to prove that humans are not worth being appointed as the vicegerent on earth (Q. 30–33). Therefore, she tries to find out the most effective way to deal with her problem within the framework of traditional healing practices. Hagar can learn from the Qur'anic warning that she needs to be alert and on guard against evil because Satan's temptations become stronger with human aid, and he cannot be strong without human weakness and lack of morality.[18] As Rahman coins it: "Satan does not exist in man except metaphorically."[19] Perhaps, the biggest contribution in Hagar's case would be teaching her idea from the Qur'an (i.e., Q. 4:76; 17:64; 4:120; 58:19) that "evil is inherently weak and truth strong is born the invincible faith of the Qur'an that falsehood and evil can and will be vanquished."[20] Therefore, Hagar can learn from the Qur'anic warning that she needs to be alert and on guard against human weakness and immorality, which will be discussed in Chapter 5 where we discuss spiritual diseases.

Folk Medicine

In addition to prophetic medicine, some Muslims also use folk medicine for relationship problems, physical and mental health problems, including satanic interference. Folk medicine is usually one of the ancient healing practices in the Muslim world and is also popular among Muslims in North America. The Muslims who come from Muslim countries such as Sudan, Egypt, Algeria, Morocco, Nigeria, the Arabian Peninsula, Iran, and other countries of Africa and the Middle East present these practices under the names such as *zar, sar, bori, tumbura, dastur*, red wind, or *shaitaini*.[21] Among Muslims, traditional healers are known by names such as *shaykh, derwish*, and *pir*[22] depending on their geographical location. Muslims from Morocco, for example, call those who practice magic as *saḥḥar* (male) or *saḥḥarah* (female).[23] Those traditional healers who heal their patients with herbs are called *hawaweej* (herbalists).[24]

Hagar's experience of the healers in her village suggests that depending on their treatment philosophies or spiritual/mystical orientation, practitioners of folk medicine may claim reliance on the divine authority by using the Qur'anic verses, recitations, and prayers from the prophetic tradition. Like Hagar, some Muslims also believe that these healers have *barakah* (a healing power of grace) that makes folk medicine powerful.

In one study,[25] for example, it is suggested that most of these healers get this healing power from belonging to an *ojak* (holy centre) or *dargah* (shrine),[26] which are specialized in treating symptoms or diseases and apply certain rituals to increase the efficiency of their remedies. For example, traditional healers who belong to the "*Sarilik ojagi*" in Turkey are known for treating jaundice by using a razor to cut and let the blood come out from the area between eyebrows; whereas healers in the "*Kutnu ojagi*" are popular treating dermatological problems using some natural formulations. The "*Temre ojagi*" treats a type of lichen infection induced by Lichen simplex either by simply spitting on the affected area or practicing some ritual treatments. The "*Ilanjık ojagi*," on the other hand, treats erysipelas infection by using a mollusk that is called "Mecca stone" and some herbal ointments. A special category of healers in this group known as "*sinikci*" applies traditional folk medicine for treating bone cracks. Yesilada argues that it is not necessary to belong to any *ojak*, but belonging to them adds a spiritual dimension or credibility of these healers among people.[27]

The folk healers also claim to heal evil eye and possession by *jinns*. In order to treat the person, the ceremonials and rituals are performed to manage the alien spirits. For example, during the *zar* ceremony in Iran, the patient afflicted by *jinn* lies down and punches himself/herself on the chest, may move along with the music chanted, and gives a sacrificial animal or something valuable such as gold or silver ornaments.[28] The patient may also be recommended to stay in isolation for up to seven days in the residence where the ritual takes place.

One of the forms of folk medicine include application of amulets and talismans against the evil eye, exorcism of evil spirits, and hygienic practices such as the practice of cupping, bloodletting, and cauterization, male and female circumcision or application of natural ingredients such as perfumes and drugs or knowledge of astrology, geomancy, and alchemy. This kind of folk medicine is also known as *al-simiya* (natural magic) or *'ilm al-rukkah* ("distaff" science or wisdom), and has received some scholarly attention because these practices are still relevant among many Muslims, who for example, believe that amulets and talismans protect and heal from diseases caused by magic, evil eye, envy, or evil spirits. Muslims, especially those who come from Turkey, Pakistan, Azerbaijan, Africa etc., accept using these healing methods, including exorcism and magical practices "as long as they are practiced in the name of God to help people . . . rather than inflict harm on them in collaboration with the devil."[29] In his *Manners and Customs of the Modern Egyptians*,[30] Edward W. Lane also described how some Muslims consider spiritual healing or *al-ruḥani* as spiritual, divine or true magic: the second type of magic was *sihr* (evil or satanic magic).[31]

Nevertheless, in Islamic jurisprudence, carrying amulets, talismans, phylacteries, *bezoars* (stomach concretion of animals), and using magic, magic stones, sorcery, and astrology as a means of healing and warding off evil spirits are considered one of the most controversial practices of traditional healing in Islam. All four schools of Islamic jurisprudence consider some folk medicine, i.e., sorcery, *haram* (forbidden), suspicious, and harmful.

For example, neither the Qur'an nor the *hadith* literature associate religious rites and prayers with magic; instead these texts warn against the application of magic. Specific chapters in the Qur'an (i.e., Q. 2:102), draw attention to an anti-social and malevolent nature of magic. Many Muslims consider such practices or heretical innovation and attribute these practices to pre-Islamic belief and practices. Both the Qur'an and the *hadith* literature also associate religious rites and prayers with magic harmful and warn against the application for magic and its malevolent nature of magic. From the perspective of *tawhid*, the Qur'an specifically emphasizes the belief that healing comes only from God. Further, as we see in Rida's contest against the practice of *ruqyah* and similar practices, attributing to the Prophet Muhammad or the deceased saints the power of divine healing has been detested. Such practices were labelled as *bid'at* (innovation) or *shirk* (ascribing something to God). The opponents of these practices argue that those who believed in the Prophet Muhammad as a healer or visited the tombs and asked the saints to intercede for them before God as a traditional healing practice act against the Prophet's tradition because they seek to heal from sources other than God. For them, *bid'at* (innovation) has always been something negative and destructive in Islamic tradition because the authentic *hadith* collection in Sunni Islam reports from the Prophet saying that if anyone introduces in Islam something that does not belong to it, it will be rejected.[32] Therefore, in Islamic psychotherapy with Hagar such practices including magic must be distinguished from religion.

Nevertheless, it is also helpful to indicate that although Prophet Muhammad had forbidden the use of some aspects of folk medicine, i.e., using amulets at the beginning of his mission, he later allowed a limited use of amulets if their contents were verses or *hadith* and the person expected healing from God and not from the amulet itself.[33] Also, many healing techniques used by the Prophet himself (i.e., cupping, honey, and so forth) are folk medicine. Therefore, some Muslims view folk medicine as an acceptable treatment method against an alternative to mainstream support and more effective than drug therapy for mental and physical health issues. Some Muslims may integrate prayer and drug therapy; however, some still trust the former for it is fast and free from side effects such as fatigue, loss of energy, and so forth. In the context of Hagar's problem of domestic violence, as Maria Sabaye Moghaddam suggests, some Muslim women look on *zar* as a temporary relief from all problems, tensions, and suppressed desires. For these women, who feel neglected, deprived, and mistreated, *zar* provides a voice and temporary relief. This is especially powerful for women who live in a remote village because, for them, the *zar* ceremony is the only place where she can voice her objection. Therefore, these practices are the "mystical defence system" against possession as a means of coping with personal suffering, emotional stress, and conflict, as coined by Ioan M. Lewis.[34]

Satanic Interference in Islamic Psychotherapy Literature

As an important aspect of the Islamic tradition, Islamic psychotherapy provides more foundation to understand Hagar's presentation of the problem of domestic violence and mental health issues. Although Islamic psychotherapy research in this area is new, this section examines how Islamic psychotherapy can help to interpret Hagar's mental health and domestic violence issues in the light of the satanic interference. Although the Islamic psychotherapy research did not fully explore the link between domestic violence and the satanic interference, it highlights how domestic violence results in mental health issues among Muslim women. It also presents the fact that many Muslims attribute relational problems, mental illnesses such as schizophrenia,[35] and physical illnesses such as epilepsy,[36] to the possession of *jinn* through the sorcery and evil eye. Therefore, Islamic psychotherapy respects both Hagar's belief that satanic interference may happen through demonic possession by evil creatures, influence by the evil eye, or magic and the fact that Hagar expects a miracle or some form of divine intervention in her healing journey.

Islamic psychotherapy and counselling literature[37] talk extensively about the nature and treatment options for cases where the satanic interference is the main counselling issue. This highlights the importance of the preference of Muslims in terms of treating satanic interference.[38] Nevertheless, some Muslim psychotherapists demonstrate a positive stance towards the use of prophetic medicine or other cultural and religious methods to tackle the satanic interference problem. Muslim psychotherapists in the past and present explain satanic interference by addressing common misconceptions about the nature and causes of mental and physical health issues such as depression, epilepsy, schizophrenia, bipolar disorder, and so forth. Hagar's case is a common case study that suggests that the cultural beliefs around physical and mental health issues still prevent many Muslims from seeking active treatment for effects of domestic violence. Hagar believes that the responsibility for domestic violence lies with Satan.

Further, Hagar's case suggests that many Muslims still tend to explain mental illness as a lack of faith or affliction of *jinn*. For example, many Arab Muslims associate the word "madness" with possession and sorcery, and some precipitating factors are intimately linked to social relationships.[39] Tahir Obeid, Abuaban Ahmad, Fawazia Al-Ghatani, Abdul Rahman Al-Malki, and Abdulaziz Al-Ghamdi[40] state that the public needs to be educated in order to correct their beliefs. In addition, the public belief about the etiology of illness is more cultural than religious.

Although research by Farah Islam and Robert A. Campbell[41] does not explore satanic interference in the context of domestic violence, they report that the Qur'an does not indicate whether *jinn* causes mental illness, whereas the *hadith* literature is rich with stories about the connection between *jinn*-possession and madness. Therefore, like Hagar, many Muslims attribute mental illness to supernatural forces. In these situations, the psychotherapist must educate their clients about the meanings of the Qur'anic verses about the *jinn*, which will produce a proper understanding of the causes of mental health issues among Muslims. Rashed,[42] on the other hand, suggests examining two main responses that some Muslims demonstrate to tackle the satanic interference which he calls "active" and "passive." The active response refers to a person's attempt to use personal coping strategies such as reading the Qur'an, performing ritual prayers, etc., and the latter means to the person's dependence on the medium, healer, or the third person to deal with psychotic experiences. Rashed uses the contemporary recovery model to frame the use of these responses in a culturally specific context. For example, central concepts of recovery such as the idea of empowerment and responsibility help people gain "control" and reclaim power and responsibility. By taking an active stance against "possession" the person claims control over or taking charge of his/her life.

Yusuf Muslim Enerborg also argues for an alternative to the religion/magic dichotomy as "an invaluable tool in helping to appreciate the essential instrumentality of the Qur'an within Islamic healing and prophylactic practices considered magical."[43] He points out that the lawful incantation has recently gained popularity among Muslim youth and has also received scholarly attention. Therefore, emphasizing the "context" rather than "content" by styling the "magical" as "scientific" to be helpful. For example, the belief in possession by *jinn* among Muslims indicates a way to cope with "psychological disturbance" and "unexplained physical symptoms."[44]

Many Muslim authors also argue that in order to be effective in psychotherapy, the psychotherapist must pay attention to some domains of their practice.[45] The application of unmodified Western theories of psychology and psychotherapy and stereotypes about Muslims can cause therapeutic failure and frustration. Such a practice may also end up with serious diagnostic errors. For example, inexperienced psychiatrists or psychotherapists may diagnose the fear of invisible creatures as psychosis, or dependence on family or community as "dependent personality disorder."[46]

These aforementioned findings in Islamic psychotherapy literature resonate with the work of Muhammad al-Ghazali (d. 1996), who has taken this approach in connection with the issue of *jinn* possession.[47] Al-Ghazali, who considers *jinn* possession to be an imaginary ailment, also recognizes the usefulness of *ruqyah* (incantation) in order to make the client more comfortable, since in his experience removing such *awham* (delusions) is a lengthy process. However, he also relies on *ta'wilat* (interpretations) and *nasihah* (counselling), using his scholarly expertise in Qur'an interpretation to object against claims of *jinn* possession, for example, based on verses that indicate that Satan may only suggest but may not exercise control over the behaviour of a person (Q. 14:22; 34:20–21).[48]

Overall, research on the perspectives, characteristics, and practices of these traditional healing practices in Islamic psychotherapy is relatively limited. Although I support the idea that some of some aspects of traditional healing practices may be controversial, they still belong to the rich Islamic tradition because since the beginning, Islam transcended cultural and ethnic identities and emphasized the relationship between God and person. Muslims established open and flexible systems that tolerated or adopted the local customs and practices of a given society as part of the Islamic tradition. Gradually, a common expression of Islamic healing traditional practices started to emerge among Muslims as a broad religious and spiritual treasure of knowledge within the global Islamic religious and spiritual landscape. Therefore, Hagar's practice of seeking help for effects of domestic violence through traditional healing cannot be labelled as against Islamic belief because the *hadith* literature also indicates that the Prophet used to practice it. However, according to the Prophetic tradition, healing does not refer to any process or activity that has a beginning or end; instead, healing is a lifelong process or journey. Moreover, it encompasses all four elements of a whole person: spirit, emotion, mind, and body. True healing happens when there is a unification of the four important aspects of a human being: body, emotion, mind, and soul. Therefore, the main goal in psychotherapy is to help Hagar to achieve this balance between mind, emotion, spirit, and body. Otherwise, the absence of healing is assumed to be caused by a fragmented sense of self.

Satanic Interference in the Social Science Literature

Regarding Hagar's preference for traditional healing over mainstream psychotherapy for satanic interference and her rejection of her diagnosis of depression with psychotic features and general anxiety disorder, clinicians and researchers have debated the boundary between mystical and psychotic experiences. These experiences are discussed under the terms of various mental health problems and diagnosis such as trance state,[49] paranormal and transcendent,[50] visionary spiritual experiences,[51] mystical experience,[52] spiritual emergence,[53] religious delusion,[54] delusions with religious content,[55] religious preoccupation,[56] problem-solving schizophrenia, positive disintegration, creative illness, spiritual emergencies, mystical experience with psychotic features, metanoiac voyages, visionary states,[57] transcendent experiences, and so forth. For example, the DSM-5 describes delusion as a false belief "based on incorrect inference about external reality" and not accepted by other members of the person's culture or sub-culture or as schizophreniform disorders that include religious preoccupation and guilty ruminations.[58] In general, in the mainstream mental health system, there is a negative and suspicious attitude towards alternative religious and spiritual healing practices.[59] Despite the improvements, the DSM-5 is also being criticized for over-diagnosis and ever-widening its borders with diagnostic labels for mental states and responses to life situations. The main reason for pathologizing religious/spiritual beliefs and practices is due to the view of psychopathology that claims that psychological health is about the absence of disordered emotional and cognitive responses.

Nevertheless, the American Psychiatric Association (APA)[60] encourages taking seriously cultural beliefs, including religious traditions, before making a diagnosis of psychotic experiences. For example, the DSM-5 category Religious or Spiritual Problem (V62.89) is not a mental disorder but is listed in the section for problems related to other psychosocial, personal, and environmental circumstances.[61] Examples for religious or spiritual problem include "distressing experiences that involve loss or questioning faith, problems associated with conversion to a new faith, or questioning of spiritual values that may not necessarily be related to an organized church or religious institution."[62] The DSM-5 also states that some ideas, experiences, and practices (i.e., hearing God's voices, witchcraft, and so forth) that might seem delusional are a normal part of religious experience.[63] Therefore, clinicians should know that distress might take the form of hallucinations or pseudo-hallucinations and overvalued ideas and pay attention to styles of emotional expression, eye contact, and body language, which vary across cultures. Further, the psychotic experiences may involve persecutory (often involving Satan), grandiose (messianic delusions), guilt delusions, etc., themes. It is suggested that powerful images like Satan should be conceived as figurative or metaphorical; in many cases, these images can also be linked to mental, emotional, or psychological traumas, memories, or complexes. For example, possession might be considered as a "trance state" with two aspects: "(i) the individual's acceptance that they have been possessed, and (ii) an altered state of consciousness. The personal psycho-physiological mechanism is both possession and trance states are dissociation."[64]

Therefore, since some mystical experiences may meet the criteria for psychotic symptoms, a recent scholarly and clinical attempt is made to discuss the resemblance and importance of differentiating between psychotic symptoms and mystical experiences: such as the relationship between desperation, mental illness, and spiritual madness which are reminiscent of the behaviour of some *crazy wisdom* teachers and saints.[65] Susan L. DeHoff, who explored how mystical religious experiences might be distinguished from brief psychotic episodes from the perspective of religion, stated that mental health professionals heavily depend on DSMs to determine the nature of non-rational experiences. She argues that there are issues that still need serious attention to the subject. These issues are: (1) the need to define mystical, (2) identifying experiences interpreted as mystical religious, (3) identifying experiences interpreted as psychotic, and (4) discovering methods and sources used to interpret reported experiences, will be presented and supported by specific examples from the interviews.[66] DeHoff states that experiences of evil spirits (such as seeing an evil [harmful] spirit, spiritual warfare, and possession by evil spirits) do not usually involve God at the centre. These experiences reflect the "darker" side of mystical religious experiences.

However, unlike psychopathological syndromes, positive mystical experiences are healthy, pleasurable, beneficial, life-transforming, ineffable, or difficult to describe with words, and are not typically associated with any observable mental illness.[67] The person may also have a strong conviction that he/she has come in contact with the Truth. These experiences also and usually go beyond

> our accustomed levels of functioning . . . such transcendental experiences appear mysterious because they arise from processes outside of our ordinary conscious awareness. . . . Hopefully, in this process, you will find that you have gained an expanded vision of human potential.[68]

The positive mystical experiences are not paranormal in nature; however, since these experiences are rare, exceptional, and mysterious, many people define them as mystical, spiritual, and transcendental. They are very significant to those who experience them. Therefore, the clinicians need to know the religious and cultural background of the patient and the shared beliefs of his/her sub-culture. For example, in his article titled "Religious Delusions," Andrew Sims suggests that religious delusions indicate a profound disturbance in the self-image of patients who try to find an answer to the question who they are and how they relate to the world. If the clinicians fail to answer these questions using patient's cultural beliefs, then the diagnosis of a mental disorder will be stigmatizing and intensifying an individual's sense of isolation and blocking his or her efforts to understand and assimilate the experience.[69] If mystical experiences are perceived only part of an illness without considering other environmental aspects of these experiences, they are less likely to adhere to psychiatric treatment.[70] The result would be, as we see in Hagar's case, failure to explore more about the nature of these experiences and tendency to prescribe more medications that show poorer clinical outcomes. At the result, these individuals have more self-injurious behaviour and wait longer to resume treatment.[71]

Hagar's complaining about her family doctor and psychiatrist suggest that mainstream mental health services may downplay the idea that traditional healing practices constitute a significant part of Hagar's healing process. In the context of the clash between Aboriginal healing practices and the mainstream mental health system, James B. Waldrum questions those who reject other forms of healing and a failure of patient's cultural belief system by mainstream health caregivers: Is this because the healing itself is ineffective? Is it possible that science currently lacks the tools (and the inclination) to see traditional healing? How do healers view the issue of efficacy? What are their goals when they undertake to heal and what measures (if any) do they employ to determine success? Is efficacy, as science understands it, an issue even for traditional healers? Is the whole idea of questioning the efficacy and developing evaluation programmes even necessary? Is it possible that to undertake these we are violating the basic principles of the healing itself? Can traditional healing ever be understood by the dominant biomedical system?[72]

Nevertheless, many contemporary psychologists, psychiatrists, psychotherapists, counsellors, and so forth, such as Hans Gunter Heimbrock,[73] M. Scott

Peck,[74] Clemmont Vontress,[75] acknowledge the role of traditional healing practices such as magic and exorcism in psychotherapy. Heimbrock, for example, draws attention to the popularity of folk non-conventional treatment options. M. Scott Peck[76] and Clemmont Vontress[77] also accept the validity of folk and traditional healing practices, and therefore, encourage practitioners to draw upon the belief system of the client in formulating a treatment plan. Peck, for example, argues that the practice of exorcism is not against science and he even encourages psychiatrists and psychologists to consider demonology as a "proper field of scientific inquiry."[78] His acknowledgment of knowing the theological foundation of demonology reflects the lack of theology in the field of psychiatry and psychology. However, his introduction of names such as "a demon of confusion," "demons of lust and hate," and so forth, indicates his belief in satanic possession in the case of confusion, lust, hate, and other undesired mental and emotional disorders.

In his article "Traditional Healing in Africa: Implications for Cross" and "Animism: Foundation of Traditional Healing in Sub-Saharan Africa," Vontress[79] also argues that traditional healing practices have a potential in cross-cultural counselling. He presents the role of the family in the healing process, diagnosis, and intervention techniques in traditional client practices, and how folk beliefs and practices integrated with Islam, Christianity, and Vodou help in situations of spiritual, psychological, social, and psychical distress. Vontress states: "People in a given culture favour certain types of therapies because the methods are compatible with their cultural values and expectations."[80] He especially gives credit to traditional healers for their holistic approach by paying attention to "the most important therapeutic consideration – the spiritual."[81]

The treatment should also start with normalizing mystical experiences in order to facilitate healing. The purpose is to help people understand their crisis in a positive context for their experiences by proving sufficient information about the process that they are going through.[82] Therefore, it is suggested that it is important to help the client get the capacity to know objects that he/she accepts as the ultimate truth. Also, it is important to be mindful of how the clinician differentiates between true mystical experiences and psychotic ones. For this purpose, some mental health practitioners suggest involving family members and/or spiritual care professionals (e.g., chaplains and clergy).[83] Religious leaders who are familiar with a variety of faith traditions may provide important insight into the patient's beliefs when making this differentiation.

Many contemporary psychologists also invite counsellors to consider traditional healing practices that address spiritual, psychological, social, and physical distress and criticize those who ascribe these practices to ignorance, limited intelligence, and a lack of knowledge of mental illness.[84] The DSM-5 also takes into consideration psychosocial and environmental factors (i.e., the intensification of beliefs and practices, experiences of guilt, mystical experiences, near-death experiences, and reactions to terminal illness) that may affect the diagnosis, treatment, and prognosis of mental disorders. In addition, explanations of illnesses also change in response to context based on the fact of who is interviewing, where the interview takes place, and so forth.[85] In general, healing practices are accepted as specific coping strategies and help-seeking behaviours. Martin La Roche and Devon E. Hilton define coping as the techniques that individuals use to deal with the problem; whereas, seeking help refers to the specific ways the individuals seek assistance for the problem from others.[86] For example, if people think that their problems are psychological, they tend to visit their psychiatrists; however, if they think that they are related to physical health issues, they consult with their family doctors. In these situations, assessing coping and help-seeking patterns allows the clinician to obtain useful information about what the clients want to gain from the current treatment and/or why they tend to avoid the mainstream treatment. Also, clients may have a lack of confidence and trust because they did not find previous psychological or psychiatric treatment helpful.[87] Therefore, clients may find accessing traditional healing practices easier than accessing mental health services.

Although Carla Bellamy's[88] work does not predominantly describe women's healing practices, it describes how women seek healing for their problems, including physical and mental illnesses, disabilities, family problems, financial, and relationship issues, etc. First, the women "develop new identities" through participating in the ritual and everyday life of the holy shrines.[89] Second, although in these traditional healing practices the women might seem to be at the mercy of the practitioner and the malevolent spirit, they also provide a space for women for consciousness changing. Regardless how these women seek help, their use of traditional healing practices suggests that women tend to reflect and create "systems of power," such as the ritual activities of dominant and subaltern groups. For example, in the context of one specific traditional healing practice, *khuli haziri* is "religious practice in a manner similar to meditation (alteration of one's consciousness through breath and body control) or prayer (a request)."[90]

One of the important questions might be how traditional healing practices are meaningful for women who are subject to domestic violence. As one who is familiar with these traditional healing practices know that these practices may not directly relate to the dominant narrative of domestic violence. The women might even not to choose to share or tell their experience of domestic violence. However, these healing practices involve a series of sub-narratives, stories, anecdotes, and tropes that also purposefully rekindle the desire "to respond to a context that the process of healing takes place."[91] Regardless whether Hagar chooses the dominant narrative of her life to be domestic violence, she might feel that the elements of her narrative are meaningfully connected with the narratives in traditional healing practices.

Also, one of the questions is related to the process of the traditional healing process that quires a thorough reflection. According to Bellamy, the connection between the dominant narrative and sub-narratives occur on the level of being acquainted with the stories and tropes of the healing places to experience the multiple formulations of truth and express opinions and ideas; and on the level of "juxtaposition of general expressions of pain, protestation, and threat and incoherent cries of suffering and anger."[92]

In sum, the successful healing practice allows the person "to conceptualize healing regarding the successful resumption of social roles."[93] As Thomas J. Csordas[94] notes:

> Therapeutic efficacy in religious healing is typically analyzed by extrapolating from ritual procedure to expected effect, without specifying conditions for success or failure regarding concrete experience of participants. Taking such experiential data as primary in the therapeutic process should allow for the definition of minimal conditions of therapeutic efficacy, including incremental change and inconclusive results.[95]

From the perspective of Csordas, like any therapy models, the traditional healing process for women who are subject to domestic violence is long-term and requires long preparations that involve different contributors. Traditional healing practices are also only about a moment that makes healing experiences powerful and meaningful which can only be understood in their greater context. It is indeed a fact that that most often these women develop a lifelong relationship with these places of healing, and come back for help for new or old problems. The women who usually visit these places return saying: "I came, I prayed, I got better. . . ." Therefore, exorcism and psychotherapy may be the result of physical and psychological changes and "the desired transformation itself is also said to be effected by engaging emotions."[96] However, unlike psychoanalytic or other therapeutic models, traditional healing allows for the possibility of recovery without learning or consciously acknowledging the causes of the distress.[97] In addition, one also should note that traditional healing should not be paralleled to Western psychotherapy. One example of such difference is the fact that in some non-Western cultures, emotions are conceptualized bodily. In traditional healing practice, "healing is a process of discipline and self-erasure, not conscious self-exploration."[98] Also, healing which women who are victims of domestic violence expect may not be recognizable as it is based upon how that individual feels. For the women who choose traditional healing,

> the measure of healing both the medium of the experience of healing and the sources recognized as affecting the recovery – is not the body and cannot be the body, since, from the perspective of those with a healer, the body is experienced as little more than a heap of vulnerabilities. This alone should give pause to researchers inclined to liken forms of spirit possession to forms of psychoanalysis or therapy.[99]

However, this does not suggest that the Western psychotherapeutic models are not helpful to understand the phenomenon of traditional healing practices if these models take into consideration the cultural construction of illness and cure. In the context of the healing through exorcism, Dwyer suggests that "By understanding the first [Western psychotherapies], it may be possible to illuminate the second [exorcism] and vice versa."[100]

The recent attempt for a sensitive approach to psychotic episodes encourages discovering and using religious traditions in understating mystical religious experiences, including spiritual and religious factors in treating this kind of mental health issues.[101] Therefore, when Hagar seeks traditional healing approaches, her attempt must be conceived from the angle of her cultural beliefs, worldviews, and expectations in the counselling practice.

Interventions to Address Satanic Interference

Hagar's dilemma, in this case, is to choose the right treatment option for the effects of domestic violence. Hagar responds to domestic violence by seeking traditional healing practices for the satanic interference; thereby, she attempts to reclaim control over violence and re-formulate her identity. Even though Western approaches to the healing practices are controversial as they view these practices as something suspicious and harmful, Hagar views these practices as Islamic. Such a step should be accepted as her personal accomplishment because she is not passive towards violence. These actions are consistent with the recovery process. Therefore, Hagar might have three choices, either: (1) prefer traditional healers, (2) use only the conventional medicine, or (3) try to integrate the conventional medicine with traditional healing practices. The last option is consistent with the prophetic tradition, which encourages Muslims to seek various ways for healing and finding solutions to problems. For example, Prophet Muhammad said: "There is no disease that Allah has created, except that He also has created its treatment."[102] However, the challenge of Muslim psychotherapist is how to reframe the problem in such a way that it enables Hagar to reclaim her identity and establish skills to resist domestic violence.

Islamic psychotherapy prefers the third approach to treatment practices, i.e., integrating traditional healing practices and mainstream counselling, and encourages Muslims to encounter, engage, and exchange ideas and best practices in other traditions. Therefore, while Islamic psychotherapy may seek to educate Hagar about various opinions and interpretations of the Qur'an about satanic interference and benefits and risks of traditional healing because she maintains a strong attachment to cultural healing methods, the Muslim psychotherapist should also find an appropriate intervention both from Western psychotherapeutic approaches and traditional healing in order to be effective with Hagar who still views traditional healing as more powerful than Western counselling therapies. For example, to some degree, the Muslim psychotherapist can address Hagar's interpretation of domestic violence as a satanic interference by applying the externalizing technique found in narrative therapies.

Narrative therapy views knowledge as locally produced and related to networks of power. Therefore, the process of change starts with deconstructing ideas, concepts, and interactions. Individuals come to the therapy to present negative, dead-end stories. The counsellor deconstructs the familiar ideas of what something is or what it means rather than someone being deficient. The role of the psychotherapist is to work with clients so as to replace unhelpful stories with helpful ones, explore alternative stories, make new assumptions, and open new possibilities for re-authoring stories.

As Catrina Brown suggests, in unhelpful stories, the psychotherapist needs to take a stance, form an opinion, develop an analysis, or take responsibility for knowledge and power, and move out from the "not-knowing" stance to the expert position.[103] The founder of narrative therapy Michael White also states that the counsellor "cannot waive responsibility and accountability for the influence of our own knowledge and power in the therapeutic work by claiming to 'not know' or to be responsible only for 'expert' knowledge about process."[104]

Therefore, the Muslim narrative psychotherapist should address social justice issues and take a stance against oppression and social inequity by blending modernist and postmodernist ideas to adopt a vision for social change without claiming an absolute truth as all claimed moral truths depend on the special contexts of their followers. By applying a narrative or discursive approach to therapy, the Muslim counsellor can enable Hagar's experiences and sense of self to be re-authored. She might gain an understanding of her ambivalence and struggles. She can start telling positive stories in her tradition that might be more empowering than anything else (i.e., pharmaceutical interventions) to enable her to develop alternative and more empowering ways of thinking about herself.

Narrative therapy welcomes "problem-saturated" stories, which can also become "identity stories" that are conceived beyond the boundaries of "normalcy" and does not try to correct these stories for the client. It allows women to express and reclaim their identities, trace their journeys through the violence, and then explore insights into their situation. This provides options for the telling and retelling of preferred stories of people's lives, including their solutions, deconstructing the disempowering stories through finding exceptions, strengths, and resources (even if they are small and tangential) and externalization techniques. For example, when clients talk about the narratives of satanic forces, they do not rush to correct the clients' beliefs. Instead, they acknowledge that these narratives are important in the life of the client because through them they find meaning in their experience.[105]

The narrative psychotherapist uses the method of first engaging the client in a therapeutic conversation; second, externalizing the problem so that the problem is not in one particular person but in the family system; third, enabling the clients to see and develop their personal agency by deconstruction of ideas, concepts, and interactions; and fourth, reflecting with a team of experts other than the psychotherapist to offer their perceptions and therapeutic conversations to the client on his/her strengths and possible directions.[106] First, the Muslim psychotherapist uses the word "narrative" which refers to the stories of people's lives and the differences that can be made through particular narrative and encourage the client to retell these stories. These narratives are so powerful that in a broader context they are affecting Hagar's life. The Muslim psychotherapist first asks Hagar to name the problem and personify the problem and attribute oppressive intentions and tactics to it. The Muslim narrative psychotherapist encourages women to focus on their identity, meaning, and resistance, and helps them construct their responses to violence through active listening. Such listening without bias and judgement helps women find meaning in their experience, and follow interventions that can emanate and liberate women.[107] The underlying position of the Muslim narrative psychotherapist is not that of the expert, all-knowing therapist or its mirror twin, but that of the "not-knowing therapist." Both the counsellor and the client are "partial knowers."[108] In addition, they both perceive her stories within its context and create a new meaning, which Hagar tells from a subjective experience.

Second, both the Muslim psychotherapist and Hagar investigate how the problem has been disrupting, dominating, or discouraging the person and the family. Through this investigation, both may discover moments when Hagar has not been dominated or discouraged by the problem or when life has not been disrupted by the problem. This process leads to finding historical evidence to create a new view of the person as competent enough to have stood up to, defeated, and escaped from the dominance of the problem. By applying externalization technique, which refers to helping the client who is preoccupied with the problem-saturated stories, the Muslim psychotherapist takes that problem beyond the self and locates it within cultural practices and discourses. The Muslim psychotherapist also recognizes the importance of a meaningful avenue that offers women a sense of power and control and the need for the formation of thicker descriptions that acknowledge and honour women's emotional needs and desires that otherwise feel forbidden.[109] In this respect, externalization is similar to the process of deconstruction where ingrained cultural assumptions that contribute to the occurrence of a problem are explored in order to reconstruct or re-author a new personal narrative. Hagar might need these stories/images through which she might be connected and feel nourished. The main goal of "externalizing conversations" with Hagar is to create a discursive space where she can name, unpack, and detail the relational and ideational contexts of her problems and imagine and experience a sense of active agency.[110]

Third, the Muslim psychotherapist asks Hagar to identify her disqualified or suppressed voices that others need to know in order to encourage her to see the fact that she was afraid to seek out help because she was afraid to express herself and the possible consequences. For instance, the Muslim psychotherapist can ask Hagar to reflect on what she has heard, and her "reflections then become part of [her] narrative . . . this process is a vivid example of the social construction of reality."[111] Finally, then both find or create an audience of reflecting team for perceiving the new identity and new story.[112]

This intervention might help Hagar to see there is a gendered context in her domestic violence experience because her culture requires her not to complain, to act satisfied, and to be happy and content. One advantage of the externalization process is that Hagar is encouraged to narrate her experience of domestic violence by linking it to the satanic interference, and see her identity as separate from the plot of her story. She might come to the conclusion that she is not the "problem" but the satanic interference is actually within the dominant patriarchal culture, which is the problem that causes all her troubles. Interpreting cultural and social actions such as seeking healing for domestic violence through traditional healing are also related to the cultural interpretations of the problem that locate the problem outside the men and hold them unaccountable for their actions because from this perspective these men are themselves victims of unseen creatures. Such interpretation of cultural practices might help Hagar to locate her problem within the larger social context of their lives rather than "owning" the problem.

However, the Muslim psychotherapist should also pay attention to the weakness of this therapy: it may not be an effective tool to solve Hagar's basic needs such as food, shelter, safety, and physical health, but narrative therapy is suitable for issues related to self-concept, interpersonal relationships, and personal growth. Narrative therapy separates people from their problems and attempts to help the client to create or discover new purposes for living that may be more suitable to the client's unique nature.[113] Nevertheless, the Muslim narrative psychotherapist assumes that Hagar has many skills, competencies, beliefs, values, commitments, and abilities that will assist her in reducing the influence of problems in her life.

Conclusion

In sum, narrative therapy privileges the feminist perspective and dictates that the psychotherapist needs to pay careful attention to the patriarchal narratives in these parables/stories/images. Therefore, Hagar's problems are conditions of emotional or material suffering resulting from narratives saturated with negative assumptions. These problems are products of cultural practices that are oppressive to the development of Hagar's functional life narratives. Hagar is vulnerable to the oppressive cultural narratives that include forces of oppression, such as sexism that assumes that she was supposed to not only heal herself but also her husband. However, it does not mean that the Muslim psychotherapist takes a harsh stance to criticize Hagar's belief system or cultural practices: instead, he/she displays more respectful curiosity and persistence, empathy and a listening ear and does not "jump" to find solutions as he/she looks for other ways to tell these solutions differently or to understand the client's problems in other ways. In doing so, the Muslim counsellor should put Hagar's problem outside of the individual, thus externalizing it. This is the beginning of the process of re-authoring that "requires moving beyond simply telling and retelling stories to an active deconstruction of oppressive and unhelpful discourses."[114] Unpacking unhelpful stories and creating alternative preferred stories involves recognizing the relationship between knowledge and power, as knowledge and power are joined through discourse. This kind of intervention builds freedom, resilience, and a sense of empowerment as Hagar moves from being a victim to claiming authorship.

Notes

1. Abdulla, "Islam and Counseling," 42–55.
2. Among the Muslim scholars who wrote on this subject, the most famous Muslim scholars are: Muhammad ibn Ahmad ibn 'Uthman ibn Qayyum 'Abu 'Abd Allah Shams ad-Din al-Dhahabi, known as Al-Dhahabi (1274–1348) (*Al-tibb al-nabawi* [Prophetic Medicine]) and Muhammad ibn Abu Bakr, also known as Ibn al-Qayyim or Ibn Qayyim al-Jawziyyah (1292–1350) (*Al-tibb al-nabawi*); Muḥammad al-Mahdawi ibn 'Ali ibn Ibrahim al-Sanawbari (d. 1412) (*Kitab al-Rahman fi al-tibb wa-l-hikmah* [The Book of Mercy Concerned With Medicine and Wisdom]); Jalal al-Din al-Suyuti (1445–1505) (*al-Manhaj al-sawi wa-al-manhal al-rawi fi al-tibb al-nabawi* [An Easy Manual and Refreshing Source for the Medicine of the Prophet]); al-Shaykh Abu al-'Abbas, Ibn al-Milaq or al-Maylaq (15th century); and others.
3. Sahih-Bukhari, trans. by M. Muhsin Khan (New Delhi, India: Kitab Bhaban, 1984). Accessed on December 30, 2015 from http://sunnah.com/muslim/52.
4. See Mohammed M. Ghaly, "Physical and Spiritual Treatment of Disability in Islam," *Journal of Religion, Disabilty & Health*, 12 (2) (2008), 126.
5. See Khadher Ahmad, Ishak Suliaman, and Sedek Ariffin, "Sorcery Treatment on Ibn Qayyim al-Jawziyya's (691H/1292M-751H/1350M) Perspective and The Reality in Islamic Medical Centre in Malaysia: A Comparative Studies," *Al-Bayan: Journal of Qur'an and Hadith Studies* 10 (1) (2012): 63–83.
6. Whitney S. Bodman, *The Poetics of Iblis: Narrative Theology in the Qur'ān* (Cambridge, MA: Harvard University Press, 2011), 59.
7. See Bodman, *The Poetics of Iblis*, 57. Also see verses Q. 2:168–169; 17:64; 7:17; 4:120, and so forth.
8. Ghaly, "Physical and Spiritual Treatment of Disability in Islam," 127.
9. See Bodman, *The Poetics of Iblis*; Fazlur Rahman, *Major Themes in the Qur'an* (Minneapolis, MN: Bibliotheca Islamica, Inc., 1989); Muhammad Rashid Rida and Muhammad Abduh, *Tafsīr al-Qur'an al-hakim al-shahr bi-tafsir al-Manår*, 12 vols. (Bayrut: Dår al-Ma ̧rifah, n.d.); Andrew Rippin, "Devil," in *Encyclopaedia of the Qur'an*, ed. by Jane Dammen McAuliffe (Leiden: Brill, 2001), 1: 524–527.
10. Rania Awaad and Sara Ali, "Obsessional Disorders in al-Balkhi's 9th Century Treatise: Sustenance of the Body and Soul," *Journal of Affective Disorders* 180 (2015): 185–189.
11. Ahmad N. Amir, Abdi O. Shuriye, and Ahmad F. Islamic, "Muhammad Abduh's Scientific Views in the Qur'an," *International Journal of Asian Social Science* 2 (11) (2012): 2034–2044; Jacquelline Youssef and Frank P. Deabe, "Arabic-Speaking Religious Leaders' Perception of the Cause of Mental Illness and the Use of Medication for Treatment," *Australian and New Zealand Journal of Psychiatry* 47 (11) (2013): 1041–1050.
12. Ghaly, "Physical and Spiritual Treatment of Disability in Islam,"128.

13. Rahman, *The Major Themes in the Qur'an*, 123–125.
14. Ibid., 128.
15. Bodman, *The Poetics of Iblis*, 69.
16. Rahman, *The Major Themes in the Qur'an*, 127.
17. Ibid., 133.
18. Ibid., 124.
19. Ibid., 128.
20. Ibid., 125.
21. Maria Sabaye Moghaddam, "Zar Beliefs and Practices in Bandar Abbas and Qeshm Island in Iran," *Anthropology of the Middle East* 7 (2) (2012): 19–28.
22. Carla Bellamy, *The Powerful Ephemeral: Everyday Healing in an Ambiguously Islamic Place* (Berkeley, CA: University of California Press, 2011), 17.
23. Edward Westermarck, *Ritual and Belief in Morocco*, 2 vols. (London: Routledge, 1926/1968).
24. See Erdem Yesilada, "Contribution of Traditional Medicine in the Healthcare System of the Middle East," *Chinese Journal of Integrative Medicine* 17 (2) (2011): 95–98.
25. Ibid., 95–98.
26. Bellamy, *The Powerful Ephemeral*, xix.
27. Yesilada, "Contribution of Traditional Medicine in the Healthcare System of the Middle East," 97.
28. Moghaddam, "Zar Beliefs and Practices in Bandar Abbas and Qeshm Island in Iran," 19–28.
29. Ihsan Al-Issa, "Mental Illness in Medieval Islamic Society," in *Al-Junun, Mental Illness in the Islamic World*, ed. by I. Al-Issa (Madison, CT: International Universities Press, Madison, 2000), 64.
30. Edward W. Lane, *Manners and Customs of the Modern Egyptians* (London: J. M. Dent Co., 1836/1902).
31. Lane, *Manners and Customs of the Modern Egyptians* (London: J. M. Dent Co., 1836/1902).
32. Muhammad ibn Isma 'il Bukhari. *Sahih Bukhari*. Accessed on October 26, 2016 from http://sunnah.com/bukhari/53.
33. Ibn Qayyim al-Jawziyyah, *Healing With the Medicine of the Prophet*, trans. by Jalal abu al-Rab and ed. by Abdul R. Abdullah (Riyadh: Darussalam Publications, 1999).
34. Ioan M. Lewis, *Religion in Context: Cults and Charisma* (Cambridge: Cambridge University Press, 1986), 98.
35. M. A. Rashed, "From Powerlessness to Control: Psychosis, Spirit Possession and Recovery in the Western Desert of Egypt," *Health, Culture and Society* 8 (2) (2015): 10–26. doi:http://dx.doi.org/10.5195/hcs.2015.194.
36. Tahir Obeid, Abuaban Ahmad, Fawazia Al-Ghatani, Abdul Rahman Al-Malki, and Abdulaziz Al-Ghamdi, "Possession by 'Jinn' as a Cause of Epilepsy (Saraa): A Study From Saudi Arabia," *Seizure: European Journal of Epilepsy* 21 (4) (2012): 245–249.
37. Osman Ali and Frieda Aboul-Fotouh, "Traditional Mental Health Coping and Help-Seeking," in *Counseling Muslims*; Yusuf Muslim Eneborg, "The Quest for 'Disenchantment' and the Modernization of Magic," *Islam and Christian – Muslim Relations* 25 (4) (2014): 419–432; Yusuf Muslim Eneborg, "Ruqya Shariya: Observing the Rise of a New Faith Healing Tradition Amongst Muslims in East London," *Mental Health, Religion & Culture* 16 (10) (2013): 1080–1096; Laila M. Akhu-Zaheya and Esraa M. Alkhasawneh, "Complementary Alternative Medicine Use Among a Sample of Muslim Jordanian Oncology Patients," *Complementary Therapies in Clinical Practice* 18 (2) (2012): 121–126.
38. See Tahir Obeid, Ahmad Abulaban, Fawazia Al-Ghatani, Abdul Rahman, Abdulaziz | Al-Ghamdi, "Possession by 'Jinn' as a Cause of Epilepsy (Saraa)," *Seizure: European Journal of Epilepsy*, 21 (4) (2012): 245–249; Ashy, "Health and Illness From an Islamic Perspective"; Eneborg, "Ruqya Shariya."

39. Samir Al-Adawi, Atsu Dorvlo, Suad. Al-Ismaily, et al. "Perception of and Attitudes Towards Mental Illness in Oman," *International Journal of Social Psychiatry* 48 (4) (2002): 305–317; Mohamed Iqbal Pasha and Saxby Pridmore, "Psychiatry and Islam," *Australian Psychiatry* 12 (4) (2004): 380–385.
40. O Tahir Obeid, Ahmad Abulaban, Fawazia Al-Ghatani, Abdul Rahman, Abdulaziz | Al-Ghamdi, "Possession by 'Jinn," 245–249.
41. See Farah Islam and Robert A. Campbell, "Satan Has Afflicted Me! Jinn-Possession and Mental Illness in the Qur'an," *Journal of Religion and Health* 53 (2014).
42. See Rashed, "From Powerlessness to Control: Psychosis, Spirit Possession and Recovery."
43. Eneborg, "The Quest for 'Disenchantment' and the Modernization of Magic," 420.
44. Simon Dein, Malcolm Alexander, and A. David Napier, "Jinn, Psychiatry and Contested Notions of Misfortune Among East London Bangladeshis," *Transcultural Psychiatry* 45 (2008): 31, 49; Adarsh Vohra and Walaa M. Sabry, "Role of Islam in the Management of Psychiatric Disorders," *Indian Journal of Psychiatry* 55 (6) (2013); Louay M. Safi, "Islamization of Psychology: From Adaptation to Sublimation," *The American Journal of Islamic Social Sciences* 15 (4) (1998): 117–125.
45. Dwairy, *Counselling and Psychotehrpay with Arabs*; Sasan Vasegh, "Psychiatric Treatments Involving Religion: Psychotherapy From an Islamic Perspective," in *Religion and Spirituality in Psychiatry*, ed. by Philippe Huguelet and Harold G. Koenig (Cambridge: Cambridge University Press, 2009), 301–316.
46. Sasan Vasegh, "Cognitive Therapy of Religious Depressed Patients," *Journal of Cognitive Psychotherapy* 25 (3) (2011) 177–188.
47. See his chapter "*al-Mass al-Shaytani: Haqiqatuh wa-'Ilajuh*" (Satanic Interference: Facts and Treatment) in Muhammad al-Ghazali, *al-Sunna al-Nabawiyya bayna Ahl al-Fiqh wa-Ahl al-Hadith*, 14th ed. (al-Qahira: Dar al-Shuruq, 2006), 113–124.
48. Ghazali, *al-Sunna*, 114.
49. Roland Littlewood, "Possession States," *Psychiatry* 3 (8) (2004): 8–10.
50. Andrew Neher, *Paranormal and Transcendental Experience: A Psychological Examination* (New York, NY: Dover Publications, 2013).
51. David Lukoff, "Visionary Spiritual Experiences," in *Southern Medical Journal* 100 (6) (2007): 635–641.
52. Ibid., 636.
53. Stanislav Grof and Christian Grof, *Spiritual Emergence: When Personal Transformation Becomes a Crisis* (Los Angeles: Tartcher, 1989), 195.
54. Sigmund Freud, *Religion as a Mass Delusion*. Accessed on October 19, 2016 from www.freud.org.uk/education/topic/10573/subtopic/40005/.
55. Sarah M. Clark and David A. Harrison, "How to Care for Patients Who Have Delusions With Religious Content: To Improve Outcomes, Look Beyond Delusion Content and Enlist Spiritual Care Experts," *Current Psychiatry* 11 (1) (2012): 47–51.
56. In the *Diagnostic and Statistical Manual of Mental Disorders* (DSM-4), it is noted as a form of preoccupation under the category Obsessive Compulsive Disorder, which appears with many other preoccupations, e.g., sex, money, health, hand washing, and so forth, and for the most part fits the definition of scrupulosity.
57. Lukoff, "Visionary Spiritual Experiences," 635.
58. See American Psychiatric Association, *Diagnostic and Statistical Manual of Mental Disorders: DSM-5-TM*, 5th ed. (Washington, DC: American Psychiatric Association, 2013).
59. W. W. Meissner, "The Pathology of Beliefs and the Beliefs of Pathology," in *Religion and the Clinical Practice of Psychology*, ed. by Edward P. Shafranske (Washington, DC: American Psychological Association, 1996), 241–267. Also see Anton Boisen, *Out of the Depths*, 139–140.
60. American Psychiatric Association, *Diagnostic and Statistical Manual of Mental Disorders*, 725–726.

61. See American Psychiatric Association, *Diagnostic and Statistical Manual of Mental Disorders*; Lukoff, "Visionary Spiritual Experiences," 209.
62. American Psychiatric Association, *Diagnostic and Statistical Manual of Mental Disorders*, 725.
63. Ibid., 93, 95, 103, 304.
64. Littlewood, "Possession States," 8–10.
65. George Feurerstein, *Holy Madness: The Shock Tactics and Radical Teachings of Crazy-Wise Adepts, Holy Fools, and Rascal Gurus* (New York, NY: Paragon House, 1990); Susan L. DeHoff, "Distinguishing Mystical Religious Experience and Psychotic Experience: A Qualitative Study Interviewing Presbyterian Church (U.S.A.) Professionals," *Pastoral Psychology* 64 (1) (2015): 21–39.
66. DeHoff, "Distinguishing Mystical Religious Experience and Psychotic Experience," 21.
67. Mike Jackson and K. W. Fulford, "Spiritual Experience and Psychopathology, Philosophy," *Psychiatry and Psychology* 4 (1) (1997): 41–65.
68. Neher, *Paranormal and Transcendental Experience*, 2–3.
69. Lukoff, "Visionary Spiritual Experiences," 209.
70. Sylvia Mohr, Laurence Borras, Isabelle Rieben, and Phillip Huguelet, "Evolution of Spirituality and Religiousness in Chronic Schizophrenia or Schizo-Affective Disorders: A 3-Years Follow-Up Study," *Social Psychiatry and Psychiatric Epidemiology* 45 (2010): 1095–1103; Sylvia Morh, Lawrence Borras, Jennifer Nolan, et al. "Spirituality and Religion in Outpatients With Schizophrenia: A Multi-site Comparative Study of Switzerland, Canada, and the United States," *International Journal of Psychiatry in Medicine* 44 (1) (2012): 29–52; Sylvia Mohr, Nader Perroud, Christine Gilleron, et al. "Spirituality and Religiousness as Predictive Factors of Outcome in Schizophrenia and Schizo-affective Disorders," *Psychiatry Research* 186 (2011): 177–182.
71. Sarah M. Clark and David A. Harrison, "How to Care for Patients Who Have Delusions With Religious Content," 47–51.
72. James B. Waldrum, "But Does It Work? Traditional Healing and Issues of Efficacy and Evaluation," in *Widening the Circle: Collaborative Research in Mental Health Promotion in Native Communities*. Proceedings of the Conference September 26–28, 1997, Montreal.
73. Hans Gunter Heimbrock, "Healing, Magic and the Interpretation of Reality," in *Happiness, Well-being and the Meaning of Life: A Dialogue of Social Science and Religion*, ed. by V. Brümmer and M. Sarot (Kämpen: Kok, 1996), 42, 46–47.
74. See M. Scott Peck, *Glimpses of the Devil: A Psychiatrist's Personal Accounts of Possession, Exorcism, and Redemption* (New York, NY: Free Press, 2005).
75. Clemmont Vontress, "Traditional Healing in Africa: Implications for Cross," *Journal of Counseling and Development* 21 (4) (1990), 326–336; "Animism: Foundation of Traditional Healing in Sub-Saharan Africa," in *Integrating Traditional Healing Practices Into Counseling and Psychotherapy*, ed. by Roy Moodley and William West (Thousand Oaks, CA: Sage Publications, 2015), 124–131.
76. See Peck, *Glimpses of the Devil.*
77. Vontress, "Traditional Healing in Africa: Implications for Cross," 326–336; "Animism: Foundation of Traditional Healing in Sub-Saharan Africa," 124–131.
78. Peck, *Glimpses of the Devil*, 239.
79. Vontress, "Animism: Foundation of Traditional Healing in Sub-Saharan Africa," 124–137.
80. Ibid., 134–135.
81. Ibid., 134.
82. Lukoff, "Visionary Spiritual Experiences," 211.
83. Lukoff, "Visionary Spiritual Experiences," 211; Clark and Harrison, "How to Care for Patients Who Have Delusions With Religious Content."
84. Humair Yusuf, "Traditional Healing: A Culmination of Clemmont Vontress's Ideas," in *Counseling Across the Cultural Divide: The Clemmont E. Vontress Reader*, ed.

by Roy Moodley, Lawrence Epp, and Humair Yusuf (Herefordshire: PCCS Books), 211–215; Roy Moodley and William West, *Integrating Traditional Healing Practices Into Counseling and Psychotherapy* (Thousand Oaks, CA: Sage Publications, 2005).

85. See American Psychiatric Association, *Diagnostic and Statistical Manual of Mental Disorders*; Roberto Lewis-Fernandez, Neil Krishan Aggarwal, Ladson Hinton, Devon Hinton, and Laurence J. Kirmayer, *DSM-5: Handbook on the Cultural Formulation Interview* (Washington, DC: American Psychiatric Association, 2016), 15.
86. Martin La Roche and Devon E. Hilton, "Supplementary Module 7: Coping and Help Seeking," in *DSM-5*, 136.
87. Ibid., 137.
88. Bellamy, *The Powerful Ephemeral*.
89. Ibid., 21.
90. Ibid., 27.
91. Ibid., 50.
92. Ibid., 50–51.
93. Ibid., 51.
94. Thomas J. Csordas, "Elements of Charismatic Possession and Healing," *Medical Anthropology Quarterly* 14 (4) (1988): 121–142.
95. Ibid., 121.
96. Graham Dwyer, *The Divine and the Demonic: Supernatural Affliction and Its Treatment in North India* (London: Routledge Curzon, 2003), 111.
97. Ibid. Also see Bellamy, *The Powerful Ephemeral*, 134.
98. Bellamy, *The Powerful Ephemeral*, 63.
99. Ibid.
100. Dwyer, *The Divine and the Demonic*, 5.
101. Roche and Hilton, "Supplementary Module 7."
102. Bukhari, *Sahih al-Bukhari*. Accessed on October 26, 2016 from http://sunnah.com/bukhari/76.
103. Catrina Brown, "Situating Knowledge and Power in the Therapeutic Alliance," in *Narrative Therapy: Making Meaning, Making Lives*, ed. by Catrina Brown and Tod Augusta-Scott (Thousand Oaks, CA: Sage Publications, 2007). Accessed on October 26, 2016 from http://sk.sagepub.com.myaccess.library.utoronto.ca/books/narrative-therapy/n1.xml.
104. Ibid.
105. Clive Baldwin, "Narrative, Ethics and People With Severe Mental Illness," *Australian and New Zealand Journal of Psychiatry* 39 (2005): 119–122.
106. Thomas S. O'Connor, "Climbing Mount Purgatory: Dante's Cure of Souls and Narrative Family Therapy," *Pastoral Psychology* 47 (6) (1999): 445–457.
107. See Mary Allen, *Narrative Therapy for Women Experiencing Domestic Violence: Supporting Women's Transition From Abuse to Safety* (London: Jessica Kingsley Publishers, 2012).
108. Brown, "Situating Knowledge and Power in the Therapeutic Alliance."
109. Catrina Brown, "Talking Body Talk: Merging Feminist and Narrative Approaches to Practice," in *Narrative Therapy*. Accessed on October 26, 2016 from http://sk.sagepub.com.myaccess.library.utoronto.ca/books/narrative-therapy/n14.xml.
110. Ibid.
111. Jill Freedman and Gene Combs, *Narrative Therapy: The Social Construction of Preferred Realities* (New York, NY: Oxford University Press, 1996), 186.
112. See James R. Bitter, *Theory and Practice of Family Therapy and Counseling* (Belmont, CA: Brooks/Cole, 2009).
113. See Joseph Walsh, *Theories for Direct Social Work Practice* (Pacific Grove, CA: Brooks/Cole Publishing Company, 2010).
114. Brown, "Situating Knowledge and Power in the Therapeutic Alliance."

5 Spiritual Diseases

Sarah was a 23-year-old woman who was born in New York to parents who had immigrated to the United States from the rural areas of Syria. Since her childhood, she prayed five times a day and attended the spiritual gatherings in the local community where she learned to practice *taqwa* (God-fearing; God-consciousness). When she was 19, her parents arranged her marriage to a 28-year-old man who was from the local Arab community, claiming that he was "a very good Muslim who cares about his religion." However, her husband turned violent during their ten years of marriage, and his personality changed. He stopped praying five times a day and reading the Qur'an. He controlled where she went and what she did and limited her access to the phone or the car.

Sarah was young, naive, and ill prepared for engaging in relationships, which left her vulnerable to manipulation by a violent partner. In the beginning of the cycle of violence, Sarah interpreted his behaviour as a sign of his love; therefore, she avoided confrontation with him. However, in the end, the cycle of violence became intolerable due to his insecurity, possessiveness in the relationship, and managing her every step. Further, he humiliated her, criticized her, and treated her so badly that she was embarrassed for her family to see it. She could not talk to her parents about his ill treatment because she did not want them to be upset that her husband was not actually "a good person at all" as they assumed before. Furthermore, he checked her phone calls, text messages, e-mails, and even the car mileage to "detect" her "faults" even when she tried to attend the local religious/spiritual celebrations and events. He blamed her for causing instability in the family life. He ignored her desire to go to her mother's place so that her mother could help her care for the children.

There were times that she confronted him and reminded him about the importance of being nice in the prophetic tradition. However, he excused and explained his attitude by his desire to protect his family and teach them to fear God. He told her that when she attended family parties and religious events without his permission, she neglected him. At other times, he would usually respond, "*I am a man!*" or "*You need only me!*" When she complained that he was acting like *munafiq* (hypocrite), he was reckless, tried to jump to conclusions about her and blamed her for being unfaithful and having *marad* (sickness) in her heart (spiritual diseases).[1] He also claimed that she needed to say more *shukr* (gratitude; thankfulness) and demanded she practice *qana 'a* (contentment).

Gradually, Sarah felt constantly tired, cried often, and worried about how she was going to get through the day. She noticed that symptoms had been worsening for months. She had trouble falling asleep almost every night and lost the ability to take proper care of her children and husband by cooking, cleaning, doing laundry, and teaching her children a proper way of Islam. She also felt a deep hurt because her husband simply ignored her contributions to their relationships. She felt worried and unenthusiastic about her faith, and observed diminished pleasure and poor concentration in daily prayers. However, she also worried about her husband because she believed that due to spiritual diseases in his heart, he fell prey to his *nafs* (ego, self, soul). At the end, his *ruh* (spirit) became more disturbed. Sarah blamed him for not being spiritually strong; if he was, he would not abuse her. She believed that the more violent he was, the more his heart became spiritually dead because his *nafs* defeated him, and as a result, his spirit had collapsed. She also believed that his spiritual disease had an immediate impact on her spiritual health, as she became more irritable, angry, tending to be too "lazy" to perform her prayers in a timely manner or to not being able to focus when she prayed.

When Sarah finally disclosed to her family the challenging relationship she had with her husband, she felt a lot of pressure from them to be a good mother and wife. Her parents also encouraged her to forget and forgive her husband, reminding her how God is most merciful and compassionate, even towards those who do *zulm* (injustice). They also told her that otherwise, she would be to blame for her hardened heart. They also blamed her for being reckless and jumping to conclusions about her husband easily and gave her the example from the Qur'an that God does not like people who are reckless. She perceived the underlying message from an interaction with them that if she did not behave the way they wanted her to behave, they would not accept her. When she did what they wanted her to do, she saw herself as a mere "hypocrite." She felt that if she did not forgive her husband, she would be a bad Muslim. It stressed her out. She was convinced that she had made a mistake that would lead to eternal punishment.

Finally, Sarah decided to seek help from a Muslim psychotherapist who was also practicing *tasawwuf* (Sufism). She stated that she was previously a regular attendant of the mosque, but she had quit attending prayers in the local mosque because she felt her faith was "weak." She also wanted to know whether her husband or she had *marad* in the heart (spiritual diseases) and whether her husband's violence towards her was due to these spiritual diseases. She said that she wanted to have space where she can discuss her spiritual problems, advance her *ruhaniyyah* (spirituality), and find a cure for "spiritual diseases" which believed was a serious problem that caused all kinds of disturbances.

Spiritual Disease and Distress in Islamic Studies and Islamic Psychotherapy Literature

In this case, Sarah presents domestic violence as spiritual violence. Spiritual violence can be defined broadly and includes any kind of abuse that uses religious and spiritual tradition to condone violence, forcing the victim to forgive, forcing attendance at religious gatherings, or preventing the person from attending religious gatherings. The case study suggests that Sarah complains about her husband's spiritual diseases and undesired character traits as one of the causes of domestic violence. However, Sarah also complains about herself as she thinks that she is also not immune from spiritual diseases. She assumes that violence against her triggered her own spiritual diseases or at least caused them. In the Islamic tradition, the theme of spiritual violence needs a thorough understanding in the context of the nature, symptoms, and descriptions of the spiritual diseases. Perhaps a more common illustration of this issue is in the Sufi tradition of Islam.

Sufism and Its Definition of Spiritual Diseases

The Sufi tradition does not directly link spiritual diseases to domestic violence or suggest that spiritual diseases breed domestic violence. However, the Sufi tradition provides a detailed account of nature common spiritual diseases that directly or indirectly cause domestic violence, especially in the context of the Sufi understanding of soul development. Furthermore, not all spiritual diseases may be the root cause of domestic violence.

In this section, I use the Sufi literature to provide the definition of spiritual diseases that Sarah is curious about and how these diseases can trigger or cause domestic violence. A general Sufi perspective of spiritual diseases presents violence as a choice made by individuals with low spiritual and moral standards. From this perspective, men who are violent towards their wives are characterized as people who are driven by their *nafs al-ammarah bi'l-su'* (the soul that urges evil; the animal soul). I also highlight how such a perspective naturally leads to the idea that the treatment for violence might progress the animal soul to the upper stages of soul development.

First of all, according to the Sufi tradition, by *fitrah* (inner character; nature),[2] humans are inherently good and free from spiritual diseases. Generally, it is also assumed that the body is healthy if the spirit is healthy, and the spirit is healthy if it is not in conflict with the divine purpose. Otherwise the person loses a sense of wholeness.[3] Nevertheless, when *fitrah* is misused for purely worldly reasons, especially with a purpose to subdue another person's will, inherently good human nature becomes toxic due to extreme preoccupation with material benefits such as power, money, etc., and leads to reprehensible morals and deeds or demoralization in general, including any kind of violence. Such demoralization causes the soul to suffer from maladies like forgetfulness of the Divine presence, greed, jealousy, hypocrisy, grandiose ideas, laziness, and so forth, and the body also has its own ailments, such as ailments of skin, joints, kidneys, brain, and other organs. For example, in Sarah's case, her husband's spiritual diseases were evident in his maintaining inconsistent, or perhaps even hypocritical, behaviour that conflicts with the inherent human nature to be genuine, honest, and sincere. His reprehensible morals and values such as claiming superiority over Sarah placed priority on his choice of violence to gain dominance in his relationship with Sarah. His animal soul commanded evil and allowed indulgences, blameworthy actions, sins, anger (Q. 12:53; 79:40; 5:30–20; 95:6), and bitterness against Sarah, as he tended to criticize, judge, or denigrate her as he saw her powerless and helpless, and satisfied with his envy and greed.

Further, his following spiritual diseases, such as *al-kibr* (conceit), *al-ghill* (malice), *al-hasad* (envy), *al-riya'* (ostentation), *su' al-zann* (having a bad opinion [of someone]), *i 'tiqad su' al-damir* (believing in the evil of the conscience), *al-mudahana* (fallacious flattery), *hubb jam ' al-mal* (the love of accumulating wealth), *al-takathur* (excess), *al-tafakhur* (bragging and the love to hear praise), and *hubb al-sharcf mahmada* (the love of rank) have also affected Sarah. These spiritual diseases of the animal soul are products of ignorance, ungratefulness, the lack of *hubb* and *wudd* (love), *al-ghafla* (heedlessness), *al-sahw* (forgetfulness), extreme adherence to *ittiba' al-hawwa* (the desires), and *al-shahawat* (sexual appetites).

The Sufi tradition acknowledges *al-hawa* (the desires) and *al-shahawat* (appetites for women, and excess of food, drinks, clothing, etc.) are inherent feelings in all human beings and does not reject the fact that the human body should not be completely deprived from fulfilling their "earthly" needs. For al-Muhasibi, uncontrolled desires for earthly goods breed the spiritual diseases by extreme indulgence in forbidden appetites and results in physical, emotional, psychological, and spiritual destruction. In the Sufi tradition, appetites are classified in two categories: "hidden appetites" (*al-shahawat al-khafiyya*) and "manifest appetites" (*al-shahawat al-zahira*). Al-Muhasibi explained the differences as following: the appetites for foods, drinks, clothing, etc., are not evil and sin. However, these of appetites or cravings become destructive if they are uncontrollable and extreme: the love of power, prestige; the attainment of rank; the love of good reputation and to be praised for the righteous deeds one has performed.[4] Also, as a basic human trait, ungratefulness is a source of many mental and emotional distresses (Q. 100:6). The Qur'an explains that the cause of ungratefulness is the desire to achieve more material resources (Q. 17:83). The other reason for this ungratefulness is boredom and annoyance, which may be due to material and psychological needs (Q. 10:12).

Many Sufis believed that human nature tends to believe and accept the truth with experimental proofs. However, humans may disbelieve and reject the truth even when they see it with their physical eyes (Q. 6:111). The most feasible ignorance of human nature is regarding uncontrolled sexual desires, and ignorance about the compassion and mercy of God. According to the

Qur'an, one of the reasons of human transgression is an individual's unlimited and unrealistic sense of self-sufficiency (Q. 96:7). An excessive love for the worldly life is one of the reasons of transgression (Q. 79: 37–38). Also ignorance and forgetting the weaknesses of human nature can lead to transgression (Q. 59:19). Qushayri narrates from Salih al-Murri that "If one keeps knocking on the door persistently, it will eventually open for one." To this Rabi'a al- 'Adawiyya responded, saying: "For how long will you continue saying this? Has the door ever been closed, so that one had to request that it be opened?" Salih replied: "An old man [like myself] has shown ignorance (*jahila*), while a woman has shown [true] knowledge (*'alimat*)."[5]

Therefore, all famous Sufi masters detested the spiritual diseases because these diseases occupy the person's entire sphere of attention leaving no room for spirituality. For instance, for Qushayri (986–1074), the deficiencies of Sarah's husband might fall into two categories: first, the acquired or chosen deficiencies, which is "earned" by acts of disobedience against the Divine Law and sins such as being violent, belittling her, calling her names, etc.; second, the low morals and imperfections such as pride and grandiosity, wrath, spite, envy, bad temper, lack of tolerance, etc. Both categories of these deficiencies are blameworthy in the Islamic tradition. Further, from al-Ghazali's perspective (d. 1111), who is also well-known with his works on spiritual diseases, Sarah's husband's animal soul displays (1) ferociousness, (2) beastliness, (3) Satanity, and (4) lack of godliness. For al-Ghazali, people who possess the destructive nature of rage and uncontrolled sexual desires are dangerous not only to themselves but also to people around them:

> If rage controls the person he displays beastly behaviours. He will become furious, and attack the people around him. When sexual instincts rules over him, he will act upon his lustful desires, and will be addicted to overeating and over engaging in sexual relations.[6]

In the context of domestic violence, the Sufi teachings also acknowledge that desperation to acquire power over someone else at the expense of abusing them is a kind of spiritual disease. In the Sufi tradition, this kind of spiritual disease is called *takabbur* (narcissism and grandiosity), which is "neurogenic behaviour" in contemporary psychiatry.[7] The more the person indulges in entertaining high hopes for limitless and uncontrolled power, the worse they become. Although domestic violence might also be explained with a loss of control over temperament, frustration, and anger, as Sarah's case presents, domestic violence is the struggle for power and authority in the relationship through an abusive behaviour. His claim that "*I am a man!*" or "*You need only me!*" clearly demonstrated that Sarah's husband made this choice himself to dominate her, who already had less power and authority in the relationship at the expense of everything, including depriving her from going to religious/spiritual events and having her own financial means.

The animal soul also tends to any kind of spiritual violence that uses religious/spiritual traditions to compel a victim to forgive, to impose attendance at religious gatherings, or to prevent a person from attending religious gatherings. The outcomes of such a caustic combination cause spiritual diseases and distress for women. For example, in Sarah's case, her family demanded her to forgive her husband, not to be controlled by her sense of recklessness and jump to conclusions easily. They advised her to practice patience and to avoid being reckless in difficult situations. As a result, their admonishments and their wrong application of the Qur'anic message confused Sarah: "So make no haste against them, for We but count out to them a (limited) number (of days)" (Q. 19: 84). Her family simply ignored the fact that the Qur'anic warning against being reckless is for the protection of the person who might suffer undesired results and does not mean forcing the victim to forgive and forget without requiring justice for herself. In addition, multiple Qur'anic verses include messages of the genuine form of justice that starts with repentance of the wrongdoer who committed violence against the helpless and innocent beings (Q. 24:22; 2:173; 3:31).

Remedies in the Sufi Tradition

Sarah might benefit from the Sufi teachings about the necessity of repentance of the wrongdoers without pushing the victim to forgive. For example, a famous Sufi master Abu'l-Husayn al-Nuri (d. 907), extensively talked about "the two-fold rain" in the process of dealing with injustice and forgiveness: one is *rahma* (grace and mercy) (Q. 17:110), and the second is *ghadb* (divine wrath and anger) (Q. 1:7) or *naqma* (revenge) (Q. 3:4; 5:95; 7:136; 15:79: 24:6–9), that require a pure repentance. For Nuri, repentance is required to vanish the thunderstorm of revenge which

> sends the thunder of rupture into the hearts of the idolaters, the lightning of hatred into the hearts of the hypocrites, the rains of enmity into the hearts of the oppressors, and the wind of the veiling screen into the hearts of those who transgress the law.[8]

For example, Sarah may choose the first option, which is grace and mercy, if her husband chooses to repent. This does not imply that she should be pushed to reconcile with her husband; instead, Sarah's husband has a chance to start his journey of *jihad* or a war on the animal soul. In the Sufi tradition, the battle against the animal soul is necessary. This idea existed since the time of the Prophet who invited Muslims to practice *al-jihad al-akbar* or the greater inner *jihad as* "the worst enemy you have is [the *nafs*] between your sides."[9] In this regard, he might benefit from learning that God nurtures the human soul to avoid the destructive tendencies of the soul. For this purpose, many Sufi masters paid significant attention to self-awareness and awareness of people and things around them. They used spiritual counselling to transform the destructive forces into positive forces by teaching self-awareness.

Sarah would also be empowered by the teachings of another Sufi master, al-Fudayl bin 'Iyad (d. 803), who taught that the following five signs of injustice require a sincere repentance. These injustices are: the coarseness of the heart, the ruthlessness of the eye, the paucity of shame, desire for this world, and expecting too much of it.[10] From the perspective of these teachings, it is undeniable that domestic violence against women displays all these five signs of injustice because women are unfairly treated due to the coarseness of the heart and ruthlessness of their husbands. The outcomes of their injustice are very often dangerous for the powerless members of the family, including children. In this case, Sarah's husband's intentional use to control or dominate Sarah through threats, intimidation, and coercion is against the Qur'anic teachings (Q. 28:70; 31:14; 2:231), which condemn any violence and destructive behaviours that disturb peace; therefore, the struggle for power, especially in marriage, is a blameworthy act and poignant spiritual disease that disturbs peace and contentment in the relationship between the husband and wife.

Therefore, by violating the principle of justice, Sara's husband transgresses the boundaries and rebels against the code of conduct prescribed by Divine Order, which especially emphasizes compassion and mercy toward fellow human beings, especially those who are related to each other, and living a virtuous and righteous life. Further, by insisting not to get "treated" for his spiritual diseases, Sarah's husband goes against the principle of *adab* (a praiseworthy, effective norm of conduct or a code of manners, courtesies) that is supposed to be followed in every aspect of human life, including relationship with others, to demonstrate the integration of faith and belief with social and communal aspects of living.

On the other hand, the Sufi tradition offers Sarah's husband how to "treat" his spiritual diseases through strenuous and uninterrupted efforts to achieve perfection[11] that are consistent with Islam's spiritual and moral model or punitive method against violence. For this purpose, the Sufi masters developed a plan of action and a critical mind as a significant medicine for spiritual diseases.[12] Their suggestions for treating spiritual diseases were codified under the concept of *tazkiyat al-nafs* (treating spiritual diseases by purifying the soul; the purification of the soul), which is the most used spiritual intervention offered within the Sufi tradition.[13]

The concept of purification of the soul emphasizes accountability and acceptance of responsibility as prerequisites to purification of the soul. The underlying assumption in the Sufi tradition is that those who engage in domestic violence choose to behave that way. Such a perspective puts responsibility on the violent husbands, and encourages them that there is a cure for violence if they assume their responsibility without providing an excuse to continue using violence as a means of power and control, and commit themselves to elevating their moral and spiritual status. In the process of the purification of the soul, the main attention is given to the destruction of the soul; its procrastination regarding the performance of righteous acts; its wickedness because they are the causes of the repugnant behaviours, i.e., *jinayat al-nafs* (offences) and *'uyub al-nafs* (faults of the soul). The assumption is that the *nafs* tends to conceal and keep the diseases hidden to avoid public criticism. Such a pattern of thinking and behaviour then leads to the deception of the self, deceit, and falsehood and plots.[14]

Misuse of the Sufi Tradition

The process of a true repentance requires a deep self-awareness and feeling remorse for the violence against others. Sarah's husband might not be ready for such process as he is adamant to accept his fault. In the case if Sarah's husband refuses to repent sincerely and engage in the process of purification of his soul, then Sarah has the right to make the second choice, i.e., *ghadb*, which Nuri suggested, to deal with her husband's violence. In this case, Sarah might refuse to pardon and forgive her husband. Also, Sarah might openly reject her family's suggestion that she needs to forgive her husband; otherwise, she will be blameworthy for a hardened heart or spiritual disease and being ungrateful. Her family's extreme emphasis on forgiveness without holding the violent husband accountable made Sarah view herself as a Muslim with a weak faith. In the case of ungratefulness, the expectation that Sarah should be grateful and content with her condition – even in the context of violence – may be more harmful than helpful. As we see in Sarah's case, she experienced the effects of spiritual disease in the family system and often felt bewildered and was forced to forgive her husband's violence, even when she did not feel that reconciliation was warranted.

Pushing women to forgive when they are not ready to do so leads to spiritual distress – a complex group of signs and symptoms that include spiritual pain, spiritual alienation, spiritual anger, spiritual anxiety, spiritual guilt, spiri tual loss, and spiritual despair.[15] This vicious cycle is exacerbated when access to spiritual resources is either denied or limited. Therefore, Sarah's refusal to pardon her husband does not imply that she denies the capacity to forgive as an exalted personal characteristic trait in the Islamic tradition. The Sufi masters encourage but do not blame those who find it hard to forgive. Furthermore, being grateful even in the context of injustice contradicts the nature of the Qur'an, which makes it obligatory on humans to seek justice (Q. 2:188; 4:58; 5:1).

In the process of the purification of the soul, the Sufi tradition also warns that the people who progress to the stage of blaming soul from the stage of animal soul as they may relapse because this process is a very painful and challenging spiritual journey. For example, Sarah repeatedly excused her husband for his violence. However, his repetitive and remorseless attitudes and behaviours of violence suggested that his hypocrisy and the lack of integrity must also concern the person who has it because it threatens the inner self.

Moreover, the danger involved in his character trait also involves the threat to the faith or unity of Muslim community.

However, the Sufi tradition suggests that hypocrisy as a character deficiency is treatable and the common "prescription" for hypocrisy is acquisition of *ikhlas* (sincerity). They believed that by instilling *al-takhwif* (fear) in the animal soul the person can shun the worldly life, its pleasures, and appetites, to inculcate wisdom and restrict the animal soul from extreme indulgence to its desires.[16] Such a prescription for reviving the spirit has potential to awaken the person by engaging them in the piety practices. Until this occurs in some measure, we have guilt as a sign of alienation from the self and self-rejection. In the beginning of the purification of the soul, the person's predominant attitude is a negative self-reference. Only gradually, in the process of purification, does it begin to become positive.

In addition to acquisition of sincerity, one of the aspects of the purification of the soul is love and appreciation of others. In this regard, the prophetic tradition might be exemplary for Sarah's husband.[17] In fact, in the purification of the soul, love is one of the most important concepts in the development of the soul because the lack of love causes many problems. Sufism teaches that the first rule of caring in any relationship is love,[18] which has always been at the centre of the Islamic tradition.[19] The second rule of caring is *rahma*, mercy or compassion. The Qur'an encourages extending these attributes to every aspect of life. In the *hadith* literature and contemporary Islamic scholarship, it refers to a motherly quality.[20]

Thus, failure to love or lack of love and empathy is one of the spiritual diseases of the heart, because when the heart is empty of love it is filled with evil that makes the person turn away from the self and others. The Sufi tradition offers both Sarah and her husband the purification of the soul to treat spiritual diseases by taking into consideration the Islamic concept of *fitrah* that always inclines towards the depth of the moral and spiritual world despite the stains of acquired sin on the soul. Sufism also preaches that the deformation of *fitrah* starts only after the person comes under the influence of external sources. However, as one of the great medieval Islamic scholars of the Qur'an and Arabic language, Abu Qasim Husain b. Muhammad, who was known as Raghib Isfahani (d. 1108), suggests, humans are also created with *fitrah* that gives them the ability to improve their attitudes and behaviours, to distinguish between right and wrong or to deform their inherent goodness.[21] Therefore, the Sufi tradition instils hope that humans (even violent men) have the capacity to overcome their challenges and spiritual diseases with a strong commitment to change thoughts and attitudes that breed violence.

Islamic Feminist Response

As Sarah's case presents, spiritual diseases breed domestic violence and cause spiritual distress: first, by reducing women's access to spiritual resources (i.e., spiritual gatherings in Islamic centres); second, by blaming them for not having *taqwa* (God-consciousness; God-fearing); and third, by triggering their emotional problems such as anger, depression, and so forth. For example, Sarah's case clearly indicates that she feels bewildered and forced to forgive her perpetrator, and when she does not want to do so, she is viewed as a Muslim with weak faith or blamed for not having modesty.

Although many Islamic feminists do not directly talk about the relationship of spiritual diseases and fundamental issues as the main causes of misogynist practices against women (such as the Creation story, female autonomy, and the principle of modesty), they extensively talk about the impact of these practices on the health of Muslim women. For example, an extreme emphasis on women's attitudes in the family and society to please men forces them to give up their individual autonomous consciousness for the sake of the balance with social heteronymous action (socially imposed norms), while seeking equilibrium with Allah's guidance. These Muslim feminist scholars argue that the attempt of the patriarchal society to exclude women from an active role in spiritual, religious, and public life was against the Qur'anic instruction of God's creation of man and woman as a pair and equal in status. Such misreading of the Islam's key sources causes spiritual diseases in the society because such understanding creates a potential for domestic violence, trouble, risk, injury, danger, destruction, harm, loss, endangerment, and so forth, that goes against the Qur'anic image of Islam. As Sarah's case clearly demonstrates, in fact, violence causes serious disturbances in the soul development. She felt that her spirit has been "collapsed and smashed" by her traumatic experience and the spiritual diseases of her husband. Domestic violence she experienced triggered the "negative" side of her soul; however, her reflection on it is a path towards achieving perfect morals. This is especially important because Sarah complains that her husband tried to prevent her from attending the religious rituals in the community.

Sa'diyya Shaikh's presentation of gender discourses is helpful in Sarah's case as she tries to answer to the questions of Muslim women such as "Who am I?" and "What is the nature of existence?" using the philosophical and Sufi constructs of Islam. Although Shaikh clearly states that she does not claim that Sufism "automatically cure[s] people of sexism," she finds Sufism more inclusive and empowering to answer to these questions. She specifically uses the ideas of Ibn 'Arabi (d. 1240), especially his idea of *wahdat al-wujud* (unity of being) and *insan-i kamil* (the perfect human or universal human) that transcends gender constructs "in relation to the ultimate nature of reality."[22] For example, Ibn 'Arabi used traditionally "feminine" and "masculine" metaphors (such as "fathers," "mothers," pregnancy and birthing) for divine creativity and relationality.[23] Further, he rendered the tripartite structure of Islam's moral obligation – *islam* (outward conformity), *iman* (inward faith), and *ihsan* (virtuous excellence) – to transcend gender, sex, race, ethnicity, etc., discourses, challenge normative boundaries, and provide gender-egalitarian spaces.

Although this is not the subject of this paper, it is helpful to mention that in addition to aforementioned tripartite structure of Islam, Ibn 'Arabi's idea of *insan-i kamil* can be more empowering in Sarah's case because this concept contests what Sarah's husband believes (he saw Sarah in lower status because she was a woman).[24] The purpose of *insan-i kamil* is to fulfil the need of the universe as the macrocosm, for – as an ethical and ideal self – *insan-i kamil* has knowledge of how to influence the equilibrium of representation of divine attributes in order to give life/spirit to the universe and transform it "into a polished mirror of the divine attributes."[25] Ibn 'Arabi argues that each person has the potential to become *insan-i kamil*; however, their lack of proper behaviour and spirituality and morality prevents them from attaining this capacity: only the prophets and the friends of God, or *awliya*, belong to the category of the sublime human archetype. Nonetheless, Ibn 'Arabi is not pessimistic. He also provides the way to success in elevating oneself to the status of *insan-i kamil*. For example, he writes that success on the path to become *insan-i kamil* depends on training the self in relationship to the divine name Jamal, for *jamali* qualities of mercy, compassion, and love are the key qualities to transforming human life by taming unrefined *jalali* instincts of *nafs al-ammara* (lower self that represent animalistic drives of self).

Furthermore, the concept of *insan-i kamil* can empower Sarah in many ways. For example, Sarah might open her heart to divine inspiration and blessing, which can be attained with excellent morals and behaviours. In the case of her husband, if he begins his journey to become a perfect man he might become more beneficial to his wife and humanity in general. Second, the concept can be used to help both Sarah and her husband achieve moral perfection through improving the inner qualities (*khuluq*) or nature, learn Islamic rituals to purify their carnal souls that are impossible without reflecting on the true meaning of Islam and Muslim. Such a reflection starts with reflecting on the meaning of Islam that helps the follower to become pious, God-conscious and God-fearing, which is the basic awareness of the dangers of sin. Although we explored this in the previous section, it is helpful to point out here again that preventing women from gaining the true meaning of Islam is sin and spiritual disease of the patriarchal cultures as it is a grave lie to claim that it is the divine order for women to show their submission to their husbands just because they are men. Misinterpreting or misrepresenting the key sources in this regard runs counter to the basic principles of Islam on justice and equality. In fact, the Qur'an does not grant special privileges to men just being biologically men; instead, it supports equality between women and men. Therefore, violating this important principle is the indication of spiritual diseases of the heart.

In sum, Ibn 'Arabi's perspective of spiritual development suggests that Sarah should possess both *jamali* and *jalali* qualities on the path to becoming a perfect human being. In addition, for Sarah, this also has a social significance because it makes it almost mandatory for Sarah's husband to become perfect human being and possess human qualities such as love, mercy, compassion, and gentleness. Perhaps, this journey for Sarah's husband starts with a deep contemplation of the meaning of *islam*, the first step of tripartite structure of

Islam's moral obligation.[26] Otherwise, Sarah's husband acts against the core meaning of being a human and a Muslim in Islam. Nevertheless, when the concept of spiritual diseases of the Sufi tradition is used in Islamic psychotherapy, Muslim counsellors also need to show clinical sensitivity. This will allow the Muslim counsellor to consider what prevents the individual from achieving spiritual progress, which in turn, it is hoped, will help Muslim women to deal with domestic violence. Therefore, I consider that Islamic feminist framework provides an important perspective on how to use the Sufi understanding of spiritual diseases in a sensitive manner in Islamic psychotherapy..

Spiritual Diseases in the Social Science Literature

After discussing the Sufi understanding of spiritual diseases, one might also wonder what the social science literature offers to understand Sarah's issues in Islamic psychotherapy. Therefore, this section discusses whether spiritual diseases are lack of morality as the Sufi tradition of Islam suggests or mental illness.

In some cases, spiritual disease might fall in the category of emotional and/or mental health disturbances, or as a religious abuse. Nevertheless, the domestic violence literature defines religious abuse as the abuse of religious beliefs: "by applying unsound explanations to religious values, erroneous interpretations to religious roles or other certain perspectives of religion and faith, one justifies or allows for various insults and accusations, sometimes even physical."[27] Further, those who use religion to legitimize their violent behaviour tend to maintain a positive self-image by denying responsibility and mitigating feelings of guilt after their violent behaviour. The violent man who is more religious than their partners also uses theological/religious arguments and explanations for violence: he may use these arguments to make his victims feel fear, guilt, shame that ultimately leads these victims to feel alone, distressed, worthless, neglected, or even cursed. In domestic violence literature such spiritual violence may also be discussed under the concept of emotional violence. For example, Barbara Simoni , Tina Rahne Mandelj, and Rachel Novsak state that that both emotional and physical abuse may occur in the name of God, and point out that the abuse of religious beliefs leads to emotional maltreatment such as: spurning (rejecting or degrading behaviour), terrorizing (threatening injury, death, or abandonment), isolating (refusing opportunities to interact), exploiting/corrupting (encouraging engagement in inappropriate behaviours), and denying emotional responsiveness (ignoring human needs for interaction and affection). Therefore, they identify spiritual/religious violence as emotional violence, which manifests itself not only in people with religious/spiritual beliefs but also in all clients. Nevertheless, they also acknowledge that spiritual/religious violence has its specific features and aspects that make it stand out from other forms of emotional violence.[28]

In Sarah's case, the Power and Control Wheel shows the relationship of physical violence to other forms of violence and the cycle of violence. Each part of this wheel, including emotions, economics, children, social isolation, etc., shows how violent men try to control or gain power over women. The wheel particularly shows how men use their male privilege in violence against women. For example, in Sarah's case, this wheel is relevant as it shows how he made the big decisions himself, acted like the master, and defined the gender roles in their relationship. In all these acts of violence, Sarah's husband usually excused, rationalized, justified, and minimized domestic violence against Sarah.

Violence and aggression can be related to personality traits and mental health issues, even in the case of religious/spiritual violence.[29] In this respect, there is a strong correlation between the Sufi tradition of Islam and the social sciences, especially in regard to the concept of narcissism and how it is linked to the concept of spiritual diseases, i.e., grandiosity in the Sufi tradition.

Under the concept of ego libido, narcissism was first explored by Sigmund Freud (1856–1939) as the natural development of active-egoistic and passive-altruistic tendencies in the individuals. Freud presented it as a sexual instinct but also as emotional and mental health problems as originating from a lack of development within the human personality. He argued that when people with narcissistic personality traits are not fully developed they can show destructive and unhealthy behaviours.[30] Freud also related but also differentiated between the concepts of narcissism and egoism. For him, narcissism is the libidinal complement to egoism; whereas, egoism is not related to the libidinal satisfaction. Also, egoism is self-evident and constant, while narcissism is the variable element. Narcissistic people can be egoistic in their pursuit of fullfilling direct sexual satisfaction, or other needs.[31]

From Freud's perspective, Sarah's belief in spiritual diseases is an example of faulty myths, a comforting illusion, part of the mythological view of the person, and her husband's narcissism and egoism is related to his unmet sexual needs. In his *The Future of an Illusion*, he claims that psychoanalysis can respond to the challenges of these myths by exploring traumatic unconscious memories that threaten the person's mental and physical well-being. As we see in his interpretation of his patient Ida Bauer (1882–1945), known by a pseudo name Dora, who was diagnosed with hysteria, he would see it as "the uncertainty in regard to the boundaries of what is to be called normal sexual life."[32] From his perspective, Sarah's belief that her problems are due to evil forces is the product of her *id*, which is inherited, is present at birth, and also originates from the somatic organization.

However, with respect to Sarah's concern of her husband's spiritual diseases, the current psychiatric and psychological concepts suggest that the tendency to claim a grandiose self-image, the need for admiration, and a lack of empathy is Narcissistic Personality Disorder,[33] which can be overt and covert: overt narcissism is related to a grandiose sense of self and results from parental overindulgence; whereas, covert narcissism is associated with a vulnerable sense of self, i.e., self-doubting, hypersensitivity, craving for attention, and inability to trust or depend on others.[34] Four fundamental personality dimensions (impulse control, affect regulation, narcissism, and paranoid cognitive personality style) of narcissism are especially tied with the risk of violence. For example, low impulse control and affect regulation, which is strictly criticized in the Sufi tradition, increase the risk for violence across disorders, especially for primary and comorbid substance abuse disorders. Paranoid cognitive personality style and narcissistic injury, on the other hand, increase the risk for violence, especially in persons with schizophrenia spectrum disorders and individuals with personality disorders.

Similarly, in previous studies, L. K. Hamberger and J. E. Hastings also suggested that men with mental health issues such as the schizoid/borderline, narcissistic/anti-social profile, and dependent/compulsive profile are prone to domestic violence.[35] They pointed out that individuals with schizoid/borderline profile are usually withdrawn and asocial individuals who are moody and hypersensitive to interpersonal slights. These men are usually highly volatile and over-reactive to trivial interpersonal friction.

The patients with narcissistic/anti-social profile, on the other hand, have an exaggerated sense of importance as well as a self-righteous insistence. They claim that others are supposed to act in accordance with their wishes; if not, these men act violently until they force others to obey to their demands. The patients with dependent/compulsive profile are usually anxious, passive people who lack self-esteem, and therefore, are extremely "needy" in their primary interpersonal relationships. These men may also become hostile and violent when their relationship needs are not met.

In their study with 63 currently dating couples, Kathryn M. Ryan, Kim Weikel. and Gene Sprechini[36] also point out the correlation between narcissism and domestic violence. They present three forms of narcissism (the exploitativeness/entitlement factor of overt narcissism, i.e., a grandiose sense of self, covert narcissism, i.e., a vulnerable self-concept, and sexual narcissism) in courtship violence in seriously dating couples. For women, narcissism is strongly associated with exploitativeness/entitlement and the relative over-reporting of their partner's sexual coercion. However, for men, narcissism was correlated with physical assault and sexual narcissism was correlated with their partner's sexual coercion.

Spiritual disturbances hinder growth and development. However, some studies suggest that narcissism, even with pathological narcissistic traits and dimensions, is a motivating factor because it can contribute to exceptional and remarkable accomplishments in higher-functioning people.[37] Nevertheless, the circumstances that lead to narcissism or spiritual disease can also encourage the person to reflect for spiritual and emotional growth.[38] In general, the narcissistic men usually demand constant positive feedback, but tend to give negative feedback, and express grandiosity. They also display extreme vulnerability, and symptoms of lack of conscious, lack of empathy, lack of remorse. When their self-image or grandiose self-concept is threatened, they tend to be more violent. Therefore, narcissistic men usually perceive violence more socially desirable and acceptable.[39]

Interestingly, narcissistic females may also be accepting of violence. However, the notion that narcissistic females tend to remain in violent relationships is controversial. Therefore, the correlation between clinical disorders and domestic violence is questionable; furthermore, making such connections is misleading and problematic.[40] For example, according to Judith Herman, some of the psychological disorder models present the women victims of domestic violence as frigid, aggressive, indecisive, and passive because they tolerate domestic violence and use it to fulfil their "masochistic needs."[41] She points out that, in the 1980s, a group of male psychoanalysts in the United States mistakenly labelled these women with masochistic personality disorder. This disorder is used to diagnose someone "who remains in a relationship in which others exploit, abuse, or take advantage of him or her, despite opportunities to alter the situation."[42] In addition, other conditions, such as somatization disorder, borderline personality disorder, and multiple personality disorder, were once diagnosed as hysteria, typically known as a "female disease." Even now, women who are victims of domestic violence are often labelled or blamed for their crazy, disturbed, and/or bizarre behaviours. Some studies relate this tendency to female narcissism or covert narcissism.[43] Unfortunately, those who tend to blame the women victims do not make the connections between the behavioural disturbances, personality disorders, and/or domestic violence. Oddly, however, it has been noted that when women leave the abusive relationship, the bizarre behaviour ceases.

In general, prolonged abuse negatively affects the characteristics of personhood and leads to personality changes. Many people who are exposed to prolonged abuse experience challenges in the areas of relatedness and identity. Herman proposes a more accurate diagnosis – complex post-traumatic stress disorder (C-PTSD).[44] This disorder will be discussed in more depth below when the impact of domestic violence is addressed. Also, the idea that the narcissistic females tend to remain in violent relationship does not fully explain Sarah's initial acceptance of her husband's violence; instead, such theories put blame on Sarah rather than on her husband. The examination of her case suggests that her initial acceptance should be explained with the fact that victims of spiritual violence often present a sense of personal inadequacy, seeing themselves as sinful and blaming themselves for the chaos that develops within the home environment. Islamic psychotherapists should recognize and assess the symptoms of spiritual violence, disease, and distress to engage appropriate interventions that ameliorate the process of growth and recovery while decreasing the incidence of further spiritual damage and unhealthy consequences.

Even though the relationship between psychological disorders, including narcissistic personality disorder, and domestic violence remains a controversial diagnosis, personality and other psychological disorders need more attention in domestic violence literature, especially to explore how narcissistic psychopathology relates to violent men and distinguishes between overt and covert narcissism. It is also equally important to find out why narcissists are generally more accepting of anti-social and violent behaviours.

Interventions to Address Spiritual Disease and Spiritual Distress

Taking into account that many Muslims in various forms follow the Sufi tradition, Islamic psychotherapy is open to using Sufi teachings in its interventions and is keen to explore impact of these teachings and interventions on the mental well-being of patients in mental healthcare clinical settings. Being inspired by the Sufi tradition, one of the assumptions of Islamic psychotherapy is that any violence and deviant behaviour is the result of spiritual diseases of the heart and various interventions are required to deal with these diseases. Generally, these interventions range from conventional approaches to the problem, to religious/spiritual approaches.[45] Also, these interventions, including prayers, are used for various problems such as for divine love, to be forgiven for sins, to remove evil thoughts, to ease a woman's birth-pangs, to heal sickness, to lengthen life, to solve financial problems, and so forth.[46]

Islamic psychotherapy offers various ways of purification of the soul for Muslim women who bring their concerns over spiritual diseases of their soul due to domestic violence. It is accepted that there is no unifying opinion about the duration of the purification of the soul. Nevertheless, some argue that the minimum period for completing the process of perfection is the average lifespan of the human being; and the maximum period takes place over 50 thousand years (Q. 70:4).[47] It is also accepted that this process must not be interrupted; otherwise, the succession of the spiritual stages may not be complete.

In general, the process of purification in Islamic psychotherapy might comprise three steps: (1) confession, (2) forsaking the sin that causes spiritual disease, and (3) divine purification of the effects of sin. The order of the steps for treating spiritual diseases may also vary. However, this is a sample model that might benefit psychotherapy practice with Muslim women who are subject to domestic violence, and their husbands. The following section explains each step in full detail.

The Act of Confessing Sin – Repentance (Tawbah)

In a situation such as domestic violence, Muslim men and women may not be aware of the true intention of the Qur'anic verses on domestic violence that may require the act of confession and repentance. This is especially important for violent men who are forgetful that they have taken on the responsibility for the well-being of their family. Nevertheless, a human being is not only ignorant because he/she accepted to undertake the responsibility that the other parts of creation refused to undertake. As the Qur'an declares, knowing the truth but neglecting to apply it in one's personal and social life also leads the person to ignorance (Q. 46:23). However, the Qur'an (Q. 7:23) also describes humans as having the ability to distinguish just from unjust, and to repent and correct what is unjust. Therefore, seeking forgiveness is a remedy for unjust behaviour in domestic violence. In this situation, Sarah's husband has two obligations: first, to ask forgiveness from her; and second, to ask forgiveness from God.

In Islamic psychotherapy with Muslim women who are subject to domestic violence, the therapy for the act of confession starts with self-awareness and critical reflection of the violent partner and the situation. This is also a stage of self-realization. Regarding the importance of self-awareness and critical reflection in treatment of spiritual diseases, almost all Sufi masters addressed this issue to explain misunderstanding of certain Islamic belief and practices. Al-Ghazali, for example, argues that many Muslims do not live Islamic beliefs sincerely; instead they are hypocritical.[48] A critical reflection requires developing a sincere intention of striving to know and love God, and understanding the true purpose and inner dimension of Islam, including its branches (i.e., *shari 'a*). When the person reflects on the true purpose of Islamic belief and practices, he/she acknowledges that he/she did something wrong and that behaviour must be modified. In the case of the perpetrator of domestic violence, this leads to the process of censuring of the soul (*mu 'atabat al-nafs*) regarding its inadequacy (*tafritiha*). The person rebukes the *nafs* for sins and breaching the divine commands. However, in the case of the survivor of domestic violence, it is a stage when the woman begins to reflect on the real obstacles such as habits, fear, etc., that nurture the behaviour of a mere submission to injustice, aggression, tyrannies, corruptions, and excesses.

However, the process of confessing sin and repentance is a personal matter. There is no requirement for an intermediator to act between the person and God. Most Muslims perform this act almost every day. Muslims use certain prayers in the Qur'an and *hadith* literature to perform this important devotional liturgy. One of the well-known prophetic prayers is: "O Allah! Make me from those who constantly repent to You, and from those who purify themselves,"[49] or *astaghfirullah* (O God, forgive me!). The importance of this step for Muslim women is to make them aware of the abuse of this tradition in some religious communities and their husbands who blame them for not forgiving and even forcing them to repent for their own "disobedience" towards their husbands. They may have a chance to find out that the demand for unlimited and unconditional forgiveness of their perpetrators is an abuse of the Islamic tradition. In addition, they may be empowered by being informed about the spiritual diseases of their husbands.

The Act of Forsaking Sin – The Stage of Commitment

The second process of the purification of the soul is the act of forsaking sin completely or gradually, but the purpose is to achieve a desirable behavioural change by focusing more on the good drives and instincts to ascend to a higher state of the soul: *nafs al-lawwama*.

The more the person is committed to freedom and capacity the more moral growth occurs. During this stage, the person actively engages in reflecting on the dangers of following one's desires. In the case of the survivor of domestic violence, this means that Muslim women begin to be mindful about their desires of submitting to the will of their perpetrators. In the classic Sufi tradition, some practical ways on how one should begin this process are as follows:

> The first stage of opposing the desires (*mukhalafat al-hawa*) is to gain control over one's stomach, since if the devotee can control his stomach he will have charge of his limbs; he will have full knowledge of his heart; taking his soul to account (*al-muhasaba*) will become easy and he will be able to oppose his soul in everything it desires, if God wills. However, if you lose control of your stomach then the issue will become difficult for you, your limbs will go astray, your heart will overstep the bounds and be misguided, you will not truly know your state and you will not be able to take your soul to account.[50]

Besides controlling how much and what one eats and drinks, a number of other devices that help in the process of restricting the desires are as follows: remaining silent instead of indulging in vain talk; lowering one's gaze; avoiding backbiting; the avoidance of indulging in sins and excesses, as well as contemplation and remembrance of God, as all of these acts preoccupy the soul from its desires.[51] This stage also involves developing awareness and mindfulness of past sins because due to them, faith becomes weak. Applying these principles of this process in Islamic psychotherapy is a process of providing psychoeducation to the survivors of domestic violence on how to nurture their bodies, minds, and souls with healthy food, positive thoughts, and spiritual practices.

One of the promising aspects of this stage regarding Muslim women who are subject to domestic violence is educating them about the Qur'anic emphasis on the caution against the rights of others (Q. 49:6–12; 3:159). In classical Sufi counselling theories and techniques, this aspect is especially highlighted. For example, when al-Muhasibi discusses how to reform the soul (*islah al-nafs*), he also instructs how to be carefully observant about being concerned with the faults of others: "It is sufficient a fault in a person that he brings to light in people that which is hidden from himself in his own soul."[52] The violence towards women in the family often occurs because men are too indulged with judging women. Some Muslim men may consider that their wives deserve abuse because they failed to perform their wifely duties in a proper manner. This suggests that these men are quick to point out what their wives are doing or not doing, and they recognize the right for themselves to "discipline" their wives. These abusive men may also introduce themselves as practicing faithful men who only follow the Qur'anic instructions. However, they fail to notice their own behaviours and their own role in the "problem." Applying the Sufi understanding of responsibility in Islamic psychotherapy shows how to invite Muslim women to think about the responsibility of their husbands for their violent attitudes and behaviours. For example, psychotherapists can ask Muslim women to be critical of their husbands who consider themselves "ideal" but consider their wives to be "failures." A sample of questions for developing this awareness is: "What is the responsibility of your husband for this problem?" "What did your husband do to help you to fulfil your duties?" "As a man, did your husband always fulfil what he promised to you?" "What is he going to do to improve the situation?"

These questions help Muslim women to consider that those who force them to repent and forgive their perpetrators are not doing proper counselling. Instead they are supposed to invite their perpetrators to repent continuously. This exercise of responsibility with violent husbands should instil fear into the *nafs* of the perpetrator, or bring some awareness about the importance attached to rights in relationships.

The potential promise of this kind of approach is that consequently, in the light of the feeling of sin and guilt and continuous process of repenting and renewing intention, it will change violent husbands psychologically and spiritually. They will also learn that they have the freedom to choose between two results of the process: either to grow as a man of virtue or be doomed as a violent man on the Final Day.

The Act of Divine Purification on the Effects of Sin

The third and final act of purification is the divine purification that aims to eliminate the effects of the sin on the soul of Muslim women who are subject to domestic violence. Almost all Muslim scholars agree that eliminating the negative effects of spiritual diseases is important for spiritual development and preparation for the Final Day or Return. Although Muslim scholars vary in their understanding of the Return (whether this will happen in physical body or it is a purely spiritual Return, or both), this term is very important regarding the perfection of the spirit. It is no wonder that Muslim scholars have devoted – and continue to devote – a considerable amount of attention to this subject. For example, Ostad Elahi even pointed out that the effects of sin may delay the return of the spirit immediately after death to the world of *barzakh* (the intermediate world). He stated that the spirits of those who commit suicide, or die a sudden death, from insanity, and so forth, remain in the world for a certain period in a state of bewilderment or disorientation, which delays their return to the intermediary world.[53] However, the souls that need further purification are granted a chance to do so in the world of *barzakh* that may be equipped with means like earthly surroundings.

Most Sufi masters suggest accomplishing this stage before death for the desired result. Therefore, they recommend the person to engage in the practice of contemplating death to be aware that one day the soul will be extracted and he/she will be returned to God. This practice is indeed a motivating factor for Muslims, because fear of the Day of Judgement is eternally imbedded in their spirit. The key sources of Islam, such as the Qur'an and the *hadith*, also instil this fear. When one reads the Qur'an, he/she will notice that one of the major themes is related to warning humans against eternal damnation. One of the promising aspects of this practice is that many Muslims, men or women, are inclined to follow religious obligations and spiritual purification to avoid eternal damnation, even though the Qur'an emphasizes more hopes of being rewarded with paradise.

Nevertheless, Muslim psychotherapists also need to be careful when they implement this process with Muslim women whose souls are sensitive to hopelessness and fear about their future. It may put additional stress on them with respect to their inability to reach paradise. However, this process has great potential to treat violent men in Islamic psychotherapy. Since the belief in the Return is such an important objective for Muslims, those Muslim men who violate their wives may strive to avoid the harsh judgement of God and gain the rewards of paradise by avoiding violence against their spouses. To avoid extreme feelings of hopelessness in both men and women in abusive situations, Islamic psychotherapy teaches that God gives them many chances to improve their situations. Although past events are important in the process of repentance, the intention and action to improve one's attitudes and behaviours promises eternal rewards.

Conclusion

In sum, regardless the application of the mainstream therapy interventions, the Sufi tradition can be incorporated in Islamic psychotherapy to deal with spiritual violence. For example, if the Muslim psychotherapist uses cognitive behaviour therapy, the Sufi themes of patience, trust in God, contentment, and God as the ever-forgiver can change the negative cognitive schemas through the application of the Sufi practices of remembrance of God and thankfulness. Transpersonal psychotherapy is also open to application of spiritual practices such as yoga, qigong, and aikido for the treatment of abnormal grief, spiritual crises, psychotic disorders, and substance use disorders. Although it is also important to consider that application of the Sufi tradition in Islamic psychotherapy requires Muslim psychotherapists trained in the Sufi tradition, Sufi beliefs, and practices into the therapeutic process in general may increase the utilization of mental health services by Muslims. However, since the purification of the soul in the context of domestic violence is primarily based on the Sufi sources, the conclusions and recommendations from this chapter are tentative. Further study is required to find out the benefits, risks, and psychotherapy guidelines for Muslim psychotherapists and their clients and, how this model might help in Islamic psychotherapy. This is especially important to minimize any androcentric assumptions and misogynistic biases in counselling with Muslim women who are subject to domestic violence. Any future study on this three-step model should also address the questions on the misapplication of this model by someone who is not familiar with the Sufi tradition.

Notes

1. For the sake of clarity, I will use spiritual diseases to describe the diseases of the heart; otherwise, in the modern context, it might be understood in the context of the physical illness.
2. See Shalahudin Kafrawi, "Fitrah," in *The Oxford Encyclopedia of the Islamic World*, ed. by John Esposito (Oxford: Oxford University Press, 2009). Accessed October 20, 2016. http://www.oxfordislamicstudies.com.myaccess.library.utoronto.ca/article/opr/t236/e1151?_hi=2&_pos=7
3. See Ostad Elahi, *Knowing the Spirit*, trans. and with an Introduction by James Winston Morris (Albany: State University of New York Press, 2007).
4. See Picken, *Spiritual Purification in Islam*, 177.
5. See Bayraktar Bayrakli, *İslamda Eğitim:* Batı *Eğitim* Sistemleri ile Mukayeseli (*Education in Islam and Its Comparison to the Western Education Systems*), 2nd ed. (Istanbul: Marmara Üniversitesi İlahiyat Fakültesi, 1983), 113; Abu'l Qasim al-Qushayri, *The Epistle on Sufism*, trans. by Alexander D. Knysh (Reading: Garnet Publishing Limited, 2007), 227.
6. See Bayrakli, *Education in Islam and Its Comparison to the Western Education Systems*, 108.
7. See William Barrett, *The Illusion of Technique: A Search for Meaning in a Technological Civilization* (New York, NY: Anchor Press/Doubleday, 1978), 75, 104, 232, 261, 167, 343. It is also described as "ontic self-aggrandizement." See Moshe Halevi Spero, *Judaism and Psychology: Halakhic Perspective* (New York, NY: KTAU Publishing House, Inc., Yeshiva University Press, 1980).
8. Schimmel, *Mystical Dimensions of Islam*, 60.
9. Ibid., 112.
10. al-Qushayri, *The Epistle on Sufism*, 229.
11. Ibid.,154.
12. Bayrakli, *Education in Islam and Its Comparison to the Western Education Systems*,112.
13. See Picken, *Spiritual Purification in Islam*,123.
14. Ibid.,185.
15. Mary Elizabeth O'Brian, "The Need for Spiritual Integrity," in *Human Needs and Nursing Process*, ed. by Helen Yura and Mary B. Walsh (Norwalk, CT: Appleton-Century-Crofts, 1982).
16. Picken, *Spiritual Purification in Islam*, 187.
17. Mohamad V. A. Ashrof, *Islam and Gender Justice: Questions at the Interface* (Delhi: Kalpaz Publications, 2005), 204.
18. See William C. Chittick, "Love in Islamic Thought," *Religion Compass* 8 (2014): 229–238; Hoel Nina and Sa'diyya Shaikh, "Sexing Islamic Theology: Theorising Women's Experience and Gender Through abd allah and khalifah," *Journal for Islamic Studies* 33 (2013): 127–151.
19. William C. Chittick, *Divine Love: Islamic Literature and the Path to God* (New Haven, CT: Yale University Press, 2013).
20. Sachiko Murata, *The Tao of Islam: A Sourcebook on Gender Relationships in Islamic Thought* (Albany, NY: State University of New York Press, 1992), 215–216. Also, see Hassan, "Feminism in Islam."

21. See Oliver Leaman, *The Biographical Encyclopaedia of Islamic Philosophy* (London: Thoemmes Continuum, 2006).
22. Shaikh, *Sufi Narratives of Intimacy*, 10.
23. Ibid., 30.
24. See Shaikh, *Sufi Narratives of Intimacy*; Schimmel, *Mystical Dimensions of Islam*, 224.
25. Shaikh, *Sufi Narratives of Intimacy*, 80.
26. For Nevin Reda, Muslims are supposed to reflect the meaning of the word Islam, which refers to "wholeness making, peacemaking, well-being making, and safety making." Nevin Reda, "The 'Good' Muslim, 'Bad' Muslim Puzzle? The Assertion of Muslim Women's Islamic Identity in the Sharia Debates in Canada," in *Debating Sharia: Islam, Gender Politics, and Family Law Arbitration*, ed. by Anna C. Korteweg, and Jennifer A. Selby (Toronto: University of Toronto Press, 2012), 243.
27. Barbara Simonič, Tina Rahne Mandelj, and Rachel Novsak, "Religious-Related Abuse in the Family," *Journal of Family Violence* 28 (2013): 339.
28. Ibid., 347.
29. See McCue, *Domestic Violence*; Jacobson and Gottman, *When Men Batter Women*; Paul Nestor, "Mental Disorder and Violence: Personality Dimensions and Clinical Features," *The American Journal of Psychiatry* 159 (1) (2002): 1973–1978; Kathryn M. Ryan, Kim Weikel, and Gene Sprechini, "Gender Differences in Narcissism and Courtship Violence in Dating Couples," *Sex Roles* 58 (2008): 802–813; Nicole Buck, Petronella Leenaars, Paul Emmelkamp, and Hjalmar Marle, "Personality Traits Are Related to Intimate Partner Violence Among Securely Attached Individuals," *Journal of Family Violence* 29 (3) (2014): 235–246; Victoria Blinkhorn, Minna Lyons, and Louise Almond, "Drop the Bad Attitude! Narcissism Predicts Acceptance of Violent Behaviour," *Personality and Individual Differences* 98 (2016): 157–161; Simonič, Mandelj, and Novsak, "Religious-Related Abuse in the Family," 339; Dutton and Bodnarchuk, "Through a Psychological Lens: Personality Disorder and Spouse Assault."
30. Sigmund Freud, *Moses and Monotheism* (New York, NY: Vintage Book, 1938/1955), 537.
31. Phillip Crockatt, "Freud's 'On Narcissism: An Introduction'", *Journal of Child Psychotherapy* 31 (1) (2006): 4–20; Kelso Cratesly, "Revisiting Freud and Kohut on Narcissism," *Theory and Psychology* 26 (6) (2016): 333–359.

   American Psychiatric Association, *Diagnostic and Statistical Manual of Mental Disorders*, 669–672; Elsa Ronningstam, "New Insights Into Narcissistic Personality Disorder," *Psychiatric Times* 33 (2) (2016): 11. Accessed on October 14, 2016 from www.psychiatrictimes.com/special-reports/new-insights-narcissistic-personality-disorder.
32. See Sigmund Freud, *Fragment of an Analysis of a Case of Hysteria* (London: Hogarth Press, 1905/1975), 50.
33. American Psychiatric Association, *Diagnostic and Statistical Manual of Mental Disorders*, 669–672; Ronningstam, "New Insights Into Narcissistic Personality Disorder," 11.
34. Nestor, "Mental Disorder and Violence: Personality Dimensions and Clinical Features," 244.
35. L. Kevin Hamberger and James E. Hastings, "Personality Correlates of Men Who Abuse Their Partners: A Cross-Validation Study," *Journal of Family Violence* 1 (1986): 323–341.
36. Ryan, Weikel and Sprechini, "Gender Differences in Narcissism and Courtship Violence in Dating Couples," 802–813.
37. Ronningstam, "New Insights Into Narcissistic Personality Disorder."
38. Hood Morris, "A Spiritual Well-Being Model: Use With Older Women Who Experience Depression," *Issues in Mental Health Nursing* 17 (1996): 439–455.
39. Blinkhorn, Lyons, and Almond, "Drop the Bad Attitude! Narcissism Predicts Acceptance of Violent Behaviour," 157.

40. Edward W. Gondolf, "A Comparison of Re-Assault Rates in Four Batterer Programs: Do Court Referral, Program Length and Services Matter?" *Journal of Interpersonal Violence* 14 (1999): 41–61.
41. Judith Herman, *Trauma and Recovery – The Aftermath of Violence From Domestic Abuse to Political Terror* (New York, NY: Basic Books, 1997).
42. Ibid., 117.
43. See Blinkhorn, Lyons, and Almond, "Drop the Bad Attitude! Narcissism Predicts Acceptance of Violent Behaviour"; Nestor, "Mental Disorder and Violence: Personality Dimensions and Clinical Features."
44. Herman, *Trauma and Recovery*, 119.
45. See Ashy, "Health and Illness from an Islamic Perspective"; Md Zain Azhar and Shashjit L. Varma, "Religious Psychotherapy in Depressive Patients," *Psychotherapy and Psychosomatics* 63 (1995): 165–173; Md Zain Azhar, Shashjit L. Varma, and Abdulla S. Dharap, "Religious Psychotherapy in Anxiety Disorder Patients," *Acta Psychiatrica Scandinavica* 90 (1994): 1–3; Shamsul Nizamie, Mohammed Zia Ul Haq Kathsu, and N Ahamed Uvais, "Sufism and Mental Health," *Indian Journal of Psychiatry* 55 (6) (2013), 215–223.
46. Ernst, *Sufism*, 89.
47. Elahi, *Knowing the Spirit*, 98–99.
48. David Buchman, "Translator's Introduction," in Al-Ghazali, *The Niche of Lights*, A parallel English-Arabic test, trans., introduced and annotated by David Buchman (Provo, UT: Brigham Young University Press, 1998), xxvi.
49. See *Jami at-Tirmidhi*. Accessed on November 11, 2016 from http://sunnah.com/tirmidhi/1/55.
50. al-Muhasibi, cited by Picken, *Spiritual Purification in Islam*, 176.
51. Picken, *Spiritual Purification in Islam*, 176.
52. Ibid., 178.
53. Elahi, *Knowing the Spirit*, 139.

6 Honour and Shame

Noor is a 25-year-old woman from United Arab Emirates (UAE). She moved to Canada with her parents from UAE when she was 19 years old and was immediately married to a man from her community. She did not experience any major adjustment issues after her immigration as she was already familiar with English at high school and university where she studied food engineering. Nevertheless, she did not enjoy her life as her husband prevented her from contacting her friends and working in her field, a situation which was resolved when she was finally allowed to apply for jobs and get her desired job in the food industry because her husband's income alone was not enough to pay the expenses.

Unfortunately, Noor was not able to see important warning signals in their relationship. For example, she did not realize that by preventing her from contacting the people she wanted to see, he was laying the foundation for control and manipulation. Also, when he forbade her attendance at *Jum'ah*, the Friday prayers in the local mosque, she did not understand his rationale, but obeyed to avoid conflict and because she believed a woman's place was at home. In deference to his knowledge about Islam, she stopped questioning him and eventually, she could not differentiate between his interpretations of Islam and the actual tenets of her faith.

Gradually, when her husband became hyper-critical of her, Noor could not understand his behaviour. When she asked him for clarification, he repeatedly shut her out, simply ignored her points and made a face as if telling her, "How dare you question me!" Gradually, he berated her for doing things "wrong" just because she did things in her own way. He also called her names and put her down, e.g., "a woman without *namus* (chastity), *haya* (decency), *'ird* (honour) and *sharaf* (dignity)."[1] Consequently, she gave up her dream of being a happy woman and sacrificed herself for her children's (who were 2 and 4 years old) sake hoping that she would be rewarded for her patience and sacrifice. This sacrifice of self was reinforced by what she had learned from her family of origin that women should compromise and sacrifice their ambitions and desires for the sake of the family. Also, she learned from her mother that if the husband beats the wife, she must be "asking for it" as she failed to be desirable, lovable, and pleasing to her husband.

However, the more she sacrificed, the more he became violent. He treated her like a slave instead of an equal partner and she concluded that she was only needed for cooking, cleaning, raising his children, sex, and giving all her income to him to buy their family home under his name.

However, Noor did not dare to challenge him openly and she learned how to talk carefully in order not to irritate her husband by making "mistakes." Most of the time, she avoided the areas in the home where he would usually spend his time. Nevertheless, she felt guilty for avoiding her husband because she believed that a "good wife" was supposed to be physically attractive to and verbally affectionate with her husband and demonstrate her honour and decency. Sadly, the pattern of violence escalated and he began hitting and slapping her in the face. After the first incident of physical violence, she was in shock and wondered how a good Muslim husband could do this to his wife. His actions towards her conflicted with what he preached to others about kindness, mercy, gentleness, and forgiveness. Noor felt that her husband failed to carry out his responsibilities as enjoined by the Qur'an.

She thought of divorce but was afraid as she assumed this process to be complicated and difficult as her husband might refuse to cooperate with lawyers, provide financial support, and give her rights over their family property. When she turned to her extended family for support, and told them that she wanted to go to the local imam for help but her husband might become angry with her for having disclosed her husband's "secret," her family sided with him, telling her that a mild slap and shouting were permissible between a husband and a wife. They even cited the Qur'an[2] and criticized her for her plan to leave her husband and seek the custody of her children. They also warned her that they would not accept her as she had already left the house a long time ago when she married. In addition, she was admonished that in case of the divorce, she would not have the right over her children and property as in their tradition it is only men who enjoy these rights. She also was reminded to be a good wife and not visit the imam because she was not supposed to meet any man; otherwise, she would be considered to be violating the honour of the family. Gradually, Noor became more isolated and the violence escalated. At one point, she felt that she was a scapegoat; her pleas for help were turned against her and she became a target for retribution.

Finally, Noor sought some guidance in the local mosque because she believed that imams might be influential in addressing marital problems. Initially, the imam offered suggestions for engaging with her abusive husband, and he reinforced the mutual rights and duties of couples in Islam. He also provided emotional support by listening and encouraging her to express her emotions. He also promised to talk to her husband in the mosque and demand him to stop his violent behaviours and focus on caring for his wife. As might be expected, Noor begged the imam not to talk to her husband because she knew that he would accuse her of betraying the secrets of the family with another man; obviously, he considered the imam more as a man than a professional religious leader. Noor was also tormented by her thought that she did something wrong by asking for help from the imam. She thought that her actions brought shame to her husband in the eyes of the community.

However, her husband became so physically violent that she almost wanted to call 9–1–1, but she did not because she felt ashamed of her bruised eyes and face. She decided to go to a shelter for women, but she changed her mind as she did not want to hear people to say that the reason why she was being violated is because of her religion. Noor considered herself a devoted follower of Islam and did not want her faith to be the centre of blame, and she wanted to be in a place where she could have a space to pray and not have an issue with the food. In addition, she was afraid that her parents would blame her for dishonouring their name.

Soon Noor found out that there was one Muslim shelter in the city that was run by a local Islamic community and provided access to a Muslim psychotherapist for women's healing, change, and empowerment. One day, she fled there for help without taking her children, as she did not want to burden her children with new challenges. In this shelter, people usually took their shoes off at the door, there was no pork served in the kitchen, and a section of the house was reserved for prayers. Although she found the shelter to be a sanctuary and an escape from the abuse, she cried almost every day because she had to leave her children behind. Although she phoned them every day, she could not stop their voices in her head. Because of intense pressure on her shoulders and ambiguity of her situation, Noor could not find peace and felt her soul bent under the heavy burden of her sorrow. Almost every night, she woke up screaming: she complained of unpleasant dreams in which her husband was attacking her and her children. Noor suffered in silence and fear that was slowly tearing her soul apart. She was struggling with trauma due to domestic violence and suffered from symptoms such as extreme anxiety and fear, guilt, shame, self-blame, denial, and questioning her faith.

To get rid of her trauma symptoms, she wanted to meet with a Muslim counsellor in the shelter to know her rights under *Shari 'ah* (the Islamic law) as she wanted to reconcile with her faith. Noor wanted to be assured that she did not embarrass her husband nor her extended family in the eyes of the community. The only person who should be blamed was her husband, because he embarrassed her in the community and damaged her soul. She wanted to know whether the Islamic law allows her husband to beat her and control her. She had a sense that her husband manipulated Islam's sacred sources that contributed to her tolerance to abuse. For her, whatever he said was "sacred." Since she wanted to be faithful to her religion, she did not question her husband's misinterpretation of Islam; otherwise, she would feel as if she had disobeyed the word of God, even if she was in an abusive relationship. In psychotherapy with the Muslim psychotherapist, she also wanted to know whether the Islamic Family Law endorses her rights to get the children returned to her care, to receive child and spousal support, and her share from the family property.

Honour and Shame in Islamic Studies and Islamic Psychotherapy Literature

Noor's story highlights the difficulty leaving the violent relationship and many reasons why Muslim women stay in violent relationships and/or work so hard at making the relationship work. The most important questions in this case are linked to Noor's quest to find out whether she violates the honour of her family:

1. by questioning the physical violence, willing to leave the violent husband, and
2. her rights for child custody, child and spousal support under the Islamic Family Law.[3]

Since Noor comes belongs to a collectivist society, she knows that personal and family reputations are of paramount importance for her family. Therefore, her questions with respect to honour and shame not only have a personal/individual dimension but also "imply a public dimension, as *maintaining face* or *losing face* (i.e., maintaining or losing reputation and dignity) in front of one's community can be a matter of life or death."[4] The public dimension of her dilemma puts intense social pressure on her shoulders and makes her feel extremely distressed and "trapped, without adaptive means to regain their sense of dignity."[5]

In the context of her questions we need to examine how the concepts of honour and shame are directly linked to the legal aspects of domestic violence. Noor is afraid that if she complains and seeks out help for the violence she experiences at home outside the established family norms or seeks a divorce, she might be blamed for dishonouring her family and deprived of her rights and children, and be subject to honour violence. Indeed, she is right to be cautious as many honour- and shame-related incidents involve crimes and offences against women (such as acid throwing, death threats, rape, burning, beatings, stoning, suffocating, depriving the women of the essentials for their lives and progress) in the context of domestic violence.[6]

This section highlights why it is important for Noor to find answers to her questions before and/or after she wants to leave her violent partner within the framework of the Islamic Family Law of Shari 'ah, i.e., what the Islamic Family Law says with respect to beating the wife, women's rights in marriage and after divorce, and whether there is any indication of the code of "honour" in the Islamic Family Law. Since those who commit this violence against women use the Islamic Family Law[7] to justify themselves, I begin with providing an overview of the Islamic Family Law, then address Noor's question whether her husband's physical violence is endorsed in the Qur'an as he claimed and discuss Noor's rights for family property, spousal, and child custody using the Islamic Family Law as a main resource. I also highlight the Islamic Family Law's response to domestic violence with respect to honour violence in relationship to gender inequality, cultural values, and religious norms. A discussion of the various cultural understandings of honour will be followed by a feminist response to Noor's case.

The Islamic Family Law: A Brief Introduction

Unlike the classical Islamic laws, the reformed Islamic Family Law allows women to exercise more rights to divorce, custody, and claims after divorce.[8] Despite the reforms in the Islamic Family Law, many aspects such as polygamy, *talaq* (divorce), registration of marriage and divorce, post-divorce financial provisions, and the minimum age for marriage remain unchanged.[9] In addition, Islamic Family Law is very diverse and fluid regarding its doctrines and principles, and there is no clear demarcation between the mundane and secular, and moral and legal aspects of family relationships, which makes the case more complicated.

Noor's case demonstrates that many Muslim women understand Islamic Family Law not only as a legal code but also a moral code (even a code of "honour") that provides a framework for the individual's relationship with God in the context of the social, moral, and legal framework.[10] *Qadis* or the Muslim judges treat the Islamic law as a set of social, moral, and legal imperatives. It is impossible to imagine the court process "remote from the social world of the disputants."[11] The aim is to restore the social roles embedded in the social and moral compromise and seek legal response to an irreparable or serious breach of social harmony and the moral code.[12]

As outlined before, the violation of the Shari 'ah objectives[13] involved *hudud* (the prescribed penalties) (i.e., capital punishment for murder). The intention of classifying these objectives of the Shari 'ah is to provide "a holistic approach, to establish the fundamental coherence of the whole corpus of *ahkâm* to clarify the stakes in the practice of *fiqh*."[14] In the context of these rules, the majority of Muslims jurists have provided some protection for women. For example, Islamic laws concluded that a woman's physical virginity was not the requirement for a valid marriage contract and that she cannot be accused of wrongdoing.[15] The Islamic Family Law also implemented a severe penalty for slandering women and attempted to protect women's privacy and honour against the defamation of her chastity.

The Islamic Family Law and Wife-Beating

As Noor's case explicitly demonstrates, women who are subject to domestic violence live a deep sense of shame and feel that their honour was violated. However, due the societal, cultural, and religious interpretations, the Islamic Family Law does not pay attention to these emotional and psychological factors. It might also give an impression that instead of their husband, the women themselves should feel shame for dishonouring their husbands and their families. In Noor's case, her family uses the Islamic legal traditions and their interpretation of Q. 4:34 "as a proof text for supporting the right of husbands to physically hit their wives."[16] Therefore, Noor wonders if she has behaved "badly" and "deserves" punishment. In this context, it is very natural for Noor to inquire about the Islamic Family Law's position on wife-beating to find out the truth about this conception in Islam.

The task to reveal the truth behind the claim that the husbands do not have the right to physically discipline their wives is not an easy matter as some provisions of the Islamic Family Law may seem to support the husband's accusations against the wife in cases of her *nushuz* (an act of rebelliousness) verse (Q. 4:34). Some schools may even support the husband against the wife if she leaves the matrimonial house without his permission. However, each of these legal traditions was guided by different principles when addressing marital disputes.[17]

The Hanafi jurists also made sure that the authority of husbands in marriage was not challenged: therefore, their legal rulings protected husbands from legal accountability even in the worst cases of extreme violence. Whereas, the Maliki jurists limited the disciplinary privilege (such as beating, hitting) of husbands by restricting and even applying penalties in cases of *darar* (harm), including physical, even verbal and emotional abuse – without suspending the hierarchal status in the marital relationship. The intention of these prescriptions in the Maliki School of jurisprudence was to ensure that wives were protected from excessive abuse by exercising judicial supervision over the authority of husbands in marriage. The Shafi ʿi jurists sought to find a middle ground between the Hanafi and Maliki positions by reconciling between these two schools: they also supported the sequence of trio-scheme offered in Q. 4:34, but also imposed penalties (in case of extreme hitting), and intrusion of social actors/mediators if it necessitated.[18]

In his *Jami'al-bayan*, al-Tabari (d. 923), who established his own school of law after he separated himself from the Shafi ʻi school of law, also challenged the notion of the husband's authority over women. He put a limitation to this authority stating that women's responsibility to obey their husbands is only in those matters that God ordered them to, i.e., being good to their husband's families and preserving their husband's wealth.[19] In addition, al-Tabari cites a hadith from Ibn Abbas (d. 687) and concludes that even in cases where the husband accuses his wife in disobedience, he has to forgive her because he has *rutba wa -manzila* (a "rank and a status"). Similarly, al-Razi also reported:

> the superiority of men over women is established in these matters, and it is clear that women are like helpless captives in men's hands. Therefore, [Muhammad] said, peace and blessings be upon him, "treat women well, for they are your captives" and in another narration, "Be God-fearing in your treatment of two weak ones: orphans and women."[20]

He also cautioned men for not abusing their status because when someone is in apposition of power, they might hurt and harm the one who has less power. Further, al-Tabari and al-Razi also expressed their vision of a Muslim marriage, which, for them, should be coherent, bounded, and a strong system. In this regard, the Shafi 'i scholar al-Suyuti (d. 1505) also emphasized the husband's duties towards their wives.

At the far end of the spectrum of the Islamic schools of jurisprudence, the Ḥanbali jurists took an even more radical approach in their legal rulings: they extended the list of the wife's act of rebelliousness that might be subject to physical punishment. Furthermore, their legal rulings protected "husbands from liability in cases of excessive violence by denying wives clear legal recourse."[21] Nevertheless, the Hanbali scholars, i.e., Ibn Qudamah (d. 1223), also recognized the wife's right to seek divorce if her husband violated her rights mentioned in the marriage contract.[22] Thus, despite the controversies related to the interpretation and application of the Islamic Family Law, in classical schools of thought, it will be a limited approach to assume that the classical Muslim scholars' only concern was to protect the position of the husband in the marital hierarchy: they also raised their concerns with respect to the husbands' correct and ethical behaviour towards their wives in cases of separation and divorce. The Islamic Family Law, for example, also included provisions that protected women against violence of their husbands.

Contemporary Muslim scholars who maintain traditionalist or neo-traditionalist perspectives share similar interpretations of Q. 4:34 as the pre-modern Muslim jurists. For example, Yusuf Al-Qaradawi, a prominent contributor to Islamic studies and jurisprudence, draws on the classical texts of Islamic jurisprudence to address questions regarding *halal* (lawful) and *haram* (forbidden) in the areas of worship, business transactions, marriage and divorce, family, and social ethics.[23] When discipline is required, al-Qaradawi advocates using the steps from Q. 4:34 in an incremental fashion.[24] However, al-Qaradawi establishes clear limitations. He permits a husband to beat his wife, "lightly with his hands, avoiding her face and other sensitive areas. In no case should he resort to using a stick or any other instrument which might cause pain and injury."[25] He strictly prohibits striking on the face since this "is an insult to her human dignity as well as being a danger to the most beautiful part of her body."[26]

Nevertheless, al-Qaradawi's recommendation may still encourage the violent husband to beat his wife on other parts of her body and bruises on the remainder of the body can be hidden by clothing. Nevertheless, al-Qaradawi also argues that for the sake of the marriage, a husband's ill treatment of his wife (i.e., being cruel, causing injuries, and damaging her interests) in the context of divorce is *haram* (forbidden). To avoid dysfunctional relationships within the marriage, he reminds couples that the divine purpose of marriage is love and affection and "the nurturing of affection and tenderness among the children under the loving care of their parents."[27] Another contemporary Muslim scholar, Jamal Badawi, suggests that "beating" women may be done in moderation; however, he interprets Q. 4:34 as "more of a symbolic gesture than a punitive one."[28] However, Dr. Taha Jabir al-Alwani, one of the well-known Muslim jurists, does not think that the wife-beating is the best solution to marital problems.[29]

As we see, for Muslim scholars, regardless of their religious views and orientation, the underlying question was how to maintain marital hierarchy and balance between duties and obligations between the spouses. In the light of the authority of a husband, they offered various interpretations of how to apply the three levels of strategies (admonishment, abandonment, and physical force) prescribed by Q. 4:34. Some of them treated the levels as steps and adopted an incremental approach, while others made no such distinction and allowed the steps to be used in any combination or simultaneously. Therefore, when we examine the Islamic Family Law's response to wife-beating in Islamic psychotherapy, the problem should not be only what the Muslim scholars said "(which is, at times, entirely predictable), but why they said it."[30]

In general, the Islamic Family Law's "perceptions" of the wife-beating were influenced by societal norms and their interpretations of the Qur'an. In addition, they aimed to protect the family and create and maintain peace, love, and companionship between the spouses but at the expense of the women's safety and sacrifices.[31] For this purpose, Muslim scholars used various sources of information and knowledge to arrive at a conclusion. We, for example, notice that social customs or culture were used as normative along the sacred texts of Islam as they also played an important role to achieve this goal. However, Muslim scholars mainly concluded that the Islamic Family Law set out more ethical and legal norms for the husband's attitudes and behaviours as they have more responsibility and accountability because of their higher status in the patriarchal society.

Islamic Feminist Responses

In response to the patriarchal interpretation of Q. 4:34, Islamic feminist scholarship offers a new understanding of Noor's question whether her husband can use the sacred text to justify his violent behaviour. Although we have already provided a detailed account of Islamic feminist response to this question in the chapter where we discussed domestic violence and Islam's exegetical tradition, it is helpful here to mention that except the controversial Q. 4:34, the Qur'an in general does not endorse any violence against women.

Muslim feminist scholars argue that historically, the Islamic Family Law was not immune from patriarchal interpretations and applications that sacrificed women's rights to men's. They questioned some aspects of the Islamic Family Law and offered progressive readings of the Qur'an and other sources of the Islamic tradition in their socio-economic and cultural context. For example, the husband's privilege in the Islamic Family Law needs to be examined from the framework of gender egalitarianism and new feminist hermeneutical understanding of the Qur'anic concepts of *khilafah* (vicegerent), *wilayah* (governance, administration), and *qawwamah* (protection, maintenance).[32] Although *khilafah* is a privilege given to humans, regardless of their gender, sexuality, race, ethnicity, etc., it also refers to human responsibility and accountability and conscious governance. On the other hand, *wilayah*, which is also a genderless concept and expressed in various forms in the Qur'an and other sources of Islam, such as *awliya* (allies), *al-wala'* (closeness, friendship, loyalty, and fidelity), *wilayah 'ammah* (political governance), etc., refers to alliance, mutual assistance, and mutual reinforcement. In the legal context, it refers to the one who manages the affairs of a minor or serves as a guardian over someone "to manage, govern and be entrusted, among other things with affairs of state."[33]

Similarly, *qiwamah* which comes from the Qur'anic term *qawwamun* or *qawwamin*, is not only legal but also an ethical concept and at least has 30 meanings, including, "stand up," "comply," "carry," "take on," "proceed," "rise up," "provide for," "revolt," "endure," "lift up," and so forth, that refer to the successful performance or implementation of justice in *qiwamah 'ammah* (the public sphere) and *qiwamah khassah* (the private sphere).[34] Unfortunately, disregarding the ethical aspects of the concept, most scholars have interpreted this concept to mean "maintainers," "care takers," "protectors," "in charge of," "keeping check on them," "having an authority over them and concluded that this word refers to men's guardianship over women at home, in the society, and in all spheres."[35] It is not *tashrif* (an honour) or *fadl* (the favour) but *taklif* (responsibility), especially during women's most vulnerable times such as during pregnancy, confinement, and nursing when the husbands are responsible for moral and material security of their families.[36]

As a result, the interpretations of these key terms influenced by the patriarchal norms lead to gender inequality and the root cause of domestic violence. Of course, it should be outlined that gender inequality is not a specifically "Muslim" problem, because it operates in almost all corners of the world. However, its implication in the context of domestic violence against Muslim women is very significant. More specifically, to compound the problem of gender inequality, many Muslim societies do not recognize women as equal partners of men and domestic violence as a crime.

Nevertheless, despite the divergence in the Islamic Family Law (i.e., the wife's obedience to her husband as a *Shari 'ah*-based obligation), Islamic feminism also tries to find a practical solution to women's issues. A sensitive approach to the Islamic Family Law can be explained with the fact that this law, including other aspects of *Shari 'ah*, act as a symbol and "a central defining characteristic of Muslim self-awareness."[37] For example, a fresh and new exegetical understanding of male violence against women that distils the pre-modern Islamic legal tradition, educates Muslim women about their choices within the legal tradition. For this purpose, *Muslim & Canadian Family Law: A Comparative Primer* produced by Canadian Council of Muslim Women (CCMW) provides practical and ground-breaking research that compares Muslim law with Canadian Family Law.[38] Also, the Peaceful Families Project in the United States also initiated the similar project in the United States.[39]

The Faith Trust Institute developed this resource in order to help American Muslims understand and access the complex American legal system, and inform Muslim women of their rights both in civil and religious laws. The findings of these projects suggest that despite the Islamic Family Law's underlying principle to provide protection and support to women at all stages of life, the Muslim women in the United States might also find it helpful to compare their rights under the law systems in the United States.

In general, both projects conclude that overall, the North American laws enhance the rights of women in the context of domestic violence by declaring domestic violence a crime against women. For example, the violent husband is removed from the house, detained and charged with violating the rights of his wife. In addition, the women can seek help from the courts and community resources that provide legal and financial advice. However, one also should consider that many North American laws, legislative and policy initiatives may be providing formal rather than substantive protection for women. For example, the Canadian laws also respect contracts, including marriage contracts, and assume that adults sign away these contracts with responsibility and awareness of their risks and negative consequences. In the United States, some attorneys may also accept the *mahr* in Islamic marriage contracts as prenuptial agreements. However, recently, in the US, Islamic marriage contracts are also being enforced as simple contracts rather than prenuptial agreements.[40] Nevertheless, it also depends whether Islamic marriage contract is accompanied by a civil marriage licence, and if it has been registered in the US or overseas. This might be a "laudable principle in theory," it does not take into consideration the interests of vulnerable women who might sign away these contracts under the pressure of their abusive husbands.[41]

The protection that the Canadian laws offer might be minimally accessible to women from marginalized communities. For example, although according to the Canadian laws, women can initiate separation and divorce at any time, it takes years to get the final divorce certificate, especially in cases when the women do not have financial means to hire a lawyer to defend her rights. Further, women who are financially eligible to use the Legal Aid of Ontario (LAO) may be disappointed that the legal aid does not help women in all matters, i.e., property division because "LAO takes the position that lawyers can be paid out of the property being divided between the parties."[42] In cases the courts asks for evidence that they did so, these women might have difficulty to prove it. Also, courts in United States and Canada do not enforce Muslim men to fulfil gender roles or domestic chores outlined in the Islamic marriage contracts because they consider these to be personal service agreements.[43] In addition, the Muslim women's perspective of safety and a sense of belonging might be misinterpreted.[44]

Therefore, by using all these resources, Islamic psychotherapy might help Noor to understand that both the Islamic Family Law and the North American laws recognize a woman's right to seek divorce or to end a marriage to extricate herself from a harmful situation. However, there are many factors that prevent women from seeking divorce in conservative Muslim families. For example, a woman may be pressured to remain in abusive family relations because of social expectations and/or a lack of financial means. Although Shari 'ah functions as a framework for Islamic norms and values and administering Muslim family affairs such as marriage, divorce, custody, and inheritance, multiple interpretations of the Law are often influenced by state power in Muslim societies. In some cases, interpretations of Shari 'ah clearly prohibit violence within the family; in other cases, aggression is sanctioned. With respect to the precept of *qawwamah* in the context of the responsibility of men to protect and provide for women, this principle offers shelter for women, but on the other hand, women are not afforded equal rights because they are expected to obey their husbands, fathers, or other male heads of family.

The Muslim psychotherapist might also consider some contemporary scholarship that takes a distinctly anti-traditionalist approach to the issue of domestic violence in Muslim families and clearly blames the Islamic legal tradition for perpetrating oppression and injustice towards women.[45] In this regard, the role of the Muslim psychotherapist is to assess Noor's preference of the legal tradition, search for empowering and women-friendly legal rulings, and understand why she prefers what she chooses.

Islamic Family Law and the Honour Violence

One of the emerging questions in Islamic psychotherapy in this case is to counsel Noor with respect to the issue of honour in the Islamic Family Law as she finds her husband's attitude to blame her as a woman without honour traumatic and dangerous as the honour charges against women must be taken seriously because it may lead to honour violence against women. Therefore, one of the tasks in Islamic psychotherapy with Noor should focus on properly assessing the threats and risks of honour violence in the family.

The Qur'an or *hadith* categorically prohibits torturing or killing female members of the family. The Islamic Family Law also describes the honour violence as an illegal punishment and outlaws it. For example, in the case when the husband accuses his wife of dishonouring him, the Islamic Family Law recognizes the right of both parties to *li'an* or *al-mula'nah* (an oath made by the husband and wife to speak the truth) and support his accusations by four witnesses.[46] Taking into considerations the power of the husband, the Islamic Family Law recognizes the wife's right to take an oath of innocence (as prescribed in Q. 24:6–10) to protect her honour against her husband's accusations.[47]

Unfortunately, despite the clear instructions in the Islamic Family Law regarding the honour of the wife and the husband, honour violence is still practiced in many Muslim countries and among Muslims in North America.[48] In general, honour violence is a complicated issue as it cuts deep into the history of Muslim societies and is linked to multiple oppressive practices against women. One of the forms of such violence against Muslim women is harassment that can also be in the form of the husband spreading rumours of immorality that threatens a woman's credibility and ability with intention "to garner family and community support, or to remarry."[49] Due to the extreme harm and violation of women's rights in the name of the Islamic Family Law, many Muslim scholars voiced their concern and issued legal rulings against it.[50]

Nevertheless, it is agreed that the honour violence is more a cultural rather than religious issue because it is more practiced in collectivistic communities where an individual must put the community needs above the individual needs.[51] Further, there are other factors that make the honour violence more prevalent among individuals who have lower levels of education, more economic and social stress, and adhere to rigid patriarchal structures and extended kinship groups. A strong gender and generational hierarchy, a degree of proximity, status, and knowledge are also one of the main causes of the honour violence. In these groups, gender is the main factor that defines the role of individuals in the family and society. For example, in these societies, women and young generations usually have a lower status than males and elders.

In some Muslim cultures, confinement and alienation of women is also a normal cultural practice. Women are expected to marry within the extended family and take care of domestic affairs. Some cultures may expect women to give birth to many children. Any abuse towards women is accepted as a "family business" meaning that violence against women should not be disclosed to "strangers." Although with a rapid cultural transformation in the Muslim world, many women also enter the workplace, they still must carry "their traditionally mandated household and childcare duties."[52] Although in these communities, humility and interdependence are the major qualities promoted by the collectivistic nature of the societies, any deviation from these qualities may also be interpreted as violating honour and causing shame or guilt to the family and community. Therefore, even for survival, any attempt to challenge the collectivistic system may cause undesired results. In these societies, honour violence is used against women who are believed to "contravene" the code of sexual behaviour (i.e., premarital or extramarital sexual relationships), marry someone against the family's wishes, or seek divorce that damages honour.[53] These women are unforgivable as "women on whom suspicion has fallen are not given an opportunity to defend themselves, and family members have no socially acceptable alternative but to remove the stain on their honour by attacking the woman."[54]

In sum, both the historical and contemporary practice of honour violence should be examined in Islamic psychotherapy in terms of cultural perspectives as it is more common in collectivistic societies where family and community play a vital role in the life of the individual. The Muslim psychotherapist should assess the relationship between a firm belief in honour of the family and power of men in the society. For example, he/she should consider the degree of the patriarchal cultural mind-set of Noor's culture because it is well-known that honour violence is common in feudal and patriarchal cultures to control women, especially, not only in terms of controlling sexual power or behaviour but also fertility or reproductive power of women.[55] However, Noor might benefit from knowing that there are many attempts to reform Islamic Family Law with respect to women's right in marriage. This will empower her and finally, she may find peace with her faith that she, indeed, is not forced by Shari 'ah to obey her violent husband.

Moral Response to Islamic Family Law

The discussion of the principle of modesty in Muslim female scholarship may also provide a theoretical framework in Islamic psychotherapy. Islamic feminist literature particularly brings to the attention the necessity to reread the concept of *taqwa*[56] in reinterpreting the legal discourse of women's rights and patriarchal construction of "honour." Although the classical definition of *taqwa* is helpful, one also needs to go beyond the classical understating of *taqwa*, especially with Muslim women who might be blamed for having lack of *taqwa* when they demand their rights.

For this purpose, a new interpretation of *taqwa* offered by Fazlur Rahman can be helpful. Rahman, who agrees with the classical Islamic interpretation of *taqwa* (he prefers to translate it as a "conscience") as a "keen insight," "inner torch," and "inner insight" in humans "here and now where there is opportunity for action and progress," names this important Qur'anic concept as "an acute sense of responsibility, here and in the hereafter" or a personal act of fear of God.[57] Therefore, *taqwa* not only means protecting oneself against sin out of a simple fear of God, but it also means to be conscious of the consequences of one's actions.

According to Nimat Hafez Barazangi,[58] in the context of modesty of women, Muslim women struggle between an "individual autonomous consciousness and its balance with social heteronymous action (socially imposed norms), while seeking equilibrium with Allah's guidance (*taqwa*)." Barazangi argues that patriarchal interpretations of *taqwa* as a God-fearing character or piety excludes Muslim women from active participation in the construction of Islamic knowledge and idealization of problems. These patriarchal readings of key Islamic sources presented the Qur'anic examples for women, such as Maryam and the pharaoh's wife, "as the silent pious, the pure, the virgin, and so on"[59] and as ideal spiritual women or archetypes. Islamic psychotherapy should tackle the "ideal" image of Muslim women as obedient and silent in the context of domestic violence.

Thus, the principle of modesty is bound to specific historical, cultural, and social factors. The Sufi tradition, particularly the ideas of Ibn al-'Arabi "provides a model of engagement between ontology, law and gender ethics"[60] and address these factors cited above. Therefore, even a more thorough and deep analysis of the Islamic jurisprudence is not adequate without using the Sufi concept of the nature of human being and purpose and gender differences assumed within the traditional *fiqh* discourse. It is not an argument whether *fiqh* has dominance over Sufism but Sufism provides an ontological ground for reshaping gender ethics in emerging feminist discourse.[61] Therefore, in addition to using Shari ‘ah and its family law, Muslim psychotherapists can also apply other aspects of the Islamic tradition to address Noor's sense of shame and normalize her feelings associated with it.[62]

Honour and Shame in the Social Science Literature

The discussion of the honour violence should be integrated to our wider inquiry in the social sciences to understand specific issues for the Muslim women face in the context of domestic violence. In this section, I introduce the definition of honour violence, the causes of honour violence against women and its impact on the health of women. Nevertheless, it is also important to note here that although there is no "honour" in any violence, the term used in this section is helpful to highlight the cultural understanding of the issue as its application provides a common language to engage a wide range of views and perspectives. I specifically argue that so-called honour violence makes domestic violence against Muslim women harsh. In addition, women feeling shame for dishonouring their husbands and families makes many honour violence crimes unreported.

There are some debates around whether the issue of honour violence should be considered as domestic. Some scholars emphasize a difference between honour violence and domestic violence. According to Phyllis Chesler,[63] there are specific differences between honour violence and domestic violence. For example, honour violence is usually committed by Muslims against Muslim girls/young adult women; committed mainly by fathers against their teenage daughters and daughters in their early twenties. Wives and older-age daughters may also be victims but to a lesser extent. Honour violence includes these features:

- The planning and execution involve multiple family members and can include mothers, sisters, brothers, male cousins, uncles, grandfathers, and so forth.
- If the girl escapes, the extended family will continue to search for her to kill her.
- It is carefully planned.
- Death threats are often used as a means of control.
- The reason given for the honour violence is that the girl or young woman has "dishonoured" the family.
- The murderer(s) do not show remorse. Instead, they experience themselves as "victims," defending themselves from the girl's actions and trying to restore their lost family honour, and so forth.

Chesler argues that domestic violence is committed by men of all faiths usually against adult women; committed by an adult male spouse against an adult female spouse or intimate partner; the murder is often unplanned and spontaneous; the batterer-murderer does not claim any family concept of "honour"; the reasons may range from a poorly cooked meal to suspected infidelity to the woman's trying to protect the children from his abuse or turning to the authorities for help; the batterer-murderer is seen as a criminal; no one defends him as a hero. Such men are often viewed as sociopaths, mentally ill, or evil.

However, Chesler's differentiation of honour violence from domestic violence ignores the overlaps between these specific features of honour violence and domestic violence. Several studies suggest that non-Muslims in the Middle East and some non-Muslim families from the Middle East and India may commit this crime in the context of domestic violence. It might be true that in honour violence multiple family members are involved; therefore, in many domestic violence cases, the wife might be subject to violence not only by her husband but also by the members of his family; or the husband might maltreat his wife because of the accusations of his family members, i.e., his mother, sister, father, and so forth.

In addition, the concept of honour is one of the reasons why many Muslim women do not report the violence they face in the hands of their husbands. Nevertheless, Chesler is right when she states that a proper religious education is necessary to combat honour violence because many perpetrators understand Islam incorrectly, "either for malicious reasons or simply because they are ignorant of more tolerant Muslim exegesis or conflate local customs with religion."[64] Further, the response to honour violence as one aspect of domestic violence should be treated not only within the context of religious, national laws but also within the framework of universal values.[65]

The literature draws attention to the effects of the honour violence on the mental, emotional, and physical health of women. In the counselling literature, the culture of "honour," "shame," and "guilt" is also related to many physical and psychological health issues, specifically trauma. In one of the recent contributions to the relationship between violence and shame, Devona Gruber, Lauren Hansen, Katrina Soaper, Aaron J. Kivisto,[66] point out that shame is one of the consequences of violence victimization, which suggests a more complex, bidirectional, and interactive relationship between the two. In addition, shame leads to the development of various mental and emotional health issues such as mood and anxiety symptoms. The shame-prone individuals usually display maladaptive efforts to manage this unpleasant emotion through anger. For example, in the case of male perpetrators of domestic violence, shame is expressed in anger because it is highly related to the pain of "being exposed, uncovered, unprotected, vulnerable."[67] Shame is a painful mental feeling aroused in the context of social relationships and human's self-reflective tendencies that dictate a sense of having done something wrong or dishonourable or improper.[68]

The literature differentiates between three forms of shame: (1) shame anxiety, (2) being ashamed, and (3) the sense of shame. *Shame anxiety* is a painful affective state which is expressed in reaction to sudden exposure, especially in the face of the threat of contemptuous rejection. The feeling of *being shamed* is a complex affective and cognitive pattern in reaction to disgrace shame or shame about. The *sense of shame* is a motive of behaviour: it is a sense that adapts and/or restrains certain actions/behaviours by making the person to have a sense of modesty, reticence, or tact.[69] A wide range of responses is expected from people who are subject to the feeling of shame or the threat being exposed. For example, men who are violent can be more aggressive when they are ashamed.[70] However, people with less power such as women or people with mental health disorders tend to display sad mood, social isolation, and tendencies toward self-blame when they are ashamed especially in cases of hospitalization, ruined relationships, and financial loss.[71]

The men's aggressiveness when they are ashamed is also explained with respect to their strong feelings about their rights in the context of power and domination. In her *The Bonds of Love*, Jessica Benjamin uses psychoanalytic theory to explain that men's aggressiveness is not because of inherent and innate aggressive instinct or drive as suggested by Freud but because of domination which she interprets as "the psychological inevitability" that "can now be seen as the result of a complex process of psychic development and not as "bedrock."[72] She suggests a deeper symmetry that characterizes power relations and in which "the genesis of the psychic structure in which one person plays subject and the other must serve as his object."[73] This dualism starts from "the earliest awareness of the difference between mother and father to the global images of male and female in the culture."[74] Such a view of domination and power has a significant impact on the psyche of real relationships: if the relationships are healthy then both attunement and separateness (also reciprocity and love) are the result without domination or submission; however, if it is not then, the relationship rejects a continuing dialectic between self-assertion and recognition of the other's sovereignty. Healthy relationships begin with acknowledgment of recognizing shared responsibilities and the projection of shame on each other, men on women. For this purpose, both men and women must engage in "the double task of recognition" which refers to knowing one's own subjectivity and recognizing the other's. Although she rejects the patriarchal views in Freudian psychoanalysis (the male mastery and female submission), Benjamin argues that men's desire to dominate "begins with the attempt to deny dependency"[75] that leads to multiple problems such as shame, anxiety, and aggressiveness. This is especially problematic in cultures where masculine values are idealized and feminine values are seen as lower. For example, in the Western culture, dependency on the husband might be deeply feared and stigmatized; whereas, in the collectivist cultures, independence of women might be seen as a danger to male power, which makes it impossible for them to establish a healthy relationship based on a direct recognition and care for each others' needs. In these situations, men's loss of absolute control over women and children exposes "the vulnerable core of male individuality, the failure of recognition which previously wore the cloak of power, responsibility, and family honor."[76] Therefore, at the core of the problem or discontent is not repression or narcissism, but gender polarity that produces shame, fear, anxiety, and violence. The solution to the problem then is to accept and transform the experience of complementarity from being one of shameful participation in domination to a creative working with an opportunity.

Although Benjamin states that feminism "has opened up a new possibility of mutual recognition between men and women,"[77] she does not fully pay attention to the vulnerability of women, including its impact of women's health, because she accepts the notion of a fundamental tension between the men and women to be normal. For her, this kind of tension is a foundation for pleasure in being with the other without telling the pathology of love in the case of unbalanced exercises of power in the context of domestic violence. Therefore, I find Pamela White-Cooper's analysis of domestic violence relevant here. White-Cooper explores the subject not only from the framework of pastoral theology, but she uses the wisdom from psychoanalytic theory to highlight the impact of domination and power on women's status and health. In the case of shame that women experience, she argues that shame is interpreted as "rejection, humiliation, allowing one's boundaries to be infringed, or violation of a social norm."[78] She argues that women who are forced to shame or guilt-provoking experiences might also experience existential shame and class shame.[79] The women's existential shame arises from her vulnerability and suppressing her self-awareness about herself and the world around her; however, her class shame is the result of "the self-internalized oppression and self-blame based on racial, class, gender, or other social oppression."[80]

Noor has experienced existential and class shame in two phases. In the first phase, the "cognitive phase," she became aware of shame which took place in eight different themes or meanings:

1. matters of size, shape, ability, skill (she believed that she was not competent in dealing with violence herself);
2. dependence/independence (she depended on her family to stop the violence and felt that she was helpless without their aid);
3. competition (she felt that she was the loser in her struggle against domestic violence);
4. sense of self (she felt that as a woman she was defective);
5. personal attractiveness (she blamed herself for not being attractive and lovely enough);
6. sexuality (she thought that there was something wrong with her sexually);
7. issues of seeing and being seen (she tried to escape from her husband; otherwise, it provoked violence against her); and
8. wishes and fear about closeness (because of her fear, she did not want to be intimate and close to her husband).

In the second phase or the decision phase, Noor made a choice to adjust by either trying to alter her self-view and repair or reframe her identity in conformation with her husband's or family's desired image of a Muslim woman. Women in this phase also become defensive which usually takes four forms:

1. withdrawal (becoming mute or stopping complaining about their experience);
2. attacking oneself (blaming herself and promising to be "good");
3. avoidance (self-medicating or distracting self via unhealthy ways of coping, such as drugs, alcohol, and so forth, in order to reduce or avoid shame); or
4. attacking the other (the one who causes physical or sexual abuse, contempt, character assassination, put-downs).

In the second phase, Noor experienced the third and second forms as she tried not to complain about violence to her family and blamed herself for her husband's attitudes.

This case study also reveals the importance of family support in the lives of women who feel shame in the context of domestic violence. The strong family and friends are one of the most important sources of well-being of women who are subject to domestic violence.[81] They can provide a safe space for women by providing them and their children with a temporary shelter, keeping their belongings and important documents, and/or providing them with cars and cell phones, and so forth. Such families provide women with initial and ongoing support in crucial times. In addition, such family support provides women with comfort and a sense of safety. Women who do not have this kind of support are more exposed to dangers and obstacles. To strip them of this support, the violent partners try everything to cut their relationships with friends and family members.

Noor might have also benefitted from family support when the violence became severe and unmanageable. However, Noor's family played a negative role in her attempt to resist domestic violence. She did not directly go to the family because of the fear that she would be labelled as dishonouring them. In many cases, some women do not seek out support from their families with concern that their husbands would easily be able to locate them even though the family's support might give the women inner strength and reduce stress.

Nevertheless, the patterns of asking for help are strongly influenced by attachment to traditional and cultural values. The negative aspect of family support may also imply that women may be reluctant to use other support networks. As one study states, many Muslim women still view family, individual, and mental health issues as something shameful which means they end up dealing with depression, anxiety, and psychosis, silently and "privately in the home or with the help of extended family."[82] Therefore, Muslim women who are subject to domestic violence typically look to their extended family first for assurance and guidance on how to manage their problems related to domestic violence.

A number of studies have also proved that there is a strong correlation between honour, guilt, shame, trauma, and domestic violence.[83] For example, it is well-known that shame, the frequency of threats and honour killings negatively contribute to psychological well-being of women.[84] The experience of being controlled puts women's lives at risk as they are hesitant to seek help in a timely manner, and therefore, they are more vulnerable to developing a variety of psychiatric disorders such as PTSD, depression, and anxiety.

Traumatic events also lead to moral and spiritual injuries. These injuries can be categorized into two distinct conceptual categories and are associated with complex emotional responses: "(1) moral injury by self (perpetration), which is thought to elicit feelings of guilt and shame, and (2) moral injury by others (betrayal), which evokes anger and frustration."[85] For example, moral and spiritual injuries may result because of a transgression (an act of commission) or failing to prevent or intervene (acts of omission), gross violations of moral standards, ethical alternatives, and prescribed roles. In Noor's case, she experienced intense guilt as she struggled with what she or her family believed and what should have been done to make the relationship work. She finds herself in a dilemma: on the one hand, she regrets seeking her rights as it caused more marital problems, but on the other hand, she wants to know her rights under the Islamic Family Law. Moral injuries may also be result of betrayals by the social environment, i.e., peers, people in authority, and so forth. For example, Noor felt betrayed by her husband and family for not protecting her, and even forcing her to live in a dangerous family situation. Her experience of betrayal by her family was particularly damaging to her understanding of trust which is a very critical feeling for survival in the context of domestic violence. All these feelings and experiences "evoke guilt, shame, and potentially incapacitating self-blame."[86] Such an internalized shame, moral, and spiritual injury threatened Noor's psychological well-being and without therapeutic intervention had a potential to cause self-loathing and self-punishing behaviours (e.g., suicidal behaviours, substance abuse, and recklessness).

Nevertheless, despite the damage caused by moral and spiritual injuries, it is still not known how these injuries relate to mental health in general and mental disorders specifically. These injuries are usually associated with significant distress and impairment, but not presented as a mental disorder. However, it is generally accepted that these injuries are psychologically unhealthy mental states that cause haunting memories that evoke self-condemnation and aversive emotions (e.g., anxiety about potential social censure, shame, and dysphoria), leading to avoidance, emotional numbing, and social isolation. People who experience these injuries tend to distance themselves from others or the environment to prevent rejection. However, they may not be that successful to deal with internal feelings such as depression, anxiety, shame, and guilt feelings, and further, they also yearn for unconditional love and life affirmation. In some cases, morally and spiritually injurious events can also exacerbate PTSD, anxiety, and depression. These people may also question their religious and spiritual identities and their attempt to find meaning in their experiences may diminish their sense of the power that further exacerbates their feelings of frustration and anger.

Interventions to Address Honour and Shame

In Islamic psychotherapy, addressing honour-related problems requires a sensitive approach. Therefore, the assessment process with Noor should start with reviewing and assessing family and cultural norms, how they extensively influence/d her, and how her family perceives and responds to domestic violence. For example, in families that highly value female submission to male authority, a woman who has been assaulted may often be blamed or stigmatized for being disobedient that caused "disciplinary action" by her partner. In some cases, family members may reject women who use various support networks other than the family. Similarly, in some cultures women's openness to complain about the violence in the family is not welcomed; therefore, disclosure regarding domestic violence is perceived as a "threat" against cultural and family taboos. Such norms prevent women from revealing domestic violence incidents for fear of being rejected, isolated, or humiliated. In these families, silence of women often becomes a habit for self-protection and further victimization. Therefore, some scholars recommended three consecutive steps such as:

> (i) creation of a refuge where their secret can be safely disclosed, (ii) risk assessment consisting of assessing the degree of the young women's anxiety, the risk of disclosure of the secret and the risk of repercussions if the secret is disclosed and (iii) worry-reducing measures, which may take the form of four different strategies: empowerment, keeping the secret, mediation and secondary prevention, depending on the result of the worry analyses.[87]

In this regard, empowerment of women in Islamic psychotherapy is very important in helping them deconstruct and reconstruct the narratives of honour and shame to create meaning in their lives.

Also, since there is a strong relationship between PTSD and the experience of honour and shame,[88] trauma work is also essential in providing care for women who have been subjected to domestic violence.[89] Trauma in domestic violence includes various forms of individual, family, social, and community violence, including trauma because of physical, sexual, or psychological abuse in an intimate relationship. However, the literature also identifies the importance of extending the scope of trauma and describing it in the context of poverty, physical health issues, and discrimination related to immigration, race/ethnicity, homophobia, or disability concerns.[90] Such an approach encourages multisystem advocacy and culturally responsive services as well as individual healing to address systemic challenges that Muslim women face when they deal with domestic violence.

Further, since Noor comes from collectivistic culture, for her the attempt to reveal the "family secret" about the violence in the family is a tremendously heavy burden and trauma on her shoulders. Dwairi brings to light the consequences of the involvement of state enforcement institutions and suggests a sensitive approach to domestic violence issues. He states that an abused partner who seeks help outside the family and community support (i.e., the police) may face additional challenges. The violent partner may become more defensive, or the community may see that person as a victim and the violated wife as the abuser in the eyes of her community. The result will end with more victimization of the violated wife.[91] The impact of trauma will be even more devastating if these women find out that what they go through is domestic violence that threatens their and their children's well-being.

Therefore, the Muslim psychotherapist should not only ask the question "What happened to you?" but also "Who are you?" with an emphasis on Noor's identity, strengths, and context. Such approach to psychotherapy will demonstrate the counsellor's ability of cultural competence and to contextualize the problem as we will highlight more in the chapter *Future Recommendations*. However, it is helpful to mention here that cultural competence is an essential and fundamental value of trauma-informed practice.[92] An effective application of trauma-focused treatments in counselling should also target reducing feelings of guilt and shame by "*contextualizing* the moral and spiritual injury events to elicit possible explanatory contextual factors through nondirective post-exposure reflective listening or a specific focus on cognitive restructuring skills."[93] During the application of contextualizing, the goal is to help the client differentiate her past behaviour from her present identity. Reframing women's feelings of shame might be deconstructed through meaning-making to process post-exposure or cognitive restructuring.

Further, Noor's exposure to multiple trauma experiences because of domestic violence, she might be at greater risk of developing Post-Traumatic Stress Disorder (PTSD). The Muslim counsellor might also consider using Rapid Eye Movement Desensitization Reprocessing (EMDR) treatment, which has been found to be especially helpful for female survivors of sexual abuse who are coping with symptoms of complex PTSD. Integrating EMDR into other therapeutic techniques is possible as such a practice is not strange: the founder of the EMDR therapy F. Shapiro and many psychotherapists indeed prefer to incorporate EMDR into their existing modalities rather than practicing EMDR alone.[94]

As "an interactive, intrapsychic, cognitive, behavioural, body-oriented therapy" EMDR targets "to rapidly metabolize the dysfunctional residue from the past and transform it into something useful."[95] During at least six 90-minute individual therapy sessions through the interventions such as visualization, guided imagery, and hypnosis, EMDR proved to be helpful in reducing trauma-specific anxiety, trauma-specific post-traumatic stress, depression, and negative beliefs.[96] In the initial EMDR session with Noor, a Muslim counsellor should get a detailed narrative description of the traumatic episodes, including information about the features of the traumatic event, date and location of the stressor(s), and names of individuals who witnessed or were involved in the traumatic incident. Further, the assessment should include details about Noor's subjective emotional reaction and behavioural response during and after the trauma; her view of perceived consequences of the traumatic event, including abrupt changes in behaviour, adjustment, and well-being; and whether Noor attended other healthcare facilities for PTSD treatment, where her trauma-related injuries might be assessed. A thorough assessment of the problem will allow the Muslim counsellor to develop a care plan to define the specific targets on which to apply EMDR. For this purpose, the Muslim counsellor can use the Posttraumatic Stress Disorder Checklist (PCL-C) tool as an effective measurement tool for symptoms of PTSD and measure current PTSD status. This tool allows the Muslim counsellor to measure the frequency and intensity of distress associated with PDST symptoms, such as the occurrence of flashbacks, unpleasant dreams about the event.

With its unusual use of eye movements, EMDR can be unique and one of the most successful therapy treatment models with Noor to address a range of problems, which Noor presented, including panic disorder, somatic disorders, chronic depression, obsessive-compulsive disorder, anxiety disorder, traumatic memories, and so forth. Although EMDR borrows elements from cognitive-behavioural therapies, it is not a theory-driven intervention. EMDR therapists usually speculate that the nature of the problem of PTSD is the unprocessed and blocked memories or information of trauma, which leads to the development of pathologies. Therefore, the goal of the therapy is to overcome blocked neural patterns, mimicking REM sleep, and reciprocal inhibition.[97] By applying accelerated information processing, EMDR therapists consider it important to work with "parts" of the personality. For this purpose, he/she first integrates ego-state therapy of a psychodynamic approach to resolving conflicts between the various ego states existing within the individual and then aims to attain unity of the ego and not uniformity of the various ego states.[98]

Although EMDR can be an effective treatment for Noor struggling with symptoms of PTSD, there is also a risk of inadvertently re-traumatizing Noor as she addresses her post-trauma symptoms. Further, there are cultural factors to consider. Although the PCL-C can be administered in many languages, all assessment tools developed can be biased. Even though most counsellors try to be culturally sensitive and inclusive, there are always "blind spots" that could go undetected. We have explored that such a sensitive approach is important because we already know that Noor wants to use folk healing and prophetic medicine for physical, mental, emotional, and spiritual distress, and illness. Therefore, exploring culturally appropriate and beneficial interventions can be integrated into Islamic psychotherapy to help Noor live transcendence and mystery to reach the highest levels of imagination. Although the Muslim psychotherapist also needs to pay attention to which aspects of the Islamic tradition hold the most benefits for their well-being and improve spiritual distress due to their feelings of shame and guilt, using spiritual interventions based on the teachings of Islam could be potentially beneficial for Noor.

Further, the Muslim counsellor should also consider that the traditional PTSD treatment may not be effective with survivors of the traumatic event, including the women who experience shame and guilt due to "honour" culture in their cultures.[99] In the traditional PTSD treatment, the individual is encouraged to remember and discuss the details of the original trauma with the therapist. Therefore, a traditional approach to trauma work during individual or group sessions may adversely affect the mental and emotional health of the survivor.[100] There are times that the ability to forget versus inability to forget is a gift that helps people to move on because it enables them to overcome difficult and painful losses. Otherwise, the victims might become hypersensitive to their symptoms and become too disabled to move on.

Conclusion

The Muslim psychotherapist should consider the fact that women who want to leave the violent relationship are in the most dangerous stage of their relationships.[101] It is important to determine whether women stay or return to a violent relationship either because they want to survive the threats or they have limited resources available to protect their and their loved ones' safety. The general recommendations for sensitive support for these women require a tremendous amount of patience and cultural knowledge. General questions about the family life and decision-making process in the family may help professionals to have a certain picture about the status of women in the family. Socio-cultural factors should also be considered how they influence women's responses and willingness to disclose violence against them. However, one also needs to be aware of biases and stereotypes to avoid making faulty conclusions. Building rapport and trust before making a thorough assessment and clinical intervention is important. Specific situations may also prevent women from coming forward. For example, some of them may fear or distrust of officials, including police and doctors. They may refuse to sign forms, even confidentiality forms or consent for treatment, or disclose personal and family details, i.e., the name of their partners, their addresses, and so forth. Nevertheless, these women who lose family support may also be empowered by being connected to other services, resources, and support networks. These resources and support networks include domestic violence programmes that provide legal advice, referrals to legal resources, crisis intervention, financial assistance, individual and family counselling, premarital counselling, imam counselling, support groups, and job placement.[102]

Notes

1. See Barbara Lois Helms, "Honour and Shame in the Canadian Muslim Community: Developing Culturally Sensitive Counselling Interventions/Honneur et honte dans la communauté musulmane au Canada: Élaborer des modes d'intervention et de counseling tenant compte des cultures," *Canadian Journal of Counselling and Psychotherapy* 49 (2) (2015): 163–184.
2. > Men are the protectors and maintainers of women, because Allah has given the one more (strength) than the other, and because they support them from their means. Therefore, the righteous women are devoutly obedient, and guard in (the husband's) absence what Allah would have them guard. As to those women on whose part ye fear disloyalty and ill-conduct, admonish them (first), (Next), refuse to share their beds, (And last) beat them (lightly); but if they return to obedience, seek not against them Means (of annoyance): For Allah is Most High, great (above you all).
   >
   > (Q. 4:34)
3. Islamic Family Law is defined as

   > those laws upon which the Muslim family is founded and which govern the relationship among its members. It includes laws relating to marriage, to the rights of children and relatives, and to the finances of the family, including expenses, the distribution of inheritances, bequests, waqfs, and related matters.

   See Muhammad Abu Zahra, cited by Lynn Welchman, "Qiwamah and Wilyah as Legal Postulates in Muslim Family Laws," in *Men in Charge: Rethinking Authority in Muslim Legal Tradition*, ed. by Ziba Mir-Hosseini, Mulki Al-Sharmani, and Jana Rumminger (London: Oneworld Publications, 2015), 150. Also see Abdullahi Ahmed An-Na'im, "Shari'a and Islamic Family Law: Transition and Transformation," *Ahfad Journal* 23 (2) (2006): 2–30.
4. Lois Helms, "Honour and Shame in the Canadian Muslim Community," 164; Olubunmu Basirat Oyewuwo-Gassikia, "American Muslim Women and Domestic Violence Service Seeking," *Affilia*, 31 (4) (2016): 450; D. Hassouneh-Phillips, "American Muslim Women's Experiences of Leaving Abusive Relationships," *Health Care for Women International* 22 (2001): 415–432; Dena Saadat Hassouneh-Phillips, "'Marriage Is Half of Faith and the Rest Is Fear Allah': Marriage and Spousal Abuse Among American Muslims," *Violence Against Women* 7 (2001): 927–946; Dena Saadat Hassouneh-Phillips, "Strength and Vulnerability: Spirituality in Abused American Muslim Women's Lives," *Issues in Mental Health Nursing* 24 (2003): 681–694.
5. Helms, "Honour and Shame in the Canadian Muslim Community," 164.
6. See Rana Husseini, "Honor Killings," in *The Oxford Encyclopedia of Islam and Women*. Accessed on December 23, 2016 from www.oxfordislamicstudies.com.myaccess.library.utoronto.ca/article/opr/t355/e0130.
7. Islamic Family Law is that part of Shari'ah that regulates family relations, including marriage, divorce, custody, spousal support, etc. It is also called *Shari'at al 'ahwal al-shakhsiyah* (Muslim Personal Status Law). See An-Na'im, "Shari'a and Islamic Family Law," 2–30. It is generally accepted that the Islamic Family Law is the most developed area of Shari 'ah but was formed under the highest monopoly of the

traditional, patriarchal Muslim scholars who regulated the law and assumed that the family issues were the private matters of religion. Since the 19th century, Muslim reformers, such as Muhammad Abduh and Jamaluddin al-Afghani, initiated a call to reform the Shari 'ah, including the codification of the Islamic Family Law in several Muslim countries, i.e., Egypt, Jordan, and Morocco. See Ramadan, *Radical Reform*, 13, 24. Also see Valentine M. Moghadam, *Modernizing Women, Gender and Social Change in the Middle East* (Boulder, CO: Lynne Rienner Publishers, 1993); Ziba Mir-Hosseini, *Marriage on Trial: A Study of Islamic Family Law: Iran and Morocco Compared* (London: I. B. Tauris, 1993); Essam Fawzy, "Muslim Personal Status Law in Egypt: The Current Situation and Possibilities of Reform Through Internal Initiatives," in *Women's Rights & Islamic Family Law: Perspectives on Reform*, ed. by Lynn Welchman (London: Zed Books, 2004), 15–17; Fatima Z. Rahman, "Gender Equality in Muslim-Majority States and Shari'a Family Law: Is There a Link?" *Australian Journal of Political Science* 47 (3) (2012): 347–362.

8. Among Muslim countries, Tunisia carried out major reforms of the Islamic Family Law in 1957 and 1993; whereas, Morocco made only superficial reforms in 1993. It is also worth mentioning that the Islamic Family Law in the Muslim-majority states incorporate laws based on the predominant school of law in the state. For example, the Hanafi School is predominant in South Asia, the Levant, the Balkans, Turkey, and Egypt; while the Maliki School predominates in North Africa (except for Egypt), West Africa, and Kuwait. The Shafi 'i School is the main school of law in Southeast Asia, Somalia, and Yemen. However, the Hanbali School is more predominant in Saudi Arabia and Qatar. Following the changes to the Islamic Family Law, there were substantial differences between Tunisia and Morocco in fertility rates and gender equality outcomes.
9. Raihanah Abdullah, Taslima Monsoor, Fuadah Johari, and Wirdati Mohd Radzi, "Financial Support for Women Under Islamic Family Law in Bangladesh and Malaysia," *Asian Journal of Women's Studies* 21 (4) (2015): 363–383. doi:10.1080/12259276.2015.1106853.
10. Zainab Alwani, "The Qur'anic Model for Harmony in Family Relationships," in *Change From Within: Diverse Perspectives on Domestic Violence in Muslim Communities*, ed. by Maha B. Alkhateeb and Salma Elkadi Abugideiri (Great Falls, VA: The Peaceful Families Project, 2007), 33–66.
11. See Hallaq, *Sharī'a*, 62.
12. Therefore, the Muslim judges who interpreted the Islamic law in the court process

    > mediated dialectic between, on the one hand, the social and moral imperatives – of which he was an integral part – and, on the other, the demands of legal doctrine which in turn recognized the supremacy of the unwritten codes of morality and morally grounded social relations.
    >
    > (ibid., 62)

13. The main classical objectives in Shari 'ah include: "(1) protection of al-din [religion]; (2) protection of life (al-nafs); (3) protection of dignity or lineage (al-'ird); (4) protection of intellect (al-'aql); and (5) protection of property (al-mal)." See Afridi, "Maqasid al-Shari'ah and Preservation of Basic Rights," 275–285; Hallaq, *Sharī'a*, 65.
14. See Ramadan, *Radical Reform*, 61. In addition to these five objectives of the Shari 'ah, according to the Maliki jurist Shihab al-Din al-Qarafi (d. 1285), the sixth fundamental *maqasid* (objectives, purpose) of Shari 'ah is the protection and preservation of *'irḍ* (honour, dignity), which was approved by Taj al-Din 'Abd al-Wahhab ibn al-Subki (d. 1370) and Muhammad ibn 'Ali al-Shawkanî (1834). See Mohammad Hashim Kamali, *Maqasid al Shariah: The Objectives of Islamic Law*. Accessed on January 23, 2017 from http://islam101.net/index.php/shariah/141-maqasidalshariah.
15. Even al-Shafi 'i stated that

> if a man marries a woman on the condition that she is beautiful, young or a virgin, and he finds afterward that she is not, the marriage still takes effect, for marriage is not like a [contract of] sale, in which the buyer has an option [to return the goods].
>
> (ibid., 35)

16. Chaudhry, *Domestic Violence and the Islamic Tradition*, 98.
17. Marwa Sharafeldin, "Reformulating Qiwamah and Wilayah for Personal Status Law Reform Advocacy in Egypt," in *Men in Charge*, 172. Also see Chaudhry, *Domestic Violence and the Islamic Tradition*. For example, one of the earliest and famous eighth-century Muslim scholars Muqatil (d. 767) said that since men are *qawwamun* over women, they also have an authority to discipline them and the husbands should not be held accountable for beating them except in cases if they kill or wound them. See Muqatil, *Tafsir*, cited by Karen Bauer, *Gender Hierarchy in the Qur'an: Medieval Interpretations, Modern Responses* (New York, NY: Cambridge University Press, 2015), 171.
18. Chaudhry, *Domestic Violence and the Islamic Tradition*, 112.
19. Bauer, *Gender Hierarchy in the Qur'an*, 180.
20. Ibid., 188.
21. Ibid., 99.
22. Lynda Clarke and Pamela Cross, *Muslim & Canadian Family Law: A Comparative Primer* (Ottawa, ON: Canadian Council of Muslim Women, 2006), 14.
23. Yusuf Al-Qaradawi, *The Lawful and the Prohibited in Islam* (Al- Halal Wal-Haram fil Islam), trans. by Kamal El-Helbawy, M. Moinuddin Siddiqui and Syed Shukry (Washington, DC: American Trust Publications, 1980), 19–20. For Yusuf al-Qaradawi, the Qur'an is a primary source, for only God "has the right to make lawful or to prohibit a matter, either through His Book, or through the tongue of His Messenger." He interprets an act of rebelliousness as a wife's failure to fulfill duties of sexual satisfaction and is spiritually and legally prohibited in the Qur'an and the *hadith*; a wife's duty towards her husband is to please him and fulfill his needs any time he wishes. He states, "The man is the head of the house and of the family. He is entitled to the obedience and cooperation of his wife, and accordingly it is not permissible for her to rebel against his authority, causing disruption." Al-Qaradawi, *The Lawful and the Prohibited in Islam*, 205.
24. Al-Qaradawi, *The Lawful and the Prohibited in Islam*, 19–20. Al-Qaradawi interprets an act of rebelliousness as a wife's failure to fulfill duties of sexual satisfaction and is spiritually and legally prohibited in the Qur'an and the *hadith*; a wife's duty towards her husband is to please him and fulfill his needs any time he wishes. He states, "The man is the head of the house and of the family. He is entitled to the obedience and cooperation of his wife, and accordingly it is not permissible for her to rebel against his authority, causing disruption." Al-Qaradawi, *The Lawful and the Prohibited in Islam*, 205. Al-Qaradawi states,

> he [the husband] should try his best to rectify her attitude by kind words, gentle persuasion, and reasoning with her. If this is not helpful, he should sleep apart from her, trying to awaken her agreeable feminine nature so that serenity may be restored and she may respond to him in a harmonious fashion. If this approach fails, it is permissible for him to beat her lightly with his hands.
>
> (ibid., 205)

25. Ibid., 205.
26. Ibid., 203.
27. Al-Qaradawi, *The Lawful and the Prohibited in Islam*, 194.
28. Jamal Badawi, *Wife Beating*. Accessed from http://islamic-world.net/sister/wife_beating.htm.

29. Taha Jabir al-Alwani states that

> jurists consider the purposes of marriage when deriving rulings from these verses. The general purposes of marriage include fulfilling the conditions needed for living in tranquility and harmony, building family relationships and networks, and procreation. Application of teachings from the Qur'an must not undermine these goals. Sometimes, jurists apply the literal meaning of a verse when that meaning will achieve these goals; other times they apply the spirit of a verse if the literal meaning hinders the achievement of these goals . . . in modern societies today, the third step in the process ("beating" the wife, is not to be applied because the circumstances of today's society are different from the society in which the Qur'an was revealed. . . . Emphasis is placed on the spirit of the verse, which is the protection of the family unit from a real threat to its survival. In today's world, beating one's wife would surely lead to the very destruction of the family unit that this verse seeks to preserve.

Taha Jabir al-Alwani, cited by Salma Elkadi Abugideiri and Zainab Alwani, *What Islam Says About Domestic Violence* (Herndon, VA: FAITH, 2003), 105.

30. Bauer, *Gender Hierarchy in the Qur'an*, 165.
31. See Salma Elkadi Abugideiri, "Domestic Violence Among Muslims Seeking Mental Health Counseling," in *Change From Within*, 71.
32. Ayesha S. Chaudhry, "A Case Study of Guardianship (Wilayah) in Prophetic Practice," in *Men in Charge*, 103; Asma Lamrabet, "An Egalitarian Reading of the Concepts of Khilafah, Wilayah and Qiwamah," in *Men in Charge*, 71–77. The concepts of protection, maintenance, and governance are the key terms in the Islamic Family Law that define gender relations and rights. However, these concepts should be understood from the perspective of ethical principles. Asma Lamrabet, for example, suggests that the role of *khilafah* (vicegerent), for instance, requires the qualities such as *'ilm* (knowledge), *'adl* (justice), *'aql* (reason), *hurriyyat al-mu'taqad* (freedom of belief), *ikhtilaf* (diversity), and *mahbah* (love). See Lamrabet, "An Egalitarian Reading of the Concepts of Khilafah, Wilayah and Qiwamah," 67.
33. Lamrabet, "An Egalitarian Reading of the Concepts of Khilafah, Wilayah and Qiwamah," 72.
34. Ibid., 78–79.
35. al-Zeera, "Violence Against Women in Qur'an 4:34: A Sacred Ordinance?" 222. Due to patriarchal social pressures, the word *qiwamah*, therefore, was wrongfully translated into "authority": *qiwamah 'ammah* (the public sphere) gradually turned into political autocracy and *qiwamah khassah* (the private sphere) into husband's authority which both were accepted as a sacred order. Therefore, the real and authentic meaning of *qiwamah* means the husband's "moral and material responsibility of providing for the needs of his wife and family." Ibid., 82.
36. Ibid., 83, 85.
37. Brad Archer, "Family Law Reform and the Feminist Debate: Actually-Existing Islamic Feminism in the Maghreb and Malaysia," *Journal of International Women's Studies* 8 (4) (2007): 49–59.
38. This publication arose in response to a three-year long controversial debate that focused on the application of religious laws in family matters in Ontario. It helps clarify confusion and misconceptions about Islamic law and examines the position of Muslim women vis-à-vis Islamic classical jurisprudence, tackling especially contentious subjects such as the abuse of women that arises because of interpretations of an act of rebelliousness of a disobedient wife. In addition, CCMW also provided a brief guide to the Canadian laws to help Muslim women be aware of the various strategies for mitigating domestic violence. This guide helps Muslim women compare the Islamic Family Law with the Canadian laws. See Lynda Clarke and Pamela

Cross, *Muslim & Canadian Family Law: A Comparative Primer* (Canada: Canadian Council of Muslim Women, 2006); Pamela Cross, *Violence Against Women: Health and Justice for Canadian Muslim Women* (Ottawa: CCMW, 2013).

39. For example, *Islamic Marriage Contracts* is a resource guide for legal professionals, advocates, imams, and communities. Marwa Zeini, "A Legal Guide to Marriage and Divorce for the American Muslim Women," in *Change From Within*, 203.
40. Maha B. Alkhateeb, *Islamic Marriage Contracts*" (Great Falls: The Peaceful Families Project, 2012), , 29.
41. Clarke and Cross, *Muslim & Canadian Family Law*, 108.
42. Ibid., 99.
43. Alkhateeb, *Islamic Marriage Contracts*, 30.
44. In this regard, Mohammed Baobid states that Muslim women who seek help face four dilemmas: (1) the high price they must pay for revealing the secret of abuse, because of the collectivist nature of their community; (2) the pressure they will feel if the service provider insists on a focus of gender inequality rather than a focus on treating the violence; (3) the lack of support from mainstream service providers for women's self-determined goals, which may include a goal for them to stay in their home or community; and (4) being challenged by the service provider in their belief that they are partially responsible for the violence against them. See Mohammed Baobid, "Guidelines for Service Providers: Outreach Strategies for Family Violence Intervention with Immigrant and Minority Communities: Lessons Learned from the Muslim Family Safety Project," *The Centre for Children and Families in the Justice System*, 32. Accessed on January 10, 2017 from www.lfcc.on.ca/MFSP_Guidelines.pdf.
45. In this regard, Chaudhry proposes an egalitarian cosmology that is both progressive and emancipatory. According to Chaudhry, "modern rhetorical overtures to the 'Islamic tradition' are tempered by the historical, emotional, and psychological experiences of colonialism." See Chaudhry, *Domestic Violence and Islamic Tradition*, 7. Clearly, any discussion of the Islamic legal tradition on domestic violence in Muslim families is complex and highly dependent on differing – and often opposing – values (traditional, egalitarian/reformative, or Western, for instance). On one end of the spectrum, idealists maintain that the Islamic legal tradition provides an appropriate response to every aspect of life; by contrast, Muslim feminist scholars argue that it discriminates against women.
46. Alwani, "The Qur'anic Model for Harmony in Family Relations," 59; Keilani Abdullah, "A Peaceful Ideal, Violent Realities: A Study on Muslim Female Domestic Violence Survivors," in *Change From Within*, 71.
47. Alwani, "The Qur'anic Model for Harmony in Family Relations," 59. In this respect, Keilani Abdullah says, "with the implementation of *li'an* a woman is not at the mercy of her husband's word, whether true or not, that would have otherwise overridden hers in a patriarchal society." Abdullah, "A Peaceful Ideal, Violent Realities: A Study on Muslim Female Domestic Violence Survivors," 71.
48. See Martin Lau, "Honour, Crimes, Paradigms and Violence Against Women," *Yearbook of Islamic and Middle Eastern Law Online* 11 (1) (2004): 471–472; Azman Mohd Noor, "Rape: A Problem of Crime Classification in Islamic Law," *Arab Law Quarterly* 24 (4) (2010): 417–438; Pascale Fournier, "Introduction: Honour Crimes and the Law – Public Policy in an Age of Globalization," *Canadian Criminal Law Review* 16 (2) (2012): 103–115.
49. Abdullah, "A Peaceful Ideal, Violent Realities: A Study on Muslim Female Domestic Violence Survivors," 83.
50. For example, Sheikh Atiyyah Saqr, former head of the al-Azhar University Fatwa Committee, issued a legal ruling in which he stated that Islam strictly prohibits murder and killing without legal justification. He also stated that the so-called honour crimes are based on ignorance and disregard of morals and laws. Saqr suggests

that this kind of crime cannot be abolished except by disciplinary punishments. Kroslak Daniel, "Honor Killings and Cultural Defense (with a Special Focus on Germany)," *Mil'niky Práva v Stredoeurópskom Priestore* (June 19, 2009); Islamic Law and Law of the Muslim World Paper No. 09–71. Accessed on December 21, 2016 from http://ssrn.com/abstract=1422503.

51. Helms, "Honour and Shame in the Canadian Muslim Community," 165.
52. Nasir, "Globalization, Health and Culture."
53. Helms, "Honour and Shame in the Canadian Muslim Community," 166.
54. Amnesty International, *Pakistan: Violence Against Women in the Name of Honour* (AI Index: ASA 33/17/99 1999).
55. Suzanne Ruggi, "Commodifying Honor in Female Sexuality: Honor Killings in Palestine," *Middle East Research and Information Project*. Accessed on October 20, 2016 from www.merip.org/mer/mer206/ruggi.htm. Also see Dwairy, "The Arab/Muslim Culture"; Keshavarzi and Haque, "Outlining a Psychotherapy Model for Enhancing Muslim Mental Health Within an Islamic Context," *The International Journal for the Psychology of Religion* 23 (2013): 230–249; Abugideiri, "Domestic Violence"; Baobaid and Hamed, *Addressing Domestic Violence in Canadian Muslim Communities*; Sana al-Khayyat, *Honour and Shame: Women in Modern Iraq* (London: Saqi, 1992); Aylin Akpinar, *Male's Honour and Female's Shame: Gender and Ethnic Identity Constructions Among Turkish Divorcees in the Migration* (Uppsala, Sweden: Dept. of Sociology, Uppsala University, 1998).
56. The word *taqwa* is usually translated as "piety," "fear of God" in the context of its root word that means "to protect from getting lost or wasted" and "to guard against peril."
57. For Rahman, *taqwa* is a central concept of Islam similar to the concept of love in Christianity in the context of human response to the ultimate reality. Also, he points out that "When a man or a society is fully conscious of this while conducting himself or itself, he or it has true *taqwa*. This idea can be effectively conveyed by the term 'conscience,' if the object of conscience transcends it." Rahman, *Major Themes of the Qur'an*, 29. According to Abdel Haleem, the root word of *taqwa* is w q y and in the Qur'an, it refers to "mindfulness." See Muhammad A. S. Haleem, *The Qur'an* (New York, NY: Oxford University Press, 2008). Accessed on January 23, 2017 from https://archive.org/stream/TheQuranKoranenglishEbook-AbdelHaleem-BestTranslationInThe/the_QURAN-abdel-haleem-ebook-english_djvu.txt.
58. Barazangi, *Woman's Identity and the Qur'an*, 6.
59. Ibid., 40.
60. Sa'diyya Shaikh, "Search of al-Insan: Sufism, Islamic Law, and Gender," in *Muslima Theology*, 273. Nevertheless, a feminist reading of the past may produce "the methodological spectrum of anachronism" and one may question whether such a reading is a right approach to the past from the perspective of contemporary lens to patriarchy, feminism, or gender equality. To resolve the dilemma, Sa'diyya Shaikh uses Rita Gross's concept of a "usable past," especially regarding Sufism. Along with using a feminist and egalitarian perspectives, Shaikh suggests applying Sufi discourses as "substantial resources for more relevant, enriching and benevolent interpretations of the *Shari 'ah* and the related understandings of human nature reflected in the Quran than do the prevailing *fiqh* discourses." Ibid., 107.
61. Shaikh argues that Sufi concepts presented by great Sufi thinkers such as Rabia al-Adawiyya (d. 801), Muhydi al-Din Ibn al-Arabi (d. 1240), and so forth, reject any other authority except God's absolute sovereignty and counters the idea of power over the other, including "male claims to authority over women." Ibid., 117. Also see, Shaikh, *Sufi Narratives of Intimacy*.
62. For example, the problem of honour is highly correlated with the concept of *kibr*, *kibriya'*, *takabbur*, *istikbar* (arrogance and haughtiness), *mufakhara*, *tafakhur*, *munaẓara*, *munafara*, and *tafaḍul* (self-praise), and *'ujb*, *i'jab* (pride, vanity, and smugness). The

Qur'an and the *hadith* literature present these practices as the worst feature of the pre-Islamic times of ignorance: the Arab tribes used to engage in the poetical jousts of glorification to demonstrate their arrogance, glories, pride, and honour above others in terms of the worldly gains. See Q. 4:36; 40:71–75; 7:75–76; 57:23–24; 102:1; 27:27, 35; 16:29; 39:60, 39:72; 40:76; 59:23. In addition, arrogance and pride is associated with Satan and Pharaoh (Q. 2:34; 7:13; 74–76; 10:75; 23:45–46; 28:39). In his various instructions and admonitions, ʿAli b. Abi Ṭalib, the Prophet's cousin and the fourth caliph warned against behaving arrogantly and in pride. See Claude Gilliot, "Arrogance," *Encyclopedia of Islam*, 3rd ed., ed. by Kate Fleet, Gudrun Kramer, Denis Matringe, John Nawas, and Everett Rowson (Boston, MA: Brill, 2008). Accessed on January 25, 2016 from http://referenceworks.brillonline.com.myaccess.library.utoronto.ca/entries/encyclopaedia-of-islam-3/arrogance-COM_26355?s.num=0&s.f.s2_parent=s.f.book.encyclopaedia-of-islam-3&s.q=honour. Many Sufi masters also cautioned against these aspects of human nature. For example, al-Muhasibi narrated from the Prophet Muhammad that God said: "Majesty *(kibriyaʾ)* is My cloak, and grandeur *(ʿaẓama)* My girdle. Whoever contends with Me in either one of these, him shall I cast into Hell *(jahannam)*." Also, see Picken, *Spiritual Purification in Islam*. A famous Mu 'tazila theologian al-Jahiz (d. 869) devoted some of his works, e.g., *al-Nubl wa-l-tanabbul wa-ḍhamm al-kibr* (True and Affected Nobleness, and Censure of Pride), *Fakhr al-Sudān ʿala l-biḍan* (The Pride of Blacks over Whites), on differentiation between the true/acceptable pride and unacceptable pride. In al-Ghazali's *Ihya*, there is one special section devoted to this subject: *Dhamm al-kibr wa-l-ʿujb*, "Condemnation of pride and conceit." See al-Ghazali, *Revival of Religious Leaning*. In general, arrogance in the Islamic tradition is described as one of the great sins. See al-Qushayri, *The Epistle on Sufism*; Picken, *Spiritual Purification in Islam*.

63. See Phyllis Chesler, "Are Honor Killings Simply Domestic Violence?" *Middle East Quarterly* 16 (2) (2009): 61–69.
64. Ibid., 69.
65. See "Combating Patriarchal Violence Against Women – Focusing on Violence in the Name of Honor," The Swedish Ministry of Justice and the Swedish Ministry for Foreign Affairs, Stockholm, December 7–8, 2004, 51.
66. Devona Gruber, Lauren Hansen, Katrina Soaper, and Aaron J. Kivisto, "The Role of Shame in General, Intimate and Sexual Violence Perpetration," in *Psychology of Shame: New Research*, ed. by Kevin G. Lockhart (New York, NY: Nova Science), 39–62.
67. Carl D. Schneider, "Shame," in *Dictionary of Pastoral Care and Counseling*, ed. by Rodney J. Hunter (Nashville, TN: Abingdon Press, 1990), 1160–1163.
68. Stephen P. Hinshaw, *The Mark of Shame: Stigma of Mental Illness and an Agenda for Change* (Oxford: Oxford University Press, 2009), 36.
69. Ibid., 1160.
70. Gruber, Hansen, Soaper, and Kivisto, "The Role of Shame," 60.
71. Hinshaw, *The Mark of Shame*, 36.
72. Jessica Benjamin, *The Bonds of Love: Psychoanalysis, Feminism, and the Problem of Domination* (New York: Pantheon Books, 1988), 7.
73. Ibid.
74. Ibid., 114.
75. Ibid., 52.
76. Ibid., 181.
77. Ibid., 224.
78. Pamela Cooper-White, *Many Voices: Pastoral Psychotherapy in Relational and Theological Perspective* (Minneapolis, MN: Fortress Press, 2011), 116.
79. Also see Karen G. Weiss, "Too Ashamed to Report: Deconstructing the Shame of Sexual Victimisation," *Feminist Criminology* 5 (3) (2010): 286–310; Jenny Mouzos and Toni Makkai, *Women's Experiences of Male Violence: Findings From the Australian*

Component of the International Violence Against Women Survey (IVAWS) (Canberra, ACT: Canberra Australian Institute of Criminology Research and Public Policy Series, 2004).

80. Cooper-White, *Many Voices*, 116.
81. See McCue, *Domestic Violence*, 2008; See Abdul Basit and John Tuscan, "The Spiritual Dimensions of Trauma Healing," in *Religion and Psychology*, ed. by Michael T. Evans and Emma D. Walker (New York, NY: Nova Science Publishers, 2009), 70.
82. Khadija Khaja and Chelsea Frederick, "Reflection on Teaching Effective Social Work Practice for Working With Muslim Communities," *Advances in Social Work* 9 (1) (2008): 1–7.
83. See Cooper-White, *Many Voices*, 114–117. Also see J. P. Wilson, B. Drozdek, and S. Turkovic, "Post-traumatic Shame and Guilt," *Trauma, Violence and Abuse* 7 (2) (2006): 122–141.
84. See Nima Ghorbani and P J Watson, Mehdi Salimian, and Zhuo Chen, "Shame and Guilt: Relationships of Test of Self-Conscious Affect Measures With Psychological Adjustment and Gender Differences in Iran," *Interpersona* 7 (1) (2013): 97–109. doi:10.5964/ijpr.v7i1.118. UN Commission on Human Rights, *Cultural Practices in the Family That Are Violent Towards Women* (UN Doc. E/CN.4/2002/83, 2002); Bellal Joseph, Mazhar Khalil, Bardiya Zangbar, Narong Kulvatunyou, et al., "Prevalence of Domestic Violence Among Trauma Patients," *Journal of Emergency Medicine* 50 (4) (2015): 1177–1183.
85. Jennifer H. Wortmann, Alyssa Boasso, Yonit Schorr, Maria M. Steenkamp, and Brett T. Litz, "Facilitating Recovery From Moral and Spiritual Injuries," in *Handbook of Psychosocial Interventions for Veterans and Service Members: A Guide for the Non-Military Mental Health Clinician*, ed. by Nathan D. Ainspan, Craig Bryan, and Walter E. Penk (Oxford: Oxford University Press, 2016), 255.
86. Ibid., 251.
87. Venus Alizadeh, Ingrid Hylander, Tahire Kocturk, and Lena Törnkvist, "Counselling Young Immigrant Women Worried About Problems Related to the Protection of 'Family Honour' – From the Perspective of Midwives and Counsellors at Youth Health Clinics," *Scandinavian Journal of Caring Sciences* 24 (1) (2010): 34. doi:10.11 11/j.1471-6712.2009.00681. x.
88. Donald J. Robinaugh and Richard J. McNally, "Autobiographical Memory for Shame or Guilt Provoking Events: Association With Psychological Symptoms," *Behaviour Research and Therapy* 48 (7) (2010): 646–652; Sally Lakkary, Barbara Franke, Dina Shokri, Sven Hartwig, Michael Tsokos, and Klaus Püschel, "Honor Crimes: Review and Proposed Definition," *Forensic Science, Medicine, and Pathology* 10 (1) (2014): 76–82.
89. Joshua M. Wilson, Jenny E. Fauci, and Lisa A. Goodman, "Bringing Trauma-Informed Practice to Domestic Violence Programs: A Qualitative Analysis of Current Approaches," *American Journal of Orthopsychiatry* 85 (6) (2015): 586–599; Gina Dillon, et al. "Mental and Physical Health and Intimate Partner Violence Against Women: A Review of the Literature," *International Journal of Family Medicine* 2013 (2013): 313909.
90. Wilson, Fauci, and Goodman, "Bringing Trauma-Informed Practice to Domestic Violence Programs," 588.
91. Dwairi, *Counselling and Psychotherapy With Arabs and Muslims*, 118.
92. Wilson, Fauci, and Goodman, "Bringing Trauma-Informed Practice to Domestic Violence Programs," 588.
93. Wortmann, Boasso, Schorr, Steenkamp, and Litz, "Facilitating Recovery From Moral and Spiritual Injuries," 253.
94. Tonya Edmond, Allen Rubin, and Kathryn G. Wambach, "The Effectiveness of EMDR with Adult Female Survivors of Childhood Sexual Abuse," *Social Work Research* 23 (2) (1999), 114.

95. F. Shapiro, *Eye Movement Desensitization and Reprocessing: Basic Principles, Protocols, and Procedures* (New York, NY: Guilford Press, 1995), 52–53.
96. Edmond, Rubin, and Wambach, "The Effectiveness of EMDR," 113.
97. R. Greenwald, "Eye Movement Desensitization and Reprocessing (EMDR): An Overview," *Journal of Contemporary Psychotherapy* 24 (1) (1994): 15–34.
98. Paul William Miller, *EMDR Therapy for Schizophrenia and Other Psychoses* (New York, NY: Springer Publishing Company 2016), 107.
99. Cathy Cave and Terri Pease, *Culture and Inclusion Within the Context of Trauma-Informed Domestic Violence Services and Organizations* (National Center on Domestic Violence, Trauma, and Mental Health, 2013). Accessed on October 28, 2016 from www.nationalcenterdvtraumamh.org/trainingta/webinars-seminars/2013-practical-strategies-for-creating-trauma-informed-services-and-organizations.
100. Basit and Tuscan, "The Spiritual Dimensions of Trauma Healing," 66; Jill Price , *The Woman Who Can't Forget* (New York, NY: Free Press, 2008).
101. McCue, *Domestic Violence.*
102. Alkhateeb and Abugideiri, "Introduction," 9.

7 Future Recommendations

Muslim women who are victims of domestic violence often turn to Islamic psychotherapy for assistance. This assistance can either be help from the imam who provides psychotherapy or formal or informal counselling, advice and information giving, and so forth, from the sister's group in Islamic institutions, or from Muslim psychotherapists, social workers, spiritual caregivers, psychologists, and so forth. Therefore, there is a need for Islamic psychotherapy to enhance the network for Muslim women who are subject to domestic violence to break down their isolation, promote their mental and physical health, and link them with community-based agencies and available mainstream support agencies.

Domestic violence disrupts Muslim women's support networks and leaves them in social isolation. The loss of these support networks create more stress. Muslim women who are separated from their usual formal and informal support networks may have more difficulty in challenging mental, emotional, and spiritual crisis due to domestic violence. When Muslim women are able to re-establish their support network, they are better equipped to handle the crisis situations that derive from domestic violence. Support networks promote Muslim women's health by enhancing their self-esteem and buffering stress and isolation that results from domestic violence. Muslim psychotherapists must discern how to engage such diverse Muslim communities in the recovery and empowerment of Muslim women.

The help-seeking strategies which Muslim women employ depend on the availability of support within their socio-economic circumstances and the response they receive from these support networks. Their efforts to seek formal or informal support for problems related to domestic violence may be impeded by a variety of factors including: lack of immediate protection, trust, racism, Islamophobia, cultural barriers, issues with regard to confidentiality and privacy, stigma and family dynamics, lack of awareness of available sources of help, and so forth.

There are various support networks available for Muslim women who experience domestic violence. These sources can be divided into two categories: formal and mainstream supports such as shelters, medical, psychological and counselling support, legal aid, etc.; and informal or traditional supports, which include community help, traditional healing services, the extended family, and so forth. The degree of assistance varies depending on the resources available and the individual circumstances.

Regardless of the support available for Muslim women, research findings indicate that Muslim women are susceptible to being trapped in a violent relationship due to their fear and shame of using these support networks. The cultural norms and experiences influences Muslim women's behaviour in seeking support and their views about domestic violence and the problems related to it. As we have seen, in collectivistic Muslim societies, the most appropriate source of support is the family and the community; in these situations, the community – including family and friends – is obliged to assist disadvantaged members. Women from collectivistic societies may be reluctant and cautious to seek help outside these community support networks. Nevertheless, as we mentioned before, Muslim women represent a diversity within and among themselves. Any generalizations about Muslim women – even those from the same ethnic backgrounds – should be avoided. Rather than assuming that all women who come from collectivistic societies will not seek help outside their own family and community, some Muslim women adjust well to individualistic social conditions and accept outside support more freely. In other situations, Muslim women do not seek help within the family or the community for fear of being the target of a problem within the family. For many reasons, enhancing the support network for Muslim women who experience domestic violence is a vital strategy. What follows are recommendations that can be implemented within the practice of Islamic psychotherapy.

The Muslim Community

One of the emerging themes in our case studies was the community involvement in tackling domestic violence against Muslim women. Muslim women use community sources such as sister's groups, imams, etc., as alternative sources of help when they are subject to domestic violence. The Muslim community is a central concept in the lives of Muslim women, especially those who suffer from mental health problems, poverty, unemployment, stigmatization, and discrimination due to domestic violence. This fact is repeatedly referenced in our case studies. Therefore, Islamic psychotherapy should emphasize the role of the community in the recovery of people with mental health problems. Although the involvement of the Muslim community in Islamic psychotherapy is complex, at the same time it is important. Therefore, the involvement of the Muslim community in Islamic psychotherapy is not only about recovery but also about acknowledging belonging which has been emphasized in the stories of Muslim women who are subject to domestic violence.

The Muslim psychotherapist also needs to know that in Canada, it has taken a long journey to transform the Muslim community response to domestic violence. Indeed, this study once more presents a mere fact that the Muslim man alone is not responsible for domestic violence against Muslim women. For example, some androcentric religious interpretations and cultural practices remove responsibility from men for their violence. There were – and are – Muslim leaders who ignore the issue of domestic violence, too. Nevertheless, many of the mainstream Muslim organizations in North America have realized that religious leaders play a significant role in maintaining the values that support or eradicate domestic violence towards women.[1]

Furthermore, few Muslim organizations exist to provide support and resources to Muslim women who are victims of domestic violence. Many Muslim shelters across North America provide telephone helplines, individual and family counselling, free legal advice, free bus services for the school children, vocational skills training, and many outreach and education programmes.

Many Muslim women organizations also promote awareness of gender violence against women by organizing workshops and leading research projects in the field. Their resources represent one of the most noteworthy attempts to raise awareness about the "pathology" of domestic violence in Muslim communities. The CCMW in Canada and the Peaceful Families Project (PFP) in the US define and address four forms of violence against Muslim women: domestic violence, femicide (honour-based violence), forced marriage, and female genital cutting/mutilation (FGM/FGC), and analyze the international and North American context of these practices. They educate Muslims and non-Muslims (both male and female) regarding the causes and the impact of violence against women. Their basic approach to the problem is that any form of violence committed against women in the name of religion or Islam cannot be tolerated and must be resisted.

Altogether the recent scholarship on domestic violence and community activism to tackle the problem provides a framework for Islamic psychotherapy to explore domestic violence against Muslim women from legal, political, economic, social, and religious perspectives. Their contributions are the most reliable source for psychotherapists to understand Muslim women's perspectives on Islam's key sources. However, in addition to exploring theological and spiritual aspects of domestic violence in the Islamic tradition, instead of focusing on the misogynistic aspects of Q. 4:34, the question is also whether we can look at this verse from a psychological perspective. For example, can we see the recommendations in the Q. 4:34 as a "time out" strategy? A "time out" strategy implies that when the man observes certain risk factors or cues that indicate the possibility for violence (i.e. the men who fear abandonment observe symptoms of fear and anxiety), they need to take a one-hour "time out" for cooling off.[2] During this period, the men should engage in healthy activities, such as walking, listening to music, visiting a friend, or engaging in anything that helps him vent his rage and anger.

In general, Muslim women who are subject to domestic violence still see themselves as an organic part of the Muslim community. This suggests that by transforming community response to domestic violence, Islamic psychotherapy will be able to mobilize the community resources for Muslim women who are subject to domestic violence. The elimination of stereotypes that legitimize domestic violence against women in the Muslim community is an example for such transformative practices. For example, transforming malicious gossip against Muslim women who come forward and report abuse against themselves, into community awareness and vigilance, and empathy will promote the well-being of Muslim women in the community. It will also lead to new initiatives to increase capacity of community support services (i.e. sister's groups, counselling services in Islamic organizations) to support Muslim women who are subject to domestic violence. We have already seen the power of belonging to the community. In addition, the community is also the place where Muslim women reconnect to their spiritual and cultural foundations.

Therefore, Muslim psychotherapists need to map the status and dynamics of the community and assess the community's capacity for empowering Muslim women. In addition, they should transform Islamic psychotherapy to be a resource for the community to build the capacity to deal with domestic violence against Muslim women: they can develop training guidelines and manuals for Islamic organizations on how to address domestic violence, and modify attitudes and behaviours in the community.

Mainstream Support Services

One of the resources for the Muslim psychotherapists is their collaboration with the mainstream support services. This is because the number of Muslim women who utilize social and health services in Canada is growing. Cultural awareness, knowledge and skills, and acknowledging the limitations of support services may increase the effectiveness of these services to Muslim women who are subject to domestic violence.

Muslim women who are subject to domestic violence need legal, economic, physical, emotional, spiritual, and psychological support because domestic violence harms their essential support systems. They need immediate access to healthcare and support services to deal with the immediate effects of violence. Economic, social, legal, psychological, and other support services will also help them deal with longer-term needs. This study suggests several principles for effective and sufficient support services will promote the well-being, safety, and economic security of Muslim women; ensure that they have access to immediate and appropriate services; ensure that service providers have cultural awareness to address Muslim women's needs and risk factors for domestic violence; and cooperate and coordinate all services in such a manner that empowers Muslim women.

However, when the Muslim psychotherapist collaborates with the mainstream support services, they also need to know that to avoid cultural encapsulation and several barriers to addressing spiritual dimensions of Muslim women, the providers of these services need to have three core emotional and interpersonal dimensions in a helping relationship with Muslim women. These core characteristics are empathy, respect, and genuineness.[3] Empathy is the ability to accurately perceive what people are experiencing and to communicate that perception to the client. Respect is a positive regard and the indication of a deep and honest acceptance of the worth of persons apart from behaviours. Genuineness is the ability to be honest with self and others. An additional core condition of "warmth" is about treating people in a way that makes them feel safe, accepted, and understood. For Derek Truscott and Kenneth H. Crook, four aspects of cross-cultural competence are important: openness, awareness, knowledge, and services. Openness means that when the therapist provides services to culturally diverse clients, he/she needs to be willing to accept that others may possess a different worldview; therefore, an attitude of openness toward other cultural views of the world and a tolerance for divergent views of right and wrong is considered a competence in multicultural counselling practice.[4] Openness is also about "curiosity and naïveté."[5] Confident and skilled therapists are sensitive and receptive to the differences between themselves and their clients and have these skills to engage their clients in therapy: working alliance, listening, attending, paraphrasing, asking open-ended questions, and using accepting non-verbal cues.[6]

Awareness as a skill is an evolving capacity within each care provider. This aspect of cross-cultural competence implies that counsellors "need to become more aware of their cultural values, assumptions, and biases about human behaviour; the lessons they learned from their own upbringing and culture."[7] Therapists learn self-awareness as a skill in their training programmes because they need to know themselves before they attempt to learn their clients. It also helps them become aware of their worldview and culture to overcome ethnocentrism and cultural encapsulation.

The requirement to respect individuals should include respect for the cultural beliefs of Muslim women. Being autonomous should not demand that Muslim women become independent, autonomous, or alienated from their cultural identity and place the interests of their families secondary to individual interests. Providing the best possible services to Muslim women is through respect for Muslim women, who want to abide by community mores and social customs. In addition, as an antecedent to ethical practice, cultural knowledge is being emphasized in many healthcare centres. Cultural knowledge implies having experience in diverse cultures, languages, historical experiences, values, spiritual and religious beliefs, customs, and lifestyles of Muslim women; awareness of cultural practices of privacy, different communication styles, body language cues, use of interpersonal space, tone of voice, eye contact, passivity/assertiveness patterns of Muslim women; an ability to identify coping strategies and help-seeking behaviours of Muslims; awareness of common misconceptions about Islam will increase knowledge about the media's distorted presentation of Islam, which exacerbates a social problem referred to as *Islamophobia*;[8] and awareness of some attempts of universalizing the dominant/hegemonic Western cultural values with Muslim women. All these suggestions assist in understanding different ways of being and of communicating with Muslim women, and in developing and delivering culturally appropriate services for Muslim women.

In addition, mainstream support networks may use spirituality to empower their Muslim women clients with a non-imposing and non-judgemental manner. This is because many Muslim women adopt some identifiable expression for their spirituality. It is expected that mainstream support services should attend to the spiritual belief systems of their clients. To ignore this dimension of care for Muslim women clients may result in negative outcomes.

It is true that dealing with religious or spiritual issues in a client's life also shows the professionalism and competence of the mainstream support services. For example, in the counselling profession, multiculturally competent counsellors need to be able to:

1. explain the relationship between religion and spirituality, including similarities and differences.
2. describe religious and spiritual beliefs and practices in a specific context.
3. engage in self-exploration of his/her religious and/or spiritual beliefs to increase sensitivity, understanding, and acceptance of his/her belief system.
4. describe one's religious and/or spiritual belief system and explain various models of religious/spiritual development across the lifespan.
5. demonstrate sensitivity to and acceptance of a variety of religious and/or spiritual expressions in the client's spiritual expression, and demonstrate appropriate referral skills and general possible referral sources.
6. assess the relevance of the spiritual domains in the client's therapeutic issue.
7. be sensitive to and respectful of spiritual themes in the counselling process as befits each client's expressed preference.
8. use a client's spiritual beliefs in the pursuit of the client's therapeutic goals as befits the client's expressed preference.[9]

Furthermore, the skill to recognize the impact of racism in diagnosis, staff assignment, treatment modality, utilization treatment duration, and attitudes is also required.[10] Biases in tests and assessments in psychology (be they in content, internal structure, or selection), may have adverse impacts on minority groups in education, hiring, diagnosis, and treatment.[11] Such practices result with minimal counselling contact, medication only, or custodial care rather than intensive psychotherapy.

Thus, regardless of the attitudes held by the mainstream support services towards religion or spirituality of Muslim women, religion and spirituality are important factors for Muslim women. Most Muslims perceive issues related to domestic violence, and any issue that relates to family, individual, and mental health, as religious.[12] They also view themselves either as religious, favouring strict Islamic observance or are moderate observants. Those Muslims who are strongly religious may be less likely to seek mainstream support services because they want their concerns addressed from an Islamic point of view. Nevertheless, Muslims are not a homogenous group because of their adherence to various Islamic schools of law, sympathy to Sufism, and the relationship of human freedom and divine determination. Therefore, demographic changes in society have huge implications for the inclusion of Muslim women's beliefs in support and care for them.

Therefore, the psychotherapist may question how the dominant culture gives religious privilege to the dominant religious group and bans or outlaws the religious beliefs and practices of a subordinate group. For example, the therapist may question why young Muslim girls were prevented from wearing the hijab when playing soccer while other children could wear their religious symbols (e.g. crucifixes, the Star of David, or a kippah). The advantage of such a critical approach in psychotherapy with Muslim women is the establishment of a safe space for clients for the expression of their needs, which helps identify coping strategies and the impact of problems on the mental health status of the client.

However, it does not mean that psychotherapists should ignore some cultural and religious beliefs and practices that breed or endorse domestic violence against Muslim women. Furthermore, despite her challenging views, Susan Moller Okin's[13] perspective suggests that psychotherapists need to be aware of cultures that disadvantage women and children or refuse to accept mainstream values or norms such as human rights, democracy, and so forth. Therefore, the psychotherapist should explore social relations and cultural forms on micro, mezzo, and macro levels to assess risks and threats to Muslim women. They need to be aware that an uncritical approach to certain patriarchal practices towards women may indicate that tolerance to certain practices may not always hold potential for Muslim women, who are subject to violence.

Nevertheless, some support service providers do not have adequate training and experience when dealing with Muslim women clients who seek their help, even though increasing demand for helping professions requires that these support services should happen from the context of the personal culture of the client. This implies that the service providers need to integrate theoretical knowledge and professional skills to set appropriate goals that are consistent with the life experiences and cultural values of their client. For example, when service providers see Muslim women, who are subject to domestic violence, and who are different from them, do they balance the importance of individualism versus collectivism in assessment, diagnosis, and treatment? The religious and cultural values and biases of the service providers should not negate or belittle those of the client. Furthermore, service providers need to be aware of the client's culture, and willing to bring culture into the discussion during interactions with clients.

A few Muslim women who are victims of domestic violence consider using psychological and emotional support from non-Muslim psychotherapist, social workers, psychiatrists, and so forth. For example, Muslim women who are victims of domestic violence may have an impression that the mainstream psychotherapy was not Islamic or at least, not compatible with Islam. They were not specific whether their social workers, psychotherapists, psychiatrists, and so forth, made any attempt to universalize Western psychotherapy theories without a critical approach to their limitations. However, the literature review suggests that any attempt to universalize these theories and techniques are not effective with non-Westerners for various reasons. Although, there were a few attempts to produce a strong critique of the Eurocentric approach, constructing racial identity theories and developing cultural competencies, the clinical understanding of the culture of clients of an ethnic minority, specifically racism, sexism, power, differentials, and identity politics has not changed. Therefore, few psychotherapists and mental health workers have competency:

1. to critically examine racism, sexism, misogyny, homophobia, and economic oppression;[14]
2. to provide clinically useful information within which psychotherapists understand the subjective distress of their clients, and their cure seeking expectations;[15]
3. to understand individual cultural healing contexts;
4. to examine fully client-therapist differences; and/or
5. to consider the socio-cultural processes relating to the client-therapist alliance.[16]

Thus, uncritical acceptance of Western theories and techniques with Muslim women may impede trust of the client to their counsellor. Nevertheless, a critical approach to the role of counsellor in professional counselling literature acknowledges the importance of trust in the counselling process. The establishment of trust begins with the process of unmasking of violence and oppression towards minority groups. Furthermore, it is enhanced with competencies that enable the counsellor to commit the professional counselling practice to fulfilment, liberation, and mutuality in intercultural relationships. If the counsellor fails to acknowledge how the cultural differences are constructed on micro, mezzo, and macro levels, these differences or "otherness in relation," as Bannerji[17] calls it, become a projected and objectified ethical issue. Therefore, it is important to address issues such as counselling values and cultural knowledge in relation to Muslim women who are subject to domestic violence.

Notes

1. An example of such an activism is the ongoing efforts of the prominent national as well as local Muslim organizations, community leaders, and activists, as well as imams

from across Canada, who joined together to issue a "Call to Action to Eradicate Domestic Violence." Canadian Muslims, in their call, highlighted six ways to combat domestic violence: 1. Working within our community and with other communities to raise awareness of the harmful (and sometimes lethal) attitudes that lead to this violence. 2. Working within our communities to raise awareness about the serious psychological, judicial, social, and religious consequences of such practices, through Friday sermons, public lectures, workshops, and other means. 3. Morally opposing the use of the word "honour" when describing honour killings to ensure no positive connotation is implied directly or indirectly in connection to such heinous crimes. Working with community leaders and imams to ensure that they are equipped with the necessary resources and training so that they can offer mediation, conflict resolution, and domestic violence counselling in a manner that reflects professional standards, contemporary research and religious scholarship, and so on. CAIR-Can, *Canadian Muslims Issue Call to Action to Eradicate Domestic Violence* (Toronto, 2013). Accessed from www.caircan.ca/itn_more.php?id=3134_0_2_0_C.

2. Bruce Wood and Robert Kiyoshk, *Change of Seasons: A Training Manual for Aboriginal Men Who Abuse Their Partners/Spouses* (Squamish and North Vancouver, BC: Change of Seasons Society, 1994).
3. Carl Ransom. *The Therapeutic Relationship and Its Impact: A Study of Psychotherapy With Schizophrenics* (Madison, WI: University of Wisconsin Press, 1967).
4. Truscott and Crook, *Ethics for the Practice of Psychology in Canada*, 118.
5. Elise Cole, "Navigating the Dialectic: Following Ethical Rules Versus Culturally Appropriate Practice," *The American Journal of Family Therapy* 36 (2008): 430.
6. Ibid.
7. Truscott and Crook, *Ethics for the Practice of Psychology in Canada*, 119.
8. Amber Haque and Najeeb Kamil, "Islam, Muslims, and Mental Health," in *Counseling Muslims: Handbook of Mental Health Issues and Interventions*, ed. by Sameera Ahmed and Mona M. Amer (New York, NY: Taylor & Francis Group, 2012), 4, 9, 10.
9. Burke, cited in Kobeisy, *Counseling American Muslims*, 96.
10. Ibid.
11. Dwairy, *Counseling and Psychotherapy With Arabs and Muslims*, 76.
12. Kobeisy, *Counseling American Muslims*.
13. Susan Moller Okin, *Is Multiculturalism Bad for Women?* (Princeton, NJ: Princeton University Press, 1999).
14. Roy Moodley, "Double, Triple, Multiple Jeopardy," in *Antidiscriminatory Counselling Practice*, ed. by C. Lago and B. Smith (London: Sage Publications, 2003), 120–134.
15. Roy Moodley, "Representation of Subjective Distress in Black and Ethnic Minority Patients: Constructing a Research Agenda," *Counselling Psychology Quarterly* 13 (2000): 159–174.
16. Ibid.
17. Himani Bannerji, *The Dark Side of the Nation: Essays on Multiculturalism, Nationalism and Gender* (Toronto, ON: Canadian Scholars', 2000), 90.

Conclusion

Domestic violence does not discriminate against different ethnic, religious, social, economic, and cultural groups. However, the responses to domestic violence vary from group to group. Due to misunderstanding of the key sources of the Islamic tradition(s), in Muslim culture(s) certain elements of domestic violence (such as it is still viewed as a private matter) might be seen more normative without adequate reflection of the harmful effects of domestic violence. For example, psychological, physical, spiritual, and emotional trauma of domestic violence has destructive impact on the overall well-being of Muslim women, including their quality of life. Many Muslim women confront the challenges of domestic violence within their communities, mistakenly confining domestic violence to physical behaviour that results in bruises and broken bones, and unfortunately dismissing other forms of abuse – economic or emotional control, for example – that are as detrimental to women's health.[1]

Although this research study provides basic information about Muslim women who experience domestic violence, more research is required so that the phenomenon of domestic violence can be understood more comprehensively, especially with the field of Islamic psychotherapy. Through the heuristic case studies, this research showed how Muslim women might find Islamic psychotherapy helpful but it should be based on theological and social sciences founded on the Islamic tradition.

As a branch of emerging Islamic practical theology, Islamic psychotherapy is the Muslim term to describe religiously based spiritual care and counselling offered by religious leaders, e.g. imams, to the members of their congregation or by Muslim mental health professionals (social workers, psychologists, counsellors, psychotherapists) to their clients in various settings. Historically, effective Islamic psychotherapy is based on the concept that views human beings as an integral composite of physiological, psychological, social, and spiritual components. Muslims in the past sought counselling alongside medical attention. The Prophet's practice and teaching also viewed a healthy body and spirit as a gift and a trust from God. From this framework, the Muslim therapist's role during this process is to help the client go through the re-examination process without feeling guilt, and achieve good mental and spiritual health through natural balance within the individual and the practice of social and religious obligation.

To find out how Islamic psychotherapy helps Muslim women I applied various methodological elements from Islamic theology, social sciences, and practical theology[2] as a very important foundation of this study. I hope the dialogue between the Islamic practical theology and the social sciences allowed critical and fresh analysis of the lived experience of Muslim women who are victims of domestic violence.

I used the heuristic case studies to present the rich description of beliefs and attitudes of Muslim women toward domestic violence, an overview of the definition of domestic violence using the key terms and concepts in the Islamic tradition and the social sciences literature. Each story begins with problems and asks how Islamic psychotherapy should provide help in the problem at hand and how it can help these women who are subject to domestic violence. The stories represent emotional, passionate, suspicious, and desperate situations of Muslim women who are subject to domestic violence and their need for Islamic psychotherapy for empowerment using their faith and tradition. In this regard, the heuristic case studies of the Muslim women have provided some insight into potential clinical implications of spirituality and domestic violence in Islamic psychotherapy. First, many Muslim women who require Islamic psychotherapy might explicitly be religious and spiritual. Some of them are spiritual but not religious. These women want clinicians to deal with or at least understand their religious and spiritual issues. Also, in Islamic psychotherapy, even if the psychotherapist is Muslim, she/he might hold different beliefs, values, and practices from his/her clients. Very often they need to be informed about the clients' belief system by exploring religious and spiritual issues with them. Sometimes we witness a rich tradition of religious and spiritual themes that we are left with making two decisions: (1) reject them by assuming that these themes are not directly linked to our psychotherapy practice or (2) explore and educate ourselves to be more efficient in our practice.

This study also concludes that there is a need for Muslim therapists to take domestic violence against women more seriously. For example, what was interesting is that while I created the heuristic case studies and tried to understand the uniqueness of the experiences of Muslim women, I felt that I was immersed in their dilemmas as well. I often had to reflect on my own feelings, perspectives, biases, expectations, and values, and closely monitor my responses (such as feeling angry and saddened by injustices in case studies) in the light of the rich insights from my advisors. I also realized that Islamic psychotherapy has a great potential to address domestic violence that is frequently employed to control and dominate a woman. For example, Islamic psychotherapy cannot only educate Muslim women with respect to various aspects of domestic violence but also can offer an alternative treatment option for those Muslim women who seek help based on their belief systems. Unfortunately, there is still much insufficient research on the positive effects of the Islamic psychotherapy interventions and how these interventions help Muslim women restore their wellness, claim control over their lives, and motivate them to reclaim their position in the family and community.

To be more effective, Muslim psychotherapists should be trained to understand the relationship between violence and its impact of women's health. For example, they should pay attention to the spiritual health of these women because spirituality constitutes a special position in Islamic psychotherapy with Muslim women. Spirituality is directly linked to the Muslim women's sense of identity and has remained fixed in their psychology and behaviour since the emergence of Islam. For example, a famous narration from the Prophet that states "*Man 'arafa nafsahu faqad 'arafa Rabbahu*" ("Whosoever knows himself knows his Lord") has left a permanent imprint in the psyche of Muslims by encouraging them to achieve a greater self-identity and self-awareness. This alone proves that in Islamic psychotherapy, spirituality is not only about traditional religious experiences but it goes beyond it.

Further, for Muslim women, spirituality invokes extremely deep feelings of Divine Proximity, eternity, inwardness, and interiority, permanent abiding rather than the transient and passing,[3] and immense contemplation that their sense of self is not limited to the identification with the physical body alone, but with something that is spiritual and mystical. However, it also implies that in all our experiences, including domestic violence situations, the Muslim women's identity is not limited even to our intelligence or our spiritual awareness but goes beyond it.[4] For example, for Muslim women there is some aspect that attracts them to the existential meanings of existence. Therefore, they have a strong sense of moral and spiritual perfection and beauty of the soul. Thus, the above-mentioned explanations suggest the overwhelming importance of spirituality in Islamic psychotherapy. In this context, there is a strong feeling of being connected to a transcendent being or force.

Spiritual and religious dimensions and attitudes, such as forgiveness, religious coping, devotion, contemplation, etc., might also help Muslim women who are subject to domestic violence. For example, Islamic psychotherapy can help Muslim women who consider the negative life events into opportunities for spiritual growth. This approach towards negative life events relates to the Sufi understanding of the use of our struggles. For example, the Sufi masters used their disciples' struggles and internal conflicts to facilitate their spiritual development. However, when we use this approach to Muslim women who are victims of domestic violence we must also be cautious because we may give an impression that domestic violence is something positive and leads to more spiritual maturity.

The case study of divine testing and suffering examined the meaning in suffering and empowering Muslim women. The analysis concluded with the idea that Islamic theology suggests to take more responsibility for ending the suffering although many Muslim women believe that their suffering is a divine testing and trial from God. Therefore, these Muslim women may prefer to endure their suffering by *tawakul* (resigning to the Will of God) with a hope to attain a state of peace and tranquillity. Therefore, Muslim therapists must keep in mind that these attitudes may not always be helpful; indeed, they may be more harmful and damaging. Thorough spiritual and religious assessments must be conducted before making any decision about the use of these dimensions in Islamic psychotherapy. Islamic psychotherapy can also integrate mainstream techniques, i.e., existential therapy.

The results of this case study suggest that to do an effective intervention, we first need to explore, for example, what "suffering in the face of evil" means in Islam. Although suffering is universal, the definitions of suffering are myriad. Since Muslims are very diverse in terms of their ethnic, religious, and spiritual backgrounds, their approach to suffering also varies from person to person. Nevertheless, at the heart of their approach to suffering lies the definition of suffering in Islamic thought. Therefore, Islamic psychotherapy depends heavily on the theological arguments of suffering. Without an adequate knowledge and information about this issue, it would be impossible to understand Muslim women's concern with respect to suffering. For example, unhealthy spiritual practices and "toxic" spirituality among Muslims, such as Muslim women's passive acceptance of domestic violence and unnecessary suffering as a religious duty and virtue, are a direct result of the articulation of the problem of suffering in Islamic theology, patriarchal readings of the Qur'an, and the perception of mental illness among Muslims. Finally, Muslim therapists need to apply the correlational approach to Islamic psychotherapy to provide effective intervention in the case of the woman who questions her experience as divine suffering.

Muslim psychotherapists also need to be clear that the suffering does not mean to endorse injustice. The Qur'an and *hadith* call men to practice justice, compassion, and kindness to women. Resigning to the Will of God does not mean not taking a firm action against injustice and oppression and search for relief from suffering.[5] To avoid giving false impressions, the Muslim psychotherapist must engage in asking questions if the clients want to reflect on the impact of domestic violence instead of seeking divine wisdom behind it. Further, if the Muslim women are not ready for such intervention, the Muslim psychotherapist must avoid giving any advice how to use domestic violence and other negative life events for spiritual growth.

Some cases, (i.e., where we discussed viewing domestic violence as a satanic interference), might also require a review of the significant influences of traditional customs and culture that arise when addressing the complex issue of domestic violence against Muslim women. In this study, Islamic culture was examined as a way of life that includes the religious and cultural practices of Muslims. The various case studies showed that undoubtedly, Islamic culture varies considerably around the world and local customs contribute to a complex diversity of cultural expressions. As social systems evolve, traditions and time-honoured practices are sometimes discarded, like outworn and useless "baggage."[6] By contrast, some customs are fiercely protected even though they no longer make sense in contemporary society. In many cases, there are cultural factors that are intrinsic to Muslim men and women that make it nearly impossible for Islamic counsellors to tackle the issues of domestic violence. For example, some Muslim men believe that their actions ultimately protect the family from "outside" influences and keep it pure from an Islamic point of view; they do not respect Canadian laws that protect abused women from assault by any man, including family members. Some Muslim women believe that their husbands have the right to beat them and that subjecting themselves to this form of "discipline" holds out a potential for spiritual reward.[7] For the most part, cultural customs and religious practices are inextricably bound to each other in a seemingly "parallel world." When addressing issues of domestic violence against Muslim women, Islamic counsellors need to conduct a comprehensive assessment of these complex cultural and religious factors to determine an appropriate treatment plan.

When the Muslim psychotherapist assesses the context of domestic violence, he/she also needs to take into consideration that there is diversity within and among Muslim women regarding their attempts and use of support networks. For example, our examination of the second case study suggests that integrating traditional healing practices and mainstream counselling may help some Muslim women who want healing from satanic interference. Traditional healing practices in Islam carry several potential meanings for Muslim women who are subject to domestic violence. These practices refer to healing from wounds and problems associated with domestic violence by applying traditional methods of healing using religious and spiritual activities, and folk healing. Some Muslim women prefer to seek care through both Islamic traditional healing and conventional medicine with a hope that they could benefit from both.

In the Spiritual Diseases chapter, the application of the Sufi tradition can also be powerful in Islamic psychotherapy to deal with spiritual violence. For example, the Sufi technique of the purification of the soul with careful consideration of androcentric assumptions and misogynistic biases can be powerful. Taking into consideration the importance attached to healing practices and Sufi rituals, Islamic traditional healing methods should be included within Islamic psychotherapy. Although traditional healing practices do not replace conventional mainstream counselling techniques and medicine, especially in the countries where access to a healthcare system is easy and fast, the traditional healing techniques are important for Muslim women. Explaining the benefits and risks of traditional healing can also help Muslim women choose an appropriate intervention both from Western psychotherapy and traditional healing. Furthermore, a detailed intake interview and assessment must focus on the healthy and unhealthy spiritual practices and beliefs. In some cases, these practices must also be used as alternative and additional treatment options. Therefore, it is crucial for the Muslim psychotherapist to explore the cultural assumptions and experiences of Muslim women, who are subject to domestic violence, behind the psychotherapy theories to avoid unethical situations, especially misinformation, biased thinking and assumptions about clients who belong to a minority culture. To make the theories work, the Muslim psychotherapist also needs to ask "why" questions to understand and explore value charged issues and their impact on the clients. In elucidating these cultural and spiritual distinctions, Islamic psychotherapy offers unique opportunity to these women because Islamic psychotherapy is a space where it harmonizes different worldviews on treatment and helps psychotherapists integrate or at least build a positive and meaningful partnership between the conventional and traditional healing practices.

In the case study on honour and shame, Muslim psychotherapists might need to explore domestic violence from the perspective of Shari 'ah – the Islamic legal tradition. Historically, Islam's legal tradition was influenced by continuous intellectual reinterpretation of the legal rulings depending on the socio-political, economic, and cultural needs of the people although for a long time "Islamic law" did not signify a geography, a living sociology, or a materially engaged culture but a religion, a religious culture, a religious law, a religious civilization, or an irrationality (hence the presumed "irrational nature" of this law).[8] As might be expected, some Muslims employ patriarchal interpretations of Shari 'ah, and cultural practices to justify domestic violence against women. Nevertheless, despite the inherent misogynistic and androcentric characteristics of Shari 'ah, the Islamic law can also act as a potent source of empowerment to prevent such violence because its truth cannot be fettered.

Also, providing information from the Islamic exegesis was also important. Therefore, Muslim psychotherapists need to know that pre-modern Islamic exegetical traditions continue to influence legal rulings on marital disputes. As we discussed in previous chapters, in classical interpretations of the Qur'an, disciplining a wife for disobedience is considered a just and religious duty. Pre-modern exegetes "never curtailed the right of husbands to engage in corporal punishment or questioned the right of husbands to serve as spousal disciplinarians."[9] Interpretations like this effectively impede attempts to address domestic violence against Muslim women. Unfortunately, this pre-modern classical exegetical tradition still has a considerable impact in the contemporary world. As we have witnessed, Muslim feminist scholarship, however, questions and investigates the assumptions in both classical and secular sources, constructing innovative interpretations of the Qur'an that support and empower Muslim women who are victims of domestic abuse.

One of the important conclusions of this study is that Muslim women who are subject to domestic violence also suffer from trauma. They suffer from low self-esteem and usually have negative images of themselves. The indicators of such negativity are the negative images of God; negative images of the Day of Return; feelings of unworthiness; feelings of being punished by God through the hands of their violent partners; fears of losing relationships with their children, families, community; fears of being abandoned by God; and so forth. They also want to know their rights under the Islamic law. The case study also reveals the trauma of the honour-related problems within the context of domestic violence. Any trauma needs a careful and sensitive approach. With Muslim women, the assessment of trauma should take into consideration family norms, like cultural norms, their impact of the identity of Muslim women. In addition, we need to know whether there is a risk for the life of women who are blamed or stigmatized for being disobedient that may involve "disciplinary action" by her partner. In some cases, Muslim women might not be open about their experience: they might choose silence to avoid further victimization. In these cases, the Muslim psychotherapist needs to know that for the families of these women, disclosure regarding domestic violence is perceived as a breach of the family or cultural norms. The women who do not comply with these norms are subject to rejection, isolation, and/or humiliation. Islamic psychotherapy may use powerful resources of Islamic law to tackle these issues by reconstructing clients' self-image; however, the Muslim counsellor should also inform them about their rights in Canadian family law.

Aside from physical and psychological needs of Muslim women who are subject to domestic violence, a broad range of other social determinants affects the health of these women. Some of the determinants are shelter, education, food, income, social justice, equity, social support, and access to services. Social determinants play an important role in mental well-being of individuals. When these conditions are not met, Muslim women who are subject to domestic violence suffer from mental illness that in turn leads to serious social problems, such as poverty, oppression, racism, violence, and homelessness and contribute to vulnerabilities and risks for the development of more mental health problems. This study suggests the goals and objectives of Islamic psychotherapy must be based upon this understanding as well.

Finally, Muslim psychotherapists need to develop a critical framework using the Islamic feminist perspective that suggests questioning patriarchal readings of the Islamic tradition, particularly the Qur'an. Attention should be given to the application of historical, cultural, and societal measures in Islamic psychotherapy practice in general, while considering the biological, psychological, social, emotional, and spiritual needs of Muslim women and paying attention to how their needs differ from those of men. Taking into consideration the patriarchal-theological context of domestic violence against Muslim women as a spiritual and religious duty of Muslim men and submissiveness to abuse as a spiritual practice among Muslim women, Islamic psychotherapy needs to address not only internal (for instance, cultural or religious) sources of unhealthy spiritual practices but also external sources and forms that support it.

Although Islamic feminist perspective yet needs to be integrated in Islamic psychotherapy, from the perspective of Islamic feminism, the questions raised in the heuristic case studies cannot be fully grasped without a critical approach to the advantages and disadvantages of current interventions and treatment modalities and the importance of Islamic psychotherapy. For example, these case studies display how different spiritual practices – even unhealthy ones – may help build resilience towards suffering and may act as a buffer against difficult times. It is important to remember that some spiritual practices may encourage the client to ignore negative messages that come from the relationship and create optimism in addressing causes of suffering and generate hope and competence and self-efficacy. However, Muslim psychotherapists (both Muslim and non-Muslim) also need to engage in exploring discussions about the role of spirituality and religion in the treatment and address questions and doubts raised by the clients. It is insisted throughout this study that such an open and honest approach will enhance therapeutic outcomes. In addition, I suggest that a lack of spiritual maturity and understanding might generate risk of domestic violence in some families. With these findings in mind, Islamic psychotherapy may engage in educating individuals about the Universalist message of Islam. Islamic psychotherapy must also engage clients in dialogue around controversial but very often salient issues of Islamic faith, and encourage clients to nurture their spirituality and improve their religious education.

The Islamic feminist-centred approach to Islamic psychotherapy may promise new avenues in deconstruction of the misogynist beliefs and unhealthy spiritual practices among Muslim women in these areas of life. However, there is still a genuine need for more case studies and research to give power and voice to Muslim women in Islamic psychotherapy theory and practice. We need a methodology that provides tools for analyzing current practices in Islamic psychotherapy and how they fail the needs of Muslim women, and what these needs are overall. This will benefit the field by expanding the understanding and experience of Muslim psychotherapists, and equip them with tools to address the specific needs of Muslim women.

Thus, this study is encouraging in many ways. First, it aims to nurture dialogue in Islamic psychotherapy practice. I do not claim that I added a new source of fresh ideas; instead, I tried to use the basic sources of the Islamic tradition, practical theology, and the social sciences to bring alternative perspectives of interventions in Islamic psychotherapy with Muslim women. In doing so, this study brings diverse voices from various disciplines into play in Islamic psychotherapy. Second, this study provides thick description of fear, anger, frustration, violence, trauma, and other painful experiences, and the hopes of Muslim women who experience domestic violence. However, even though Islamic psychotherapy is an important way to promote Muslim women's well-being and safety after, before, and during domestic violence and aims to promote safety, well-being, and self-esteem of Muslim women, this study also suggests that there's room for improvement in Islamic psychotherapy practice with Muslim women who are subject to domestic violence. Nevertheless, this study is just a beginning of the process of understanding practical theology issues, and in time further developments in Islamic psychotherapy with Muslim women are bound to occur.

Notes

1. Baobaid and Hamed, *Addressing Domestic Violence in Canadian Muslim Communities.*
2. As I mentioned previously, I give high priority to literature produced by Muslim feminist scholarship. Nevertheless, relevant material from mainstream Islamic research and practice is reviewed to understand how Islamic counselling empowers or disempowers Muslim women who are victims of domestic violence.
3. Seyyid Hossein Nasr, *Islamic Spirituality: Foundations* (New York: Crossroad, 1987), xvii.
4. Ingrid Mattson, "Dignity and Patient Care: An Islamic Perspective," *The Yale Journal for Humanities in Medicine* (2002). Accessed on March 16, 2016 from http://yjhm.yale.edu/archives/spirit2003/dignity/imattson.htm.
5. Rafia M. Hamid, "Domestic Violence in Muslim Communities," *Religion and Men's Violence Against Women* (2015), 334.
6. Tylor, *Primitive Culture*, 16.
7. Baobaid and Hamed, *Addressing Domestic Violence in Canadian Muslim Communities*, 2.
8. Hallaq, *Sharīʿa*, 5.
9. Chaudhry, "The Ethics of Marital Discipline," 126.

Bibliography

Abdul-Raof, Huseein. *Theological Approaches to Qur'anic Exegesis: A Practical Comparative-Contrastive Analysis*. New York: Routledge, 2012.

Abdullah, Keilani. "A Peaceful Ideal, Violent Realities: A Study on Muslim Female Domestic Violence Survivors." In *Change From Within: Diverse Perspectives on Domestic Violence in Muslim Communities*, edited by Maha B. Alkhateeb and Salma Elkadi Abugideiri, 69–90. Alexandria, VA: The Peaceful Families Project, 2007.

Abdullah, Raihanah, Monsoor, Taslima, Johari, Fuadah and Radzi, Wirdati Mohd. "Financial Support for Women Under Islamic Family Law in Bangladesh and Malaysia." *Asian Journal of Women's Studies* 21 (4) (2015): 363–383. doi:10.1080/12259276.2015.1106853.

Abdullah, Somayya. "Islam and Counseling: Models of Practice in Muslim Communal Life." *Journal of Pastoral Counseling* 42 (2007): 4.

Abrahamov, Binyamin. "Scripturalist and Traditionalist Theology." In *The Oxford Handbook of Islamic Theology*, ed. Sabine Schmidtke. Oxford: Oxford University, 2016.

Abrahamov, Binyamin. "Al-Ghazālī's Theory of Causality." *Studia Islamica* 67 (1988): 75–98.

Abu Bakr, Omaima, "Islamic Feminism: What's in a Name? Preliminary Reflections." *AMEWS Review* xv, xvi (Winter/Spring 2001): 1.

Abugideiri, Salma Elkadi. "Domestic Violence." In *Counseling Muslims: Handbook of Mental Health Issues and Interventions*, edited by Sameera Ahmed and Mona M. Amer, 309–328. New York, NY: Routledge, Taylor & Francis Group, 2012.

Abugideiri, Salma Elkadi, and Alwani, Zainab. *What Islam Says About Domestic Violence*. Herndon, VA: FAITH, 2003.

Abu-Odeh, Lama. "Modern Family Law, 1800–Present. Arab States." In *Encyclopaedia of Women in Islamic Cultures*, vol. 2, edited by Joseph Su'ad, 459-462. The Hague: Brill 2.005.

Abu Zayd, Nasr Hamid. *Falsafat al-ta'w/l*. Dår al-Bayda': al-Markaz al-Thaqåf al-Arab, 1996.

Abu Zayd, Nasr Hamid. *al-Na, wa al-,ulƒah wa al-aaqiqah*. Dår al-Bayda': al-Markaz al-Thaqåf al-Arab, 2000.

Afridi, Muhammad Adil Khan. "Maqasid al-Shari'ah and Preservation of Basic Rights Under the Theme 'Islam and Its Perspectives on Global & Local Contemporary Challenges.'" *Journal of Education and Social Sciences* 4 (2016): 275–285.

Ahmad, Khadher, Suliaman, Ishak, and Ariffin, Sedek. "Sorcery Treatment on Ibn Qayyim al-Jawziyya's (691H/1292M-751H/1350M) Perspective and The Reality in Islamic Medical Centre in Malaysia: A Comparative Studies." *Al-Bayan: Journal of Qur'an and Hadith Studies* 10 (1) (2012): 63–83.

Amir, Ahmad N., Shuriye, Abdi O., and Islamic, Ahmad F. "Muhammad Abduh's Scientific Views in the Qur'an." *International Journal of Asian Social Science* 2 (11) (2012): 2034–2044

Ahmed, Leila. *Women and Gender in Islam: Historical Roots of a Modern Debate* (New Haven, CT: Yale University Press, 1992.

Ahmed, Shahab. *What Is Islam.: The Importance of Being Islamic.* Princeton: Princeton University Press, 2016.

Ahmed, Sameera, and Mona M. Amer, eds. *Counseling Muslims: Handbook of Mental Health Issues and Interventions.* New York, NY: Routledge, Taylor & Francis Group, 2012.

Akhu-Zaheya Laila M., and Alkhasawneh, Esraa M. "Complementary Alternative Medicine Use Among a Sample of Muslim Jordanian Oncology Patients." *Complementary Therapies in Clinical Practice* 18 (2) (2012): 121–126.

Akpinar, Aylin. *Male's Honour and Female's Shame: Gender and Ethnic Identity Constructions Among Turkish Divorcees in the Migration.* Uppsala, Sweden: Dept. of Sociology, Uppsala University, 1998.

Ajouaou, Mohamed. *Imam Hebind Bars: A Case Stufy of Islamic Spiritual Care in Dutch Pirson Towards the Development of a Professional Profile.* North Charleston, SC: CreateSpace Publishing Platform, 2014.

Al-Adawi, Samir, Atsu Dorvlo, Suad. Al-Ismaily, et al. "Perception of and Attitudes Towards Mental Illness in Oman." *International Journal of Social Psychiatry* 48 (4) (2002): 305–317.

al-Afendi, Muhammad Hamid, and Nabi Ahmed Baloch, eds. *Curriculum and Teacher Education.* Jiddah, Saudi Arabia: Islamic Education Series, 1980.

Al-Allaf, Mashhad. "Islamic Theology." In *The Bloomsbury Companion to Islamic Studies*, edited by Clinton Bennett, 119–134. London: Bloomsbury, 2013.

al-Alwani, Taha Jabir. "The Islamization of Methodology of Behavioral Sciences." *American Journal of Islamic Social Sciences* 6/2 (1989): 227–238.

al-Badawi, Mostafa. *Islamic Psychotherapy? Man & the Universe: An Islamic Perspective.* Amman: Wakeel Books, 2002.

al-Dhahabi, Muhammad ibn Ahmad. *Al-Tibb al-Nabawi.* Beirut: Dar Ihyaa al-Uloom. Al-Azraq, *Tahsil al-Manafi'* (Medical Benefits Made Accessible). Cairo, 1963.

al-Faruqi, Ismail R. "Towards a New Methodology for Qur'anic Exegesis." *Islamic Studies* 1 (1) (1962): 36–52.

al-Ghazali, Abu Hamid. *Al-Munqidh min al-dalal* (The Rescuer From Error). Edited by J. Saliba and K. Ayyad. Damascus: Maktab al-Nashr al-'Arabi, 1934.

al-Ghazali, Abu Hamid. *Mishkat al-Anwar* (The Niche of the Lights). Edited by A. Afifi. Cairo: Dar *al*-Qawmiya lil-Tab'a wa *al*-Nashr, 1964.

al-Ghazali, Abu Hamid. *Mizan al-'amal* (The Balance of Action). Edited by S. Dunya. Cairo: Dar al-Ma'arif, 1964.

al-Ghazali, Abu Hamid. *Revival of Religious Learning* (Ihya Ulum-id-Din). Translated by Fazl ul-Karim. Karachi: Darul-Ishaat, 1993.

al-Khayyat, Sana. *Honour and Shame: Women in Modern Iraq.* London: Saqi, 1992.

Ali, Parveen Azam and Naylor, Paul B. "Intimate Partner Violence: A Narrative Review of the Biological and Psychological Explanations for Its Causation." *Aggression and Violent Behaviour* 18 (3) (2013): 373–382.

Ali, Kecia. *Sexual Ethics and Islam: Feminist Reflections on Qur'ān, Hadith and Jurisprudence.* Oxford: Oneworld Publications, 2006.

Ali, Kecia. *Marriage and Slavery in Early Islam.* Cambridge, MA: Harvard University Press, 2010.

Ali, Osman M., and Aboul-Fotouh, Frieda. "Traditional Mental Health Coping and Help-Seeking." In *Counseling Muslims: Handbook of Mental Health Issues and Interventions*, edited by Sameera Ahmed and Mona M. Amer, 33–47. New York, NY: Taylor & Francis Group, 2012.

Al-Issa, Ihsan. "Mental Illness in Medieval Islamic Society." In *Al-Junun, Mental Illness in the Islamic World*, edited by I. Al-Issa, 64. Madison, WI: International Universities Press, 2000.

Alizadeh, venus, Hylander, Ingrid, Kocturk, Tahire, and Lena Törnkvist, Lena. "Counselling Young Immigrant Women Worried About Problems Related to the Protection of 'Family Honour' – From the Perspective of Midwives and Counsellors at Youth Health Clinics." *Scandinavian Journal of Caring Sciences* 24 (1) (2010): 34. doi:10.1111/j.1471-6712.2009.00681.

al-Jawziyyah, Ibn Al-Qayyim. *Healing With the Medicine of the Prophet.* Translated by Jalal Abu al-Rab and edited by Abdul R. Abdullah. Riyadh: Darussalam Publications, 1999.

Al-Jazairi, Abu Bakr Jabir. *Minhajul Muslim*, 3rd ed. Morocco: Dârul baidâ' n.d.

Al-Jilani, Abd al-Qadir. *The Secret of Secrets*, trans. by Shaykh Tonsun Bayrak al-Jerrahi al-Halveti. Cambridge: The Islamic Texts Society, 1994.

Al-Jilani, Abd al-Qadir. *Utterances (Malfuzat).* Translated by Muhtar Holland. Kuala Lampur: S. Abdul Majeed & Co., 1992.

Alkhateeb, Maha B., and Abugideiri, Salma Elkadi. "Introduction." In *Change from Within: Diverse Perspectives on Domestic Violence in Muslim Communities*, edited by Maha B. Alkhateeb and Salma Elkadi Abugideiri. Great Falls: The Peaceful Families Project, 2007.

Alkhateeb, Maha B. *Islamic Marriage Contracts.* Great Falls: The Peaceful Families Project, 2012.

Jamal Badawi, *Wife Beating.* Accessed from http://islamic-world.net/sister/wife_beating.htm.

Al-Krenawi, Alean., and Graham, John R. "Spirit Possession and Exorcism in the Treatment of a Bedouin Psychiatric Patient." *Clinical Social Work Journal* 25 (1997): 211–222.

Allen, Mary. *Narrative Therapy for Women Experiencing Domestic Violence: Supporting Women's Transition From Abuse to Safety.* London: Jessica Kingsley Publishers, 2012.

Al-Qaradawi, Yusuf. *The Lawful and the Prohibited in Islam* (Al- Halal Wal-Haram fil Islam). Translated by Kamal El-Helbawy, M. Moinuddin Siddiqui, and Syed Shukry. Washington, DC: American Trust Publications, 1980.

al-Qushayri, Abu'l Qasim. *The Epistle on Sufism.* Translated by Alexander D. Knysh. Reading: Garnet Publishing Limited, 2007.

al-Razi, Abu Bakr Muhammad ibn Zakariya. *The Spiritual Physick of Rhazes.* Translated from the Arabic by Arthur J. Arberry. London: John Murray, 1950.

Al-Sharmani, Mulki, and Jana Rumminger. "Understanding Qiwamah and Wilayah Through Life Stories." In *Men in Charge: Rethinking Authority in Muslim Legal Tradition*, edited by Ziba Mir-Hosseini, Mulki al-Sharmani and Jana Rumminger, 219–255. London: Oneworld Publications, 2016.

Al-Uthaymin, Muhammad bin Salih. *An Explanation of Shayhkh al-Islam Ibn Taymiyyah's Introduction to the Principles of Tafseer Explanation by Shaykh Muhammad Ibn Salih al-Uthaymin.* Birmingham, UK: Al-Hidaayah Publishing Ltd., n.d.

Alwani, Zainab. "The Qur'anic Model for Harmony in Family Relations." In *Change From Within: Diverse Perspectives on Domestic Violence in Muslim Communities*, edited by Maha B. Alkhateeb and Salma Elkadi Abugideiri, 33–66. Great Falls, VA: Peaceful Families Project, 2007.

Al-Zeera, Rabha Isa. "Violence Against Women in Qur'an 4:34: A Sacred Ordinance?" In *Muslima Theology: The Voices of Muslim Women Theologians*, edited by Ednan Asla, Marcia J. Hermansen, and Elif Medeni, 217–230. New York, NY: Peter Lang Edition, 2013.

Alziari, Gabriela. *Is Domestic Violence Acceptable?* Accessed from https://authoristo.wordpress.com/2011/12/17/verse-434-is-domestic-violence-acceptable/.

American Psychiatric Association. *Diagnostic and Statistical Manual of Mental Disorders*. 5th ed. Arlington, TX: American Psychiatric Publishing, 2013.

Ammar, Nawal H. "Simplistic Stereotyping and Complex Reality of Arab-American Immigrant Identity: Consequences and Future Strategies in Policing Wife Battery." *Islam and Christian – Muslim Relations* 11 (1) (2000): 51–70.

Amnesty International. *Pakistan: Violence Against Women in the Name of Honour*. AI Index: ASA 33/17/99 1999.

Anees, Munawar A. "Al-Majusi's Observations and Instruction on Medical and Public Health." In *Health Sciences in Early Islam*, edited by S. Hamaerneh and M. Anees, 313–331. E-Book: Zahra Publication, 1984. Accessed from http://www.zahrapublications.com/pdf/HealthSciencesInEarlyIslamVolume1-HaeriTrust-ZP-Sample.pdf

An-Na'im, Abdullahi Ahmed. "Shari'a and Islamic Family Law: Transition and Transformation." *Ahfad Journal* 23 (2) (2006): 2–30.

Archer, Brad. "Family Law Reform and the Feminist Debate: Actually-Existing Islamic Feminism in the Maghreb and Malaysia." *Journal of International Women's Studies* 8 (4) (2007): 49–59.

Archer, John. "Testosterone and Human Aggression: An Evaluation of the Challenge Hypobook." *Neuroscience and Biobehavioral Reviews* 30 (3) (2006): 319–345.

Asad, Muhammad. *The Message of the Qur'an*. Gibraltar: Andalus Press, 1980.

Asad, Talal. *The Idea of Anthropology of Islam*. Washington, DC: The Center for Contemporary Arab Studies at Georgetown University, 1986.

Ashrof, Mohamed V. A. *Islam and Gender Justice: Questions at the Interface*. Delhi: Kalpaz Publications, 2005.

Ashy, Majed A. "Health and Illness From an Islamic Perspective." *Journal of Religion and Health* 38 (3) (1999): 241–258.

Auda, Jasser. *Maqasid Al-Shariah: An Introductory Guide*. Herndon, VA: IIIT, 2008.

Awaad, Rania and Ali, Sara. "Obsessional Disorders in al-Balkhi's 9th Century Treatise: Sustenance of the Body and Soul." *Journal of Affective Disorders* 180 (2015): 185–189.

Aydin, Mehmet S. "The Problem of Theodicy in the *Risale-i Nur*." In *Islam at the Crossroads: On the Life and Thought of Bediuzzaman Said Nursi*, edited by Ibrahim M. Abu Rabi, 215–228. New York, NY: State University of New York Press, 2003.

Ayyub, Ruksana. "Domestic Violence in the South Asian Muslim Immigrant Population in the United States." *Journal of Social Distress and the Homeless* 9 (3) (2000): 237–248.

Azhar, Md Zain., and . Varma, Shashjit L. "Religious Psychotherapy in Depressive Patients." *Psychotherapy and Psychosomatics* 63 (1995): 165–173.

Azhar, Md .Zain, Varma, Shashjit L., and Dharap,Aabd S. "Religious Psychotherapy in Anxiety Disorder Patients." *Acta Psychiatrica Scandinavica* 90 (1994): 1–3.

Badran, Margot. "Towards Islamic Feminisms: A Look at the Middle East." In *Hermeneutics and Honor: Negotiating Female "Public" Space in Islamic/ate Societies*, edited by Asma Afsaruddin, 159–188. Cambridge, MA: Harvard Middle Eastern Monographs, 1999.

Badri, Malik. *Contemplation: An Islamic Psychospiritual Study*. London: IIIT, 2000.

Bakhtiar, Laleh. "The Sublime Qur'ān: The Misinterpretation of Chapter 4 Verse 34." *European Journal of Women's Studies* 18 (4) (2011): 431–439.

Baldwin, Clive. "Narrative, Ethics and People With Severe Mental Illness." *Australian and New Zealand Journal of Psychiatry* 39 (2005): 119–122.

Ballard, Paul. "The Use of Scripture." In *The Wiley-Blackwell Companion to Practical Theology*, edited by Bonnie J. Miller-McLemore, 163–172. Malden, MA: Blackwell Publishing Limited, 2012.

Bannerji, Himani. *The Dark Side of the Nation: Essays on Multiculturalism, Nationalism and Gender*. Toronto, ON: Canadian Scholars', 2000.

Baobaid, Mohammed. "Guidelines for Service Providers: Outreach Strategies for Family Violence Intervention with Immigrant and Minority Communities: Lessons Learned from the Muslim Family Safety Project." *The Centre for Children and Families in the Justice System*, 32. Accessed January 10, 2017, from www.lfcc.on.ca/MFSP_Guidelines.pdf

Baobaid, Mohammed, and Gahad Hamed. *Addressing Domestic Violence in Canadian Muslim Communities: A Training Manual for Muslim Communities and Ontario Service Providers*. London, ON: Muslim Resource Centre for Social Support and Integration, 2010.

Barazangi, Nimat Hafez. *Woman's Identity and the Qur'an: A New Reading*. Gainesville, FL: The University Press of Florida, 2006.

Barlas, Asma. *Believing Women in Islam: Unreading Patriarchal Interpretations of the Qur'an*. Austin, TX: University of Texas Press, 2002.

Barnett, Laura, and Greg Madison, eds. *Existential Therapy: Legacy, Vibrancy and Dialogue*. New York, NY: Routledge, 2012.

Barnett, Laura, and Greg Madison. "Introduction." In *Existential Therapy: Legacy, Vibrancy and Dialogue*, edited by Laura Barnett and Greg Madison, 1–5. New York, NY: Routledge, 2012.

Barrett, William. *The Illusion of Technique: A Search for Meaning in a Technological Civilization*. New York, NY: Anchor Press/Doubleday, 1978.

Basit, Abdul and John Tuscan. "The Spiritual Dimensions of Trauma Healing." In *Religion and Psychology*, edited by Michael T. Evans and Emma D. Walker, 63–76. New York, NY: Nova Science Publishers, 2009.

Bauer, Karen. *Gender Hierarchy in the Qur'an: Medieval Interpretations, Modern Responses*. New York, NY: Cambridge University Press, 2015.

Baugh, Carolyn. "Ibn Taymiyya's Feminism? Imprisonment and the Divorce Tafwas." In *Muslima Theology: The Voices of Muslim Women Theologians*, edited by Ednan Aslan, Marcia Hermansen and Elif Medeni, 181–196. New York, NY: Peter Lang Edition, 2013.

Bayrakli, Bayraktar. *İslamda Eğitim* (Batı *Eğitim* Sistemleri ile Mukayeseli) (*Education in Islam and Its Comparison to the Western Education Systems.*) 2nd ed. Istanbul: Marmara Üniversitesi İlahiyat Fakültesi, 1983.

Bellamy, Carla. *The Powerful Ephemeral: Everyday Healing in an Ambiguously Islamic Place*. Berkeley, CA: University of California Press, 2011.

Benjamin, Jessica. *The Bonds of Love: Psychoanalysis, Feminism, and the Problem of Domination*. Ann Arbor, MI: The University of Michigan Pantheon Books, 1988.

Bhat, Mansoor Ahmad. *The Sufi Thought of Shaikh Sayyid Abdul Qadir Jilani and Its Impact on the Indian Subcontinent*. New Delhi: D.K. Printworld, 2010.

Bitter, James R. *Theory and Practice of Family Therapy and Counseling*. Belmont, CA: Brooks/Cole, 2009.

Blackman, Winifred S. *The Fellahīn of Upper Egypt*. Cairo: American University Press, 1927/2000.

Blinkhorn, Victoria, Minna Lyons, and Louise Almond. "Drop the Bad Attitude! Narcissism Predicts Acceptance of Violent Behaviour." *Personality and Individual Differences* 98 (2016): 157–161.

Bodman, Whitney S. *The Poetics of Iblis: Narrative Theology in the Qur'ān*. Cambridge, MA: Harvard University Press, 2011,

Boisen, Anton. *Out of the Depths: An Autobiographical Study of Mental Disorder and Religious Experience*, 1st ed. New York, NY: Harper & Brothers, 1960.

Book, Angela S. Starzyk, Katherine B., and Quinsey, Vermon L. "The Relationship Between Testosterone and Aggression: A Meta-Analysis." *Aggression and Violent Behavior* 6 (2001): 579–599.

Brown, Sally A. "Hermeneutical Theory." In *The Wiley-Blackwell Companion to Practical Theology*, edited by Bonnie J. Miller-McLemore, 112–122. London: Wiley-Blackwell, 2012.

Browning, Don. *A Fundamental Practical Theology: Descriptive and Strategic Proposals*. Minneapolis, MN: Fortress, 1991.

Browning, Don, and F. Schüssler Fiorenza, eds. *Habermas, Modernity and Public Theology*. New York, NY: Crossroad, 1992.

Buck, Nicole, Petronella Leenaars, Paul Emmelmap, and Hjalmar Marle. "Personality Traits Are Related to Intimate Partner Violence Among Securely Attached Individuals." *Journal of Family Violence* 29 (3) (2014): 235–246.

Bukhari, Muhammad ibn isma 'il. *Sahih Bukhari*. Accessed October 26, 2016, from http://sunnah.com/bukhari/53.

CAIR-Can. *Canadian Muslims Issue Call to Action to Eradicate Domestic Violence*. Toronto, 2013. Accessed from www.caircan.ca/itn_more.php?id=3134_0_2_0_C.

Campanini, Massimo. "The Mu 'tazila in Islamic History and Thought." *Religion Compass* 6 (1) (2012): 41–50.

Canadian Council of Muslim Women [CCMW]. *Violence Against Women – Health and Justice for Canadian Muslim Women*. Toronto, 2013. Accessed on February 22, 2016 from http://ccmw.com/violence-against-women-health-and-justice-for-canadian-muslim-women/.

Carré, Justin M. and McCormick, Cheryl M. Aggressive Behavior and Change in Salivary Testosterone Concentrations Predict Willingness to Engage in a Competitive Task." *Hormones and Behavior* 54 (3) (2008): 403–409.

Cave, Cathy and Pease, Terri. *Culture and Inclusion Within the Context of Trauma-Informed Domestic Violence Services and Organizations*. National Center on Domestic Violence, Trauma, and Mental Health, 2013. Accessed October 28, 2016, from www.nationalcenterdvtraumamh.org/trainingta/webinars-seminars/2013-practical-strategies-for-creating-trauma-informed-services-and-organizations.

Chabbi, Jacqueline. "'Abd al-Qadir al-Jilani." In *Encyclopaedia of Islam: Three*, edited by Kate Fleet, Gudrun Krämer, Denis Matringe, John Nawas, and Everett Rowson. Brill Online, 2015. Accessed March 10, 2016, from http://referenceworks.brillonline.com.myaccess.library.utoronto.ca/entries/encyclopaedia-of-islam-3/abd-al-qa-dir-al-ji-la-ni-COM_22592.

Chaudhry, Ayesha S. "A Case Study of Guardianship (Wilayah) in Prophetic Practice." In *Men in Charge: Rethinking Authority in Muslim Legal Tradition*, edited by Ziba Mir-Hosseini, Mulki Al-Sharmani and Jana Rumminger, 88–105. London: Oneworld Publications, 2015.

Chaudhry, Ayesha S. *Domestic Violence and Islamic Tradition: Ethics, Law, and the Muslim Discourse of Gender*. Oxford: Oxford University Press, 2013.

Chaudhry, Ayesha S. "The Ethics of Marital Discipline in Premodern Qur'anic Exegesis." *Journal of the Society of Christian Ethics* 30 (2) (2010): 123–130.

Chaudhry, Ayesha S. "'I Wanted One Thing and God Wanted Another . . .': The Dilemma of Prophetic Example and Wife-Beating." *Journal of Religious Ethics* 39 (3) (2011): 416–439.

Chesler, Phyllis. "Are Honor Killings Simply Domestic Violence?" *Middle East Quarterly* 16 (2) (2009): 61–69.

Chittick, William C., ed. *The Inner Journey: Views From the Islamic Tradition*. Sandpoint, ID: Morning Light Press, 2007.

Chittick, William C. "Love in Islamic Thought." *Religion Compass* 8 (2014): 229–238.

Chittick, William C. *The Sufi Path of Knowledge: Ibn al-'Arabi's Metaphysics of Imagination*. Albany, NY: State University of New York Press, 1989.

Chittick, William C. *Sufism: A Short Introduction.* Oxford: Oneworld Publications, 2001.

Chittick, William C. "Love in Islamic Thought." *Religion Compass* 8 (2014): 229–238.

Chittick, William C. *Divine Love: Islamic Literature and the Path to God.* New Haven, CT: Yale University Press, 2013.

Clarke, Lynda, and Cross, Pamela. *Muslim & Canadian Family Law: A Comparative Primer.* Ottawa, ON: Canada: Canadian Council of Muslim Women, 2006.

Cole, Elise. "Navigating the Dialectic: Following Ethical Rules Versus Culturally Appropriate Practice." *The American Journal of Family Therapy* 36 (2008): 430.

"Combating Patriarchal Violence Against Women – Focusing on Violence in the Name of Honor." The Swedish Ministry of Justice and the Swedish Ministry for Foreign Affairs, Stockholm, December 7–8, 2004.

Cook-Masaud, Carema, and Marsha I. Wiggins. "Counseling Muslim Women: Navigating Cultural and Religious Changes." *Counseling and Values* 55 (2) (2011): 247–259.

Cooper-White, Pamela. *The Cry of Tamar: Violence Against Women and the Church's Response.* Minneapolis, MN: Fortress Press, 2012.

Cooper-White, Pamela. "Suffering." In *The Wiley-Blackwell Companion to Practical Theology*, edited by Bonnie J. Miller-McLemore, 23–31. Malden, MA: Blackwell Publishing Limited, 2012.

Cooper-White, Pamela. *Many Voices: Pastoral Psychotherapy in Relational and Theolgoical Perspective.* Minneapolis, MN: Fortress Press, 2011.Corey, Gerald. *Theory and Practice of Counseling and Psychotherapy.* 9th ed. Belmont, CA: Brooks/Cole Cengage Learning, 2008.

Corey, Gerald. *Theory and Practice of Counseling and Psychotherapy*, 9th ed. Belmont, CA: Brooks/Cole Cengage Learning, 2008.

Couture, Pamela D. "Social Policy." In *The Wiley-Blackwell Companion to Practical Theology,* edited by Bonnie J. Miller-McLemore. Maldan, MA: Wiley-Blackwell, 2012, 153–162.

Couture, Pamela D. "Introducing Practical Theology to English Canada." *Toronto Journal of Theology* 29 (1): 143–144.

Couture, Pamela D. *Child Poverty: Love, Justice, and Social Responsibility.* St. Louis, MO: Chalice Press, 2007.

Craig, Erik. "Existential Psychotherapy, Discipline and Demarche: Remembering Essential Horizons." In *Existential Therapy: Legacy, Vibrancy and Dialogue*, edited by Laura Barnett and Greg Madison, 7–20. New York, NY: Routledge, 2012.

Cratesly, Kelso. "Revisiting Freud and Kohut on Narcissism." *Theory and Psychology* 26 (6) (2016): 333–359.

Crockatt, Phillip. "Freud's 'On Narcissism: An Introduction.'" *Journal of Child Psychotherapy* 31 (1) (2006): 4–20.

Csordas, Thomas J. "Elements of Charismatic Possession and Healing." *Medical Anthropology Quarterly* 14 (4) (1988): 121–142.

Dabashi, Hamid. *Theology of Discontent: The Ideological Foundation of the Islamic Revolution in Iran.* New York: New York University Press, 1998.

Daneshpur, Manijeh. "Family Systems Therapy and Postmodern Approaches." In *Counselling Muslims: Handbook of Mental Health Issues and Interventions*, edited by Sameera Ahmed and Mona M. Amer, 119–134. New York, NY: Routledge, Taylor & Francis Group, 2012.

Daniel, Kroslak. "Honor Killings and Cultural Defense (with a Special Focus on Germany)." *Míľniky Práva v Stredoeurópskom Priestore*, June 19, 2009.

Dellenbor, Liselott. "A Reflection on the Cultural Meanings of Female Circumcision: Experiences From fieldwork in Casamance, Southern Senegal." In *Re-Thinking*

Sexualities in Africa, edited by Signe Arnfred, 79–96. Uppsala: Nordic Africa Institute, 2004.

Dein, Simon, Alexander, Malcolm, and Napier, A. David "Jinn, Psychiatry and Contested Notions of Misfortune Among East London Bangladeshis." *Transcultural Psychiatry* 45 (2008): 31, 49.

Deuraseh, Nurdeen., and Abu Talib, Mansor. "Mental Health in Islamic Medical Tradition." *The International Medical Journal* 4 (2005): 76–79.

Dhami, Sangeetha, and Sheikh, Aziz. "The Family: Predicament and Promise." In *Caring for Muslim Patients*, edited by Sheikh A. Gatrad. Abingdon: Radcliffe Publishing, 2000.

Dharamsi, Sabnum, and Abdullah Maynard. "Islamic-Based Interventions." In *Counselling Muslims: Handbook of Mental Health Issues and Interventions*, edited by Sameera Ahmed and Mona M. Amer, 135–160. New York, NY: Taylor & Francis Group, 2012.

Dillon, Gina, Hussain, Raffat, Loxton, Deborah, and Rahman, Saifur. "Mental and Physical Health and Intimate Partner Violence Against Women: A Review of the Literature." *International Journal of Family Medicine* 2013 (2013): 313909.

Dobash, Emerson., and Dobash, Russel P. *Violence Against Wives: A Case Against the Patriarchy*. New York, NY: Free Press, 1979.

Dol, Michael. *Majnun: The Madman in Medieval Islamic Societies*. Oxford: Clarendon Press, 1992.

Domestic Violence Protection Act, *2000, S.O. 2000, c. 33 – Bill 117*. Accessed February 21, 2017, from www.ontario.ca/laws/statute/S00033.

Douglass, Bruce G., and Moustakas, Clark. "Heuristic Inquiry." *Journal of Humanistic Psychology* 25 (3) (1985): 45–46.

D'Sousa, Diane. *Shia Women: Muslim Faith and Practice*. New Delhi: Zubaan, 2012.

Dutton, Donald. G., and Bodnarchuk, Mark. "Through a Psychological Lens: Personality Disorder and Spouse Assault." In *Current Controversies on Family Violence*, edited by D. R. Loseke, R. J. Gelles and M. M. Cavanaugh, 5–18. 2nd ed. Thousand Oaks, CA: Sage Publications, 2005.

Dwairy, Marwan. *Counselling and Psychotherapy With Arabs and Muslims: A Culturally Sensitive Approach*. New York, NY: Teachers College Press, 2006.

Dwyer, Graham. *The Divine and the Demonic: Supernatural Affliction and Its Treatment in North India*. London: Routledge Curzon, 2003.

Edmond, Tonya, Rubin, Allen, and Wambach, Kathrun G. "The Effectiveness of EMDR with Adult Female Survivors of Childhood Sexual Abuse." *Social Work Research*, 23 (2) (1999), 109–116.

Egan, Gerald. *The Skilled Helper: A Problem-Management Approach to Helping*, 6th ed. Pacific Grove, CA: Brooks/Cole, 1998.

Elahi, Ostad. *Knowing the Spirit*. Translated and with an Introduction by James Winston Morris. Albany, NY: State University of New York Press, 2007.

El-Fadl, Khaled Abou. *Speaking in God's Name: Islamic Law, Authority and Women*. Oxford: Oneworld, 2001.

El Omari, Racha. "Theology." In *The Princeton Encyclopedia of Islamic Political Thought*, edited by Gerhard Böwering and Patricia Crone. Princeton, NJ: Princeton University Press, 2013.

El-Rouayheb, Khaled. "Al-Māturīdī and the Development of Sunni Theology in Samarqand." *Journal of Near Eastern Studies* 75 (2) (2016): 413–416.

Eneborg, Yusuf Muslim ."The Quest for 'Disenchantment' and the Modernization of Magic." *Islam and Christian – Muslim Relations* 25 (4) (2014): 419–432.

Eneborg, Yusuf Muslim. "Ruqya Shariya: Observing the Rise of a New Faith Healing Tradition Amongst Muslims in East London." *Mental Health, Religion & Culture* 16 (10) (2013): 1080–1096.

Ernst, Carl W. *Sufism: An Introduction to the Mystical Tradition of Islam*. Boston, MA: Shambhala, 2011.

Esposito, John L. *The Oxford Dictionary of Islam*. New York, NY: Oxford University Press, 2003.

Esposito, John L. *The Oxford Encyclopedia of the Islamic World*. Oxford: Oxford Unviersity Press, 2009.

Ess, Josef van. *The Flowering of Muslim Theology*. Cambridge, MA: Harvard University Press, 2006.

Esack, Farid. *Qur'an, Liberation and Pluralism: An Islamic Perspective on Inter-Religious Solidarity Against Oppression*. Oxford: Oneworld, 1997.

Esack, Farid. *The Qur'an: An Introduction*. Oxford: Oneworld, 2002.

European Association for Psychotherapy (EAP). *Definition of the Profession of Psychotherapy [Web page]*, 2003. Accessed on March 4, 2016 from www.europsyche.org/contents/13219/definition-of-the-profession-of-psychotherapy.

Feurerstein, George. *Holy Madness: The Shock Tactics and Radical Teachings of Crazy-Wise Adepts, Holy Fools, and Rascal Gurus*. New York, NY: Paragon House, 1990.

Fiorenza, Elizabeth Schussler. *Bread Not Stone: The Challenge of Feminist Biblical Interpretation*. Boston, MA: Beacon Press, 1995.

Fiorenza, Elizabeth Schussler. *But She Said: Feminist Practices of Biblical Interpretation*. Boston, MA: Beacon Press, 1992.

Fortune, Marie M. *Violence in the Family: A Workshop Curriculum for Clergy and Other Helpers*. Cleveland, OH: Pilgrim Press, 1991.

Fawzy, Essam. "Muslim Personal Status Law in Egypt: The Current Situation and Possibilities of Reform Through Internal Initiatives." In *Women's Rights & Islamic Family Law: Perspectives on Reform*, edited by Lynn Welchman, 15–17. London: Zed Books, 2004.

Frager, Robert. *Heart, Self, and Soul: The Sufi Psychology of Growth, Balance and Harmony*. Wheaton, IL: Quest Books, 1999.

Frankl, Viktor. *Man in Search of Meaning*. Phoenix, AZ: Zeig, Tucker, and Theisen, 2003.

Frankl, Viktor. *The Will to Meaning*. Phoenix, AZ: Zeig, Tucker, and Theisen, 2003.

Freedman, Jill, and Combs, Gene. *Narrative Therapy: The Social Construction of Preferred Realities*. New York, NY: Oxford University Press, 1996.

Freud, Sigmund. *Fragment of an Analysis of a Case of Hysteria*. London: Hogarth Press, 1905/1975.

Freud, Sigmund. *Moses and Monotheism*. New York, NY: Vintage Book, 1938/1955.

Freud, Sigmund. *Religion as a Mass Delusion*. Accessed October 19, 2016, from www.freud.org.uk/education/topic/10573/subtopic/10005/.

Fournier, Pascale. "Introduction: Honour Crimes and the Law – Public Policy in an Age of Globalization." *Canadian Criminal Law Review* 16 (2) (2012): 103–115.

Gadamer, Hans-George, *Truth and Method*, 2nd rev., edited/translation revised by Joel Weinsheimer and Donald G. Marshall, Wahrheit und Methode. New York, NY: Continuum, 2004.

Gerkin, Charles. *Widening the Horizons: Pastoral Response to a Fragmented Society*. Philadelphia: Fortress Press, 1986.

Gerkin, Charles. *The Living Human Document: Re-Visioning Pastoral Counseling in a Hermeneutical Mode*. Nashville, TN: Abingdon Press, 1984.

Ghaly, Mohammed. "Physical and Spiritual Treatment of Disability in Islam." *Journal of Religion, Disabilty & Health*, 12 (2) (2008): 105–143.

Ghaly, Mohammed. "Prophetic Medicine." In *Muhammad in History, Thought, and Culture: An Encyclopedia of the Prophet of God*. 2 Vols., Vol. II, edited by C. Fitzpatrick and A. Walker, 502–506. Santa Barbara, CA: ABC-CLIO, 2014.

Ghorbani, Nima, Watson, Paul, J., Salimian,Mehdi., and Chen, Zhuo. "Shame and Guilt: Relationships of Test of Self-Conscious Affect Measures With Psychological Adjustment and Gender Differences in Iran." *Interpersona* 7 (1) (2013): 97–109. doi:10.5964/ijpr.v7i1.118.

Gilliat-Ray, Sophie, Mansur M. Ali, and Stephen Pattison. *Understanding Muslim Chaplaincy*. Surrey: Ashgate, 2013.

Gilliat-Ray, Sophie. "Body-Works and Fieldwork: Research With British Muslim Chaplains." *Culture and Religion* 11 (4) (2010): 413–432.

Gilliot, Claude. "Arrogance." In *Encyclopedia of Islam*. 3rd ed., edited by Kate Fleet, Gudrun Kramer, Denis Matringe, John Nawas, and Everett Rowson. Boston, MA: Brill, 2008, Accessed on January 25, 2016 from http://referenceworks.brillonline.com/browse/encyclopaedia-of-islam-2.

Glaz, Maxine, and Jeanne Moessner Stevenson. *Women in Travail and Transition: A New Pastoral Care*. Minneapolis, MN: Fortress Press, 1991.

Gnanadason, Aruna, and The World Council of Churches. *No Longer a Secret: The Church and Violence Against Women: Risk Book Series*. Geneva: WCC Publications, 1993.

Goffman, Erving. *Stigma: Notes on the Management of Spoiled Identity*. New York, NY: Simon and Schuster Inc., 1963.

Goldziher, Ignaz. *Introduction to Islamic Theology*, translated by Andras and Ruth Hamori. Princeton, NJ: Princeton University Press, 1981.

Gondolf, Edward W. "A Comparison of Re-Assault Rates in Four Batterer Programs: Do Court Referral, Program Length and Services Matter?" *Journal of Interpersonal Violence* 14 (1999): 41–61.

Graham, Elaine. "Feminist Theology." In *The Wiley-Blackwell Companion to Practical Theology*, edited by Bonnie J. Miller-McLemore, 193–203. Malden, MA: Blackwell Publishing Limited, 2012.

Green, Nile. *Sufism: A Global History*. Malden, MA: Willey Blackwell, 2012.

Green, Thomas A. *Folklore: An Encyclopedia of Beliefs, Customs, Tales, Music, and Art*. Santa Barbara, CA: ABC-CLIO, 1997.

Greenwald, Ricky. "Eye Movement Desensitization and Reprocessing (EMDR): An Overview." *Journal of Contemporary Psychotherapy* 24 (1) (1994): 15–34.

Grof, Stanislav, and Grof, Christian. *Spiritual Emergence: When Personal Transformation Becomes a Crisis*. Los Angeles: Tartcher, 1989.

Gruber, Devona, Lauren Hansen, Katrina Soaper, and Aaron J. Kivisto. "The Role of Shame in General, Intimate, and Sexual Violence Perpetration." In *Psychology of Shame: New Research*, edited by Kevin G. Lockhart, 39–62. New York, NY: Nova Science, 2014.

Haj-Yahia, Muhammad. "Implications of Wife Abuse and Battering for Self-Esteem, Depression, and Anxiety as Revealed by the Second Palestinian National Survey on Violence Against Women." *Journal of Family Issues* 21 (4) (2000): 435–463.

Hajjar, Lisa. "Domestic Violence and Sharia: A Comparative Study of Muslim Societies in the Middle East, Africa, and Asia." In *Women's Rights and Islamic Family Law: Perspectives on Reform*, edited by Lynn Welchman, 233. New York, NY: Zed Books, 2004.

Haleem, .Muhammad A. S. *The Qur'an*. New York, NY: Oxford University Press, 2008. Accessed January 23, 2017, from https://archive.org/stream/TheQuranKoranenglish

Ebook-AbdelHaleem-BestTranslationInThe/the_QURAN-abdel-haleem-ebook-engish_djvu.txt.

Hallaq, Wael. *Sharī'a: Theory, Practice, Transformations.* Cambridge: Cambridge University Press, 2009.

Halverson, Jeffry R. *Theology and Creed in Sunni Islam: The Muslim Brotherhood, Ash'arism, and Political Sunnism.* Basingstoke, UK: Palgrave Macmillan, 2010.

Hamberger, L. Kevin, and Hastings, James E. "Personality Correlates of Men Who Abuse Their Partners: A Cross-Validation Study." *Journal of Family Violence* 1 (1986): 323–341.

Hamjah, Salasiah Hamin, and Noor Shakirah Mat Akhir. "Islamic Approach in Counseling." *Journal of Religion and Health* 53 (2014): 279–289.

Haque, Amber. "Psychology From Islamic Perspective: Contributions of Early Muslim Scholars and Challenges to Contemporary Muslim Psychologist." *Journal of Religion and Health* 43 (4) (2004): 357–377.

Haque, Amber, and Najeeb Kamil. "Islam, Muslims, and Mental Health." In *Counseling Muslims: Handbook of Mental Health Issues and Interventions*, edited by Sameera Ahmed and Mona M. Amer, 3–14. New York, NY: Taylor & Francis Group, 2012.

Hamid, Rafia M. "Domestic Violence in Muslim Communities." *Religion and Men's Violence Against Women* (2015): 319–342.

Harrigan, Marcia. P. "Major Depression." In *Challenges of Living: A Multidimensional Working Model for Social Workers*, edited by E. D. Hutchison, H. C. Matto, M. P. Harrigan, L. W. Charlesworth and P. A. Viggiani, 267–300. Thousand Oaks, CA: Sage Publications, 2007.

Hassan, Riffat. "Feminism in Islam." In *Feminism and World Religion*, edited by Arvind Sharma and Katherine K. Young, 248–278. Albany, NY: State University of New York Press, 1999.

Hassouneh-Phillips, Dena Saadat. "American Muslim Women's Experiences of Leaving Abusive Relationships." *Health Care for Women International* 22 (2001): 415–432.

Hassouneh-Phillips, Dena Saadat. " 'Marriage Is Half of Faith and the Rest Is Fear Allah': Marriage and Spousal Abuse Among American Muslims." *Violence Against Women* 7 (2001): 927–946.

Hassouneh-Phillips, Dena Saadat. "Strength and Vulnerability: Spirituality in Abused American Muslim Women's Lives." *Issues in Mental Health Nursing* 24 (2003): 681–694.

Heimbrock, Hans Gunter. "Healing, Magic and the Interpretation of Reality." In *Happiness, Well-Being and the Meaning of Life: A Dialogue of Social Science and Religion*, edited by V. Brümmer and M. Sarot, 42–47. Kämpen: Kok, 1996.

Helms, Barbara Lois. "Honour and Shame in the Canadian Muslim Community: Developing Culturally Sensitive Counselling Interventions/Honneur et honte dans la communauté musulmane au Canada: Élaborer des modes d'intervention et de counseling tenant compte des cultures." *Canadian Journal of Counselling and Psychotherapy* 49 (2) (2015): 163–184.

Herman, Judith. *Trauma and Recovery – The Aftermath of Violence From Domestic Abuse to Political Terror.* New York, NY: Basic Books, 1997.

Hinshaw, Stephen P. *The Mark of Shame: Stigma of Mental Illness and an Agenda for Change.* Oxford: Oxford University Press, 2009.

Hodgson, Marshall. *The Venture of Islam: Conscience and History in a World Civilization.* Chicago, IL: The University of Chicago Press, 1974.

Hoeft, Jeanne. *Agency, Culture, and Human Personhood: Pastoral Theology and Intimate Partner Violence.* Eugene, OR: Princeton Theological Monograph, Pickwick Publications, 2007.

Husaini, Sayyid Waqqar Ahmed. "Humanistic–Social Sciences Studies in Higher Education: Islamic and International Perspectives." In *Social and Natural Sciences: The Islamic Perspectives*, edited by Ismāʿīl Rājī al-Fārūqī and Abdullah Omar Nasseef, 148–166. Jiddah: Islamic Education Series, 1981.

Hussein, Abdul-Raof. *A Practical Comparative-Contrastive Analysis*. London: Routledge, 2012.

Huseein, Abdul-Raof, *Theological Approaches to Qur'anic Exegesis: A Practical Comparative-Contrastive Analysis*. New York: Routledge, 2012.

Hussain, Amjad. "Muslim Theology and Religious Studies: Relational, Practical, and Inter-Faith Dimensions." *Religious Education: The Official Journal of the Religious Education Association* 104 (3) (2009): 239–242.

Husseini, Rana. "Honor Killings." In *The Oxford Encyclopedia of Islam and Women*, edited by John Esposito. Accessed on December 23, 2016 from www.oxfordislamicstudies.com.myaccess.library.utoronto.ca/article/opr/t355/e0130.

ibn Taymiyyah, Taqi al-Din Ahmad b. ʻAbd al-Halim. *Mukhtasar al-fatawa al-misriyya*. Cairo: Dar *al*-Kutub *al*-Misriyya, 1980.

ibn Taymiyyah, Taqi al-Din Ahmad b. ʻAbd al-Halim. *The Relief From Distress*. Birmingham: Daar us-Sunhah Publishers, 2006.

ibn Taymiyyah, Taqi al-Din Ahmad b. *Majm'at al-rasa'il wal-masa'il*. Bayrut: Dår al-Kutub al-Ilmiyyah, 1983.

ibn Taymiyyah, Taqi al-Din Ahmad b. *Muqaddimah fi usul al-tafsir*. Edited by Adnan Zarzour, 2nd ed. Bayrut: n.p. 1972.

ibn Taymiyyah, Taqi al-Din Ahmad b. An Explanation of Shayhkh al-Islam Ibn Taymiyyah's Introduction to the Principles of Tafseer Explanation by Shaykh Muhammad Ibn Salih al-Uthaymin. Birmingham, UK: Al-Hidaayah Publishing Ltd., n.d. Accessed from http://alsiraat.co.uk/wp-content/uploads/2014/12/Ibn-Taymiyahs-Principles-of-Tafseer.pdf.

Idriss, Mohammad Mazher, and Abbas, Tahir. *Honour, Violence, Women and Islam*. New York, NY: Routledge, 2011.

International Organization for Migration (IOM). *Introduction to Basic Counselling and Communication Skills: IOM Training Manual for Migrant Community Leaders and Community Workers*, 2009. Accessed on March 4, 2016 from www.iom.int/jahia/webdav/site/myjahiasite/shared/shared/mainsite/activities/health/pandemic_manual.pdf.

Iqbal, Muhammad. *The Reconstruction of Religious Thought in Islam*. Lahore: Shaikh Muhammad Ashraf, 1934/1962.

Isgandarova, N. "The Role of Practice Based Education in Islamic Spiritual Care: The Clinical Pastoral Education (CPE) Training." *The Muslim World 108* (1) (2018).

Isgandarova, N. "Practical Theology and Its Importance for Islamic Theological Studies." *Ilahiyat Studies: A Journal on Islamic and Religious Studies* 5 (2) (2014). doi.org/10.12730/13091719.2014.52.109

Isgandarova, N. "Music in Islamic Spiritual Care: A Review of Classical Sources." *Religious Studies and Theology* 34 (1) (2015). doi: 10.1558/rsth.v34i1.26326

Isgandarova, N. "The Crescent of Compassionate Engagement: Theory and Practice of Islamic Spiritual Care." In *Multifaith Views in Spiritual Care*, edited by Daniel S. Schipani, 109–130. Waterloo, Belgium: Pandora Press, Society for Intercultural Pastoral Care and Counseling, 2013.

Isgandarova, N. "Muslim Spiritual Care and Counselling." In *The Spiritual Care GiversGuide to Identity, Practice and Relationships: Transforming the Honeymoon,* edited by T. O'Connor, E. Meakes, and C. Lashmar, 135–256. Waterloo, Belgium: WLU Press, 2008.

Isgandarova, N. "Islamic Spiritual Care in a Health Care Setting." In *Spirituality and Health: Multidisciplinary Explorations*, edited by A. Meier, T. O'Connor, and P. VanKatwyk, 85–104. Waterloo, Belgium: WLU Press, 2005.

Isgandarova, N. "Canadian Licensing Changes and the Anticipated Impact on Islamic Spiritual Care and Counseling Practice in Ontario." *Journal of Pastoral Care and Counseling* 68 (3) (2014): 1–9. doi: 10.1177/154230501406800307

Isgandarova, N., and O'Connor, Thomas St. James. "A Redefinition and Model of Canadian Islamic Spiritual Care." *Journal of Pastoral Care and Counseling* 66 (2) (2012): 1–8. doi: 10.1177/154230501206600207

Isgandarova, N. "Effectiveness of Islamic Spiritual Care: Foundations and Practices of Muslim Spiritual Care Givers." *The Journal of Pastoral Care & Counseling* 66 (3) (2013): 1–16. doi: 10.1177/154230501206600304

Islam, Farah., and Campbell, Robert A. "Satan Has Afflicted Me! Jinn-Possession and Mental Illness in the Qur'an." *Journal of Religion and Health* 53 (2014): 229–243.

Izutsu, Toshihiko. *The Structure of the Ethical Terms in the Koran: A Study in Semantics.* Tokyo: Keio Institute of Philological Studies, 1959.

Jacobson, Neil S., and John M. Gottman. *When Men Batter Women: New Insights Into Ending Abusive Relationships.* New York, NY: Simon and Schuster, 1998.

Jackson, Mike, and Fulford, K. W. J. "Spiritual Experience and Psychopathology, Philosophy." *Psychiatry and Psychology* 4 (1) (1997): 41–65.

Jackson, Sherman A. *Islam and the Problem of Black Suffering.* New York, NY: Oxford University Press, 2009.

James, Nelson. *Understanding Male Violence: Pastoral Care Issues.* 1st ed. St. Louis, MO: Chalice Press, 2003.

Jenkins, Allen. *Invitations to Responsibility: The Therapeutic Engagement of Men Who Are Violent and Abusive.* Adelaide, AU: Dulwich Centre Publications, 1990.

Jiwani, Yasmin. *Discourses of Denial: Mediations of Race, Gender, and Violence.* Vancouver, BC: UBC Press, 2006.

Johansen, Thor. *Religion and Spirituality in Psychotherapy: An Individual Psychology Perspective.* New York, NY: Springer, 2010.

Joseph, Bellal, Khalil, Mazhar, Zangbar, Bardiya, Kulvatunyou, Narong, et al., "Prevalence of Domestic Violence Among Trauma Patients." *Journal of Emergency Medicine* 50 (4) (2015): 1177–1183.

Kafrawi, Shalahudin. "Fitrah." In *The Oxford Encyclopedia of the Islamic World*, edited by John Esposito. Oxford: Oxford University Press, 2009. http://www.oxfordislamicstudies.com.myaccess.library.utoronto.ca/article/opr/t236/e1151?_hi=2&_pos=7

Kamali, Mohammad Hashim. *Shari'ah Law: An Introduction.* Oxford: Oneworld, 2008.

Kamali, Mohammad Hashim. *Maqasid al Shariah: The Objectives of Islamic Law.* Accessed January 23, 2017, from http://islam101.net/index.php/shariah/141-maqasidalshariah

Kamali, Mohammad Hashim. *Principles of Islamic Jurisprudence.* Cambridge: Islamic Texts, 1991.

Kemp, Simon, and Strongman. K. T. "Anger Theory and Management: A Historical Analysis." *The American Journal of Psychology* 108 (3) (1995): 397–417.

Keshavarzi, Hooman, and Amber Haque. "Outlining a Psychotherapy Model for Enhancing Muslim Mental Health Within an Islamic Context." *The International Journal for the Psychology of Religion* 23 (2013): 230–249.

Khaja Khadiji., and Frederick, Chelsea. "Reflection on Teaching Effective Social Work Practice for Working With Muslim Communities." *Advances in Social Work* 9 (1) (2008): 1–7.

Kobeisy, Ahmed Nezar. *Counseling American Muslims: Understanding the Faith and Helping the People*. Westport, CT: Praeger Publishers, 2004.

Kobeisy, Ahmed Nezar. "Faith-Based Practice: An Introduction." *Journal of Muslim Mental Health* 1 (2006): 57–63.

Kottak, Conrad Phillip. *Windows on Humanity*. New York, NY: McGraw Hill, 2007.

Kroeber, Alfred L., and Kluckhohn, Clyde. *Culture: A Critical Review of Concepts and Definitions*. Cambridge: Peabody Museum Papers, 1952. Accessed on September 2, 2016 from www.pseudology.org/Psyhology/CultureCriticalReview1952a.pdf.

Lakkary, Sally, Barbara Franke, Dina Shokri, Sven Hartwig, Michael Tsokos, and Klaus Püschel. "Honor Crimes: Review and Proposed Definition." *Forensic Science, Medicine, and Pathology* 10 (1) (2014): 76–82.

Lamrabet, Asma. "An Egalitarian Reading of the Concepts of Khilafah, Wilayah and Qiwamah." In *Men in Charge: Rethinking Authority in Muslim Legal Tradition*, edited by Ziba Mir-Hosseini, Mulki Al-Sharmani, and Jana Rumminger, 65–87. London: Oneworld Publications, 2015.

Lane, Edward W. *Manners and Customs of the Modern Egyptians*. London: J. M. Dent Co., 1836/1902.

Lau, Martin. "Honour, Crimes, Paradigms and Violence Against Women." *Yearbook of Islamic and Middle Eastern Law Online* 11 (1) (2004): 471–472.

Leaman, Oliver. *The Biographical Encyclopaedia of Islamic Philosophy*. London: Thoemmes Continuum, 2006.

Leaman, Oliver, and Rizvi, Sajjad. "The Developed Kalam Tradition (Part II: Later Shi'i Theology)." In *The Cambridge Companion to Classical Islamic Theology*, edited by Tim Winter, 77–96. Cambridge: Cambridge University Press, 2008.

Leibniz, Gottfried Wilhelm. *Theodicy: Essays on the Goodness of God, the Freedom of Man and the Origin of Evil*. La Vergne, TN: Lightning Source Incorporated, 2006.

Lewis, Bernard. "Some Observations on the Significance of Heresy in the History of Islam." *Studia Islamica* 1 (1953): 44.

Lewis-Fernandez, Roberto, Aggarwal, Neil Krishan, Hinton, Ladson, Hinton, Devon, and Kirmayer, Laurence J. *DSM-5: Handbook on the Cultural Formulation Interview*. Washington, DC: American Psychiatric Association, 2016.

Lewis, Ioan M. *Religion in Context: Cults and Charisma*. Cambridge: Cambridge University Press, 1986.

Littlewood, Roland. "Possession States." *Psychiatry* 3 (8) (2004): 8–10.

Lukoff, David. "Visionary Spiritual Experiences." *Southern Medical Journal* 100 (6) (2007): 635–641.

MacIntyre, Alasdair. *After Virtue*, 3rd ed. Notre Dame, IN: University of Notre Dame Press, 2007.

Mahoney, Annette, Layal Abadi, and Kenneth I. Pargament. "Exploring Women's Spiritual Struggles and Resources to Cope With Intimate Partner Aggression." In *Religion and Men's Violence Against Women*, edited by Andy J. Johnson, 45–59. New York, NY: Springer, 2015.

Makdisi, George. *The Rise of Colleges: Institutions of Learning*. Edinburgh: Edinburgh Unviersity Press, 1981.

Marcotte, Roxanne D. "Ibn Miskawayh's Tartib al-Saadat (The Order of Happiness)." In *Monotheism and Ethics: Historical and Contemporary Intersections Between Judaism, Christianity, and Islam*, edited by Y. Tzvi Langermann, 141–162. Leiden: Brill, 2012.

Mattson, Ingrid. *The Story of the Qur'an: Its history and Place in Muslim Life*. Oxford: John Wiley & Sons, 2012.

Mattson, Ingrid. "Dignity and Patient Care: An Islamic Perspective." *The Yale Journal for Humanities in Medicine* (2002). Accessed March 16, 2016, from http://yjhm.yale.edu/archives/spirit2003/dignity/imattson.htm.

Mawdudi, Sayyid Abul A'la. *Towards Understanding the Qur'an*, translated by Zafar Ishåq Ansari. Leicester: Islamic Foundation, 1995.

McCue, Margi Laird. *Domestic Violence: A Reference Handbook*. Santa Barbara, CA: ABC-CLIO, 2008.

McFague, Sallie. "The Theologian as Advocate." In *The Making and Remaking of Christian Doctrine: Essays in Honour of Maurice Wiles*, edited by Sarah Coakley and David A. Pail, 79–97. Oxford: Clarendon Press, 1993.

Macfarlane, Julie. *Islamic Divorce in North America: A Shari'a Path in a Secular Society*. Oxford: Oxford University Press, 2012.

Macfarlane, Julie. *Understanding Trends in American Muslim Divorce and Marriage: A Discussion Guide for Families and Communities*, 25–26. The Institute for Social Policy and Understanding, 2013. Accessed March 16, 2016, from www.ispu.org/getreports/35/2399/publications.aspx.

Merchant, Munira. "A Comparative Study of Agencies Assisting Domestic Violence Victims: Does the South Asian Community Have Special Needs?" *Journal of Social Distress and the Homeless* 9 (3) (2000): 249–259.

Mernissi, Fatima. *The Veil and the Male Elite: A Feminist Interpretation of Women's Rights in Islam*. Reading, MA: Addison-Wesley Publishing, 1987.

Michel, Thomas S. J. "The Resurrection of the Dead and Final Judgment in the Thought of Said Nursi." In *Theodicy and Justice in Modern Islamic Thought: The Case of Said Nursi*, edited by Ibrahim M. Abu-Rabic, 29–40. Surrey: Ashgate, 2010.

Miller, Paul William. *EMDR Therapy for Schizophrenia and Other Psychoses*. New York, NY: Springer Publishing Company, 2016.

Miller-McLemore, Bonnie J. "Five Misunderstandings About Practical Theology." *International Journal of Practical Theology* 16 (1) (2012): 5–26. Accessed from http://dx.doi.org/10.1515/ijpt-2012-0002.

Miller-McLemore, Bonnie J. "Introduction: The Contributions of Practical Theology." In *The Wiley-Blackwell Companion to Practical Theology*, edited by Bonnie J. Miller-McLemore, 1–20. Maldan, MA: Wiley-Blackwell, 2012.

Miller-McLemore, Bonnie J. *Christian Theology in Practice: Discovering a Discipline*. Grand Rapids, MI: Wm. B. Eerdmans Publishing, 2012.

Miller-McLemore, Bonnie J. "Toward Greater Understanding of Practical Theology." *International Journal of Practical Theology* 16 (1) (2012): 104–123. Accessed from http://dx.doi.org/10.1515/ijpt-2012-0009.

Mir-Hosseini, Ziba. "Towards Gender Equality: Muslim Family Laws and the Shari'ah." In *Wanted: Equality and Justice in the Muslim Family*, edited by Zainah Anwar, 23 63. Petalig Jaya: Musawah, 2009.

Mir-Hosseini, Ziba, *Marriage on Trial: A Study of Islamic Family Law: Iran and Morocco Compared*. London: I. B. Tauris, 1993.

Mir-Hosseini, Ziba, Al-Sharmani, Mulki, and Rumminger, Jana. (Eds). *Men in Charge? Rethinking Authority in Muslim Legal Tradition*. London: Oneworld Publications, 2015.

Moessner, Jeanne Stevenson, and Glaz, Maxine. "Introduction: I Heard a Cry." In *Women in Travail and Transition*. Minneapolis, MN: Fortress Press, 1991.

Moghadam, Valentine M. *Modernizing Women, Gender and Social Change in the Middle East*. Boulder, CO: Lynne Rienner Publishers, 1993.

Mohd, Noor Azman. "Rape: A Problem of Crime Classification in Islamic Law." *Arab Law Quarterly* 24 (4) (2010): 417–438.
Moghaddam, Maria Sabaye. "Zar Beliefs and Practices in Bandar Abbas and Qeshm Island in Iran." *Anthropology of the Middle East* 7 (2) (2012): 19–28.
Morh, Sylvia, Lawrence Borras, Nolan, Jennifer, et al. "Spirituality and Religion in Outpatients With Schizophrenia: A Multi-Site Comparative Study of Switzerland, Canada, and the United States." *International Journal of Psychiatry in Medicine* 44 (1) (2012): 29–52.
Mohr, Sylvia, Perroud, Nader, Gilleron, Christine, et al. "Spirituality and Religiousness as Predictive Factors of Outcome in Schizophrenia and Schizo-Affective Disorders." *Psychiatry Research* 186 (2011): 177–182.
Moodley, Roy. "Double, Triple, Multiple Jeopardy." In *Antidiscriminatory Counselling Practice*, edited by C. Lago and B. Smith, 120–134. London: Sage Publications, 2003.
Moodley, Roy. "Representation of Subjective Distress in Black and Ethnic Minority Patients: Constructing a Research Agenda." *Counselling Psychology Quarterly* 13 (2000): 159–174.
Moodley, Roy, Lawrence Epp, and Humair Yusuf, eds. *Counseling Across the Cultural Divide: The Clemmont E. Vontress Reader*. Herefordshire: PCCS Books, 2012.
Moodley, Roy, and William West. *Integrating Traditional Healing Practices Into Counseling and Psychotherapy*. Thousand Oaks, CA: Sage Publications, 2015.
Morris, Hood. "A Spiritual Well-Being Model: Use With Older Women Who Experience Depression." *Issues in Mental Health Nursing* 17 (1996): 439–455.
Moustakas, Clark. *Heuristic Research: Design, Methodology, and Applications* (Newbury Park, CA: Sage Publications, 1990.
Mouzos, Jenny. and Makkai, Tony. *Women's Experiences of Male Violence: Findings From the Australian Component of the International Violence Against Women Survey (IVAWS)*. Canberra Australian Institute of Criminology Research and Public Policy Series, 2004.
Mubarak, Hadia. "Breaking the Interpretive Monopoly: Re-Examination of Verse 4:34." *Hawwa* 2 (3) (2005): 261–298.
Murad, Abdal Hakim. *The Mantle Adorned*. London: The Quilliam Press Ltd., 2009.
Murata, Sachiko. *The Tao of Islam: A Sourcebook on Gender Relationships in Islamic Thought*. Albany, NY: State University of New York Press, 1992.
Murata, Sachiko, and William C. Chittick. *The Vision of Islam*. New York, NY: Paragon House, 1994.
Nasir, Laeth Sari. "Globalization, Health and Culture." In *Caring for Arab Patients: A Biopsychosocial Approach*, edited by Lateth Sari Nasir and Arwa Kyaed Abdul-Haq, 19–26. Oxford: Radcliffe Publishing, 2008.
Nasr, Seyyed Hossein. *Islamic Spirituality: Foundations*. New York: Crossroad, 1987.
Nasr, Seyyed Hossein. *The Garden of Truth: The Vision and Practice of Sufism*. San Francisco, CA: Harper, 2007.
Nasr, Seyyed Hossein. "The Teaching of Philosophy." In *Philosophy, Literature, and Fine Arts*, edited by Seyyed Hossein Nasr, 3–21. Jiddah: Islamic Education Series, 1981.
Nawas, John A. "A Re-examination of Three Current Explanations for al-Mamun's Introduction of the Mihna." *International Journal of Middle East Studies* 26 (4) (1994): 615–629.
Neher, Andrew. *Paranormal and Transcendental Experience: A Psychological Examination*. New York, NY: Dover Publications, 2013.
Nestor, Paul. "Mental Disorder and Violence: Personality Dimensions and Clinical Features." *The American Journal of Psychiatry* 159 (1) (2002): 1973–1978.

Neuger, Christie Cozad, ed. *The Arts of Ministry: Feminist-Womanist Approaches*. 1st ed. Louisville, KY: Westminster John Knox Press, 1996.

Neuger, Christie Cozad. *Counseling Women: A Narrative, Pastoral Approach*. Minneapolis, MN: Fortress Press, 2001.

Neuger, Christine Cozad. "Women's Depression: Lives at Risk." In *Women in Travail and Transition: A New Pastoral Care*, edited by Maxine Glaz and Jeanne Stevenson Moessner, 146–161. Minneapolis, MN: Fortress Press, 1991.

Nina, Hoel and Shaikh, Sa'diyya. "Sexing Islamic Theology: Theorising Women's Experience and Gender Through abd allah and khalifah." *Journal for Islamic Studies* 33 (2013): 127–151.

Nizamie, Shahsul, Kathsu, Mohammed Zia, and Uvais, N. Ahamed. "Sufism and Mental Health." *Indian Journal of Psychiatry* 55 (6) (2013): 215–223.

Nursi, Bediuzzaman Said. *The Words: The Reconstruction of Islamic Belief and Thought*. Translated by Hesyin Akarsu. Clifton, NJ: The Light, Inc., 2005.

Obeid, Tahir, Abulaban, Ahmad, Al-Ghatani, Fawazia, Al-Malki, Abdul Rahman, and Al-Ghamdi, Abdulaziz. "Possession by 'Jinn' as a Cause of Epilepsy (Saraa)." *Seizure: European Journal of Epilepsy*, 21 (4) (2012): 245–249.

O'Brian, Mary Elizabeth. "The Need for Spiritual Integrity." In *Human Needs and Nursing Process*, edited by Helen Yura and Mary B. Walsh, 198. Norwalk, CT: Appleton-Century-Crofts.

O'Connor, Thomas S. "Climbing Mount Purgatory: Dante's Cure of Souls and Narrative Family Therapy." *Pastoral Psychology* 47 (6) (1999): 445–457.

Okin, Susan Moller. *Is Multiculturalism Bad for Women?* Princeton, NJ: Princeton University Press, 1999.

Olubunmu Oyewuwo-Gassikia, Basirat. "American Muslim Women and Domestic Violence Service Seeking." *Affilia*, (31) (4) (2016): 450.

Oregon Domestic Violence Council. *A Collaborative Approach to Domestic Violence: Oregon Protocol Handbook*. Portland, OR: Domestic Violence Council, 1995.

Ormsby, Erik L. *Theodicy in Islamic Thought: The Dispute Over al-Ghazali's 'Best of All Possible Worlds'*. Princeton, NJ: Princeton University Press, 1984.

Pasha, Mohamed Iqbal, and Pridmore, Saxby. "Psychiatry and Islam." *Australian Psychiatry* 12 (4) (2004): 380–385.

Paladın, Angelisa V. "Ethics and Neurology in the Islamic World: Continuity and Change." *Italian Journal of Neurological Science* 19 (1998): 255–258.

Pattison, Stephen, and James Woodward. "An Introduction to Pastoral and Practical Theology." In *The Blackwell Reader in Pastoral and Practical Theology*, edited by James Woodward and Stephen Pattison, 1–19. Oxford: Blackwell, 2000.

Pessagno, Jerome Meric. "The Uses of Evil in Maturidian Thought." *Studia Islamica* 60 (1980). 65.

Picken, Gavin. *Spiritual Purification in Islam: The Life and Works of al-Muhasibi*. London: Routledge, 2011.

Poling, James N. *Understanding Male Violence: Pastoral Care Issues*. 1st ed. St. Louis, MO: Chalice Press, 2003.

Price, Jill. *The Woman Who Can't Forget*. New York, NY: Free Press, 2008.

Rahman, Fatima Z. "Gender Equality in Muslim-Majority States and Shari'a Family Law: Is There a Link?" *Australian Journal of Political Science* 47 (3) (2012): 347–362.

Rahman, Fazlur. *Islam*. Chicago, IL: University of Chicago Press, 1966.

Rahman, Fazlur. *Islam and Modernity: Transformation of an Intellectual Tradition*. Chicago, IL: The University of Chicago Press, 1982.

Rahman, Fazlur. *Major Themes in the Qur'an.* Minneapolis, MN: Bibliotheca Islamica, Inc., 1989.

Rahman, Fazlur. "Approaches to Islam in Religious Studies." In *Approaches to Islam in Religious Studies,* edited by Richard C. Martin, 151–163. Tucson: University of Arizona, 1985.

Rahman, Fazlur. *Revival and Reform in Islam*, edited by Ebrahim Moosa. Oxford: Oneworld, 2000.

Rahman, Fazlur. "Towards Reformulating the Methodology of Islamic Law: Sheikh; Yamani on 'Public Interest' in Islamic Law." *New York University Journal of International Law and Politics* 12 (2) (1979): 219–224.

Ramadan, Tariq. *Radical Reform: Islamic Ethics and Liberation.* Oxford: Oxford University Press, 2009.

Ramsay, Nancy J. "Emancipatory Theory and Method." In *The Wiley-Blackwell Companion to Practical Theology*, edited by Bonnie J. Miller-McLemore (Maldan, MA: Wiley-Blackwell, 2012), 183–192.

Rapp, Christof. "Aristotle's Rhetoric." In *The Stanford Encyclopedia of Philosophy*, edited by Edward N. Zalta. Spring 2010 Edition.

Rashed, M. A. "From Powerlessness to Control: Psychosis, Spirit Possession and Recovery in the Western Desert of Egypt." *Health, Culture and Society* 8 (2) (2015): 10–26. doi:http://dx.doi.org/10.5195/hcs.2015.194

Rassool, G. Hussein. *Islamic Counselling: An Introduction to Theory and Practice.* New York, NY: Routledge, 2016.

Reda, Nevin. "The 'Good' Muslim, 'Bad' Muslim Puzzle? The Assertion of Muslim Women's Islamic Identity in the Sharia Debates in Canada." In *Debating Sharia: Islam, Gender Politics, and Family Law Arbitration*, edited by Anna C. Korteweg and Jennifer A. Selby, 231–256. Toronto, ON: University of Toronto Press, 2012.

Ricoeur, Paul. *The Rule of Metaphor.* New York: Routledge, 2004.

Rida, Muhammad Rashid, and ʿAbduh, Muhammad. *Tafsir al-Qur'an al-hakim al-shahr bi-tafsir al-Manār*, 12 vols. Bayrut: Dār al-Ma ʿrifah, n.d.

Rippin, Andrew. "The Exegetical Genre '*asbab al-nuzul*': A Bibliographical and Terminological Survey." *Bulletin of the School of Oriental and African Studies* 48 (1) (1985): 1–15.

Rippin, Andrew. "Devil." In *Encyclopaedia of the Qur'an*, edited by Jane Dammen McAuliffe (Leiden: Brill, 2001) 1: 524–527.

Rizvi, Syed Azhar Ali. *Muslim Tradition in Psychotherapy and Modern Trends.* Lahore: Institute of Islamic Culture, 1989.

Robinaugh, Donald J., and Richard J. McNally. "Autobiographical Memory for Shame or Guilt Provoking Events: Association With Psychological Symptoms." *Behaviour Research and Therapy* 48 (7) (2010): 646–652.

Rogers, Carl Ranson. *The Therapeutic Relationship and Its Impact: A Study of Psychotherapy With Schizophrenics.* Madison, WI: University of Wisconsin Press, 1967.

Ruggi, Suzanne. "Commodifying Honor in Female Sexuality: Honor Killings in Palestine." *Middle East Research and Information Project.* Accessed October 20, 2016, from www.merip.org/mer/mer206/ruggi.htm.

Rudolfsson, Inga and Tidefors, Lisa. "I Have Cried to Him a Thousand Times." *Mental Health, Religion & Culture* 17(9): 910–922.

Ryan, Kathryn M., Weikel, Kim, and Sprechini, Gene. "Gender Differences in Narcissism and Courtship Violence in Dating Couples." *Sex Roles* 58 (2008): 802–813.

Sabry, W., and V. Adarsh. "Role of Islam in the Management of Psychiatric Disorders." *Indian Journal of Psychiatry* 55 (6) (2013).

Sachedina, Abdul Aziz. *Islamic Biomedical Ethics: Principles and Application*. Oxford: Oxford University Press, 2009.

Sachedina, Abdul Aziz. "Imamah." In *The Oxford Dictionary of Islam*. Accessed February 9, 2017 from www.oxfordislamicstudies.com.myaccess.library.utoronto.ca/article/opr/t236/e0357?_hi=0&_pos=1.

Saeed, Abdullah. *Interpreting the Qur'an: Towards a Contemporary Approach*. London: Routledge, 2006.

Safi, M. L. "Islamization of Psychology: From Adaptation to Sublimation." *The American Journal of Islamic Social Sciences* 15 (4) (1998): 117–125.

Sahih Bukhari. Translated by M. Muhsin Khan. New Delhi, India: Kitab Bhaban, 1984.

Sahih-Bukhari. Translated by M. Muhsin Khan (New Delhi, India: Kitab Bhaban, 1984). Accessed December 30, 2015, from http://sunnah.com/muslim/52.

Saleh, Walid. "Ibn Taymiyya and the Rise of Radical Hermeneutics: An Analysis of an Introduction to the Foundations of Qur'anic Exegesis." In *Ibn Taymiyya and His Times*, edited by Yossef Rapoport and Shahab Ahmed. Oxford: Oxford University Press, 2010.

Saleh, Walid. *The Formation of the Classical Tafsır Tradition: The Qur'an Commentary of al-Thalabi*. Leiden: Brill, 2004.

Saritorpak, Zeki. "The Creation of Evil Is Not Evil: Theological Approach to the Existence of Evil," *The Fountain* 50 (2005). Accessed September 25, 2016, from www.fountainmagazine.com/Issue/detail/The-Creation-of-Evil-is-not-Evil-Nursis-Theological-Approach-to-the-Existence-of-Evil.

Schimmel, Annemarie. *Mystical Dimensions of Islam*. Chapel Hill, NC: The University of North Carolina Press, 2011.

Schneider, Carl D. "Shame." In *Dictionary of Pastoral Care and Counseling*, edited by Rodney J. Hunter, 1160–1163. Nashville, TN: Abingdon Press, 1990.

Sells, Michael A. *Early Islamic Mysticism: Sufi, Qur'an, Mi'raj, Poetic and Theological Writings*. New York, NY: Paulist Press, 1996.

Shaikh, Sa'diyya. "Exegetical Violence: *Nushuz* in Quranic Gender Ideology." *Journal for Islamic Studies* 17 (1997): 49–73.

Shaikh, Sa'diyya. "Islamic Law, Sufism and Gender: Rethinking the Terms of the Debate." In *Men in Charge: Rethinking Authority in Muslim Legal Tradition*, edited by Ziba Mir-Hosseini, Mulki Al-Sharmani and Jana Rumminger, 106–131. London: Oneworld Publications, 2015.

Shaikh, Sa'diyya. "Search of al-Insan: Sufism, Islamic Law, and Gender." In *Muslima Theology: The Voices of Muslim Women Theologians*, edited by Ednan Asla, Marcia J. Hermansen and Elif Medeni. New York, NY: Peter Lang Edition, 2013.

Shaikh, Sa'diyya. *Sufi Narratives of Intimacy: Ibn 'Arabi, Gender and Sexuality*. Chapel Hill, NC. University of North Carolina Press, 2012.

Shaikh, Sa'diyya. "Transforming Feminism: Islam, Women and Gender Justice." In *Progressive Muslims: On Justice, Pluralism*, edited by O. Safi, 147–162. Oxford: Oneworld Publications, 2003.

Shapiro, F. *Eye Movement Desensitization and Reprocessing: Basic Principles, Protocols, and Procedures*. New York, NY: Guilford Press, 1995.

Sharafeldin, Marwa. "Reformulating Qiwamah and Wilayah for Personal Status Law Reform Advocacy in Egypt." In *Men in Charge: Rethinking Authority in Muslim Legal Tradition*, edited by Ziba Mir-Hosseini, Mulki Al-Sharmani and Jana Rumminger, 171–173, London: Oneworld Publications, 2015.

Shehu, Salisu. *Towards an Islamic Perspective of Developmental Psychology*, 2002. Accessed on March 5, 2016 from www.islamonline.net/english/Contemporary/2002/05/article7-a.shtml.

Sheikh, A., and A. A. Gatrad. *Caring for Muslim Patients.* 2nd ed. Abingdon: Radcliffe Publishing, 2000.

Siddique, Muzammil H. *Five Features of Islamic Culture.* Accessed February 15, 2017, from www.thekhalids.org/index.php/newsletter-archive/1160-5-features-of-islamic-culture.

Simonič, Barbara, Mandelj, Tina Rahn, and Novsak, Rachel. "Religious-Related Abuse in the Family." *Journal of Family Violene* 28 (4) (2013): 339–349.

Silvers, Laura. "In the Book We Have Left out Nothing: The Ethical Problem of the Existence of Verse 4:34 in the Qur'an." *Comparative Islamic Studies* 2 (2) (2006): 171–180.

Silvers, Laura. "Religion, State Power, and Domestic Violence in Muslim Societies: A Framework for Comparative Analysis." *Law & Social Inquiry* 29 (1) (2004): 1–38.

Siraj, Abu Bakr. "The Origins of Sufism." *Islamic Sciences* 13 (2) (2015): 59–76.

Soler, Hosanna, Vinayak, Preeti, and Quadagno, David. "Biosocial Aspects of Domestic Violence." *Psychoneuroendocrinology* 25 (7) (2000): 721–739.

Soroush, Abdolkairm. *Qabz o bast-e teutik-e shariat – nazariye-ye takamol-e marefat-e dini (Theory of Extension and Concentration/Evolution and Devolution of Religion – the Theory of Religious Knowledge's Development)*, 3rd ed. Tehran: Sarat, 1994.

Soroush, Abdolkarim. *Reason, Freedom, and Democracy in Islam: Essential Writings of Abdolkarim Soroush*, trans. and ed. by Mahmoud Sadri and Ahmed Sadri. Oxford: Oxford Univeristy Press, 2000.

Spero, Moshe Halvei. *Judaism and Psychology: Halakhic Perspective.* New York, NY: KTAU Publishing House, Inc., Yeshiva University Press, 1980.

Statistics Canada. *Family Violence in Canada: A Statistical Profile*, 2010. Accessed March 7, 2016 from www.statcan.gc.ca/daily-quotidien/120522/dq120522a-eng.pdf.

Statistics Canada. *Violence Against Women*, 2011. Accessed on March 7, 2016 from www.statcan.gc.ca/daily-quotidien/130225/dq130225a-eng.pdf.

Stowasser, Barbara Freyer. "Theodicy and the Many Meanings of Adam and Eve." In *Theodicy and Justice in Modern Islamic Thought: The Case of Said Nursi*, edited by Ibrahim M. Abu-Rabic, 1–18. Surrey: Ashgate, 2010.

Tabatabi, Muhammad Husayn. *Shi'ite Islam.* Herndon, VA: SUNY Press, 1975.

The United Nations Population Fund (UNPF). *Gender Equality: Empowering Women.* Accessed from www.unfpa.org/gender/empowerment.htm.

Tillich, Paul. *Systematic Theology.* Chicago: Unviersity of Chicago Press, 2013.

Tracy, David. *The Analogical Imagination: Christian Theology and the Culture of Pluralism.* New York, NY: Crossroad Publishing Company, 1981.

Tracy, David. *Blessed Rage for Order: The New Pluralism in Theology.* New York, NY: The Seabury Press, 1975.

Tracy, David. "Foundational Theology as Contemporary Possibility." *Dunwoodie Review* 12 (1) (1972): 3–20.

Tracy, David. *On Naming the Present: Reflections on God, Hermeneutics, and Church.* Maryknoll, NY: Orbis Books, 1994.

Tucker, Judith. *Women, Family, and Gender in Islamic Law.* Cambridge: Cambridge University Press, 2008.

Tylor, Edward Burnett. *Primitive Culture.* Vol. 1. New York, NY: J. P. Putnam's Sons, 1920 [1871].

United Nations General Assembly, *Declaration on the Elimination of Violence Against Women.* In the 85th Plenary Meeting. Geneva, Switzerland, 1993.

UN General Assembly, The Declaration on the Elimination 1991.

UN Commission on Human Rights. *Cultural Practices in the Family That Are Violent Towards Women*. UN Doc. E/CN.4/2002/83, 2002.

United Nations Children's Fund [UNICEF]. *Female Genital Mutilation/Cutting: A Statistical Overview and Exploration of the Dynamics of Change*. New York, NY: UNICEF, 2013. Accessed on March 7, 2016 from www.unicef.org/media/files/FGCM_Lo_res.pdf.

Utz, Aisha. "Conceptualizations of Mental Health, Illness, and Healing." In *Counseling Muslims: Handbook of Mental Health Issues and Interventions*, edited by Sameera Ahmed and Mona M. Amer, 15–32. New York, NY: Routledge, Taylor & Francis Group, 2012.

Vasegh, Sasan. "Cognitive Therapy of Religious Depressed Patients." *Journal of Cognitive Psychotherapy*, 25 (3) (2011): 177–188.

Velkley, Richard. *Being After Rousseau: Philosophy and Culture in Question*. Chicago, IL: The University of Chicago Press, 2002.

Vohra, Adarsh, and Sabry, Walaa M. "Role of Islam in the Management of Psychiatric Disorders." *Indian Journal of Psychiatry* 55 (6) (2013): 205–214.

Vontress, Clemmont. "Animism: Foundation of Traditional Healing in Sub-Saharan Africa." In *Integrating Traditional Healing Practices Into Counseling and Psychotherapy*, edited by Roy Moodley and William West, 124–131. Thousand Oaks, CA: Sage Publications, 2015.

Vontress, Clemmont. "Traditional Healing in Africa: Implications for Cross." *Journal of Counseling and Development* 21 (4) (1990): 326–336.

Wadud, Amina. *Qur'an and Woman: Rereading the Sacred Text From a Woman's Perspective*. Oxford: Oxford University Press, 1999.

Wagers, Shelly M. "Deconstructing the Power and Control Motive: Moving Beyond a Unidimensional View of Power in Domestic Violence Theory," *Partner Abuse* 6 (2) (2015): 230.

Waldrum, James B. "But Does It Work? Traditional Healing and Issues of Efficacy and Evaluation." Paper presented at the *Widening the Circle: Collaborative Research in Mental Health Promotion in Native Communities*. Proceedings of the Conference, Montreal, QC, September 26–28, 1997.

Watt, William Montgomery. *The Formative Period of Islamic Thought*. Oxford: Oneworld Publications, 1998.

Watt, William Montgomery. *Free Will and Predestination In Early Islam*. Luzac: Univrsity of Minnesota, 1948.

Weiss, Karen G. "Too Ashamed to Report: Deconstructing the Shame of Sexual Victimisation." *Feminist Criminology* 5 (3) (2010): 286–310.

Welchman, Lynn. "Qiwamah and Wilyah as Legal Postulates in Muslim Family Laws." In *Men in Charge: Rethinking Authority in Muslim Legal Tradition*, edited by Ziba Mir-Hosseini, Mulki Al-Sharmani, and Jana Rumminger, 132–162. London: Oneworld Publications, 2015.

West, Gerald. "Silenced Women Speak: Biblical Feminist Hermeneutics." In *Women Hold up Half the Sky*, edited by Denise Ackermann et al., 76–77. Pietermarizburg: Cluster Publications, 1991.

Westermarck, Edward. *Ritual and Belief in Morocco*. 2 Vols. London: Routledge, 1926/1968.

Wilson, Joshua M., Fauci, Jenny E., and Goodman, Lisa A. "Bringing Trauma-Informed Practice to Domestic Violence Programs: A Qualitative Analysis of Current Approaches." *American Journal of Orthopsychiatry* 85 (6) (2015): 586–599.

Wilson, John, Drozdek, Boris, and Turkovic. Silvana. "Posttraumatic Shame and Guilt." *Trauma, Violence and Abuse* 7 (2) (2006): 122–141.

Wood, Bruce, and Robert Kiyoshk. *Change of Seasons: A Training Manual for Aboriginal Men Who Abuse Their Partners/Spouses.* Squamish and North Vancouver, BC: Change of Seasons Society, 1994.

Wortmann, Jennifer H., Boasso, Alyssa, Schorr, Yonit Maria, et al. "Facilitating Recovery From Moral and Spiritual Injuries." In *Handbook of Psychosocial Interventions for Veterans and Service Members: A Guide for the Non-Military Mental Health Clinician*, edited by Nathan D. Ainspan, Craig Bryan, and Walter E. Penk, 255. Oxford: Oxford University Press, 2016.

Yazır, Elmalili Muhammed Hamdi. *Hak Dini Kur'an Dili* (The Qur'anic exegesis and translation of Qur'an in Turkish). Istanbul: Eser Nesriyat, 1971.

Yesilada, Erdem. "Contribution of Traditional Medicine in the Healthcare System of the Middle East." *Chinese Journal of Integrative Medicine* 17 (2) (2011): 95–98.

Yllo, K. A. "Through a Feminist Lens: Gender, Diversity and Violence. Extending the Feminist Framework." In *Current Controversies on Family Violence.* 2nd ed., edited by D. R. Loseke, R. J. Gelles, and M. M. Cavanaugh. Newbury Park, CA: Sage Publications, 2005.

Youssef, Jacquelline., and Deabe, Frank P. "Arabic-Speaking Religious Leaders' Perception of the Cause of Mental Illness and the Use of Medication for Treatment." *Australian and New Zealand Journal of Psychiatry* 47 (11) (2013): 1041–1050.

Yusuf, Humair. "Traditional Healing: A Culmination of Clemmont Vontress's Ideas." In *Counseling Across the Cultural Divide: The Clemmont E. Vontress Reader*, edited by Roy Moodley, Lawrence Epp, and Humair Yusuf, 211–215. Herefordshire: PCCS Books, 2012.

Yusuf Ali, Abdulla. *The Holy Quran-Text.* Translation and commentary. Bektsville, MD: Amana Corporation, 1989.

Zeini, Marwa. "A Legal Guide to Marriage and Divorce for the American Muslim Women." In *Change From Within: Diverse Perspectives on Domestic Violence in Muslim Communities*, edited by Maha B. Alkhateeb and Salma Elkadi Abugideiri, 203–219. Alexandria, VI: The Peaceful Families Project, 2007.

Zine, Jasmine. *Canadian Islamic Schools: Unravelling the Politics of Faith, Gender, Knowledge, and Identity.* Toronto, ON: University of Toronto Press, 2008.

Index

Abd al-Latif 19
Abduh, M. 100
Abdullah, S. 6
Abrahamov, B. 33
Abugideiri, S. E. 2, 61, 86
Abu-Odeh, L. 54
ahl al-tawhid wa'l-'adl (the people of divine justice and unity) 30, 33–34
Ahmad, A. 105
Ahmed, S. 23, 60
al-'Adawiyya, R. 126
al-a'imma ijtima'uhum hujjatun qati'atun wa ikhtilafuhum rahmatun wasi'a (divergence a divine mercy) 28
al-Alwani, T. J. 151–152, 171n29
al-'aql (intellect) 25
al-Asbahi, M. 27
al-Ash 'ari, A. 31, 76
al-Ashqar, 'U. 99
al-Aziziyya 19
al-Balkhi, A. Z. A. 19, 100
al-Bistami, A. Y. 35
al-Bukhari, A. 28
al-daruriyyat al-khams 27
al-dirayah (personal knowledge or judgement) 25
al-Farabi, A. N. 30
al-Ghamdi, A. 105
al-Ghatani, F. 105
al-Ghazali, A. 32, 77–78, 106, 126, 138
al-Ghazali, M. 20, 27, 28, 30
al-Ghumari, A. 99
Al-Hawi fi al-Tibb 19–20
Ali, A. Y. 53
al-ilaj al-nafsi 19
al-Jawziyyah 27
al-Jilani, A. 35
al-Jubba'i, A. 31
al-Junayd, A. 35
al-Juwayni, I. A. 28
al-Khattab, 'U. 56
al-Kindi, A. Y. 19
al-Malki, A. R. 105
al-Mansur 30
al-Maturidi, A. 32, 79
al-Mubarrad 18
al-Murri, S. 126
al-Nasafi, A. 79
al-Nishapuri 18
al-Nuri, A. 127
al-Qaradawi, Y. 101, 151, 170n24
al-Qarafi, S. 27
al-Razi 150–151
al-Razi, A. H. 34
al-Razi, A. Z. 34
al-Razi, F. 19, 28
al-Razi, F. A. 52
al-Sadiq, I. J. 27
al-Sarakshi, A. B. 28
al-Sha 'arawi, M. M. 27
al-Shafi'i, A. 27, 30, 81
Al-Sharmani, M. 58
al-Sufi, A. H. 34
al-Suyuti 151
Al-Tabari, A. 19, 26, 52, 77, 150–151
Al-Tabataba'i, M. 90–91
al-tabib al-ruhani or *tabib al-qalb* (spiritual physicians) 19
al-Tafsir bil-ma'thur or *al-tafsir al-naqli* (traditional exegesis) 25
al-Tafsir bil-ra'i (the school of rational exegesis) 25
Al-Turabi, H. 27
al-Zamakhshari, A. Q. 52, 77
American Psychiatric Association (APA) 108
"Animism: Foundation of Traditional Healing in Sub-Saharan Africa" 110
Aqida Wasitiyyah 28
Aquinas, T. 20
Aristotle 20
Asad, M. 53

Asad, T. 22–23
asbab al-nuzul 24
Ash 'arites 31–32; on divine testing and suffering 76–78
Avicenna 19–20

Bacon, R. 20
Badawi, J. 151
Bakhtiar, L. 57
Bandura, A. 64
Baobid, M. 172n44
Barazangi, N. H. 58, 157
Barise, A. 21
Barlas, A. 55–56, 84
Bauer, I. 134
Bellamy, C. 111
Benjamin, J. 160–161
bid'at 104
biological theories 64–65
Boisen, A. 9, 15–16n34
Bonds of Love, The 160
Bons-Storm, R. 11
British School 87
Brown, C. 114
Browning, D. 8–9, 15n32

Campbell, R. A. 105
Chaudhry, A. 10
Chesler, P. 158–159
College of Registered Psychotherapists of Ontario (CRPO) 6
commitment stage 138–140
complex post-traumatic stress disorder (C-PTSD) 136
Comprehensive Exposition of the Interpretation of the Verses of the Quran (*Jami al-bayan 'an ta'wil al-Qur'an*) 26
confessing of sin 137–138
Cooper-White, P. 11, 66, 86, 161
Corvo, K. 65
Couture, P. 11
Csordas, T. J. 112
culture: domestic violence and 58–61; Islamic psychotherapy and 36–38

Dabashi, H. 37
daraba 52–58
Dasein 16n36
Declaration on the Elimination of Violence against Women 87
DEEDS process 12
deficit theories 65
DeHoff, S. L. 108
Dharamsi, S. 6
Diagnostic and Statistical Manual of Mental Disorders (DSM-5) 107–108, 110–111
discursive tradition 22
divine purification 140–141
divine testing and suffering 72–73; Ash 'arites on 76–78; Hanbalites on 81–83; interventions to relieve 88–91; Islamic feminist response to 83–86; in Islamic studies and Islamic psychotherapy literature 73–86; Maturidites on 78–81; Mu 'tazilite school on 73–76; in social science literature 86–88
Domestic Abuse Intervention Project in Duluth (DAIP) 66
domestic violence: conclusions on 186–193; culture and 58–61; definitions in 1–3, 12n5, 13n10; divine testing and suffering and (*see* divine testing and suffering); Duluth model of 66; future recommendations for 177–184, 184–185n1; in Islamic context 51–52; Islamic feminist response to 54–58; Islamic psychotherapy and (*see* Islamic psychotherapy); Islam's exegetical tradition and 52–58; North American society and 61–63; rationale of study on 4–5; social science tradition theories for understanding 64–66
Domestic Violence Protection Act of Ontario 2000 2
Duluth Model 66
Dwairy, M. 58–60

Elahi, O. 140
Enerborg, Y. M. 106
Esack, F. 53–54
evil eye *see* Satanic interference and evil eye
exegetical tradition: domestic violence and 52–58; Islamic psychotherapy and 25–27, 191
existential therapy 87–88

Faith Trust Institute 2
family systems theories 65
fard 38n2
Fatih Trust Institute project 61
female genital mutilation (FGM) 37, 50n125
feminist practical theology 11
feminist theories 65
fitra (primordial nature) 88
fitrah (inner character; nature) 124–125
folk medicine 102–104
forsaking of sin 138–140
Foucault, M. 22

Frankl, V. 87
Freud, S. 134
Future of an Illusion, The 134
future recommendations 177–178, 184–185n1; mainstream support services 180–184; for the Muslim community 178–180

Gadamer, H.-G. 9
Gerkin, C. 9, 16n39
Glaz, M. 11
Goffman, E. 63
Goldziher, I. 30
Graham, E. 11
Gruber, D. 159

hadith 7, 15n27, 23, 25, 52, 189; divine testing and suffering and 77; folk medicine and 104; Satanic interference and 105–107
Hamberger, L. K. 135
Hanbal, A. 27
Hanbalites 35; on divine testing and suffering 81–83
Hansen, L. 159
Hastings, J. E. 135
Heidegger, M. 16n36
Heimbrock, H. G. 109–110
heuristic case studies 8
Hilton, D. E. 111
Hodgson, M. 37
honour and shame 145–147; conclusion on 167–168; honour violence and 155–157; interventions to address 164–167; Islamic feminist responses to 152–155; in Islamic studies and Islamic psychotherapy literature 148–158; in social science literature 158–164; in the social science literature 158–164
Hussain, I. 74

Ibn Abbas 150
Ibn al-'Arabi 57, 68–69n44
ibn 'Ali, I. Z. 27
Ibn 'Arabi 132
Ibn Ashur, A. 60
Ibn Qudamah 151
ibn Qutayda 34
ibn Sa 'id al-Busiri al-Shadhili, A. A. M. 19
Ibn Sina 19–20
ibn Sirin, M. 19
ibn Taymiyya, T. 26, 28, 81–83
ijma' (consensus of Muslim authoritative scholars) 23, 27–28
ijtihad (independent reasoning) 27
ilm-al nafsiyat 19
International Organization for Migration 6
interventions: to address honour and shame 164–167; to address Satanic interference 113–116; to address spiritual disease and distress 137–141; to relieve suffering 88–91; *see also* Islamic psychotherapy
ishkal wa ifsad wa tadlis (corrupt, ambiguous, and fraudulent) 28
Islam, F. 105
Islamic context, domestic violence in 51–52
Islamic counselling *vs.* Islamic psychotherapy 5–7
Islamic Family Law 148–149, 163, 168–169n7, 168n3, 191; brief introduction to 149; honour violence and 155–157; Islamic feminist responses to 152–155; moral response to 157–158; wife-beating and 149–152
Islamic feminist discourse 10–11, 192–193; on divine testing and suffering 83–86; on honour and shame 152–155; response to domestic violence 54–58; on spiritual diseases 130–133
Islamic psychology 19–20
Islamic psychotherapy 1; Ash 'arites and 31–32; based on principles of Islamic belief 18; conclusions on 186–193; culture and 36–38; current transformation into clinical discipline 21; definitions in 1–3; divine test and suffering in Islamic studies and 73–86; early accounts of 18–19; exegetical tradition and 25–27, 191; future recommendations on 177–184, 184–185n1; heuristic case studies in 8; honour and shame and 148–158; interventions to relieve suffering 88–91; *vs.* Islamic counselling 5–7; Islamic feminist discourse and (*see* Islamic feminist discourse); Islamic psychology and 19–20; Islamic tradition as primary source for 21–24, 38n2; kalam (scholastic/discursive theology) and 23, 29–30; Maturidism and 32–33; method and methodology in 7–10; Mu 'tazilites and 30–31, 45–46n78, 46–47n82; professional codes of conduct in early 20–21; rationale of study on 4–5; religious-hermeneutical methods and correlational approach in 8–9; Satanic interference and evil eye and 97–107;

Shari'ah and 27–29; spiritual disease and distress and 124–133; Sufism and 23, 34–36; theological reflections in 9–10; traditionalist school and 33–34; *see also* interventions
Islamic studies: divine testing and suffering in 73–86; honour and shame in 148–158; Satanic interference and evil eye in 97–104; spiritual disease and distress in 124–133
Islamic tradition as primary source for Islamic psychotherapy 21–24, 38n2
Islamophobia 182
istislah/maslahah (common good) 27
'Iyad, A. 128

Jackson, S. 33
Jami'al-bayan 150
Jewish Holocaust 87
Jilani, S. A. Q. 18
jinn 96–97, 100, 105–107
Jiwani, Y. 13n10, 62

kafir 23
kalam (scholastic/discursive theology) 23, 29–30
Kamali, M. H. 28
khanqah 19
Kitab al-Mansuri (The Book of Medicine) 20
Kitab al-Tawhid 33, 79
Kitab al-Uqala al-Majanin (The Wise Fools) 18
Kitab Sirr Al-Asrar wa Mazhar al-Anwar (The Book of the Secret of Secrets and The Manifestations of Light) 18
Kivisto, A. J. 159
Kluckhohn, C. 36
Kroeber, A. 36
kufr (disbelief) 28

Lane, E. W. 103
La Roche, M. 111
literature review: conclusion on 66–67; divine testing and suffering 73–86; domestic violence and culture 58–61; domestic violence and Islam's exegetical tradition 52–58; domestic violence and the North American society 61–63; domestic violence in Islamic context 51–52; honour and shame 148–164; Satanic interference and evil eye 97–113; spiritual disease and distress 124–137; theories for understanding domestic violence from the social science tradition 64–66
Logotherapy 88

MacIntyre, A. 22
Madelj, T. R. 133
madrasah 19
mainstream support services 180–184
Manners and Customs of the Modern Egyptians 103
Masalih al-Abdan wa al-Anfus (*Sustenance for Body and Soul*) 100
Maturidism 32–33; on divine testing and suffering 78–81
Maynard, A. 6
McCue 62
McFague, S. 11
Mernissi, F. 56
Miller-McLemore, B. 4, 11
Mir-Hossieni, Z. 58
Moessner, J. S. 11
Moghaddam, M. S. 104
Moustakas, C. 15n29
Muhammad, A. Q. 130
Muhammad, Prophet 7, 16n42, 18; divine testing and suffering and 84; on healing 113; prophetic medicine and 97–102; on self-identity and spirituality 188; Sufism and 35
Mu 'tazilite tradition 30–31, 45–46n78, 46–47n82; divine testing and suffering in 73–76

nafs al-lawwama 139
Narcissistic Personality Disorder 134–136
narrative therapy 114–116
nasiha 18; *see also* Islamic psychotherapy
Nasr, A. M. 20
Neuger, C. C. 65
North American society and domestic violence 61–63
Novsak, R. 133
Nursi, B. S. 77
nushuz 52, 54, 56, 58

Obeid, T. 105
orthodoxification 23

Peaceful Families Project 86
Peck, M. S. 109–110
personality disorders 134–136
post-traumatic stress disorder (PTSD) 164–167
Power and Control Wheel 66, 134
Professions of the Islamic People, and the Disagreements among Those Who Perform the Prayer, The 37
prophetic medicine and its legal-ethical context 97–102

psychoanalysis 87
psychopathology theories 64

Qasida al-Burda (the Mantle Ode) 19
qawwamun 53
qiyas (analogy) 27
Qur'an 5, 7, 16n42, 18, 189; on act of divine purification on effects of sin 140; on confessing sin 137–138; on *daraba* 52–58; exegetical tradition and Islamic psychotherapy 25–27; on forsaking of sin 138–140; God's Rule/Sovereignty and 17n46; interventions to relieve suffering and 89–90; Islamic feminist discourse and 10–11; as primary source for Islamic psychotherapy 21–24; prophetic medicine and its legal-ethical context and 97–102
Qushayri 126
Qutb, S. 27, 54

radical hermeneutics 42n53
Rahman, F. 100–101, 157, 173n57
Ramsay, N. J. 11
Rapid Eye Movement Desensitization Reprocessing (EMDR) treatment 165–166
Rassool, G. H. 21
rationalism 33, 39n9
religious-hermeneutical methods and correlational approach 8–9
repentance 137–138
restricted existence 88
Ricoeur, P. 9
Rida, R. 100
Rizvi, S. A. A. 6–7
Rumminger, J. 58
ruqyah 104
Ryan, K. M. 135

Sachedina, A. 75
safwa (chosen ones) 34
Salama, U. 56
Saleh, W. 27, 42n53
Satanic interference and evil eye 95–97; conclusion on 116–117; folk medicine and 102–104; interventions to address 113–116; in Islamic psychotherapy literature 105–107; in Islamic studies and Islamic psychotherapy literature 97–104; prophetic medicine and its legal-ethical context and 97–102; in social science literature 107–113
self-experience 15n29
semi-textualists 26
sense of shame as motive of behaviour 160
Shaikh, S. 10, 131
Shaltut, M. 101
shame *see* honour and shame
Shari'ah 23; Islamic psychotherapy and 27–29
shaykh al-khanqa 19
shaykh al-ribat 19
Shubair, M. 101
Silvers, L. 57
Simoni, B. 133
sin: confessing of 137–138; divine purification on effects of 140–141; forsaking of 138–140
situated freedom 88
Soaper, K. 159
social justice issues 114
social science literature: divine testing and suffering in 86–88; honour and shame in 158–164; Satanic interference in 107–113; spiritual diseases in 133–137; theories for understanding domestic violence in 64–66
spiritual diseases 122–123, 190–191; conclusion on 141–142; and distress in Islamic studies and Islamic psychotherapy literature 124–133; interventions to address 137–141; Islamic feminist response to 130–133; in the social science literature 133–137
Sprechini, G. 135
suffering *see* divine testing and suffering
Sufism 23, 34–36; divine testing and suffering in 80; honour and shame in 157–158; misuse of 129–130; remedies for spiritual diseases in 127–129; spiritual diseases and 123, 124–130
Sunnah 7
support services, recommendations for 180–184

tadabbur 9
ta'dib 7
tafakkur 9
Taleqani, A. M. 27
ta'lim 7
taqwa (God-fearing; God-consciousness) 122
tarbiyya 7
tasfiyat al-qulub (the purification of the heart) 34
tawhid 10; folk medicine and 104
tazkiyya 15n27

tazkiyyat al-nafs 7
tekke 19
testing *see* divine testing and suffering
Textualists 25–26
Thabit, A. H. 27
theological reflections 9–10
Tillich, P. 9
Tracy, D. 8
"Traditional Healing in Africa: Implications for Cross" 110
traditionalist school 33–34
trauma 164–167, 191–192
Tylor, E. B. 36

'Ubayd, A. 30
'Ubayd, I. H. 34
United Nations Population Fund (UNPF) 14n19

Van Deruzen 91
Velkley, R. 36
Venture of Islam, The 37
Vontress, C. 110

Wadud, A. 10, 54–55; on divine testing and suffering 83–84
Waldrum, B. H. 109
Wasil ibn 'Ata 30
Watt, W. M. 30
Weikel, K. 135
What Is Islam 60
White, M. 114

Yazi, E. H. 52–53

Zine, J. 62
zuhd (an ascetic way of life) 30